Asian America

BOOKS BY HUPING LING

Surviving on the Gold Mountain: A History of Chinese American Women and Their Lives

Chinese St. Louis: From Enclave to Cultural Community

Jinshan Yao: Meiguo Huayi Funu Shi [A History of Chinese American Women] (Winner of 1998 Ford Foundation Award for publication in the American Study Series by the Chinese Academy of Social Sciences)

Ping Piao Mei Guo: Xin Yimin Shilu [New Immigrants in America]

Voices of the Heart: Asian American Women on Immigration, Work, and Family

Chinese in St. Louis: 1857–2007

Emerging Voices: Experiences of Underrepresented Asian Americans

Asian American History and Cultures: An Encyclopedia (with Allan W. Austin)

Asian America

Forming New Communities, Expanding Boundaries

EDITED BY

HUPING LING

RUTGERS UNIVERSITY PRESS

NEW BRUNSWICK, NEW JERSEY, AND LONDON

LIBRARY OF CONGRESS CATALOGING-IN-PUBLICATION DATA

Asian America : forming new communities, expanding boundaries / edited by Huping Ling.

    p. cm

Includes bibliographical references and index.

ISBN 978-0-8135-4486-1 (hardcover : alk. paper)

ISBN 978-0-8135-4487-8 (pbk. : alk. paper)

1. Asian Americans—United States—History. 2. Asian Americans—United States—Social conditions. 3. Asian Americans—Cultural assimilation—United States. 4. Asian Americans—United States—Societies, etc. 5. Ethnic neighborhoods—United States—History. 6. Community life—United States—History. 7. United States—Ethnic relations. 8. United States—Social conditions. I. Ling, Huping, 1956—

E184.A75A816 2009

973.'0495—dc22   2008029194

A British Cataloging-in-Publication record for this book is available from the British Library.

"Reconceptualizing Asian American Communities" and "Cultural Community: A New Model for Asian American Community," by Huping Ling, includes material originally published in *Chinese St. Louis: From Enclave to Cultural Community*, by Huping Ling (Temple University Press, 2004).

"Virtual Community and the Cultural Imaginary of Chinese Americans," by Yuan Shu, is adapted from "Re-imagining the Community: Information Technology and Web-Based Chinese Language Networks in North America," in *AsianAmerican.Net: Ethnicity, Nationalism, and Cyberspace*, edited by Rachel C. Lee and Sau-ling Cynthia Wong (Routledge, 2003), 139–157. Used by permission.

Portions of "Ethnic Solidarity in a Divided Community: A Study on Bridging Organizations in Koreatown" were taken from Angie Y. Chung, *Legacies of Struggle: Conflict and Cooperation in Korean American Politics*, © 2007 by the Board of Trustees of the Leland Stanford Jr. University.

Visit our Web site: http://rutgerspress.rutgers.edu

Manufactured in the United States of America

To the Asian American communities

CONTENTS

PART THREE
Asian Communities in America:
With Cultural/Social Boundaries

PART FOUR
Asian Communities in Canada

ACKNOWLEDGMENTS

I am fortunate to have had a great number of individuals standing behind me at every stage of the making of this volume. It would have not been possible without their understanding, cooperation, and steadfast support.

The scholars who contributed chapters to the volume were most patient and supportive as I labored to conceptualize the new formations of Asian American communities. I immensely enjoyed their intellectual energy, ingenuity, and comradeship developed in the process. Leslie Mitchner, the associate director and editor in chief with Rutgers University Press, has been most enthusiastic toward the project and demonstrated unremitting support and encouragement. Rachel Friedman, Alicia Nadkarni, and other staff members at the Press have worked with me with great professionalism and efficiency throughout the production. The anonymous reviewer of the manuscript offered the most insightful and constructive suggestions and wholeheartedly endorsed the project for publication. Robert Burchfield has been a most careful and gracious copyeditor who improved the manuscript tremendously. My husband, Dr. Samiullah, has provided vital technical support and has been a valuable critic of all of my writings. I am very grateful to all of them.

Finally, I want to thank the following presses for allowing the use of materials from their titles. Portions of the introduction and chapter 6 were taken from Huping Ling, *Chinese St. Louis: From Enclave to Cultural Community*, © 2004 by Temple University. Portions of chapter 8 were adapted from "Reimagining the Community: Information Technology and Web-Based Chinese Language Networks in North America," in *AsianAmerican.Net: Ethnicity, Nationalism, and Cyberspace*, edited by Rachel C. Lee and Sau-ling Cynthia Wong (Routledge, 2003), 139–157. Portions of chapter 9 were taken from Angie Y. Chung, *Legacies of Struggle: Conflict and Cooperation in Korean American Politics*, © 2007 by the Board of Trustees of the Leland Stanford Jr. University.

Asian America

Introduction

Reconceptualizing Asian American Communities

HUPING LING

The geographic, ethnographic, and socioeconomic landscape of North America has changed dramatically since the 1960s. Asian American communities, reinforced by the newcomers from Asian countries and regions, have undergone profound transformation. While the traditional and long-established ethnic enclaves are renewed and revitalized by the influx of new immigrants, other, different types of urban or suburban communities have also emerged as a result of the socioeconomic upward mobility of native-born Asian Americans and the changing profiles of the new immigrants from Asia since the 1960s, who, such as the professionals and entrepreneurs, are better equipped with educational, monetary, and social capital. They are responsible for the formation of the new Asian American communities: suburban Asian communities, global cities, cultural communities, and cyber communities—communities with geographical or cultural/social boundaries. At the same time, refugees and immigrants from Southeast Asia (Vietnam, Laos, and Cambodia) since 1975, the end of the Vietnam War, have also constructed communities that resemble the urban enclaves of the traditional ethnic communities in the initial years following their settlement in America, and some have been able to move out of the urban enclaves and dwell in a variety of suburban Asian American communities.

The new development of Asian American communities demands academic reflection, and scholars have responded with a growing number of excellent studies on Asian communities in North America. However, most academic works to date have been local or regional studies focusing primarily on Asian communities in major metropolises;[1] few have been able to present a global depiction of Asian American communities. This volume attempts to present a comprehensive and panoramic picture of contemporary Asian American communities. It includes discussions on Asian American communities not only in the coastal metropolises but also in the hinterland; not only the commercial/residential neighborhoods but also communities with a commercial center only; not only those that can be defined as urban enclaves but also as suburban communities;

and not only geographic formations but also culturally/socially bounded communities. The volume further expands beyond the boundaries of the United States to include communities in Canada; the two sociological studies on Asian communities in Canada offer meaningful comparisons. In presenting the comprehensive and global picture of the Asian American communities, this volume explores the profound and complex socioeconomic and cultural elements in the formation of varying Asian American communities in the contexts of capitalism, transnationalism, and globalization. It examines how Asian Americans have challenged and altered the conventional borders and boundaries of a community and formed the communities best suited for their present socioeconomic needs.

Asian American Communities in Transformation: From Enclave to Cultural Community

The construction of Asian American communities has evolved from ghettolike urban enclaves to various suburban communities, defined as suburban Chinatowns, satellite cities, and "ethnoburbs."[2] In the more recent decades, propelled by their socioeconomic assimilation into the majority society, Asian American communities have further advanced to cultural communities and cyber communities, communities defined by cultural/social space or cyberspace.[3] In this section, I categorize and analyze the different forms of Asian American communities in accordance with their evolution.

Urban Enclaves

Asian immigrants, like all newcomers, first faced the challenge of survival on a foreign soil. However, the new world was more hostile to Asian immigrants than to their European counterparts. Survival in a strange and unfriendly land thus resulted in the first formation of Asian communities—urban ghettos or enclaves. Two factors are believed to be primarily responsible for the formation of Asian ethnic urban enclaves: the external discriminatory legislation and practices against Asian immigrants and the internal drive of the Asian immigrants to survive and succeed in the new world. The former restricted the socioeconomic opportunities of Asian immigrants (for instance, in the forms of the Foreign Miners' Tax passed in 1850 and 1852 and alien land laws passed between 1885 and 1921, and various discriminatory practices in the labor market) in the larger society and pushed them into limited and often service-oriented occupations (laundry, dry cleaning, restaurant, wholesale and retailing, garment, and domestic services) and dilapidated urban neighborhoods where rents were low. There they could make it largely through practical means of mutual aid and ethnic networks. Such ethnic communities historically have been in general identified as ethnic "ghettos" or ethnic "enclaves," in particular dubbed as ethnic settlements of "Chinatown," "Japantown," and

"Koreatown," or as replicas of the ethnic groups' original cultures symbolized by the names of the capital cities of the homelands, such as "Little Manila," "Little Taipei," and "Little Saigon."

Chinatowns. Chinatown is most illustrative in exhibiting the formation of Asian ethnic urban enclaves. Chinese communities in America have largely been an urban phenomenon since the early twentieth century. In the 1930 census, 64 percent of the 74,954 Chinese resided in urban centers. A decade later, the Chinese population totaled 77,504, and 71 percent of them lived in major American cities. By the 1950 census, more than 90 percent of the Chinese population resided in cities,[4] and the trend continues upward.[5] The urban presence of Chinese Americans undoubtedly warrants urban study as a significant focus within Asian American studies.

Chinatown as commercial and residential district. Like other immigrant groups, Chinese immigrants predominantly settled in gateway cities and major urban centers, where they established communities known as Chinatowns. Scholars have attempted to define Chinatown in terms of its socioeconomic and cultural functions. Historian Mary Coolidge in 1909 described San Francisco Chinatown as a "quarter" in the city formed by the Chinese to "protect themselves and to make themselves at home."[6] Sociologist Rose Hum Lee provided a similar description of Chinatown as an area organized by Chinese "sojourners for mutual aid and protection as well as to retain their cultural heritage,"[7] and Chinatowns are "ghetto-like formations resulting from the migration and settlement of persons with culture, religion, language, ideology, or race different from those of members of the dominant groups."[8] Examining Chinatown from the condition of racial discourse, anthropologist Bernard P. Wong views it as a racially closed community, while geographer Kay Anderson interprets Vancouver's Chinatown as "a European creation."[9] By far, probably the most comprehensive scholarly conceptualization of Chinatown has been made by Canadian geographer David Lai: "Chinatown in North America is characterized by a concentration of Chinese people and economic activities in one or more city blocks which forms a unique component of the urban fabric. It is basically an idiosyncratic oriental community amidst an occidental urban environment."[10] Thus, Chinatowns have generally been understood as confined urban commercial and residential districts where Chinese could find employment, housing, and cultural comfort, virtually without interacting with the larger society.

Chinatown as commercial center only. In recent decades, many Chinatowns throughout North America have transformed from ethnic enclaves for immigrants and Chinese Americans into tourist attractions to satisfy the curiosity of people with diverse backgrounds or into commercial centers for Asian cooking ingredients and culinary enjoyment of the Chinese and non-Chinese as well. In such areas, scholars are concerned that the "overuse" of architectural ethnic symbols gives these areas a flavor of superficiality and that they convey less a sense of community for Chinese Americans.[11] Nevertheless, the commercial-centered Chinatowns continue to prevail and prosper, serving as an enduring form of Chinese American communities.

Chinatown in gateway cities. The scholarship on Chinese enclaves has been dominated primarily by works focusing on Chinatowns in San Francisco and New York. The following works are representative of the many studies of San Francisco Chinatown. Victor G. Nee and Brett de Bary Nee's *Longtime Californ': A Documentary Study of an American Chinatown*, one of the early studies on San Francisco Chinatown, was based on oral history interviews of San Francisco Chinatown residents. The Nees attempted to explore the forces that created Chinatown and continued to perpetuate its existence and the sources of its cohesiveness and resilience as an ethnic community.[12] Thomas W. Chinn's *Bridging the Pacific: San Francisco's Chinatown and Its People* chronicled the history of San Francisco Chinatown by examining its social structure and the individuals who helped shape its history.[13] Chalsa M. Loo's *Chinatown: Most Time, Hard Time* was an empirical study to provide "an understanding of the life problems, concerns, perceptions, and needs of a major segment of the Chinese American population."[14] Yong Chen's *Chinese San Francisco, 1850–1943: A Trans-Pacific Community*, utilizing a wide range of primary and secondary sources, both in English and Chinese, depicts the cultural and social transformation of the Chinese in San Francisco over a century.[15] Nayan Shah's *Contagious Divides: Epidemics and Race in San Francisco's Chinatown* offers refreshing insights into a complex picture of public health and race in San Francisco from the late nineteenth century to the post–World War II era.[16]

Although New York Chinatown was formed later than San Francisco Chinatown, a number of significant works on New York Chinatown have been completed. Anthropologist Bernard P. Wong alone has contributed three books on the subject. Wong's studies analyze the dynamics of the interpersonal relationships of the Chinese and their contributions to the economic well-being and social life of the community,[17] the social organizations and ethnic identities,[18] and the formation and manipulation of the patronage and brokerage systems in the economic adaptation of the Chinese in New York.[19] Similarly, two studies by Peter Kwong, *Chinatown, New York: Labor and Politics, 1930–1950* and *The New Chinatown*, also examine the internal social structure of New York Chinatown.[20] In his first book, Kwong hails the more positive response to the Chinese in America from American society since World War II due to China's participation in the war. In his second book, Kwong categorizes Chinatown residents into two groups—"Uptown Chinese," professionals and business leaders who are engaged in property speculation, and "Downtown Chinese," manual and service workers who have to work and rent tenement apartments in Chinatown. As a result, underneath the appearance of ethnic cohesion, New York Chinatown is a polarized community.[21] Sociologist Min Zhou's *Chinatown: The Socioeconomic Potential of an Urban Enclave*, challenging the notion of Chinatown as an urban ghetto plagued by urban problems, focuses on the positive outcomes of ethnicity and ethnic solidarity. Zhou views Chinatown as an immigrant enclave with strong socioeconomic potential that would help, not retard, the new immigrants' assimilation into American mainstream society.[22]

Hsiang-shui Chen's *Chinatown No More: Taiwan Immigrants in Contemporary New York* asserts that the new Chinese residents in the Flushing-Elmhurst area of New York differ from the previous Chinese immigrants in various aspects: they are more educated and diverse in economic and class background, scatter and mix with other ethnic groups, and speak a variety of Chinese languages and dialects, not representing a homogenous ethnic group.[23] Jan Lin's *Reconstructing Chinatown: Ethnic Enclave, Global Change* recognizes New York Chinatown as an urban ethnic enclave, but examines its changes in the global context "through the conflicts and interactions of labor and capital, the community, and the state."[24]

Japantowns. While the Chinese urban enclaves have been renewed and revitalized by the incessant stream of new immigrants and thus still maintain one of the dominant forms of Chinese American communities, the Japanese urban enclaves are different from their Chinese counterparts. The Japanese urban enclaves had never been a dominant part of Japanese American communities. According to Roger Daniels's study, in 1940, when 90 percent of Chinese Americans were urban dwellers, more than half (51.4 percent) of all the Japanese males employed in the three West Coast states were in agriculture, forestry, and fishing, as were every one out of three Japanese working women. Only less than a quarter (23.6 percent) of all working Japanese were employed in wholesale and retail trade, and the remaining (17.1 percent) Japanese were working in personal service.[25]

As the postwar Japanese Americans have "structurally" assimilated into the larger society,[26] most Japanese Americans live in predominantly European American neighborhoods, work in mainstream companies, participate in social and political activities of the larger society, and have out-married to European Americans in significant numbers. For instance, in 1979, 50 percent of new marriages involving Japanese in Los Angeles were with non-Asians.[27] These characteristics of Japanese Americans, combined with other factors such as the lower rate of postwar Japanese immigration to the United States, consequently resulted in the erosion, dissolution, and even extinction of Japantowns or Little Tokyos in the United States. For this reason, I will discuss the Japanese American communities in the later section on Asian American communities with cultural/social boundaries.

Koreatowns. Korean immigrants came to the United States in three major waves. The first brought 7,226 Koreans to Hawaii as contract laborers between 1903 and 1905 to replace Japanese workers who demanded higher wages and initiated strikes.[28] Approximately 2,000 of these Korean laborers later migrated to the American mainland, and most settled on the West Coast. This early wave was halted by the Korean government in 1905, when the country lost its independence to Japan. The Japanese government intended to stop the anti-Japanese resistance movement among overseas Koreans and to eliminate the competition to Japanese immigrants from the Koreans. The second wave of Korean immigration came between the Korean War (1950–1953) and 1965. The majority of these immigrants, numbering 14,027, were war orphans or wives and relatives of American servicemen who had been stationed in Korea.[29] The third wave of Korean immigration to the United States reached the country under the 1965 Hart-Celler Act, also known as the 1965 Immigration Act, officially called An Act to Amend the Immigration and Nationality Act of 1924. The 1965 Immigration Act abolished the 1924 national quota system and established the three immigration principles of family reunion, the need for skilled workers, and the admission of refugees. The law capped the total number of immigrants from the Eastern Hemisphere at 170,000, with each country not exceeding 20,000 quota immigrants. The new wave of Korean immigration was characterized by a significant shift in the socioeconomic profile of the immigrants, who were largely middle-class professionals in the homeland.[30]

While most scholarship on the new Korean immigrants has focused on entrepreneurship and tensions between Korean Americans and African Americans in inner-city neighborhoods,[31] a few studies have explored the community structure. Sociologist Pyong Gap Min has written extensively on Korean American communities. His studies indicate that Korean immigrants possessed qualities of hard work and frugality, strong family and kinship ties, and ethnic solidarity; and such qualities helped many succeed in ethnic enterprises. He notes that Korean communities in the major metropolises of New York and Los Angeles tend to be commercial centers only.[32] Anthropologist Kyeyoung Park has in particular paid attention to the "establishment" of the Korean immigrant community in New York, the second largest concentration of Koreans in America after Los Angeles, while analyzing the small businesses. Park is sensitive to the role played by Korean women in initiating migration, in working at sewing factories or small family businesses, and in attending Korean Christian churches.[33] Jas-Hyup Lee's comparative study on Korean, Chinese, and Vietnamese American communities in Philadelphia presents a similar picture. While most Korean immigrants worked in small businesses located on North Fifth Street in Koreatown, they maintained ethnic community through preserving ethnic language and holidays and rituals, participating in ethnic organizations, and running ethnic media.[34]

Thus, the Korean urban enclaves are characterized by the separation of commercial and residential lives. The post-1965 Korean immigrants, although working in small businesses, garment factories, or services of the inner-city districts, have lived in apartment complexes outside of the business precincts and created "associational communities" formed through occupational, residential, and religious associations, as presented in Illsoo Kim's work.[35] Therefore, the separation of the commercial and residential lives of the Korean immigrants distinguishes Koreatowns from Chinatowns, which include both commercial and residential properties.

Little Manilas. Although Filipinos have been entering the United States since the 1700s, the majority have come following the liberalization of the Immigration Act in 1965. The number of Filipinos entering the United States has been increasing annually since the passage of the law. In 1973, 30,000 Filipinos were admitted to the United States. By the end of the 1980s, over 50,000 Filipinos were entering the United States annually. In 1990, there were 1.5 million Filipinos in the United States.[36] According to the 2000 census, the figure jumped to 1.8 million, making Filipinos the second largest Asian American group, behind the Chinese, in the United States.[37]

The 1965 Immigration Act alone cannot explain the influx of Filipino immigration; the U.S. presence in the Philippines has propelled and shaped this movement of human migration as well. The Treaty of Paris in 1898, which ended the Spanish-American War and made Spain cede the Philippines to the United States, and the subsequent U.S. annexation of the Philippines (1899–1913) have complicated the polity, economy, and culture of the Philippines. Prior to the passage of the 1965 Immigration Act, most Filipinos came to America as laborers or *pensionados* (students). Many Filipino men were also recruited by the navy to fight during the two world wars. Two of the largest American military installations overseas, Clark Air Base and Subic Bay Naval Base, are located in the Philippines, and most of their needs of military personnel are served by the Filipinos. In addition, the United States serves as the Philippines major trading partner, and American investment accounts for half of the country's foreign investment.[38] The military and socioeconomic ties between the United States and the Philippines have profoundly impacted the Filipino society in many ways. Academics assert that Filipino immigration to the United States has been a result of the "Americanization" of Filipino culture through American colonization.[39] The Americanization of the Filipino culture has been embodied in the government structure, educational system, language, customs, and values. The Filipino government was set up based on the American model, as was the Filipino educational system. English has been the language used in public and private schools, and Filipino television programs are inundated with American movies and soap operas.

The Filipinos were also pushed out of the country by its grave political, economic, and social conditions. Although President Ferdinand Marcos, who had instituted martial law, was ousted in 1986, the successive democratic government under President Corazon Aquino was plagued with political instability.

As a result of the Philippine's economic policy, which rested completely on the U.S. involvement in the Vietnam War, the country's economy collapsed in the 1980s. Problems of inflation and foreign debt were compounded by high unemployment, dependency on agricultural exports, and inequality in the distribution of income and wealth.[40]

The oversupply of educated people in the Philippines since the 1960s also contributed to the Filipino exodus. In 1970, 25 percent of college-age Filipinos were enrolled in colleges and universities, second only after the United States.[41] However, the country could not provide its educated people with adequate employment and pay. For instance, Filipina nurses in the United States could earn twenty times more than their counterparts in the Philippines.[42]

Since the 1960s, professional Filipinas/os have migrated to the United States in large numbers, and the majority of them are physicians, nurses, and other health practitioners as a result of the aggressive recruitment policy of the United States to fill the shortage of trained personnel in the health industry. Two-thirds of the Filipino immigrants to the United States in the 1960s were women, many of whom were nurses. By the late 1980s, 50,000 Filipino nurses were working in the United States.[43]

Academics have produced solid studies to reflect upon the transformation of Filipino American urban communities. Linda Nueva Espana-Maram's work examines how Filipino laborers in Los Angeles's Little Manila forged an ethnic identity and created a male, working-class culture from the 1920s through the 1940s.[44] Rick Bonus's ethnographic study of Filipino American communities in Los Angeles and San Diego focuses on the "Oriental" stores, the social halls, the community centers, and the community newspapers, which he defines as "alternative community spaces" that have constituted ethnic identities and transformed communities.[45] Yen Le Espiritu's work looks at the Filipino community building in a navy town, San Diego. While the pre-1965 Filipino community was small, with 5,123 people, and predominantly connected to the U.S. Navy, the post-1965 immigrants were largely middle-class professionals who swelled the community to 121,000 strong in 2000.[46]

Little Saigons. Among Asian Americans, Southeast Asians constitute the most recently formed ethnic group. Unlike earlier Asian American groups, Vietnamese, Laotian, and Cambodian Americans are refugees. Their immigration pattern and their life in America are thus inevitably intertwined with the refugee experiences.

Since 1975, when South Vietnam fell to the Communists, over 2 million refugees have fled Vietnam, Laos, and Cambodia, forming waves of refugees escaping the terror. The Southeast Asian refugee exodus was shaped by complex political and socioeconomic factors. The first wave of Vietnamese refugees primarily consisted of the elite class who left Vietnam due to the Communist takeover. This group included army officers and their families, government bureaucrats, teachers, doctors, engineers, lawyers, students, businessmen, and Catholic priests and nuns. The later flows consisted of masses of people from more modest backgrounds, including farmers and fishermen fleeing continuing regional military conflicts and deteriorating economic conditions.[47] While Vietnamese elites and professionals were joined and outnumbered by the masses of refugees who were relocated to American bases in Guam and Philippines under emergency conditions after the fall of Saigon, the elites from Laos and Cambodia were more likely to be settled in France.[48]

Orange County, California, has hosted the largest concentration of Vietnamese refugees. The population of Vietnamese Americans in the area amounts to over 400,000 out of the 1.2 million total Vietnamese Americans across the country in 2000.[49] Between 2,000 and 5,000 Vietnamese businesses in the Little Saigon area cater to the ethnic community.[50] A number of studies have focused on the origins and the initial spatial establishment of the community. Colette Marie McLaughlin and Paul Jesilow's 1998 study examines the functions of Little Saigon. Different from the earlier urban ethnic enclaves that served as both commercial and residential areas and were located in downtown districts, Little Saigon consists of ethnic commercial belts located on arterial thoroughfares. It provides Vietnamese Americans with commercial goods and services, as well as a sense of community. Meanwhile, its commercial wealth also attracts tourists of diverse backgrounds, which diminishes the sense of community.[51] Sanjoy Mazumdar and colleagues' 2000 study focuses on how architecture, daily social interaction, and public ritual events in Little Saigon can "create and sustain a sense of place, foster community identity, and structure social relations."[52]

Suburban Communities

The influx of new immigrants from Asia since 1965 resulted in a profound transformation of Asian American communities. As many of the new arrivals were better educated, better skilled, and better financed, and with better English-speaking ability, they tended to be better assimilated into the host society socioeconomically and dwell in suburban middle- or upper-middle-class neighborhoods. The new development of Asian American communities has consequently attracted scholarly attention in the recent decades. The majority of the studies explore Asian American suburban communities in the Los Angeles area.

Timothy P. Fong coins the term "suburban Chinatown." In his pioneering work *The First Suburban Chinatown: The Making of Monterey Park, California*, Fong uses ethnographic observation, archival research, oral history interviews, and sociological imagination to present the experiences of the multiethnic residents of Monterey Park and their reactions to changes in the community, and to analyze the intraethnic and interethnic political strife within the community.[53] John Horton's *The Politics of Diversity: Immigration, Resistance, and Change in*

Monterey Park, California focuses on the Chinese Americans' social, political, and cultural participation and the construction of citizenship under conditions of diversity.[54] Leland T. Saito's *Race and Politics: Asian Americans, Latinos, and Whites in a Los Angeles Suburb* examines Monterey Park, giving special attention to Asian Americans' participation in local political campaigns.[55]

Yen-Fen Tseng's essay "Chinese Ethnic Economy: San Gabriel Valley, Los Angeles County" asserts that the Chinese ethnic economy in Los Angeles has formed multinuclear concentrations in suburban communities in the San Gabriel Valley. The inflow of capital and entrepreneurs from the Chinese diaspora has made the valley's economy an integral part of the Pacific Rim economy.[56] Similarly, geographer Wei Li's work analyzes the economic structure of the Chinese ethnic economy in Los Angeles. Li proposes a model of ethnic settlement— "ethnoburbs" (ethnic suburbs), which can be recognized as suburban ethnic clusters of residential areas and business districts in large metropolitan areas.[57]

Asian American Communities with Cultural/Social Boundaries

Most studies discussed above focus on the physical space of any given Asian American community, be it urban or suburban, and thus are less adequate in addressing the new communities formed in the recent decades without visible physical boundaries. Cultural community theory and the cyber community model therefore offer alternative interpretations of Asian communities without identifiable geographical boundaries but with definable cultural/social boundaries.

Cultural Communities

While both urban enclaves and suburban Asian American communities focus on the construction of physical or geographical space of a given community with identifiable territorial boundaries, cultural communities center on the construction of cultural/social space and are defined by cultural boundaries of a given ethnic culture rather than by geographical borders. Ever since the emergence of suburban Chinese communities—such as Richmond and the Sunset District in the San Francisco Bay Area; Flushing in Queens, New York; and Monterey Park in Los Angeles—scholars have been struggling to interpret them accurately. Fong's suburban Chinatown interpretation recognizes continuity between the urban ethnic enclave and the suburban Chinese communities. Contrarily, Li's "ethnoburb" notes the contrast between the traditional urban Chinese settlement and the ethnoburbs.[58] Tseng sees that the expansive growth of upper-class professional jobs and service/petty manufacturing jobs has created dual cities in Los Angeles.[59] Similarly, Lin attributes congestion in the inner city to the emergence of "satellite Chinatowns" in the suburban areas.[60] Yet all of these models primarily focus on the geographical space of the Chinese suburban settlements, and thus are incapable of explaining an ethnic community without a geographical concentration.

Clearly, we need to study the socioeconomic structures of the suburban Asian American communities not only on their physical spatial parameters but also on their social spatial dimensions. Resting on the framework of cultural/social space, I proposed a "cultural community" model in my recent book *Chinese St. Louis: From Enclave to Cultural Community.*[61] A cultural community does not necessarily have particular physical boundaries; rather, it is defined by the common cultural practices and beliefs of its members. A cultural community is constituted by the Chinese-language schools, Chinese religious institutions, Chinese American community organizations, Chinese American cultural agencies, Chinese American political coalitions or ad hoc committees, and the wide range of cultural celebrations and activities facilitated by the aforementioned agencies and groups.

A cultural community can also be identified by its economy, demography, and geography. Economically, the overwhelming majority population of a cultural community are professionally integrated into the larger society; therefore, the ethnic economy of the community does not significantly affect the security of its members and the community as a whole. Demographically, a cultural community contains a substantial percentage of professionals and self-employed entrepreneurs whose economic well-being is more dependent on the larger economy than on an ethnic economy. The former are mostly employed by the employers of the larger society, and the latter, though self-employed, also depend on the general population for their economic success. The working-class members, in terms of population, only constitute a minor part of the Chinese American community. Geographically, a cultural community is more likely to be found in hinterland and remote areas where transnational economy has limited penetration.

The cultural community model is not limited only to St. Louis. It is applicable to communities where physical concentration of the ethnic minority groups is absent. It is applicable to communities where the ethnic minority groups have economically and professionally integrated into the larger society, but culturally have remained distinct from it. The model is especially applicable to communities where the members of ethnic minority groups are overwhelmingly professionals.

As in the cultural community model, Japanese Americans have managed to maintain their community life through preserving social relationships. Stephen S. Fugita and David J. O'Brien, in *Japanese American Ethnicity: The Persistence of Community*, argue that the persistence of Japanese American ethnicity stems from elements in traditional Japanese culture that structure social relationships among group members.[62] They explain why contemporary Japanese Americans are able to retain a high level of involvement in their ethnic community while a vast majority of them have become structurally assimilated into mainstream American life. The answer lies in their ability to perceive all members of their ethnic group as "quasi kin."[63] Similarly, Kyeyoung Park documents the importance of cultural institutions such as Christian churches and community organizations in stabilizing the Korean American communities in New York.[64] Linda Trinh Võ and Rick Bonus also extend the contemporary Asian American communities to include those of "less-territory-centered" and more "fluid" spaces.[65]

Cyber Communities

The advancement in information technology and the increase of Internet users since the 1990s have created a new type of Asian American community—the cyber community, dubbed as "virtual states," "cybersociety," or "virtual community" by various writers.[66] Various surveys indicate that more than 60 percent of Chinese Americans and Chinese Canadians own home personal computers and have Internet access.[67] The launching of the China News Digest (CND) in 1989, for instance, generated a global virtual community for its Chinese-language users. The members of the cyber community could work in any occupation and reside in any geographical locality, yet they form a spatial community through the Internet. The concept of cyber community appears plausible, explaining the many presently information technology savvy Asian Americans, especially Asian American professionals, whose professional and emotional well-being is closely tied to the Internet. Like the cultural communities, a cyber community possesses no geographical space, yet it spans the globe and provides broad cyberspace for commercial, social, academic, cultural, and recreational activities to its users, who to various degrees depend on these services/activities and could feel a sense of community in such activities.

Context of the Book

This volume includes original essays on the formation and development of the contemporary Asian American communities since the 1960s. It is the first comprehensive study on Asian communities in North America. Although a large number of scholarly works have focused on Asian American communities, few have embraced Asian American communities in various locales and across national boundaries in a single volume. It includes Asian American communities not only in the gateway cities but also in the hinterland areas. While the majority of the essays in this volume focus on the new Asian communities in the United States, two essays on Chinese Canadian communities are also included to provide comparisons. Such comparative investigation well reflects the recent academic discussions on understanding Asian American studies from a "hemispheric" perspective, that is, to investigate Asian American communities in the different locales throughout North and South America in a comparative framework.[68] This vast scope allows Asian American communities to be investigated from a broader and comparative perspective.

Second, the book incorporates various theoretical approaches, models, and paradigms on Asian American communities. It examines not only the traditional Asian American enclaves but also the newer models of suburban communities, cultural communities, and cyber communities as well. It investigates the Asian American communities with physical space as well as cultural/social space, since the latter has been a more prominent identifier for many Asian American communities in recent decades.

Third, it is a multidisciplinary study that garners results from the most recent, authoritative, and cutting-edge research by eminent scholars from various academic disciplines of American studies, education, English, geography, history, and sociology. Each chapter covers an understudied topic or represents new perspectives examining Asian American communities. All contributors have done extensive scholarly work on their respective topics. The freshness of the essays in the volume and the exceptionally high quality of contributors guarantee the relevance, accuracy, objectiveness, and readability of the book.

The volume is conceptualized and structured around the following themes: Part I. Global Views of Asian American Communities; Part II. Asian Communities in America: With Geographical Boundaries; Part III. Asian Communities in America: With Cultural/Social Boundaries; and Part IV. Asian Communities in Canada.

Part I. Global Views of Asian American Communities

Part I provides a theoretical analysis and a global overview of Asian American communities. It includes "Intragroup Diversity: Asian American Population Dynamics and Challenges of the Twenty-first Century," by Min Zhou, in which she provides a demographic overview of the Asian American population. As of 2000, at least twenty-eight national-origin groups have been officially tabulated in the U.S. census, and the ethnic population has grown to nearly 12 million, up from 1.4 million in 1970, with a median age of 31.1 years, 4.2 years younger than the general U.S. population (35.3 years). The community's sevenfold growth in the span of thirty years is primarily due to immigration, which has accelerated since the 1970s. Currently, about 60 percent (or 7.2 million) of the Asian American population are foreign-born (the first generation), another 25 percent are native-born with foreign-born parentage (the second generation), and only 15 percent are native-born with native-born parentage (the third generation), with the exception of Japanese Americans who are entering the fourth generation in America. In addition, the family is a backbone institution in the Asian American community today, as contemporary Asian immigrants from different countries of origin mostly come with their families.

Zhou points out the following patterns of contemporary immigrant adaptation. First, Asian Americans overall have made remarkable achievements in education, occupation, and median family income. Second, although a lower percentage (about 35 percent) of Asian American families lived in their own homes as compared to the national average (66 percent) and to that of the non-Hispanic whites (82 percent), Asian Americans today tend to settle in urban areas and concentrate in the West. The majority of the Asian American population is spreading out in outer areas or suburbs in traditional gateway cities as well as in new urban centers of Asian settlement across the country. Third, entrepreneurship is an alternative and effective means of social mobility in the Asian American community. Although growth in business ownership among Asian Americans is the fastest of any racial group, many Asian-owned businesses are small and rely heavily on family labor. Today, when Asian Americans have been labeled as a "model minority" or "honorary whites," Zhou notes that they still have to "constantly prove that they are truly Americans and loyal citizens."

Chapter 2, "Ethnic Solidarity, Rebounding Networks, and Transnational Culture: The Post-1965 Chinese American Family," by Haiming Liu, documents and analyzes how and why Chinese family life has rebounded as a multicultural and transnational network in the post-1965 period. Though different in content and format from the early Chinese family networks, the post-1965 Chinese family networks have once again invoked expressions of ethnic resilience, provided the basis for a culture of resistance against assimilation, and functioned as a social institution that transcends the borders and boundaries of the nation-state. Liu argues that Chinese American communities have expanded from the traditional Chinatowns to various transnational communities; transnationalism has been a dominant feature of many Chinese American families as family members reside in different spatial localities across the globe. Liu asserts that the transnational family pattern represents some of the creative and adaptive strategies used collectively by the Chinese immigrants to ensure survival and social mobility.

Part II. Asian Communities in America: With Geographical Boundaries

Part II focuses on Asian American communities with geographical boundaries. The spatial formation and transformation of the Asian American communities are examined here. In the major entry ports, whether on the West Coast or in the Midwest, Asian American communities have evolved around the business districts, at the same time the suburban communities or transnational communities have also developed rapidly, making Asian American communities more diverse and complex than ever. As we will see in this section, Asian American communities with geographical boundaries have experienced spatial transformation in terms of borders and boundaries.

Chapter 3, "Beyond a Common Ethnicity and Culture: Chicagoland's Chinese American Communities since 1945," by Ling Z. Arenson, examines the forces that transformed Chicagoland's Chinese community from a culturally and socially homogeneous urban ethnic enclave to fragmented subcommunities after World

War II. Arenson reveals a diverse group that has "not only been divided along the traditional lines such as ethnicity, gender, class, migrational differences, timing of immigration, and generational gaps," but also a group "burdened with such divisive issues as home-country politics, national loyalty, and international relations, and affected by the changing legal, political, and economic environments within the host society." Arenson also notes that the professional, political, social, economic, and national background of the new immigrants, their settlement pattern, and their interactions with the larger society in the Midwest have produced trends and consequences that are markedly divergent from the experiences of other major metropolises.

Chapter 4, "Transforming an Ethnic Community: Little Saigon, Orange County," by Linda Trinh Võ, focuses on spatial expansion, economic growth, and political developments of the Vietnamese community in Orange County, California. Challenging the prevalent perceptions that the community has remained a monolithic center for refugees and anti-Communist in its political orientation, Võ notes that the community is transforming into a second generation population and facing the same problems of other Asian American communities. She also finds most members of the community unsympathetic to the Communist regime in Vietnam, but hoping to reconnect with their relatives or being attracted by the lucrative economic opportunities there. Võ foresees that the community will have to deal with issues related to the expansion and longevity of the community, the growing entrepreneurial competition from satellite Vietnamese areas in the San Gabriel Valley and downtown Chinatown, and the diverse ethnic and racial terrain of the county.

Chapter 5, "Building a Community Center: Filipinas/os in San Francisco's Excelsior Neighborhood," by Allyson Tintiangco-Cubales, presents a new community of Filipinos who live in the Excelsior District, a working-class neighborhood bordering San Francisco and Daly City. According to the 2000 census, San Francisco is home to over 40,000 Filipinos. Today, the greatest concentration of Filipinos in San Francisco live in the southeastern neighborhoods of the city, particularly in the Excelsior/OMI, Visitation Valley, and Portola districts. Tintiangco-Cubales defines the Filipinas/os in the Excelsior neighborhood as an "ethnic community" rather than an "ethnic enclave." She also examines the experiences and needs of the community and the new development of the Filipino Community Center. She asserts that through the use of both organizing for social action and providing services, the Filipino Community Center in the Excelsior aims to create an "intentional" community.

Part III. Asian Communities in America: With Cultural/Social Boundaries

Part III looks at the Asian American communities with social/cultural and cyber boundaries. As discussed in the earlier section, Asian American communities since the 1960s have transformed not only into various suburban communities but also to communities with more flexible and invisible boundaries that cannot be identified by physical space but instead by cultural/social space. Coined as "cultural communities" or "virtual communities," the Asian American communities with cultural/social boundaries are emerging as alternatives to understanding the more diverse than ever contemporary Asian American communities.

Chapter 6, "Cultural Community: A New Model for Asian American Community," by Huping Ling, proposes a new model of the Chinese American community in St. Louis as a "cultural community." Viewing the significance of the cultural community model beyond St. Louis, Ling believes that it provides an alternative theory for understanding the complexity of contemporary Chinese American communities. It also helps one better understand the issue of cultural identity and exhibits a more advanced stage of assimilation and acculturation of ethnic groups in American society.

Chapter 7, "Chinese Week: Building Chinese American Community through Festivity in Metropolitan Phoenix," by Wei Zeng and Wei Li, documents the building of contemporary Chinese American identity and community in metropolitan Phoenix through Phoenix Chinese Week, an annual celebration of the Chinese Lunar New Year. As they observe, "due to its geographical proximity to California and its role as one of the major settlement centers in Arizona, Phoenix has been a somewhat small-scale magnet for Chinese immigrants since the late nineteenth century." Despite the long settlement history, the traditional ethnic enclave—a downtown Chinatown—was wiped out several times. Chinese Americans in Phoenix are largely a community without geographical propinquity, and they maintain their culture and identity through social networks and community events. Zeng and Li view the ethnic festival Chinese Week as a venue to understanding Chinese American culture and identity formation, through which the "cultural" or "invisible" Chinese American community is constructed.

Chapter 8, "Virtual Community and the Cultural Imaginary of Chinese Americans," by Yuan Shu, examines the function that the Internet and Web-based Chinese-language networks have performed in informing and reshaping Chinese professionals and their transnational communities in the United States. These professionals have been perceived by the general American public as foreigners and Asian Americans interchangeably, or both, and have to travel back and forth between East Asia and North America. Shu argues that the Internet and the Web-based Chinese-language networks have not only served as a medium of communication for the transnational professionals to negotiate their political power and cultural spaces in the United States but also have cultivated and performed a sense of Chineseness, a cultural imaginary that allows these professionals to achieve what cultural anthropologist Aihwa Ong describes as "flexibility" across national boundaries and "visibility" within a global context.

Chapter 9, "Ethnic Solidarity in a Divided Community: A Study on Bridging Organizations in Koreatown," by Angie Y. Chung, examines how 1.5/second generation-run Korean American organizations in Los Angeles's Koreatown cultivate and maintain ethnic political solidarity despite increasing spatial dispersion, class polarization, and ideological differences within the community. Based on ninety in-depth interviews and field observations, Chung's essay demonstrates how reliance on diverse network structures allows such organizations to expand their resource options and navigate ethnic power structures. Two case studies reveal how bridging ethnic organizations will develop diverse frameworks of ethnic political solidarity depending on how they negotiate their political agendas within traditional immigrant hierarchies. Instead of undermining ethnic political solidarity, reliance on both ethnic and mainstream networks leads to the increasing diversification and specialization of ethnic organizational structures among the next generation.

Part IV. Asian Communities in Canada

Part IV examines Asian communities in Canada to provide contrast and comparison with the Asian communities in the United States. The social construction of Chinese in Canada evolves as legal, social, and racial conditions changed throughout history, as the eminent Chinese Canadian sociologist Peter S. Li notes in his classic work *The Chinese in Canada*. The racialization of the new Chinese immigrant communities in Canada since the 1980s has erected subtle obstacles for the smooth transition and integration of Chinese communities to the host society.

Chapter 10, "The Social Construction of Chinese in Canada," by Peter S. Li, discusses the historical construction of "Chinese" and its contemporary social import in Canadian society. Historically, Canada has socially constructed the racial category of "Chinese" in relation to its territorial and social boundaries. By the end of the nineteenth century, "Chinese" in Canada carried a deep-seated meaning in law, social relations, and racial ideology. The place of Chinese in Canada improved substantially after World War II, as Canada witnessed the entrenchment of civil rights and later the Charter, which offers equal protection to all. Despite these developments, "Chinese" remains a meaningful racial category in Canada, although the content of the concept of "Chinese" changes. The new Chinese immigrants from Hong Kong in the 1980s and 1990s and from mainland China since the late 1990s contributed to the image of the new Chinese middle class in Canada. However, their mobility and ownership of property in affluent white neighborhoods also triggered racial responses from certain segments of Canadian society as presented in the controversy concerning "monster houses" in Vancouver, when Chinese were portrayed as foreign elements endangering the environment, architectural heritage, and social fabric of Canada.

Chapter 11, "Recent Mainland Chinese Immigrants in Canada: Trends and Obstacles," by Li Zong, reviews the recent changes of Canadian immigration policy and analyzes the trends, patterns, and issues of immigration from mainland China to Canada. The mainland Chinese immigration to Canada was small in the 1970s and most of the 1980s; those who came were mainly family members joining close relatives in Canada. The 1990s witnessed larger numbers of mainland Chinese immigrate to Canada. Currently, mainland China has become the top immigration source country for Canada. Zong's essay examines the changing composition of the Chinese community in Canada and analyzes some obstacles that mainland Chinese face in integrating into the Canadian society. Using survey data collected in six cities, Zong also investigates how both individual and structural factors affect occupational attainment of recent mainland Chinese immigrants in Canada. Zong criticizes the discourse that cultural diversity threatens national unity and argues that national unity can be achieved in the context of cultural diversity.

The essays in this volume, though distinctive in their specific topics, approaches, and interpretations, share a common quality—they all challenge and redefine the borders and boundaries of Asian American communities, as Asian American communities negotiate their space in a rapidly changing world complicated by capitalism, transnationalism, and globalization.

NOTES

1. See works discussed in the following section.
2. Timothy P. Fong, *The First Suburban Chinatown: The Making of Monterey Park, California* (Philadelphia: Temple University Press, 1994); Jan Lin, *Reconstructing Chinatown: Ethnic Enclave, Global Change* (Minneapolis: University of Minnesota Press, 1998); Wei Li, "Spatial Transformation of an Urban Ethnic Community from Chinatown to Chinese Ethnoburb in Los Angeles" (Ph.D. diss., University of Southern California, 1997).
3. Huping Ling, *Chinese St. Louis: From Enclave to Cultural Community* (Philadelphia: Temple University Press, 2004).
4. Percentage computed according to *U.S. Census of Population: 1950*, Vol. 4, *Special Reports*, 3B-19.
5. *U.S. Census, 1940–2000.*
6. Mary Coolidge, *Chinese Immigration* (New York: Henry Holt, 1909; reprint, New York: Arno Press, 1969), 402.
7. Rose Hum Lee, *The Growth and Decline of Chinese Communities in the Rocky Mountain Region* (New York: Arno Press, 1978), 147.
8. Rose Hum Lee, *The Chinese in the United States of America* (Hong Kong: Hong Kong University Press, 1960), 52.
9. Bernard P. Wong, *A Chinese American Community: Ethnicity and Survival Strategies* (Singapore: Chopmen, 1979), 18; Kay J. Anderson, *Vancouver's Chinatown: Racial Discourse in Canada, 1875–1980* (Montreal: McGill-Queen's University Press, 1991), 9.
10. David Lai, "Socio-economic Structures and the Viability of Chinatown," in *Residential and Neighborhood Studies in Victoria*, ed. C. Forward, 101–129, Western Geographical Series, No. 5 (Victoria: University of Victoria, 1973).

11. Colette Marie McLaughlin and Paul Jesilow, "Conveying a Sense of Community along Bolsa Avenue: Little Saigon as a Model of Ethnic Commercial Belts," *International Migration* 36, no. 1 (1998): 49–63.

12. Victor G. Nee and Brett de Bary Nee, *Longtime Californ': A Documentary Study of an American Chinatown* (New York: Pantheon Books, 1972). For other works on San Francisco Chinatown, see, for example, Helen Virginia Cather, *The History of San Francisco Chinatown* (San Francisco: R & E Research Associates, 1974); Laverne Mau Dicker, *The Chinese in San Francisco: A Political History* (New York: Dover, 1979); Rose Hum Lee, "The Recent Immigrant Chinese Families of the San Francisco–Oakland Area," *Marriage and Family Living* 18, no. 1 (1956): 14–24; Ronald Riddle, *Flying Dragon, Flying Streams: Music in the Life of San Francisco's Chinese* (Westport, Conn.: Greenwood Press, 1983); John Kuo Wei Tchen, *Genthe's Photographs of San Francisco's Old Chinatown* (New York: Dover, 1984).

13. Thomas W. Chinn, *Bridging the Pacific: San Francisco Chinatown and Its People* (San Francisco: Chinese Historical Society of America, 1989).

14. Chalsa M. Loo, *Chinatown: Most Time, Hard Time* (New York: Praeger, 1991), 3.

15. Yong Chen, *Chinese San Francisco, 1850–1943: A Trans-Pacific Community* (Stanford, Calif.: Stanford University Press, 2000).

16. Nayan Shah, *Contagious Divides: Epidemics and Race in San Francisco's Chinatown* (Berkeley: University of California Press, 2001).

17. Wong, *Chinese American Community*. For other works on New York Chinatown, see Julia I. Hsuan Chen, *The Chinese Community in New York* (San Francisco: R & E Research Associates, 1974); Chia-ling Kuo, *Social and Political Change in New York's Chinatown: The Role of Voluntary Associations* (New York: Praeger, 1977); Betty Lee Sung, *Gangs in New York's Chinatown* (New York: Office of Child Development, Department of Health, Education, and Welfare, 1977); Betty Lee Sung, *The Adjustment Experience of Chinese Immigrant Children in New York City* (New York: Center for Migration Studies, 1987).

18. Bernard P. Wong, *Chinatown: Economic Adaptation and Ethnic Identity of the Chinese* (New York: Holt, Rinehart and Winston, 1982), 107.

19. Bernard P. Wong, *Patronage, Brokerage, Entrepreneurship and the Chinese Community of New York* (New York: AMS Press, 1988).

20. Peter Kwong, *Chinatown, New York: Labor and Politics, 1930–1950* (New York: Monthly Review Press, 1979); Peter Kwong, *The New Chinatown* (Hill and Wang, 1987).

21. Kwong, *New Chinatown*, 5, 175.

22. Min Zhou, *Chinatown: The Socioeconomic Potential of an Urban Enclave* (Philadelphia, Temple University Press, 1992), xvii.

23. Hsiang-shui Chen, *Chinatown No More: Taiwanese Immigrants in Contemporary New York* (Ithaca, N.Y.: Cornell University Press, 1992), ix.

24. Lin, *Reconstructing Chinatown*, xi, 12–17.

25. Roger Daniels, *Asian America Chinese and Japanese in the United States since 1850* (Seattle: University of Washington Press, 1988), 157.

26. According to Milton Gordon's classification. Milton Gordon, *Assimilation in American Life* (New York: Oxford University Press, 1964).

27. Harry Kitano et al., "Asian-American Interracial Marriage," *Journal of Marriage and the Family* 46, no. 1 (February 1984): 179–190.

28. U.S. Immigration and Naturalization Service, *Annual Report* (Washington, D.C.: Government Printing Office, 1995).

29. Ibid.

30. Kyeyoung Park, *The Korean American Dream: Immigrants and Small Business in New York City* (Ithaca, N.Y.: Cornell University Press, 1997), 9–13; Jae-Hyup Lee, *Dynamics*

of Ethnic Identity: Three Asian American Communities in Philadelphia (New York: Garland, 1998), 39; John Stephens and Sung-Ae Lee, "Diasporan Subjectivity and Cultural Space in Korean American Picture Books," *Journal of Asian American Studies* 9, no. 1 (February 2006): 1–25; Huping Ling, *Surviving on the Gold Mountain: A History of Chinese American Women and Their Lives* (Albany: State University of New York Press, 1998), 147–148.

31. See, for example, Nancy Abelmann and John Lee, *Blue Dreams: Korean Americans and the Los Angeles Riots* (Cambridge, Mass.: Harvard University Press, 1995); Edna Bonacich, Ivan Light, and Charles C. Wong, "Small Business among Koreans in Los Angeles," in *Counterpoint: Perspectives on Asian America*, ed. Emma Gee, 436–449 (Los Angeles: Asian American Studies Center, University of California, 1976); Illsoo Kim, *New Urban Immigrants: The Korean Community in New York* (Princeton, N.J.: Princeton University Press, 1981); Illsoo Kim, "The Koreans: Small Business in an Urban Frontier," in *New Immigrants in New York*, ed. Nancy Foner, 219–242 (New York: Columbia University Press, 1987); Ivan Light and Edna Bonacich, *Immigrant Entrepreneurs: Koreans in Los Angeles, 1965–1982* (Berkeley: University of California Press, 1988); Pyong Gap Min, "A Structural Analysis of Korean Business in the United States," *Ethnic Groups* 6 (1984): 1–25; Pyong Gap Min, *Ethnic Business Enterprise: Korean Small Business in Atlanta* (New York: Center for Migration Studies, 1988); Pyong Gap Min, *Caught in the Middle: Korean Communities in New York and Los Angeles* (Berkeley: University of California Press, 1996).

32. Min, "Structural Analysis of Korean Business."

33. Park, *Korean American Dream.*

34. Lee, *Dynamics of Ethnic Identity.*

35. Kim, *New Urban Immigrants*, 226.

36. Pauline Agbayani-Siewert and Linda Revilla, "Filipino Americans," in *Asian Americans: Contemporary Trends and Issues*, ed. Pyong Gap Min, 142 (Thousand Oaks, Calif.: Sage, 1995).

37. U.S. Census, 2000.

38. Sucheng Chan, *Asian Americans: An Interpretive History* (Boston: Twayne, 1991), 149.

39. Agbayani-Siewert and Revilla, "Filipino Americans," 143.

40. Yen Le Espiritu, *Home Bound: Filipino American Lives Across Cultures* (Berkeley: University of California Press, 2003), 11; Chan, *Asian Americans*, 149.

41. Espiritu, *Home Bound*, 32.

42. Chan, *Asian Americans*, 150.

43. Ibid.

44. Linda Nueva Espana-Maram, "Negotiating Identity: Youth, Gender, and Popular Culture in Los Angeles's Little Manila, 1920s-1940s" (Ph. D. diss., University of California, Los Angeles, 1996), 3; Linda Nueva Espana-Maram, *Creating Masculinity in Los Angeles's Little Manila: Working-Class Filipinos and Popular Culture, 1920s–1950s* (New York: Columbia University Press, 2006).

45. Rick Bonus, *Locating Filipino America: Ethnicity and Cultural Politics of Space* (Philadelphia: Temple University Press, 2000).

46. Espiritu, *Home Bound*, 105–117.

47. Rubén G. Rumbaut, "The Structure of Refugees: Southeast Asian Refugees in the United States, 1975–1985," *International Review of Comparative Public Policy* 1 (1989): 97–129; Min Zhou and Carl L. Bankston III, *Growing Up American: How Vietnamese Children Adapt to Life in the United States* (New York: Russell Sage Foundation, 1998), 56.

48. Ha, interview by author, May 28 and June 14, 1999; see also Huping Ling, *Voices of the Heart: Asian American Women on Immigration, Work, and Family* (Kirksville, Mo.: Truman State University Press, 2007); James M. Freeman, *Hearts of Sorrow: Vietnamese American Lives* (Stanford, Calif.: Stanford University Press, 1989), 369–373.

49. U.S. Census, 2000.

50. Colette Marie McLaughlin and Paul Jesilow, "Conveying a Sense of Community along Bolsa Avenue: Little Saigon as a Model of Ethnic Commercial Belts," *International Migration* 36, no. 1 (1998): 49–63. See Linda Trinh Võ's chapter in this volume.

51. McLaughlin and Jesilow, "Conveying a Sense of Community."

52. Sanjoy Mazumdar, Shampa Mazumdar, Faye Docuyanan, and Colette Marie McLaughlin, "Creating a Sense of Place: The Vietnamese-Americans and Little Saigon," *Journal of Environmental Psychology* 20 (2000): 319–333.

53. Fong, *First Suburban Chinatown*. For other works on Chinese communities in suburban Los Angeles, see Joe Chung Fong, "Transnational Newspapers: The Making of the Post-1965 Globalized/Localized San Gabriel Valley Chinese Community," *Amerasia Journal* 22, no. 3 (1996): 65–77; John Horton, *The Politics of Diversity: Immigration, Resistance, and Change in Monterey Park, California* (Philadelphia: Temple University Press, 1995); Leland Saito, *Race and Politics: Asian and Latino and White in Los Angeles Suburbs* (Urbana: University of Illinois Press, 1998); Yu Zhou, "Ethnic Networks as Transactional Networks: Chinese Networks in the Producer Service Sectors of Los Angeles" (Ph.D. diss., University of Minnesota, 1996); Yen-Fen Tseng, "Suburban Ethnic Economy: Chinese Business Communities in Los Angeles" (Ph.D. diss., University of California, Los Angeles, 1994); Yen-Fen Tseng, "Chinese Ethnic Economy: San Gabriel Valley, Los Angeles County," *Journal of Urban Affairs* 16, no. 2 (1994): 169–189. For comparative studies of Chinatowns in Canada, see Anderson, *Vancouver's Chinatown*; David Lai, *Chinatowns: Towns within Cities in Canada* (Vancouver: University of British Columbia Press, 1988); Richard H. Thompson, *Toronto's Chinatown: The Changing Social Organization of an Ethnic Community* (New York: AMS, 1987).

54. Horton, *Politics of Diversity*, 8.

55. Saito, *Race and Politics*.

56. Tseng, "Chinese Ethnic Economy."

57. Wei Li, "Spatial Transformation of an Urban Ethnic Community."

58. Ibid.

59. Tseng, "Chinese Ethnic Economy."

60. Lin, *Reconstructing Chinatown*, 107–120.

61. Ling, *Chinese St. Louis*.

62. Stephen S. Fujita and David J. O'Brien, *Japanese American Ethnicity: The Persistence of Community* (Seattle: University of Washington Press, 1991).

63. Ibid., 4–5.

64. Park, *Korean American Dream*.

65. Linda Trinh Võ and Rick Bonus, *Contemporary Asian American Communities: Intersections and Divergences* (Philadelphia: Temple University Press, 2002), 6.

66. Jerry Everard, *Virtual States: The Internet and the Boundaries of the Nation States* (New York: Routledge, 2000); Steven G. Jones, "Understanding Community in the Information Age," in *Cybersociety: Computer-Mediated Communication and Community*, ed. Steven Jones, 10–35 (Thousand Oaks, Calif.: Sage, 1995); Steven Jones, "The Internet and Its Social Landscape," in *Virtual Culture: Identity and Communication in Cybersociety*, ed. Steven Jones, 7–35 (Thousand Oaks, Calif.: Sage, 1997); Yuan Shu's chapter in this volume.

67. See Yuan Shu's chapter in this volume.

68. Erika Lee, "Hemispheric Orientalism and the 1907 Pacific Coast Race Riots," *Amerasia Journal* 33, no. 2 (2007): 19–47; Lok Siu, *Memories of a Future Home: Diasporic Citizenship of Chinese in Panama* (Stanford, Calif.: Stanford University Press, 2005).

PART ONE

Global Views of Asian American Communities

1

Intragroup Diversity

Asian American Population Dynamics and Challenges of the Twenty-first Century

MIN ZHOU

Asian America began to take shape in the late 1840s when a large number of Chinese immigrants arrived in the United States as contract laborers. In the span of more than one and a half centuries, it has evolved into a vastly diverse ethnic community consisting of people whose ancestors, or who themselves, were born in more than twenty-five Asian countries. As of 2005, the estimated number of Asian Americans grew to 14.4 million, up from less than 12 million in 2000 and from 1.4 million in 1970. The group's many-fold growth in the past forty years is primarily due to immigration, which has accelerated since the passage of the Hart-Cellar Act of 1965. Based on the 2000 U.S. census, about 60 percent (or 7.2 million) of the Asian American population are foreign-born (the first generation), another 25 percent are native-born with foreign-born parentage (the second generation), and only 15 percent are native-born with native-born parentage (the third generation), with the exception of Japanese Americans who are entering the fourth generation in America based on estimates of the U.S. Current Population Survey. This chapter offers a demographic overview of the Asian American population at the dawn of the twenty-first century. It highlights the tremendous intragroup diversity in origin, socioeconomic status, and patterns of settlement and adaptation. It also discusses the challenges that this ethnic group faces in the twenty-first century, particularly the causes and consequences of the "model minority" image and its implications for Asian Americans.

Demographic Transformation

Diverse National Origins

The term "Asian American" is a socially constructed term because the variety of ethnically distinct subgroups far exceeds the similarities that these subgroups share. In 1970, the size of Asian American community was about 1.4 million, largely made up of three national-origin groups—Japanese (41 percent), Chinese

(30 percent), and Filipino (24 percent). Those who fell into the "Other Asian" category (5 percent) included mostly Koreans and Asian Indians. Since 1970, the community has been dramatically transformed by contemporary immigration.

As of 2000, at least twenty-five national-origin groups have been officially tabulated in the U.S. census. As Table 1.1 shows, Americans of Chinese and Filipino ancestries are the largest subgroups, at more than 2 million, followed by Indians, Koreans, Vietnamese, and Japanese, whose numbers surpass the 1 million mark. There are many other national-origin or ethnic groups who have made their visible presence in the United State only after the 1970s, such as Cambodians, Pakistanis, Laotians, Hmongs, and Thais. The "Other Asian" category in the 2000 census includes Bangladeshis, Indonesians, Malaysians, and Singaporeans, among others.

Immigration from Asian countries has accelerated since the 1970s. The share of immigrants from Asia as a proportion of the U.S. total inflow grew from a tiny 5 percent in the 1950s to around 35 percent in the 1980s and 1990s. Prior to 1980, no Asian country was on the United States' annual list of top ten immigrant-origin countries. Since then, however, China, the Philippines, India, Korea, and Vietnam have shown up on the list repeatedly. Between 1980 and 2000, immigration accounted for more than half of the population growth for Asian Americans (and for 70 percent of Indian growth, 63 percent of Filipino growth, and 59 percent of Vietnamese growth). National origins stretched out to more than twenty-five Asian countries, many of which had no prior settlement histories on American soil.

Table 1.2 illustrates the extent of legal immigration into the United States from six major Asian countries from 1941 to 2000. Before World War II, immigration by decade from these countries was fairly low, except for the Chinese, but it has become increasingly voluminous as the direct effect of the implementation of the Hart-Cellar Act of 1965. Compared to other Asian groups, Japanese immigration slowed down since World War II. Korean immigration slowed down significantly in the 1990s, showing less than half of the inflow from the previous decade. Filipino immigration also slowed down in the 1990s, but the inflow remained substantial.

While most of the immigrants have come directly from their ancestral homelands, others have arrived from a different country. For example, the Chinese today have immigrated into the United States not only from mainland China but also from the Chinese diaspora—Hong Kong, Taiwan, Vietnam, Cambodia, Malaysia, and the Americas. Indians have arrived not only from India but also from Fiji, Uganda, Trinidad, South Africa, and the United Kingdom.[1] Many of the Southeast Asians have been resettled in the United States after they fled their ancestral homelands and spent various lengths of time in refugee camps in other countries in Asia and Europe. Among foreign-born Asians in the United States today, about 42 percent have arrived in the United States after

TABLE 1.1

Asian American Population: 1970–2000

National Origin	1970	%	1980	%	2000	%	% Growth 1980–2000 due to Immigration
Chinese	435,062	30.2	806,040	22.7	2,858,291	24.1	47.5
Filipino	343,060	23.8	700,974	19.7	2,385,216	20.1	62.5
Japanese	591,290	41.1	700,974	19.7	1,152,324	9.7	25.5
Indian	–*	–	361,531	10.2	1,855,590	15.7	41.1
Korean	–*	–	354,593	10.0	1,226,825	10.3	57.1
Vietnamese	–*	–	261,729	7.4	1,212,465	10.2	59.6
Cambodian					212,633	1.8	–
Pakistani					209,273	1.8	–
Laotian					196,893	1.7	–
Hmong					184,842	1.6	–
Thai					150,093	1.3	–
Other Asian	70,150	4.9	364,598	10.3	215,001	1.8	–
Total	1,439,562	100.0	3,550,439	100.0	11,859,446	100.0	50.9

Source: U.S. Census of the Population, 1970, 1980, and 2000.

* Indian, Korean, and Vietnamese subgroups were not tabulated in the 1970 U.S. census.

TABLE 1.2
Immigration from Asia, 1941 to 2000

Country of Last Residence	1941–50	1951–60	1961–70	1971–80	1981–90	1991–00	Total 1941–2000
China/Hong Kong/Taiwan	16,709	25,198	109,771	237,793	444,962	528,893	1,363,326
Philippines	4,691	19,307	98,376	354,987	548,764	503,945	1,530,070
Japan	1,555	46,250	39,988	49,775	47,085	67,942	252,595
India	1,761	1,973	27,189	164,134	250,786	363,060	808,903
Korea	107	6,231	34,526	267,638	333,746	164,166	806,414
Vietnam	–	335	4,340	172,820	280,782	286,143	744,420

Source: U.S. Department of Homeland Security. 2003 Yearbook of Immigration Statistics. U.S. Government Printing Office, Washington, D.C., September 2004. Online access on November 8, 2005: http://uscis.gov/graphics/shared/statistics/yearbook/2003/2003Yearbook.pdf

1990, and 47 percent are naturalized U.S. citizens, which indicates that the Asian American population is still primarily an immigrant-dominant ethnic group.[2]

Changes in the Family

The family is a backbone institution in the Asian American community today. Most of the Asian-origin groups come from a strong tradition of extended, patriarchal family and kinship ties. Although these ties are disrupted during migration, they have been quickly rebuilt to shape family patterns in different historical periods. In the second half of the nineteenth century and the first half of the twentieth century, most immigrants from Asia were male sojourners who left their close relatives—parents, wives, and children—in the homelands and sent remittances to support them.[3] A series of anti-Asian laws following the Chinese Exclusion Act of 1882 denied the entry of immigrants from Asia while also restricting the immigration of women and family members of those already in the United States. The Asian American communities in urban areas, such as Chinatown and Little Tokyo, became bachelors' societies. In 1900, the sex ratio for Chinese was 1,385 males per 100 females and for Japanese was 487 males per 100 females.

The development of the pre–World War II Japanese American community was unique, even though it started as a bachelors' society. Because of the Gentlemen's Agreement of 1907–1908, which closed entry to laborers but permitted the entry of wives and relatives, the Japanese American community gradually evolved into a small family-based community with the departure of many first generation (*issei*) men who returned to Japan permanently between 1909 and 1924. During the same period, those Japanese who decided to settle permanently in the United States sent for their wives, or picture brides, from Japan, which gave rise to a significant cohort of U.S.-born (*nisei*) children before World War II.[4] This also explains why Japanese Americans are now entering their fourth generation in the United States, while Chinese Americans, who as a group arrived in the United States much earlier, are still primarily made up of the first and second generations, with a relatively small third generation.

Contemporary Asian immigrants from different countries of origin mostly come with their families, thanks to the Hart-Cellar Act of 1965 aiming at family reunification. Now the sex ratio of the ethnic population is nearly balanced (slightly tilted toward females for many groups), as Table 1.3 shows. Also, the population is generally younger, with few elderly, except for Japanese Americans. Because of the recentness of Asian immigration, the typical Asian American family consists of immigrant parents and their native-born children or foreign-born children who arrived in the United States before school age (also referred to as the 1.5 generation). With the exception of Japanese American families, Asian American families are generally much larger than non-Hispanic white families and are twice to four times as likely as white families to be multigenerational. Interracial and interethnic marriages and dating

TABLE 1.3

Sex Ratio, Age, Family Structure of Selected Asian Origin Groups, 2000

National Origin	Sex Ratio (Male per 100 female)	Median Age	Age (% 65 years or older)	In Husband- Wife Families %	In Multi- Generational Families %
Chinese	48	36	10	73	15
Filipino	45	36	9	73	22
Japanese	43	43	20	65	5
Indian	53	30	4	80	14
Korean	44	33	6	74	10
Vietnamese	50	31	5	70	16
Other Asian	50	27	3	74	19
All Asian	48	33	7	73	15
All White	49	38	12	67	5

Source: Adapted from tables 2 and 8 in Yu Xie and K. A. Goyette, *The American People, Census 2000: A Demographic Portrait of Asian Americans* (New York: Russell Sage Foundation Press & Washington, D.C.: Population Reference Bureau, 2004).

have been high among U.S.-born Asian Americans, particularly among Japanese Americans. Of the six largest Asian subgroups, Japanese Americans are most likely to report have mixed-race heritage (a combination of Japanese with one or more other races or Asian groups) in the 2000 census: almost a third of them are offspring of intermarriages.[5]

There are some common family values in the Asian American family that are distinguishable, such as the emphasis on the centrality of the family, filial piety, respect for the elders, and reverence for tradition and education. While these traditional values offer a strong moral basis sustaining the Asian American family, they have often clashed with dominant American cultural values and have caused emotional pain and detrimental consequences in the family and community. One common cultural clash is between the strict formality and collectivist orientation in the Asian American family and the permissiveness and individualism in the American society.

Diverse Languages and Religions

It is almost impossible to define *the* Asian American culture due to the diverse origins of Asian Americans. Except for sharing the experience of having a native homeland separated from the United States by the Pacific Ocean, there is no single ancestral language or religion that dominates the community. Each of the national-origin or ethnic groups has brought its own respective cultural traditions, including language and religion. Linguistically, Chinese, Japanese, Korean, and Vietnamese immigrants come from countries with a single official language. Filipino immigrants, in contrast, come from a country where Pilipino, a variation of the native language Tagalog, and English are both official languages, and most of the Filipino immigrants are fluent bilinguals before entering the United States.[6] Most Indian immigrants are proficient in English, as India also designates English as an official language along with more than twenty other official languages, and the most common Indian languages spoken in Indian homes include Hindi, Bengali, Telugu, Marathi, Tamil, Urdu, Gujarati, Punjabi, and others.[7] Moreover, there are many local and regional dialects spoken within each group. For example, immigrants from China, Hong Kong, and Taiwan share the same written Chinese language but speak a variety of dialects—Cantonese, Mandarin, Fujianese, Chaozhounese, Shanghainese, and Wenzhouness—that are not easily understood even within the Chinese immigrant community.

In the Asian American community, there is no single religion that unifies the pan-racial group, but religion serves as one of the most important ethnic institutions in the community. Chinese, Japanese, Korean, and Vietnamese come from non–Judeo Christian backgrounds, where Confucianism and/or Buddhism and their variations are widespread in the homelands. Western colonization in the homelands and immigration to the United States have led to a trend of conversion to Christianity prior to and after arrival. For example, less than 20 percent of the population in Korea is Protestant, but more than three-quarters of Korean Americans are Protestants.[8] Existing research suggests Protestant Koreans are more likely than others to emigrate. In Vietnam, only 10 percent of the population are Catholic, but about a third in the United States are Catholic.[9] Many Vietnamese refugees were converted to Catholicism after they fled Vietnam as a way to obtain U.S. sponsorship, largely due to the active role the Catholic Charities played in resettling Vietnamese refugees in the United States.[10] Conversion to Christianity is also noticeable among immigrants from Taiwan, but on a smaller scale than among those from mainland China and Japan.[11] The majority of Filipino Americans are Catholic, as the population in their homeland consists of 80 percent Catholics. Indian Americans come from more diverse religious backgrounds, with Hindus dominating, followed by smaller numbers of Muslims, Christians, Sikhs, and Buddhists; their conversion to Christianity is relatively rare in comparison to other major Asian subgroups.[12] Although religious practices are organized along ethnic lines, especially among immigrants, there is a trend in the second or later generations to congregate pan-racially.

Despite religious diversity, some significant common patterns can be discerned. First, religion takes on a new twist compared to that practiced in the ancestral homeland. To varying degrees, religion responds not only to uprooted immigrants' demands for reestablishing a moral order, fulfilling spiritual needs, and learning new ways of organizing individual and collective action but also to their material needs of initial settlement, survival, and social mobility.[13] For example, Korean Christian churches provide tangible resources to immigrants, such as language and job training, financial and manpower services, and counseling, while also functioning as a social status hierarchy in which religious and nonreligious positions can be achieved.[14] Those immigrants who experience downward mobility upon arrival in the United States can regain social status within their own cultural institution. Hindu organizations, such as *satsang* (religious congregation) and *bala vihar* (child development organization), offer both spiritual and secular services to immigrants and their children.[15]

Second, religion not only reorients old symbols and ways to the new environment but also provides a physical space where immigrants come together to worship, and, more important, to reconnect and reestablish social networks that are disrupted through the process of migration.[16] For example, before new immigrants are able to build their own churches, they usually congregate at suburban public high schools, rather than merge into existing American churches, where they can worship and socialize among coethnics and use their own native languages.

Third, cultural mixing in religious practices is common. For example, conversion to Christianity serves a dual function of acculturation. While it naturally promotes Christianity and thus facilitates the Americanization of immigrants from diverse origins, ethnic religious practices enable followers to selectively preserve certain elements of their ancestral culture and strengthen ethnic solidarity around a common cultural heritage.[17] When conversions occur, there emerge visible forms of "Confucianized," or "Asianized," Christianity as a means of sustaining or reaffirming ethnic identity.[18]

Contemporary Patterns of Immigrant Adaptation

Socioeconomic Characteristics

Asian Americans are diverse not only by origins but also by socioeconomic status (SES). Unlike earlier immigrants from Asia, who were mostly low-skilled laborers and disproportionately single males, today's immigrants from Asia include those who come to join their families, who invest their monies in the U.S. economy, who fill the labor market demands for highly skilled workers, and who escape war, political or religious persecution, and economic hardships. For example, scientists, engineers, physicians, and other skilled professionals tend to be overrepresented among Indians, Filipinos, Chinese, and Koreans, while less-educated, low-skilled workers tend to be overrepresented among Vietnamese, Cambodians, and Laotians, most of whom enter the United States

TABLE 1.4

Social Economic Characteristics of Asian Origin Groups, 2000

National Origin	Bachelor's Degrees or More[1] %	Management, Professional, & Related Occupations[2] %	Median Family Income $	Poverty %	Owner-Occupied Housing %
Chinese	48.1	52.3	60,058	13.5	58.4
Filipino	43.8	38.2	65,189	6.3	60.0
Japanese	41.9	50.7	70,849	9.7	60.8
Indian	63.9	59.9	70,708	9.8	46.9
Korean	43.8	38.7	47,624	14.8	40.1
Vietnamese	19.4	26.9	47,103	16.0	53.2
Cambodian	9.2	17.8	35,621	29.3	43.6
Pakistani	54.3	43.5	50,189	16.5	41.7
Laotian	7.7	17.1	43,542	18.5	52.4
Hmong	7.5	13.4	32,384	37.8	38.7
Thai	38.6	33.4	49,635	14.4	48.1
Other Asian	41.4	39.8	50,733	15.6	46.2
All Asian	44.1	44.6	59,324	12.6	53.2
Total U.S.	24.4	33.6	50,046	12.4	66.2

Source: Adapted figures 9, 11, 13, 14, and 15 from Terrance J. Reeves and Claudette E. Bennett, *We the people: Asians in the United States* (Washington, D.C.: U.S. Census Bureau, 2004).

[1] 25 years or older.

[2] 15 years or older who were in the labor force.

as refugees. Middle-class immigrants are able to start their American life with high-paying professional jobs and comfortable suburban living, while low-skilled immigrants and refugees have to endure low-paying menial jobs and ghettoized inner-city living.

In general, Asian Americans have shown remarkable achievements in key SES indicators—education, occupation, and median family income—as Table 1.4 indicates. For example, their average levels of educational and occupational attainments are much higher than those of the general American population; as of 2000, 44 percent of them held bachelor's degrees or higher, and 45 percent held managerial-professional or related occupations, as opposed to 24 percent and 34 percent, respectively, of all Americans. Their median family income was $59,000 in 1999 dollars, as opposed to $50,000 for American families. However, there were marked intragroup differences. Southeast Asian refugee groups fared poorly in all the listed SES indicators. Moreover, four of the twelve subgroups listed in Table 1.4 showed lower median family incomes, including the Koreans who fared much better than average Americans in education and occupation; and nine out of the twelve subgroups showed higher than average poverty rates, including the Chinese, who fared much better than average Americans in education, occupation, and family income.

Education as the Chief Means to Upward Social Mobility

Like all Americans, Asian Americans regard education as the most important means to social mobility. What is unique about the emphasis on education among Asian Americans lies in the family's control over educational choices and the community's institutional support. Families set high expectations for their children and instill in their children that educational achievement is a family honor as well as a means to secure future livelihood.[19] A family's educational goals are reinforced by the ethnic community. In some ethnic communities, as in the case of Chinese and Koreans, educationally oriented private institutions have become a key sector in the ethnic economy. Various SAT cram schools, after-school tutoring, music and art schools run by immigrant entrepreneurs, combined with similar services offered at ethnic churches, community cultural centers, and other nonprofit social service organizations based in the community, form an ethnic system of supplementary education to assist families and children.[20]

Tremendous family and community pressure on achieving has yielded positive results. Asian American children are indeed doing exceptionally well in school. They frequently appear as high school valedictorians and on competitive academic decathlon teams, and win prestigious awards and honors at the national, state, and local levels. They are also gaining admission to the nation's Ivy League and prestigious colleges in disproportionate numbers. In the past few years, Asian American students represented more than 20 percent of the undergraduate student population at all nine University of California (UC) campuses, close to 60 percent at UC-Irvine and 40 percent at UCLA, UC-Berkeley, and UC-Riverside. They are also visible, at 15 to 30 percent of the total undergraduate student population, at Harvard, Yale, Stanford, MIT, Cal Tech, and other Ivy League and prestigious colleges. As of 2000, Asian Americans have attained the highest level of education of all racial groups in the United States: 44 percent of Asian Americans adults (aged twenty-five and over) have attained bachelor's degrees or higher, and the ratio for those with advanced degrees (for example, master's, Ph.D., M.D., or J.D.) is one in seven.

There is a downside of overachievement. Because of family and community pressure for achieving and the burden of honoring the family, many Asian American youths have to sacrifice their own personal interests to pursue what their parents think is best for them—a career in science, medicine, or the technical professions. For example, a Chinese American college student gave up his promising singing career to enroll in medical school just to make his parents happy. Asian American youths also suffer from mental health problems, such as self-hate, depression, and suicide, which often go unnoticed until symptoms become chronic.[21]

Homeownership and Residential Mobility

Owning a home is regarded as achieving the American Dream for many immigrants in the United States. Like other Americans, Asian Americans often consider homeownership an important measure of socioeconomic mobility. As of 2000, about 53 percent of Asian American families lived in their own homes (see Table 1.4). This homeownership rate was significantly lower than the national average (66 percent) and substantially below that of non-Hispanic whites (82 percent). The disparity in homeownership may be due to the fact that Asian American families generally are more likely to be headed by the foreign-born, are younger, and have less accumulated wealth. Nevertheless, many Asian American families achieve homeownership through two typical means: the pool of family savings, including the contribution of unmarried children's incomes, and ethnic financial institutions. Through the pool of family and kin resources, many Asian American families are able to put a considerable amount (at least 25 percent of the mortgage) in down payment as a way to secure a bank loan. In some ethnic communities, such as Chinese and Korean communities, ethnic banks and other ethnic financial institutions provide an effective means to obtain home mortgage loans, especially for immigrants who may not have English proficiency, cultural literacy, and credit to navigate the mainstream banking system.[22]

Homeownership in the Asian American community is not only considered an end but also a means to an end, influencing Asian American residential patterns of settlement. Many immigrant families use homeownership to access the best possible public educational opportunities for their children. Like other middle-class Americans, one of the most important criteria in choosing a home among Asian Americans is living in a neighborhood with good public schools. Proximity to an ethnic community or coethnics is of secondary importance. In recent years, well-performing public schools are witnessing a rapid increase in the enrollment of Asian Americans in many suburbs in California, New York, New Jersey, Texas, Illinois, and the District of Columbia.

Asian Americans today tend to settle in urban areas and concentrate in the West. According to the 2000 U.S. census, one state, California, by itself accounts for 35 percent of all Asians (4.3 million) in the United States, and California also has the largest number of each of the six main national-origin groups. New York accounts for 10 percent, or 1.2 million, of all Asian Americans, second only to California. Chinese, Indians, and Koreans are heavily concentrated in New York, but not Filipinos, Japanese, and Vietnamese. Several other states deserve special mention: Texas has the second largest Vietnamese population, next to California. Illinois has the third largest Filipino population, next to California and Hawaii. Washington has the third largest Japanese population, next to California and Hawaii. And New Jersey has the third largest Indian and Korean populations, next to California and New York. Among cities with a population over 100,000, New York City, Los Angeles, and Honolulu have the largest number of Asians, while Daly City, California, and Honolulu are Asian-majority cities. Some smaller cities in California, such as Monterey Park (the first city in America that reached an Asian majority, in 1990, and remained an Asian-majority city in 2000), have also reached an Asian majority.[23]

Traditional urban enclaves such as Chinatown, Little Tokyo, Manilatown, Koreatown, Little Phnom Pen, and Thaitown have continued to exist, or have emerged, in gateway cities in recent years, but they no longer serve as primary centers of initial settlement as many new immigrants, especially the affluent and highly skilled, are bypassing inner cities to settle in suburbs immediately after arrival. For example, as of 2000, only 8 percent of Chinese in San Francisco and 12 percent in New York live in inner-city old Chinatowns. Only 13 percent of Vietnamese in Orange County, California, live in Little Saigon; 14 percent of Koreans in Los Angeles live in Koreatown; and 27 percent of Cambodians in Los Angeles live in Little Phnom Pen. The majority of the Asian American population is spreading out in outer areas or suburbs in traditional gateway cities as well as in new urban centers of Asian settlement across the country.

Ethnic Entrepreneurship

Entrepreneurship is an alternative and effective means of social mobility in the Asian American community. Historically, Chinese Americans and Japanese Americans have depended on ethnic businesses as a way to climb up the socioeconomic ladder, especially during the era of legal exclusion and labor market discrimination.[24] Since the 1970s, unprecedented Asian immigration, accompanied by the tremendous influx of human and financial capital, has set off a new stage of ethnic economic development. As of 2000, 11 percent of Asian American workers twenty-five years or older were self-employed, compared to 13 percent of white workers and 5 percent of black workers. Koreans, Chinese, Indian, and Vietnamese showed fairly high rates of self-employment (over 11 percent). Koreans in particular were nearly twice as likely as whites to be self-employed (24 percent versus 13 percent).[25]

Growth in business ownership among Asian Americans is the fastest of any racial group. Although the number of black- and Hispanic-owned businesses grew by 93 percent from 1977 to 1987, neither came close to matching the rapid expansion of Asian–owned businesses, which grew by 238 percent. From 1987 to 1997, the number of Asian-owned businesses continued to grow at a rate of 121 percent (from 355,331 in 1987 to 893,590 in 1997). As of 2002, the number of Asian-owned firms climbed to 1.1 million, employing more than 2.2 million people and generating $327 billion in revenue. Asian-owned business enterprises made up 4 percent of the total U.S. nonfarm businesses, 2 percent of their employment, and 1.4 percent of their receipts. Thirty-one percent of Asian-owned businesses operated in the category "other services"—such as personal services, repair and maintenance services, and professional, scientific, and technical services, where they owned 5.8 percent of all such businesses in the United States.[26] Overall, there was approximately one ethnic firm for every eleven Asians, but only one ethnic firm for every thirty blacks and one for every twenty-three Hispanics.

Many Asian-owned businesses are small and rely heavily on family labor. Typical Asian-owned businesses include restaurants, green grocers, garment factories, nail salons, dry cleaners, and fish markets. In New York City, there were about 500 Chinese-owned garment factories employing some 20,000 Chinese immigrant workers, and about 400 Korean-owned garment factories employing more than 14,000 Hispanic workers during the industry's peak in the late 1980s.[27] There were about 2,000 dry cleaners run by Koreans, about 1,400 Korean-owned green grocers, and about 70,000 South Indian taxi drivers in New York City in the 1990s.[28] However, Asian American entrepreneurship has also evolved out of the stereotypical mom-and-pop operations in the retail trade and labor-intensive, low-tech manufacturing operations. Many Asian entrepreneurs today offer various professional services in law, finance, real estate, and medicine, and are engaged in capital- and knowledge-intensive research and development in telecommunication, computer science, biochemistry, and biotechnology. Entrepreneurship is not only pursued by first generation immigrants, but it has increasingly been attractive to the second generation as a viable means for social mobility. Greater participation of highly skilled immigrants and the children of immigrants in entrepreneurial activity, in turn, is likely to facilitate the incorporation of the Asian American community into mainstream America.

In summary, compared with the general U.S. population, Asian Americans tend to score above average in key SES measures. In particular, their extraordinary educational achievement and hard work appear to enable them to integrate into mainstream American society. The current situation of this racial minority group seems to reinforce the image of Asian Americans as the "model minority." A simple check of the census data, however, shows clear inconsistencies with this portrait, reminding us that "Asian" is a heterogeneous category that includes a diversity of national-origin groups. Moreover, some important determinants of social mobility, such as length of U.S. residence since immigration, language usage and English proficiency, and a family's socioeconomic status, have different effects on outcomes across groups, suggesting possible interactions between these determining factors and group-specific characteristics. Furthermore, despite high levels of educational achievement, young Asian American workers are confronting a different set of barriers in the labor market from those that have been generally understood. For instance, while education is believed to be the single most important factor for occupational achievement, Asian Americans often find themselves in a situation where they must overeducate themselves in order to obtain reasonably good jobs. This simple fact suggests that even a good education may not necessarily guarantee comparable occupational achievement, and whether in the long run overeducation will translate into proportionate earnings remains uncertain. There is more behind the Asian American success.

Honorary White or Forever Foreigner

"Are Asian Americans becoming white?" For many American institutions, the answer must be yes, because they classify Asian-origin Americans with European-origin Americans for purposes of equal opportunity programs. For many Asian Americans themselves, the answer is "never." Whitening is a premature characterization of the group, given the "foreigner" image most Americans still have of Asians; it also imposes a heavy burden and reinforces a double standard upon Asian Americans.[29]

As has just been discussed, "Asian American" is a tremendously diverse racial minority group. Since all group categories are socially constructed, "Asian American" has emerged since the late 1960s as a self-proclaimed pan-racial identity in rejection of the imposed "Oriental" label. "Asian American" has now become an umbrella category that includes U.S. citizens and immigrants, who, or whose ancestors, came from the part of Asia stretching from Pakistan eastward, and has been widely applied in the public arena. However, most Asian Americans have identified themselves with it only conditionally, reflecting the nuance of this pan-racial identity as a process of being American while maintaining an ethnicity of some sort.[30] Similarly, "white" is a rather arbitrary label having less to do with biology and more to do with privilege. In the United States, groups with status and wealth generally earn "white" membership, as the Irish and Jews have done. It is hardly surprising, then, that nonwhites would seek to pass as "white," or aspire to becoming "white," a mark of their attaining middle-class status. However, becoming "white" can also mean distancing oneself from "people of color." In fact, pan-racial identities—Asian American, African American, Hispanic American—have become a way the politically vocal in any group guard against "selling out" one's ethnicity to the white establishment.[31] The ambivalence of aspiring to, versus resisting, becoming "white" may be beside the point. At issue is whether Asian Americans have achieved full citizenship through socioeconomic success.

The "model minority" categorization came into being in the mid-1960s, just at the peak of the black civil rights movement and other ethnic consciousness movements on college campuses that the civil rights movement inspired, but before the rising waves of immigration and refugee influx from Asia. Two publications in 1966—"Success Story, Japanese-American Style," by William Petersen in the *New York Times Magazine* (January 9), and "Success of One Minority Group in U.S." by the *U.S. News and World Report* staff (December 26)—marked a significant departure from the ways in which Asian immigrants and their succeeding generations had been traditionally depicted in the media and popular culture. In similar rhetoric and undertones, both articles extolled Japanese Americans and Chinese Americans for their persistence in pulling themselves up from extreme hardships and discrimination to achieve success, unmatched even by U.S.-born whites, with "their own almost totally unaided effort" and "no help from anyone else." The press attributed hard work, family solidarity, discipline, respect, delayed gratification, and nonconfrontation, but "not a welfare check," to their winning wealth and respect in the "promised land."

However, the stereotyping of Asian Americans as a "model minority" has buttressed an image of the United States devoid of racism and according equal opportunities to all. It has promoted the ideal of meritocracy and placed the blame for those lagging behind on their own inferior culture and on their own doing. Fundamentally, it carries ramifications that extend well beyond the Chinatowns and Little Tokyos of America, serving to thwart other racial minorities' claims for justice and to pit one racial minority against another.[32] On the surface, the model minority stereotype seemingly captures the Asian American success, indicating that they are on their way to becoming "white," just like the offspring of earlier European immigrants. But it is based on the judgment that many Asian Americans perform at levels above the American average. Underneath this image is thus an implicit statement about Asian Americans as different from "whites." By holding Asian Americans above rather than below "whites," the model minority categorization has set them apart from other Americans, either white or non-white, in the public mind.[33] The truth of the matter is that the larger than average size of the middle class and upper middle class in some Asian immigrant groups, such as the Chinese, Koreans, Indians, and Filipinos, helps jump start the race to the mainstream American society and paves a much smoother path for the second generation to move ahead at an accelerated pace.

At the individual level, however, most immigrants from Asia and their offspring in the United States seem to converge on a prevailing view that "white" is mainstream, average, and normal, and look to whites as their frame of reference to attain privileged social status. In much of social science and policy research, too, non-Hispanic white serves as the average against which other racial/ethnic groups are compared. This practice reflects the general assumption that white is the standard despite the fact that whites are also an extraordinarily diverse group.

Like all other immigrants to the United States, Asian immigrants tend to have a clearly defined American Dream and measure their achievements in materialist terms. In the words of one Chinese immigrant, "I hope to accomplish nothing but three things: to own a home, to be my own boss, and to send my children to the Ivy League." Those with sufficient education, job skills, or money have managed to buy into white middle-class suburban neighborhoods immediately upon arrival, while others, by working twice or many more times as hard, have accumulated enough savings to move their families out of inner-city ethnic enclaves. Immigrants strive to become "white" because of the associated privileged status and are more or less optimistic about assimilation. But in the process, they unwittingly become the celebrated "model minority," and many even seem at ease with it.[34]

Consequently, many children of Asian immigrants have lived their entire childhood in white communities, made friends with mostly white peers, and grown up speaking only English. They, too, aspired to be "white" and think "white," even though at times they pitied themselves for or felt ashamed of not looking white. In fact, Asian Americans are the most acculturated non-European-origin group in the United States. By the second generation, most have lost fluency in their parents' native languages and have switched to being almost completely English monolingual. In Los Angeles, over three-quarters of second generation Asian Americans, as opposed to about a quarter of second generation Mexican Americans, speak only English at home.[35] Asian Americans also intermarry extensively with whites and with members of other racial or ethnic minority groups. More than a quarter of all married Asian Americans have a partner of a different racial background; 87 percent of intermarried Asian Americans marry whites, and 12 percent of all Asian Americans, compared to 2 percent of whites and 4 percent of blacks, claim a multiracial background.[36]

Even though U.S.-born or U.S.-raised Asian Americans are among the most acculturated of all non-European-origin groups and their rate of intermarriage with whites is among the highest, as they grow up they are more ambivalent about becoming "white" than are their immigrant parents. Many agree that "white" is synonymous with "American," but are often cynical about it. A Vietnamese high school student in New Orleans remarked, "An American is white. You often hear people say, hey, so-and-so is dating an 'American.' You know she's dating a white boy. If he were black, then people would say he's black." But when they look to whites as a frame of reference, they reject the idea of becoming "white"—"It's not so much being white as being American." I should underscore the fact, though, that the aversion to becoming "white" is largely found among well-educated and privileged second generation college students or Asian American community activists who have access to ethnic studies courses or ethnically designated public resources rather than the second generation more generally.[37] The majority of the second generation works hard to attain socioeconomic mobility and to achieve the privileged status associated with whiteness, just like their parents.

However, second generation Asian Americans are more sensitive to the issue of whiteness than their parents' generation and more conscious about the disadvantages associated with a nonwhite group membership. A Chinese American points out from her own experience: "The truth is, no matter how American you think you are or try to be, if you have almond-shaped eyes, straight black hair, and a yellow complexion, you are a foreigner by default." This widely echoed remark prompts a sad truth: "You can certainly be as good as or even better than whites, but you will never become accepted as white." Why? The reason is not complicated. Whitening is a lived cultural phenomenon that has to do with the ideological dynamics of white America, rather than with the actual situation of Asian Americans. Speaking perfect English, effortlessly practicing mainstream cultural values, and even intermarrying members of the dominant group may help reduce this "otherness" at the individual level, but doing so has little effect on the group as a whole. Like the model minority image that is imposed upon them, new stereotypes can unwhiten Asian Americans anytime and anywhere, no matter how "successful" and "assimilated" they have become.

In fact, the stereotype of the "honorary white" has gone hand-in-hand with that of the "forever foreigner."[38] Today, globalization, U.S. involvement in Asia, and U.S.-Asia relations, combined with continually high rates of immigration, affect how Asian Americans are perceived in American society. Most of the historical stereotypes, such as the "yellow peril" and "Fu Manchu," have found their way into contemporary America, as revealed in such highly publicized incidents as the murder of Vincent Chin, a Chinese American mistaken for Japanese and beaten to death by a disgruntled white auto worker in the 1980s; the trial of Wen Ho Lee, a nuclear scientist suspected of spying for the Chinese government in the mid-1990s; the 1996 presidential campaign finance scandal, which alleged a China connection to the fund-raising practices of the Democratic Party; and the 2001 Abercrombie and Fitch T-shirts that depicted Asian cartoon characters in stereotypically negative ways, such as with slanted eyes, thick glasses, and heavy Asian accents. Ironically, the very fact that Asian Americans are accepted only conditionally prompts them to organize pan-racially to fight back—and in the end this has greatly heightened their racial distinctiveness.[39] The bottom line is: Americans of Asian ancestries still have to constantly prove that they are truly Americans and loyal citizens.

Conclusion

Asian Americans have gained remarkable inroads into mainstream America. This progress, however, is not handed over to them, but each step has been made by their conscious effort and collective struggle to fight for equality in citizenship, civil rights, and representation. The long-standing issue still relevant to the Asian American community today is racism and stereotyping. Even though Asian Americans have made extraordinary achievements and are celebrated as a "model minority" or "honorary whites," they are still perceived as "foreigners" and are targeted with such racial slurs and derogative remarks as "chink," "geek," "gook," and "go back to your own country." Moreover, Asian Americans have continued to receive unequal returns from education. They often find themselves in situations where they have to score exceptionally high in order to get into a good school and work twice or many more times as hard in order to achieve occupational and earnings parity with their non-Hispanic white counterparts. They often believe that doing just as well as everybody else is not enough: "you've got to stand out, and you've got to work much harder and do much better." Moreover, professional Asian Americans have constantly faced the glass-ceiling barriers. One consequence of the glass-ceiling effect is their underrepresentation in the ranks of executives and managers. They are often considered hard workers, competent scientists, engineers, and technicians, but not good managers. Within the Asian American community, there is also persistent inequality between the rich and the poor. Other problems that require immediate community action include a lack of political participation, cultural conflicts, youth delinquency, mental health, elderly care, and undocumented immigration.

NOTES

1. Rashmi Sharma Singh, "South Asian Diaspora in the U.S.: A Trend?" http://www.indolink.com/Living/America/a1.php, accessed December 8, 2005.

2. Terrance J. Reeves and Claudette E. Bennett, *We the People: Asians in the United States*, 2000 Census Special Report, censr-17 (Washington, D.C.: U.S. Census Bureau, 2004).

3. Sucheng Chan, *Asian Americans: An Interpretive History* (New York: Twayne, 1991).

4. M. T. Nakano, *Japanese American Women: Three Generations 1890–1990* (Berkeley, Calif.: Mina Press, 1990); Paul R. Spickard, *Japanese Americans: The Formation and Transformations of an Ethnic Group* (Farming Hills, Mich.: Twayne, 1997).

5. Yu Xie and K. A. Goyette, *The American People, Census 2000: A Demographic Portrait of Asian Americans* (New York: Russell Sage Foundation Press/Washington, D.C.: Population Reference Bureau, 2004).

6. Carl L. Bankston III, "Filipino Americans," in *Asian Americans: Contemporary Trends and Issues*, 2nd ed., ed. Pyong Gap Min, 80–203 (Thousand Oaks, Calif.: Pine Forge Press, 2006).

7. Wikipedia, "Languages of India," http://en.wikipedia.org/wiki/Indian_languages, accessed December 8, 2005.

8. W. M. Hurh and K. C. Kim, "Religious Participation of Korean Immigrants in the United States," *Journal for the Scientific Study of Religion* 29, no. 1 (1990): 19–34.

9. Min Zhou, Carl L. Bankston III, and Rebecca Kim, "Rebuilding Spiritual Lives in the New Land: Religious Practices among Southeast Asian Refugees in the United States," in *Religions in Asian America: Building Faith Communities*, ed. Pyong Gap Min and Jung Ha Kim, 37–70 (Walnut Creek, Calif.: AltaMira Press, 2002).

10. Min Zhou and Carl L. Bankston III, *Growing Up American: How Vietnamese Children Adapt to Life in the United States* (New York: Russell Sage Foundation Press, 1998).

11. Carolyn E. Chen, "The Religious Varieties of Ethnic Presence: A Comparison between a Taiwanese Immigrant Buddhist Temple and an Evangelical Christian Church," *Sociology of Religion* 63, no. 2 (2002): 215–238.

12. Prema Kurien, "Religion, Ethnicity and Politics: Hindu and Muslim Indian Immigrants in the United States," *Racial and Ethnic Studies* 24, no. 2 (2001): 264–293.

13. Zhou, Bankston, and Kim, "Rebuilding Spiritual Lives;" Pyong Gap Min, "The Structure and Social Function of Korean Immigrant Churches in the United States," *International Migration Review* 26 (1992): 352–367.

14. Min, "Structure and Social Function of Korean Immigrant Churches."

15. Prema Kurien, "Becoming American by Becoming Hindu: Indian Americans Take Their Place at the Multicultural Table," in *Gatherings in Diaspora: Religious Communities and the New Immigration*, ed. Stephen Warner and Judith Wittner, 37–70 (Philadelphia: Temple University Press, 1998).

16. Zhou, Bankston, and Kim, "Rebuilding Spiritual Lives."

17. Min, "Structure and Social Function of Korean Immigrant Churches."

18. Zhou, Bankston, and Kim, "Rebuilding Spiritual Lives."

19. Min Zhou and Susan S. Kim, "Community Forces, Social Capital, and Educational Achievement: The Case of Supplementary Education in the Chinese and Korean Immigrant Communities," *Harvard Educational Review* 76, no. 1 (2006): 1–29.

20. Ibid.

21. C. A. Chun and S. Sue, "Mental Health Issues Concerning Asian Pacific American Children," in *Struggling to Be Heard: The Unmet Needs of Asian Pacific American Children*, ed. V. O. Pang and L. L. Cheng, 75–87 (Albany: State University of New York Press, 1998).

22. Wei Li, Gary Dymski, Yu Zhou, Maria Chee, and Carolyn Aldana, "Chinese American Banking and Community Development in Los Angeles County," *Annals of Association of American Geographers* 92, no. 4 (2002): 777–796.

23. Min Zhou and John R. Logan, "Increasing Diversity and Persistent Segregation: Challenges for Educating Minority and Immigrant Children in Urban America," in *The End of Desegregation*, ed. Stephen J. Caldas and Carl L. Bankston III, 177–194 (Hauppauge, N.Y.: Nova Science, 2003).

24. Ivan Light, *Ethnic Enterprise in America: Business and Welfare among Chinese, Japanese, and Blacks* (Berkeley: University of California Press, 1972).

25. C. N. Le, "Asian Small Businesses," *Asian-Nation: The Landscape of Asian America*, http://www.asian-nation.org/small-business.shtml, accessed December 6, 2005.

26. U.S. Census Bureau, *1992 Economic Census, Survey of Minority-Owned Business Enterprises: Asian and Pacific Islanders, American Indians and Alaska Natives* (Washington, D.C.: Government Printing Office, 1996); U.S. Census Bureau, *1997 Economic Census, Survey of Minority-Owned Business Enterprises: Asian and Pacific Islanders* (Washington, D.C.: Government Printing Office, 2001; U.S. Census Bureau, *2002 Economic Census, Survey of Minority-Owned Business Enterprises: Asian and Pacific Islanders* (Washington, D.C.: Government Printing Office, 2006).

27. Margaret M. Chin, *Sewing Women: Immigrants and the New York City Garment Industry* (New York: Columbia University Press, 2005).

28. Kyeyoung Park, *The Korean-American Dream: Immigrants and Small Business in New York City* (Ithaca, N.Y.: Cornell University Press, 1997); Nazli Kibria, "South Asian Americans," in Min, *Asian Americans*, 206–207.

29. Min Zhou, "Are Asian Americans Becoming White?" *Contexts* 3, no. 1 (2004): 29–37.

30. David Lopez and Yen Espiritu, "Panethnicity in the United States: A Theoretical Framework," *Ethnic and Racial Studies* 13, no. 2 (1990): 198–224.

31. Zhou, "Are Asian Americans Becoming White?"

32. Ibid.

33. Ibid.

34. Ibid.

35. David Lopez, "Language: Diversity and Assimilation," in *Ethnic Los Angeles*, ed. Roger Waldinger and Mehdi Bozorggmehr, 139–164 (New York: Russell Sage Foundation Press, 1996).

36. Jennifer Lee and Frank Bean, "Beyond Black and White: Remaking Race in America," *Contexts* 2, no. 3 (2003): 26–33.

37. Min Zhou and Jennifer Lee, "The Making of Culture, Identity, and Ethnicity among Asian American Youth," in *Asian American Youth: Culture, Identity, and Ethnicity*, ed. Jennifer Lee and Min Zhou, 1–30 (New York: Routledge, 2004).

38. Mia Tuan, *Forever Foreign or Honorary White? The Asian Ethnic Experience Today* (New Brunswick, N.J.: Rutgers University Press, 1999).

39. Zhou, "Are Asian Americans Becoming White?"

2

Ethnic Solidarity, Rebounding Networks, and Transnational Culture

The Post-1965 Chinese American Family

HAIMING LIU

In a paper for my Asian American history class, a student wrote: "Since relatives from both of my parents' side are spread around the world, I created nicknames for all my relatives overseas based on the country they live—such as *Mei Guo Goo Ma* (An aunt from America), *Bay Lay Si Yi Yi* (An aunt from my mom's side in Belgium), *Saam Faan Si Bill Gall* (A cousin in San Francisco), *O Zhoi Yee Po* (A grandaunt in Australia), and *Ga Na Dai Sok Sok* (An uncle in Canada). At the same time, unsolved questions popped up in my mind, 'how come I have relatives all over the world?'"[1] My student's paper profiles a typical Chinese immigrant family. Instead of uprooted individuals, Chinese immigrants, both historically and today, are active participants in socially and culturally connected global migration networks, with family and kin relationship forming the organizing unit. Deeply embedded in traditional family values and lifelong obligation to each other as family members, many Chinese immigrant families had the viability to survive temporary or long physical separation, adapt themselves to the new environment, and accommodate continuities and discontinuities in the process of their social mobility. Though different from early Chinese migration in many ways, post-1965 Chinese migration is still a socially embedded, group-oriented, and family-centered movement.[2] The most interesting aspect of post-1965 Chinese migration is how Chinese family life has rebounded as multicultural and transnational networks, has once again invoked expressions of kinship solidarity, has provided the basis for ethnic resilience against assimilation, and has functioned as a social institution that transcends the borders and boundaries of the nation-state.

Family Reunification during World War II

Historically, the dynamic development of family life as a transnational network and multicultural entity was a Chinese response to the U.S. government's attempts to

control and stop Chinese migration through its racist immigration laws. During
the exclusion period (1882–1943), Chinese immigrants confronted a stark reality in
terms of their family life. Since the exclusion laws only allowed the entry of merchant immigrants or American-born Chinese, and family members of those two
categories, most Chinese were not qualified to enter. Working-class Chinese immigrants already in the United States could not send for their family members. The
Chinese population in America declined from over 105,465 in 1880 to 61,639 in
1920.[3] When the 1906 earthquake in San Francisco destroyed all immigration
records, many Chinese took the opportunity to claim to be American-born in order
to gain the right to send for their family members and the right of reentry for themselves from a home visit. After a visit to China, they could also report a forthcoming birth of a child the next year and create an entry slot, though some of them did
not necessarily have such a birth. The slot could be used to sponsor one's own
child, or sold to a potential immigrant, who would then become the sponsor's
"paper son." However, the U.S. immigration authorities established the notorious
Angel Island Detention Center in the middle of San Francisco Bay in 1910 to enforce
the Chinese exclusion laws. Every entering Chinese was subjected to a tough interrogation process. Under such circumstance, many Chinese families were in the
form of split households. While husbands worked in the United States, wives and
children remained in China. Though the "paper son" scheme sustained the survival of Chinatown during the exclusion period, Chinatown was known as a "bachelor society."

During World War II, Congress passed the Magnuson bill in December 1943.
The law repealed all Chinese exclusion acts, provided the Chinese with an
annual immigration quota of 105, and gave alien Chinese the right to gain
American citizenship. While the immigration quota was small, Chinese men
could serve in the U.S. armed forces and bring their wives over from China
through war bride laws. Since 12,041 Chinese men were drafted, many Chinese
women entered America through the War Bride Law of 1945 and the Fiancées
and Fiancés of the War Veterans Act of 1946. While 5,132 Chinese women arrived
as war brides, another 2,317 Chinese women entered because of the Chinese
Alien Wives of American Citizens Act.[4]

However, wives of Chinese veterans were strikingly different from European
war brides. The average age of Chinese war brides was 32.8, with 77 percent of
them married to their husbands for more than ten years. In comparison, the
average age of British war brides was 23 to 25.[5] While European war brides often
reflect on how American soldiers romantically dated and fell in love with foreign women, Chinese war brides told stories of long-delayed family reunification because of the exclusion policy. As the United States welcomed the
European war brides with open arms, Chinese women still went through hostile
interrogation and detainment. The entry of war brides was a continuous struggle between Chinese transnational family networks and U.S. immigration

authorities. While family reunification was the goal of Chinese immigrants, gatekeeping was the responsibility of the U.S. immigration authorities.

Being longtime immigrant wives, Chinese women knew both their rights and the risks they were confronting and were prepared for tough questions. As a carefully thought-out immigration strategy, Chinese wives brought children with them and claimed entry slots for their left-behind children during the admission process so that their paper work could be simpler while maintaining future migration opportunities for those children. Some Chinese women probably brought children or claimed children entry slots for their relatives and friends.[6] Living under the shadow of the exclusion laws for a long time, Chinese wives wanted to maximize this new immigration opportunity. Family, relatives, and friends formed the social networks to sustain Chinese migration flow against legal restrictions. The arrival of Chinese wives during World War II transformed Chinatown from a "bachelor society" into a family-centered community.

The Breaking Up of Family Networks by Cold War Warriors

The joy of family reunification did not last long for the Chinese community. The United States and China broke off their relationship when China became a Communist country in 1949. Shortly after that, the two nation-states were involved in a full-scale war in Korea. Like Japanese Americans who were labeled as "enemy aliens" and placed into internment camps during World War II, the racial background of Chinese Americans made them suspect of having political allegiance with Communist China. Beginning in the early 1950s, Chinese Americans began to confront a new racial paranoia that was politicized in the interest of the Cold War agenda.

Everett Drumwright, American consul in Hong Kong, was not only a motivated Immigration and Naturalization Service (INS) gatekeeper but also a right-wing Cold War warrior. According to his eighty-nine-page report, Communist spies could use fraudulent citizenship papers to secure American passports; Hong Kong had 123 "citizenship brokerage houses;" China sent young women to marry Chinese Americans; and sons or "paper sons" of Chinese immigrants were educated in Communist schools and served in the People's Liberation Army of China. As a China specialist, he cited child adoption, plural marriage, multiple naming, and favoring of sons in Chinese family culture as the social basis for illegal activities. He charged that many Chinese immigrants could be potential spies for China. Under Drumwright's leadership, the American consulate office required immigration applicants to take a blood test to determine paternity, to undergo x-rays to ascertain age, to submit affidavits from the American fathers in triplicate, to provide photographs from childhood onward, and to present a birth or marriage certificate. Applicants had to answer eighty-one questions in writing, including one that asked them to list "all the people who lived within houses on all sides of your last place of residence in China before you came to the U.S. and state their relationship to you if any."[7] Chinese immigrants also needed to provide a long list of secondary evidence such as old correspondence, school records, money receipts, or old Hong Kong residence documents. Sometimes these documents were trusted by American officials and sometimes not. The 1950s were one of the bleakest eras in the history of Chinese Americans, as they struggled to transcend not only a racially defined U.S. border but also a politicized cultural boundary dominated by Cold War rhetoric.

Cold War warriors were eager to dismantle Chinese transnational networks as they politicized the immigration purge and pursued a witch-hunt campaign. The Federal Bureau of Investigation (FBI) closely monitored leftist community organizations like the New York Chinese Hand Laundry Alliance and the Chinese Workers Mutual Aid Association in San Francisco, and forced many of them to cease their activities or dissolve. As part of Cold War politics, Chinese prisoners of war from the Korean War were brought over to address Chinese American community organizations. Individuals sympathetic to the new China could be deported or de-naturalized according to the McCarran Internal Security Act passed in the late 1950s. Government agencies also strengthened their collaborations. In February 1956, a task force of five investigators from the State Department's Office of Security, eight investigators from INS, and three U.S. Marshals served subpoenas on thirty-four Chinese family and district associations and ordered them to submit lists, rolls, or other records of dues, assessments, contributions, and other income of the association in twenty-four hours. They wanted even blood-test records of Chinese Americans at private doctors' offices. Chinese family networks were the very target of the Cold War warriors. All Chinese organizations and community newspapers voiced their protests against this grand jury action and won a temporary battle. On March 20, 1956, U.S. District Judge Oliver Carter granted the motion of the family association to quash the subpoenas.[8]

The government then started the "Confession Program," through which the Chinese should confess their fraudulent names in exchange for real names and permanent residency or naturalized citizenship. The Confession Program was not an amnesty but a political and psychological campaign to break and dismantle the Chinese "paper son" networks. The key component of the confession was to list names of their true and paper family members, including their whereabouts, and to surrender the entire family tree on both sides of the Pacific in order to eliminate false slots. Acting more like "social workers" than law enforcement agents, INS officers usually approached the whole family and urged them to confess. They also hired Chinese informants and formed a network of insiders to tip off the agents about the community. Under the pressure, the New York and San Francisco Chinese Consolidated Benevolent Associations called a national conference in Washington, D.C., in March 1957 and agreed to promote the Confession Program sponsored by the INS. From 1957 through 1965, about 13,895 people participated in the Confession Program, leading to the exposure of 22,083 illegal Chinese immigrants and the closure of 11,293 unused slots.[9] To confess was a painful decision as it led to betrayal of family, friends, and the community and meant eliminating the immigration opportunity for family members left behind in China. As the confessors wrote "I hereby surrender my passport," the Chinese relinquished their paper identities and false status. At the same time, they ruined the transnational family networks they and their ancestors had built and developed since 1882. Criminalizing the entire Chinese community with an "enemy alien" image, Cold War warriors successfully destroyed the long-standing migration networks among the Chinese.

The 1965 Immigration Law and Rebound of Chinese Family Networks

Pushed first by President John F. Kennedy and signed into law by President Lyndon Johnson, the Immigration Act of 1965 removed racial criteria from U.S. immigration policy for the first time in the country's history. The intention of the 1965 law was not to promote Asian immigration but to reform U.S. immigration policy. In fact, Congressman Emanuel Celler of New York, a major sponsor of the bill, assured his congressional colleagues that few Asians possessed the requisite family networks to enter as potential immigrants because the total Asian population in the United States comprised less than 0.5 percent of the total U.S. population. Asian immigrants in 1965, numbering approximately 20,683, represented only 5 percent of the total immigrant population.[10] Thus, U.S. politicians believed that the family-reunification principle in the new law would primarily benefit European immigrants. Indeed, Italians, Greeks, and Portuguese dominated immigration flows in the first decade following the 1965 immigration reform.[11]

However, as the new law provided an equal allotment to each nation-state, the annual quota of 105 for Chinese immigration jumped to 20,000. The priority of the 1965 law also favored family reunification, and the law allocated a majority of the available visas to the extended family members of U.S. citizens and to the immediate family members of permanent residents. Furthermore, immediate family members of U.S. citizens—such as spouses, minor children, or even parents—did not count against the quota. A new wave of Chinese immigrants began to arrive as they quickly took advantage of these provisions. In the next fifteen years, approximately 250,000 Chinese entered the United States.[12]

The 1965 Immigration Act divided potential immigrants into seven categories, four of which were family categories such as spouse, unmarried children of permanent residents, and married children of U.S. citizens. According to the law, 80 percent of the available visas went to the family categories. Each category had 10 to 20 percent of the total 20,000 immigration quotas, though the fifth category, which was reserved for the siblings of U.S. citizens, received 24 percent of the quota—larger than any other category. Chinese immigrants learned the immigration rules fast. They applied for U.S. citizenship as soon as possible so that their spouses, minor children, and parents could enter as part of the exempted class. The fifth category also became the most widely used and most popular preference for post-1965 Chinese immigrants. By the mid-1970s, Chinese had overtaken Italians in using the quota-exempt categories such as spouse and minor children of U.S. citizens.[13] By 1985, 81 percent of the Chinese immigrants entered in the family categories, while occupational immigrants dropped to 16 percent. Between 1965 and 1990, approximately 711,000 Chinese immigrants entered the United States.[14]

Different from the nineteenth-century Cantonese immigrants, many of the early post-1965 Chinese immigrants were students who came to pursue graduate or professional education. Though some of these students returned to China after graduation, many stayed and obtained a job or married in order to change their status into permanent residency. A typical post-1965 Chinese immigrant could be a student from Taiwan who came for his or her master's degree in science or engineering, got a job or married a U.S.-born Chinese woman or man after graduation, and became a lawful permanent resident either through work or marriage. After five years of permanent residency, he or she could apply for citizenship. As a citizen, he or she then could bring in not only quota-exempt parents, but also brothers and sisters under the fifth category of the 1965 Immigration Act. His or her siblings, most of them being adult immigrants, could in turn petition their spouses and children after they received their permanent residency or citizenship. Following the same pattern, the spouses, once their status was adjusted, could sponsor their parents under the quota-exempt category and, more important, send for their siblings also under the fifth category. It is not uncommon that many post-1965 Chinese immigrants have settled down with their siblings, siblings-in-laws, and their families in the United States.

The new Chinese immigrants followed a typical migration pattern. A potential immigrant arrived first and then sent for family members. Family and kin relationships were the key consideration when pioneer Chinese immigrants functioned as the nucleus for a family immigration network. An individual immigrant's success in adjusting his or her legal status benefited not only his or her nuclear family but his or her extended family as well. In the migration process, family and kinship networks were relocated rather than disrupted. After family relationship and kin networks were transplanted into the United States, they expanded and created new migration possibilities. The post-1965 Chinese immigrants were truly a group of socially related individuals or households that moved from one place to another through a mutual help system. Family and kinship ties became strengthened rather than weakened during the migration process. As the 1965 law functioned as a "brother and sister law" for the Chinese, their arrival in the United States became a chain migration movement in which family networks rebounded.

Chinese Migration and U.S. Foreign Policy in Asia

U.S. influence in Asia was another driving force in the rapid increase of the Chinese immigrant population. To support non-Communist regimes in Korea, Vietnam, and Taiwan, the United States sent troops, built military bases, and provided massive financial aid in these areas. Between 1953 and 1964, the United States injected an average of $100 million a year into the Taiwanese economy.[15] To help build Taiwan's economy, the United States opened its domestic market for merchandise produced in Taiwan. American influence also replaced Japanese influence in the Taiwan educational system, especially in college education. By the late 1960s and early 1970s, about 2,000 students were leaving Taiwan each year to pursue graduate degrees in America.[16] From 1950 to 1974, a total of 30,765 students from Taiwan came to American colleges and universities.[17]

The normalization of diplomatic relationship between the United States and China in 1979 marked a new era of post-1965 Chinese migration. The normalization occurred almost simultaneously with the economic and social reform in China. While normalization encouraged cultural-exchange activities between the two countries and allowed Chinese students to study in the United States, China relaxed its migration restrictions. Between 1979 and 1990, China issued 1,346,909 exit permits, and 700,000 persons actually obtained visas to enter or immigrate to foreign countries. The United States quickly became the largest receiving country of Chinese migration.[18]

U.S. immigration policy was linked to its foreign policy. When China stepped up its reunification campaign in 1980, the U.S. Congress quietly granted Taiwan a separate 20,000 quota in a 1981 defense bill that provided Taiwan with U.S. protection from China. U.S. foreign policy toward Hong Kong also influenced Chinese immigration. As a British colony, Hong Kong had a quota of its own. The 1952 Immigration Law provided a quota of 100 to colonies or dependent areas and later was increased to 600. Then the 1986 Immigration Law increased the quota for Hong Kong to 5,000. When China began to negotiate with Britain about taking over Hong Kong, the quota was quietly increased to 10,000 in 1990, and then to 20,000 in 1995.[19] The increase was obviously a political response toward Hong Kong's sovereignty transfer in 1997.

Like the post-1965 immigrants from Taiwan, many students from the People's Republic of China (PRC) stayed in the United States and became immigrants after they finished their professional and graduate studies. Initially, the PRC government austerely required its graduate students to return to China after they completed their studies. After ten years of political chaos during the

Cultural Revolution, China badly needed well-trained scientists, engineers, and scholars. To ensure their return, China requested that the United States issue J-1 (exchange scholar visas) rather than F-1 visas (international student visas) to Chinese graduate students. According to U.S. immigration rules, J-1 visa holders should return to their home country for at least two years before they are allowed to apply for permanent residency in the United States. Unwilling to damage the newly normalized U.S.-China reconciliation, the U.S. government cooperated. As graduate studies, especially doctoral programs, take a long time to complete, the PRC government allowed the spouse to join a married graduate student under the *pei-du* (student-dependent) policy. As a result, many Chinese graduate students from China had their family with them when studying in the United States.

The June 4, 1989, Tiananmen Square incident changed the fate of many Chinese graduate students and their families in the United States. Following the incident, President George H. W. Bush, as a gesture of sympathy with the angry students, announced on December 2, 1989, that the 80,000 Chinese students and their families would be allowed to stay in the United States. Furthermore, the policy permitted all of the Chinese who had arrived from China before the end of 1989 to apply for permanent residency if they wished. The *liusi luka* (June 4 Green Card) provided numerous Chinese students and scholars, and their families, with a shortcut to permanent residency.[20] Once student immigrants and their spouses adjusted their legal status, they would sponsor their parents. After their parents obtained permanent residency and citizenship in a few years, other siblings in the family could join them by using family preferences in the immigration law.

In a chain migration pattern and like student immigrants from Taiwan, these students and their spouses from mainland China functioned as the nucleus for an extended-kin migration network. When they adjusted their permanent residency and citizen status, their parents, parents-in-law, siblings, and nephews, nieces, cousins, and other extended family members began to join them. President Bush's decision had a tremendous impact on the Chinese American community. First, it significantly increased the number of Chinese Americans in the United States. Second, the arrival of new immigrants made the Chinese American community much more diverse than before because those students and their families came from all over China rather than just from Guangdong Province, a traditional migration region. Almost all the provinces had sent students and scholars to the United States before 1989. After they settled down, many new immigrants organized home-region or native-place associations according to where they came from or alumni and alumna associations according to the universities from which they graduated. In a Chinese commu-nity event like Lunar New Year banquets, Moon Festival party, or national day celebration, sponsoring organizations typically consist of both traditional Chinese American organizations like the Chinese Consolidated Benevolent Association and new immigrant organizations like the Beijing, Shanghai, and Shandong home-region associations. Mandarin has replaced Cantonese as the most popular dialect in the Chinese American community. Though arriving in large numbers only after 1989, the number of Chinese immigrants from mainland China began to catch up and surpass those from Taiwan and Hong Kong. Between 1991 and 1998, about 350,000 Chinese from China immigrated to the United States through family reunification or other visa forms.[21] Once family network became a driving force in the chain migration process, migration as a social movement developed its own momentum.

Building a Transnational Community

Coming from China, Taiwan, and Hong Kong, post-1965 Chinese immigrants are much more diverse in their social origins and class background than the nineteenth- and early-twentieth-century immigrants. Many immigrants were professionals with college educations and came from metropolitan areas in China. After their arrival, they would send for family members. Since the 1965 Immigration Act, Chinese Americans have become the largest Asian American community. According to the 2000 U.S. census, their number reached 2.4 million, with immigrant population as the majority. Whether they came from mainland China, Taiwan, or Hong Kong, many post-1965 Chinese immigrants chose or prefer to choose their residence destination in places where they could find a Chinatown. Though the Chinese population before the 1960s was small in size, the Chinese American community had long and historical roots in the United States. The Chinese were one of the pioneer immigrant groups in the American West. As early as the 1860s, Chinese immigrants constituted about 10 percent of California's population and 25 percent of the labor force. Though Chinese exclusion laws and a hostile racial environment drove many Chinese away, visible Chinatowns survived in metropolitan cities like New York, Los Angeles, and San Francisco. Those metropolitan areas have attracted numerous post-1965 Chinese immigrants and their families.

To the new immigrants, Chinatown is not only a symbol of Chinese history in America but also a place that touches their cultural sensibilities. The new immigrants, especially those with families, prefer to live close to Chinatown because it gives them a sense of familiarity, a bridge to mainstream society, and a place to pass on Chinese traditions to the children. When a Chinatown was too crowded or too small to accommodate the needs of the growing new immigrant community, as in the Los Angeles area, Chinese ethnic strip malls began to appear in the nearby cities, where the Chinese population increased. With a few restaurants as the major attraction, these strip malls feature all kinds of Chinese businesses—from Chinese supermarkets, gift shops, herbal medicine or acupuncture services,

Chinese-language video and book stores, to banks and real estate and loan offices. Monterey Park in Southern California is a case in point. When the number of Chinese residents was growing rapidly in the early 1980s, Chinese restaurants represented 75 percent of the dining business in the city and generated many other Chinese retail businesses. The city was soon dubbed "Little Taipei."

Ethnic strip malls in Monterey Park generated chain reactions and attracted even more Chinese families to the area. Beginning in the 1980s, the Chinese population and their ethnic strip malls spread to Monterey Park's neighboring cities. Immigrants from Taiwan, Hong Kong, and China began to move in large numbers into the San Gabriel Valley. By 2000, Southern California was the home of about 523,597 Chinese.[22] Monterey Park is no longer the only Chinese-dominated city in Southern California. The Chinese also predominate in San Marino, Alhambra, Arcadia, Temple City, San Gabriel, Rosemead, Rowland Heights, Diamond Bar, Walnut, and the unincorporated areas of East San Gabriel and Hacienda Heights. While Monterey Park has now over 45 percent Chinese population, San Marino has 44.2 percent; Arcadia, 37.1 percent; Alhambra, 36.2 percent; and Rosemead, 36.2 percent. All the above cities have Asians as the majority population.[23] Sociologist Wei Li has named such Chinese ethnic enclaves as the "new Chinese ethnoburbs."[24] Many Chinese families spend their weekends shopping in a Chinese grocery store, followed by a family meal in a favorite restaurant in Chinatown or at a Chinese strip mall. Praying for the blessing from the ancestors in a Buddhist temple during the Chinese Lunar New Year, consulting a feng shui master before purchasing a house, and seeing a herbalist doctor for a minor disease are all popular family activities. Obviously, post-1965 Chinese immigrant families share many cultural sensibilities with those Chinese families who have been here for many generations.

Many post-1965 Chinese immigrants have maintained their Asian lifestyle and ethnic identity while working and living in the United States. They do not see this preference as conflicting with their American life. At work, they speak English, crack jokes with their colleagues, and comfortably behave as typical Americans. At home, however, they speak Mandarin, Cantonese, Fujianese, or another Chinese dialect. About 49.6 percent of the Chinese Americans speak their native language at home when their English is not fluent. But another 35.8 percent, with fluent English ability, still use Chinese at home. Only 14.5 percent of Chinese Americans speak just English at home.[25] They also eat Chinese food, listen to Chinese-language radio stations, watch Chinese-language television channels, and/or read Chinese-language newspapers.[26] By the mid-1990s, the Southern California Chinese American community supported at least twenty-three different daily and weekly Chinese-language newspapers, and there were seven daily Chinese-language newspapers and three Chinese-language television stations in San Francisco.[27] These media outlets typically keep the Chinese American community attuned to developments in all home areas—Hong Kong,

Taiwan, and China. The Chinese media also inform the community about events related to the Chinese community in Canada, Australia, Europe, South America, and Southeast Asia, as many contemporary Chinese have relatives and friends in those places. Transnational culture is deeply rooted in Chinese family life. Ethnic resilience rather than assimilation characterizes Chinese American family life.

Post-1965 Asian immigrants, especially the Chinese, have gradually transformed the San Gabriel Valley into bustling middle-class American suburbs with a visible Asian cultural imprint. Many of the San Gabriel Valley cities have Chinese populations that make up between one-quarter and nearly half of their total residents, and therefore more and more Chinese Americans have been elected as city council members, mayors, or members of the boards of education for the local school districts. Due to the dynamic growth of the Asian population, the Asian American student population dominated more and more schools in Southern California. By 1995, at least 367 K–12 schools—5 in Los Angeles and 30 in Orange County—had Asian students as the majority. At Arcadia High School in the San Gabriel Valley, more than half of the students are of Asian descent, and many of them are Chinese.[28] The impact of Chinese cultural and political significance is deep and wide in the region. However, different from old Chinatowns, these cities are not isolated ethnic ghettos but integrated American neighborhoods with Asians as the majority. Also different from a homogeneous American neighborhood, these cities are more sensitive to cultural diversity, more informed about international events, and more dynamic in promoting the local economy. Rather than Asian American satellite cities, they are part of the global village.

Education as a Family Agenda

The influence of post-1965 Asian Americans is more visible in education than in any other area. Of the forty finalists for the Intel Science Talent Search Competition (the former Westinghouse Science Talent Search) in 2005, thirteen were Asian Americans. Among the ten winners of this prestigious precollege science award in 2004, three were Asian Americans.[29] Though Asian Americans represent only 4 percent of the total U.S. population, they constitute 10 percent of the American college student population. In 2000, they made up 14 percent of the undergraduate population at Yale, 12 percent at Harvard, and 24 percent at Stanford. In California, though Asians were only 11 percent of the state population, they constituted 25 percent of the University of California, Berkeley's undergraduate population in 1981 and 40 percent in 2000.[30] They also represented over 58 percent of the undergraduates at the University of California, Irvine. This extraordinary achievement reflects how Asian American children in the K–12 system have consistently viewed schoolwork as their life priority, and spent more hours on class assignments and were involved in more educational activities than non-Asian children. In Chinese family culture, parents view children's education as their primary obligation. In return, children are expected to do well at school and live up to their parents' expectations. Parents are often the driving force behind Chinese children's efforts.

On September 25, 2005, the *Los Angeles Times* reported how Robin Zhou, an Alhambra high school student newspaper editor, commented on the test score gap between Asian and Latino students by pointing out that "Asian students are often pushed harder and more consistently by their parents." In contrast, Hispanic parents are well meaning but less active. According to Zhou, a key factor for the difference was cultural. Many Asian parents, especially recent immigrants, push their children to move toward academic success."[31] Though highly controversial, Zhou's observation on how Asian immigrant parents are involved in their children's education is accurate. Many Chinese immigrant parents have closely monitored their children's education while struggling with their own linguistic, cultural, and career adaptation to American society.

A common practice among Chinese parents is to send their children to a Chinese-language school after their regular school hours. According to an article in the *Los Angeles Times* on June 8, 1998, every Saturday or Sunday about 50,000 Asian students attended 33 Japanese, 55 Vietnamese, 140 Chinese, and 335 Korean schools that spread from the San Gabriel Valley to San Diego. A Chinese-language school is not only an ethnic island where Chinese parents transmit Chinese culture to the younger generation but also a learning place where parents make sure that their children are doing well in their regular schoolwork. In addition to Chinese language, art, and culture, many Chinese-language schools provide classes or tutorship on English, mathematics, or science. Many also offer college preparation classes, such as a class to prepare students to take the SAT. As Chinese parents view it as another safety valve for their children to do well in education, attending Chinese-language school becomes a routine for most Chinese children. Min Zhou, former chair of the Asian American Studies Department of UCLA, has defined such schools as supplementary educational institutions.[32]

Such institutions were typically established and often staffed by a group of enthusiastic and volunteer parents, with tight budgets and small enrollments. The well-known Irvine Chinese School in the beginning only had four teachers and thirty children who gathered every week in a small, rented schoolroom. Today, its enrolment is over 1,000 aged from five to eighteen. Over the last twenty-two years, the school has developed into one of the largest Chinese cultural schools in Southern California.[33] The expansion of the Irvine Chinese School has in fact accompanied the growth of the Chinese population in Irvine. In the late 1980s, the city was consistently ranked as one of the safest cities in the United States. The master-planned city also offered high-tech jobs and housed top-rated schools. Those qualities drew many educated, professional, middle-class Chinese families. By 1990, according to the U.S. census, the Chinese made up 31 percent of its population. The pattern applies to other cities as well. The Southern California Council of Chinese Schools is an umbrella organization with over 250 schools. One of their flagship schools in Arcadia has a student enrollment of over 2,000. The Chinese School Association in the United States (CSAUS) on the East Coast, established in 1994, has more than 270 membership schools covering forty-one states and all major cities.[34] Most of the Chinese families today live in integrated neighborhoods in suburban areas. A contemporary Chinese community is no longer a solid physical Chinatown but a culturally embedded and socially connected network of Chinese families. Since education is an important family agenda in Chinese culture, Chinese-language schools bind Chinese residents in a city or suburban area together and have become an integral part of a contemporary Chinese community.

Chinese parents care about their children's education not only because of their cultural traditions but also due to the racial politics in American higher education. Chinese parents are fully aware that their children need to be more competitive in education because admission practices of many American colleges and universities set higher standards for Asian American applicants. In 2002, UCLA denied admission to Pearl Poon, Marilynn Chan, and Melissa Wang from San Marino High School in the San Gabriel Valley. All of them scored above 1,400 out of 1,600 on the SAT, and each averaged 730 or above on her three SAT II subject exams. Their high school grades were strong, too, with each taking numerous AP and honors courses. Wang's overall grade point average was 3.7 on a 4.0 point scale, Poon's was 3.5, and Chan's was 3.6. All three did community service and had many extracurricular activities. Poon, for instance, was senior class president, and Chan was the drum major of the school's marching band.[35] They would probably have been admitted if they were not Asian. Higher standards have pressured Chinese American families to spend extra time, money, and energy on children's education. That is another reason why Chinese-language schools or other after-school programs widely exist in Chinese American communities. Chinese parents view education as a major social mobility channel for their children in American society, and they urge their children to take extra training in English, math, or other subjects, and enroll in SAT test preparation courses as early as possible. Chinese-language schools often offer such courses. In short, the existence of numerous Chinese-language schools demonstrates how Chinese parents pull their resources together and are collectively involved in the younger generation's education.

Living a Transnational Life

Migration does not necessarily have a happy ending. Migration to the United States sometimes means downward mobility for educated or professional Chinese. Many post-1965 Chinese immigrants are highly educated and worked as business executives, educators, or other professionals in their place of origin. Lack of a U.S. college diploma or professional license, language barriers, and the "glass-ceiling" discrimination against Asians remain major obstacles to career success for many new Chinese immigrants. It is not uncommon that educated Chinese immigrants are employed in the service sector—restaurants businesses, bakeries, beauty shops, gift shops, and so forth. Therefore, remigration or reverse migration becomes a serious alternative consideration. Convenient modern transportation, highly developed communication technology, and the globalized economy not only stimulate migration but also remigration and reverse migration. Some of the immigrants return to Asia with their families, but many leave their spouses and children in the United States. With a split household, they live a transnational family life. The husband or the wife returns to his or her place of origin for work or business after obtaining permanent residency in America. He or she periodically flies back to the United States to visit his or her family. Such frequent air travelers are referred to as "astronaut" immigrants. Their commuting is facilitated by dozens of daily flights that link major U.S. metropolitan areas to Hong Kong, Taiwan, and major cities in mainland China. David Wong, a typical "astronaut" immigrant, for example, made the fourteen-hour flight between Hong Kong and Los Angeles twelve times a year. He usually vacationed in the United States for one or two weeks, while he mostly worked in Asia. Semiseriously, this commuter once reported his permanent address on the landing card as "Seat 1A, First Class, Cathay Pacific."[36] "Astronaut" immigrants like David Wong inhabit a space both culturally and geographically transnational.

Beginning in the late 1990s, the Chinese government began to encourage overseas Chinese professionals and scholars to return to China. Those returning scholar or professional immigrants are often dubbed "haigui pai," or "Homecoming Scholars." Some provincial or city governments have provided tax reduction policies if returning immigrants could bring in investment or establish a start-up high-tech business. Some Chinese universities have offered returning professional immigrants a high salary, good housing, and a lighter teaching load as incentives. There are also a considerable number of returning professional and business immigrants in Hong Kong and Taiwan. The United States is no longer assumed to be the immigrant's ultimate destination. When opportunities become available elsewhere, including in their home country, immigrants, sometimes including their American-born or –raised descendents, may move again. The reverse migration reflects how vibrant Asian economies have been growing in the past ten years and how the Chinese economy has deeply integrated itself into global capitalism. At the same time, developed countries, including the United States, have become increasingly de-industrialized, with labor-intensive manufacturing activities relocated overseas, including Asia. As U.S. business and employment become increasingly uninviting, reverse migration becomes increasingly appealing to Chinese professional and entrepreneur immigrants.

While modern transportation and communication technology make the Chinese transnational family a less painful choice in their family life, longtime separation between a husband and wife could cause extramarital affairs, which is not uncommon among transnational families. So, in another type of transnational Chinese family, both husband and wife return to the high-paying jobs or business in their place of origin and leave their children by themselves in the United States as "parachute or latch-key kids." According to a 1990 study, there are about 30,000 to 40,000 Taiwanese students between the ages of eight and eighteen living without the company of their parents in the United States.[37] Although physical separation between parents and children may have adverse effects on the parent-child relationship, the intense competition in college-entrance exams in Hong Kong, Taiwan, and China, the flexible and less-demanding nature of the U.S. K–12 school system, and the more marketable degrees from U.S. universities explain why upper-class and middle-upper-class families choose this transnational family life as a migration strategy. Though family members are physically separated, Internet service and cheap international calling cards allow easy communication between parents and children. Parents can closely monitor their children's school grades if they want to. Concern for the younger generation's social mobility opportunities is the key motivation for this transnational family strategy. The "parachute kids" phenomenon shows how some of the Chinese families have creatively used international resources for their children's education.

Interestingly, most "parachute kids" are doing well at school and in their social life. While some of the American-born Chinese youth are confused about their identity, "parachute kids" feel secure about their Chinese identity and proud of their ethnic background. Coming from merchant- or professional-class families in Hong Kong, Taiwan, or metropolitan areas in China, they tend to believe Chinese culture has more positive qualities than American culture and that Chinese youth are more sophisticated than American youth. Their transnational background has enabled them to form their own networks that even include immigrant students from other countries.[38] With parents working in Asia and children attending school in America, this transnational family pattern minimizes the economic sacrifices and maximizes opportunities for every member of the family.

The third type of Chinese transnational family reflects the global networks among the overseas Chinese community. As my student points out in her paper, many Chinese immigrant families in America not only maintain ties with their place of origin but also extensive international links through their family and kin relationships. In 1990, the *Los Angeles Times* told a story of a Chinese family with relatives in more than three nations. Living as a U.S. citizen in Orange County, California, Victor Chung came from China as a former Red Guard, graduated from the University of California, Berkeley, and managed a company that assembled components exported to China. Typically, Chung made ten or more trips across the Pacific a year to confer in Thailand with his grandfather—who directed family business operations in Hong Kong, Taiwan, China, and Vancouver. His grandfather had six sons and seven daughters who produced the third generation that spanned the Pacific Ocean.[39] The nuclear Chung family in California is part of the Chung clan that stretches across the Pacific. In this type of Chinese transnational family, nuclear family members are based in the United States but are closely connected with a global extended family and kin network. It shows how the Chinese in America are part of the Chinese diaspora community numbering more than 47 million and spreading to more than sixty countries, especially in Southeast Asia. Chinese traditions such as ancestor worship, herbal medicines and acupuncture, food, education, and memory of hometown in China culturally bind overseas Chinese together. Racial sentiment against the Chinese, social and political instability in a host country, economic opportunity, family and kin connections, and a bustling Chinese American community may draw them to the United States. Gerard Yang, an ethnic Chinese in Cambodia, became a refugee immigrant when the country suffered from continuous wars and Communist regimes' brutality. He arrived in America in the late 1980s and opened a 5,000-square-foot Hawaii Supermarket in 1990 in the city of San Gabriel to cater to the rapidly growing Chinese population. Wahoo's Fish Tacos is another remigration story of a Chinese family. The company was established in 1988 and operates twenty-two Mexican chain restaurants in California and Colorado. The three Lee brothers who own the company actually grew up at the beaches in Mexico. Their parents first immigrated to South America in the 1950s, and then the father and the eldest son remigrated to the United States in 1964. They were followed by the rest of the family in 1975.[40] In Los Angeles Chinatown, ethnic Chinese from Southeast Asia have already replaced those Chinese Americans who have been here for over five generations as the owners of many small businesses ranging from gift stores, ginseng shops, and jewelry stores, to restaurants. By 1996, they dominated 90 percent of this Chinatown's business. Those Chinese families often have connections in Southeast Asia and South America. All three types of Chinese transnational families demonstrate that international migration is seldom a one-way trip but often a transnational circulation of information, people, money, skills, and technology.

Conclusion

Transnational family patterns represent some of the creative and adaptive strategies used collectively by Chinese immigrants to ensure their survival and social mobility. For every flow of a human migration, there could be a reverse or remigration flow because immigrants belong to a socially connected and globally informed group that links various geographic sites across national boundaries. Reverse migration and remigration are part of the continuous flow of the population within the transnational networks established by the immigrants. The circular migration as a whole, rather than one locale, provides the cultural setting in which many Chinese immigrants organize their family life, raise their children, and develop their world outlook and ethnic identity. Post-1965 Chinese family life is still a story that transcends national boundaries.

NOTES

1. Jacqueline Li, "My Family Experience," a paper for my Asian American Experience class in Fall Quarter 2001.
2. While many early Chinese immigrants were from working class backgrounds and came from Guangdong Province, post-1965 immigrants were often educated professionals and came from Taiwan, Hong Kong, and many other parts of China.
3. Ronald Takaki, *Strangers from a Different Shore: A History of Asian Americans* (Boston: Little, Brown, 1989), 111–112.
4. Xiaojian Zhao, *Remaking Chinese America: Immigration, Family and Community, 1940–1965* (New Brunswick, N.J.: Rutgers University Press, 2002), 80.
5. Ibid., 82–86.
6. Ibid., 87–90.
7. Mae M. Ngai, *Impossible Subjects: Illegal Aliens and the Making of Modern America* (Princeton, N.J.: Princeton University Press, 2004), 207–212.
8. Zhao, *Remaking Chinese America*, 175.
9. Ibid., 183.
10. David Reimers, *Still the Golden Door: The Third World Comes to America* (New York: Columbia University Press, 1985), 92.
11. Ibid., 89.
12. Ibid., 103.
13. Ibid.
14. Bill Ong Hing, *Making and Remaking Asian America through Immigration Policy, 1850–1990* (Stanford, Calif.: Stanford University Press, 1993), 81.
15. John Liu and Lucie Cheng, "Pacific Rim Development and the Duality of Post-1965 Asian Immigration to the United States," in *The New Asian Immigration in Los Angeles and Global Restructuring*, ed. Pual Ong, Edna Bonacich, and Lucie Cheng, 76 (Philadelphia: Temple University Press, 1994).
16. Iris Chang, *The Chinese in America: A Narrative History* (New York: Viking Penguin, 2003), 286.
17. Huping Ling, *Surviving on the Gold Mountain: A History of Chinese American Women and Their Lives* (Albany: State University of New York Press, 1998), 150.
18. Min Zhou, *Chinatown: The Socioeconomic Potential of an Urban Enclave* (Philadelphia: Temple University Press), 57.
19. Hing, *Making and Remaking Asian America*, 82.
20. For discussion on Chinese students in America and their identity, see Leo Orleans, *Chinese Students in America: Policies, Issues, and Numbers* (Washington, D.C.: National Academy Press, 1988); David Iweig and Changgui Chen, *China's Brain Drain to the United States: Views of Overseas Chinese Students and Scholars in the 1990s* (Berkeley: University of California, Institute of East Asia Studies, 1995); Jianji Huang, *Chinese Students and Scholars in American Higher Education* (Westport, Conn.: Greenwood, 1997); Xiao-huang Yin, *Chinese American Literature since the 1850s* (Urbana: University of Illinois Press, 2000), 185–205.

21. Evelyn Iritani, "Chinese in U.S. Shape Economy," *Los Angeles Times*, October 17, 1999.

22. Asian Pacific American Legal Center of Southern California, *The Diverse Face of Asians and Pacific Islanders in Los Angeles County* (Los Angeles: Asian Pacific American Legal Center of Southern California, 2004), 49.

23. Ibid., 7. See also *Chinese American Data Center* (2003b and 2003c), http://members. aol.com/chineseusa/00cen4.htm.

24. Wei Li, "Spatial Transformation of an Urban Ethnic Community from Chinatown to Chinese Ethnoburb in Los Angeles" (Ph.D. diss., University of Southern California, 1997).

25. Terrance J. Reeves and Claudette E. Bennett, *We the People: Asians in the United States—Special Report*, 2000 Census Special Report, censr-17 (Washington, D.C.: U.S. Census Bureau, 2004), 11.

26. The *Los Angeles Times* 1997 survey indicated that 79 percent of the Chinese in Southern California spoke Chinese at home. K. Connie Kang, "Chinese in the Southland: A Changing Picture," *Los Angeles Times*, June 27, 1997.

27. Joe Chung Fong, "Transnational Newspapers: The Making of the Post-1965 Globalized/Localized San Gabriel Valley Chinese Community," *Amerasia Journal* 22, no. 3 (1996): 65–77; Mary Curtius, "A Coming of Age for S.F. Chinese," *Los Angeles Times*, October 11, 1999.

28. Diane Seo, "In Schools, a Minority No Longer," *Los Angeles Times*, December 26, 1995.

29. See the Intel Science Talent Search Web site http://www.sciserv.org/sts/.

30. Timothy P. Fong, *The Contemporary Asian American Experience: Beyond the Model Minority* (Upper Saddle River, N.J.: Prentice Hall, 2002), 103.

31. Jia-Rui Chong, "Morphing Outrage into Ideas," *Los Angeles Times*, October 12, 2005.

32. For a discussion on Chinese-language schools as supplementary education, see Min Zhou and Xiyuan Li, "Ethnic Language Schools and the Development of Supplementary Education in the Immigrant Chinese Community in the United States," in *New Directions for Youth Development: Understanding the Social Worlds of Immigrant Youth*, ed. Carola Suarez-Orozco and Irina L. G. Todorova, 57–73 (San Francisco: Jossey-Bass, 2003).

33. Tini Tran, "Asian Classes Introduce Kids to Ancestors, Culture," *Los Angeles Times*, October 12, 2005.

34. The information is obtained from http://www.csaus.org/.

35. Stuart Silverstein and Rebecca Trounson, "UCLA, Cal Rejections Baffle High SAT Scorers," *Los Angeles Times*, November 20, 2003.

36. Daniela Deane, "Have Job, Will Travel," *Los Angeles Times*, March 31, 1993.

37. Helena Hwang and Terri Watanabe, "Little Overseas Students from Taiwan: A Look at the Psychological Adjustment Issues" (master's thesis, University of California, Los Angeles, 1990).

38. Christy Chiang-Hom, "Transnational Cultural Practices of Chinese Immigrant Youth and Parachute Kids," in *Asian American Youth: Culture, Identity, and Ethnicity*, ed. Jennifer Lee and Min Zhou, 143–159 (New York: Routledge 2004).

39. Robert W. Gibson, "Networks of Chinese Rim Pacific," *Los Angeles Times*, July 22, 1990.

40. Marc Ballon, "Wahoo's to Become a Bigger Fish," *Los Angeles Times*, September 6, 2001.

PART TWO

Asian Communities
in America

With Geographical Boundaries

3

Beyond a Common Ethnicity and Culture

Chicagoland's Chinese American Communities since 1945

LING Z. ARENSON

The month of October is a busy time for the Chinese American communities throughout Chicagoland, unbeknownst to most non-Chinese residents in the area. The ordinary unsuspecting American shopper or diner in Chicago's Chinatown will probably fail to notice the huge banner hung across the Chinatown gateway commemorating "Double Ten," the birthday of the Republic of China. Flying outside the windows of the Hoy On Association building on Cermak Road opposite the Chinatown gateway is a sizable banner welcoming Chinese president Jiang Zemin's visit to Chicago. This familiar scene in 2001 is replayed yearly in this urban ethnic community located just south of downtown Chicago. Around the beginning of each October, certain segments of the Chinese American communities throughout the Chicago area also celebrate the National Day of the People's Republic of China through community-based activities such as entertainment and dinner parties, often attended by officials from the Chinese consulate. A Chinatown tradition is the Double Ten parade, complete with lion dances and numerous eye-catching "white sun in blue sky" national flags of the Republic of China–Taiwan. These are some of the telltale signs of a community that had become so fragmented by the last two decades of the twentieth century that we could no longer safely call it a unified ethnic community based on shared historical experience, culture, ethnicity, and identity. Instead, we witnessed the emergence of divergent, sometimes cooperative, but most of the time competing subcommunities scattered throughout Chicagoland.

The Chinese American population in the United States experienced phenomenal growth in the last two decades of the twentieth century. The demographic changes brought dynamic transformations in Chinese American communities throughout the United States. As many scholars have noted, these transformations take many forms—the emergence of revived urban ethnic communities still in transition or the gradual demise of such urban enclaves, the birth of new

suburban ethnic concentrations known as "satellite Chinatowns," and the development of cultural communities without the symbolism of Chinatowns.[1] This
essay provides a case study of the Chinese immigrant experience in a midwestern
metropolis during a time of rapid expansion and change to reflect the microdiver-
sity of the largest single national-origin group within the Asian American community. This study examines the forces that transformed Chicagoland's Chinese
American community from a relatively homogeneous urban ethnic neighborhood
before World War II to fragmented subcommunities that emerged in the second
half of the twentieth century. It reveals a pattern of community formation and
development that is unique to Chicago. We also see the impact of other familiar
issues—Chicagoland's Chinese Americans have not only been divided along traditional lines such as ethnicity, gender, class, migrational differences, period of
immigration, and generational gaps, but also burdened with such divisive issues
as home-country politics, national loyalty, and international relations, and
affected by the changing legal, political, and economic environments within the
host society. The experience of Chinese Chicagoans has important implications
for the future of Chinese Americans and Asian Americans in general.[2]

The plural form "Chinese American communities" is used here to emphasize, to a lesser degree, the geographical division, and more important, the
social, economic, political, cultural, and linguistic divisions among recent
Chinese immigrants and their descendants in Chicagoland. The geographical
boundary of this study is limited to the Chicago metropolitan area, or
Chicagoland as it is commonly called. It consists of six counties according to the
definition of both the 1960 census and the 2000 census—Cook, Will, DuPage,
Kane, McHenry, and Lake. The Chinese American communities that emerged in
Chicagoland since the 1970s radiate from three major areas—the two urban eth-
nic centers known respectively as Chinatown (or South Chinatown) and North
Chinatown, plus suburban Chinese American communities centered around
but not limited to Westmont, Naperville, Schaumburg, Arlington Heights,
Morton Grove, and Hanover Park.

A Community in Transition, 1945–1965

Like its counterparts in New York and San Francisco, the Chinese American community in Chicago evolved around an urban core—Chinatown. The earliest
Chinese immigrant community in Chicago was founded in the 1880s as a result of
secondary migration of Chinese settlers from the West Coast. The original
Chinatown was located in downtown Chicago along Clark Street between Harrison
and Van Buren. Starting from the 1910s, a notable spike in anti-Chinese sentiment,
coupled with rising rents and land values, led to the continuous relocation of the
Chinese population to a cheaper and less desirable area farther south along
Cermak Road and Wentworth Avenue. By the 1940s, a new Chinatown as we know

it today had emerged. For three decades, this growing community remained largely homogenous despite the constant interference from contentious homeland politics and community members' active involvement in native causes. Of the 3,000 residents, most were poorly educated, Cantonese-speaking male sojourners born in rural southern China and engaged in the traditional labor-intensive laundry- and restaurant-related businesses. A small number of American-born and -educated Chinese Americans, however, were able to seek white-collar jobs outside the ethnic businesses. The elite class, mostly consisting of wealthy merchants, wielded more or less absolute power in the community. Because of its historical link to the origins of the community, a single clan group, the Moys, stood out among a number of others to exert a predominant influence.[3] Despite the absence of antimiscegenation laws in Illinois and the fact that anti-Chinese sentiment never reached the level as on the West Coast, we do not see the kind of extensive racial mixing that occurred in New York's Chinatown before the 1920s or among the Filipino students-turned-immigrants in Chicago during the same period.[4] World War II only brought this fairly close-knit community even closer together. Chinese Chicagoans solidified behind the joint war effort of the United States and China against fascism, Nazism, and Japanese imperialism. A sense of community, buoyed by patriotism and nationalistic pride, reached a historical high.

The period between 1945 and the mid-1960s was a time of transition and change for most Asian immigrants and their descendants in the United States. For Chinese American communities, the convergence of two parallel movements proved especially consequential. On the national level, Congress first passed a series of acts to deal with war-related crises of refugees, displaced persons, and war brides, then initiated a process starting in 1965 that culminated in the total overhaul of the country's discriminatory immigration and naturalization laws. On the international level, the Cold War realigned the international power structure, which in turn revived and intensified factionalism and ideological divides within the Chinese immigrant communities.

The first of a series of legislative reforms set off by World War II and the Cold War was the repeal of the Chinese exclusion acts in 1943, which lifted the ban on Chinese immigration and granted a symbolic annual quota of 105 for immigration from China. The 1945 War Brides Act and the group-specific Chinese Alien Wives of American Citizens Act of 1947 enabled foreign-born wives of Chinese American war veterans and American citizens to come to the United States outside the quota restrictions and without being subjected to the previous laws that banned alien spouses who were racially inadmissible. Between 1945 and 1950, a national total of 5,728 Chinese war brides married to their returning war veteran husbands were welcomed to the excited Chinese American communities throughout the country.[5] The civil war in China and the founding of the People's Republic of China in 1949 forced another 5,000 former Nationalist government officials, merchants, professionals, and students to stay in the United States as

refugees and estranged personnel. This was made possible by the 1953 Refugee
Relief Act granting 205,000 nonquota visas to refugees from China.[6]

Chicago's Chinese American community readily embraced the first large
wave of Chinese newcomers to the Midwest, whose impact on the demographics
of the otherwise declining Chinese American community was significant.
Chinese population in Chicago's municipal area grew from 2,018 in 1940 to 3,334
in 1950 and 5,082 by 1960. That was 72 percent of the Chinese population in the
state and 1.4 percent of that in the country.[7] Based on the various census reports,
we can identify the following demographic trends in the Chicago area, which
coincide with developments elsewhere with a sizable Chinese population.

First of all, reinforcing an existing trend, more Chinese Chicagoans began to
move beyond Chinatown to parts of the city previously uninhabited by Chinese.
Some went beyond the urban confines to the suburbs throughout the ever-
expanding Chicagoland. Of the 700 Chinese professionals living in the city in 1961,
for instance, only 45 (6 percent) resided in Chinatown. The suburban Chinese
population, on the other hand, increased from 171 in 1940 to 444 in 1961, 84.2 percent
of whom were professionals.[8] Most Chinese newcomers to Chicagoland also chose
to settle down outside Chinatown. Coming from a wide range of regions in China,
they were markedly different from their predominantly rural and working-class
predecessors in Chicago. Many were college educated, professionally trained, and
relatively well-off. Being mostly Mandarin Chinese speakers with some proficiency
in English, they felt little affinity with the Taishanese speakers in Chinatown. The
end result of suburbanization in general and exodus of Chinese professionals
from Chinatown in particular was the relative decline of Chinese population in
Chinatown along with the decrease of population from all ethnic backgrounds in
the city of Chicago. Chinatown might still claim the largest concentration of
Chinese population (about 40 percent) in the city proper during the 1950s, but
the trend of outward migration was unmistakable.[9]

The coming of women and dependent children to Chicago also changed the
nature of the Chinese American community from a predominantly male society
to a family-centered community. According to the records of the Chinese
Consolidated Benevolent Association (CCBA) and the Mon San Association, out
of 2,905 foreign-born Chinese in Chicago in 1926, only 92 were women. Among
the 1,114 native-born Chinese, only 106 were women.[10] These figures indicate an
even more eschewed male-female ratio than the national figure for the same
period. By the 1960s, the sex ratio became close to even.

Political changes in China after 1949 forced many first generation Chinese
immigrants to Chicago to forgo their dreams of ever returning to China. They
became permanent settlers in and near Chinatown. This trend helped redraw the
physical boundaries of the community as a whole and Chinatown in particular.
The latter experienced phenomenal spatial expansion from the initial one
square block of Cermak and Wentworth Avenue to an area that covered seven

square blocks by the mid-1960s, defined on the north and south by Eighteenth and Twenty-fourth streets and on the east and west by Red Line EL and Canal Street. This seven-square-block area underwent discernable physical improvements with the opening up of new businesses and residential developments.[11]

Meanwhile, second generation Chinese Americans in Chicago came to age in the two decades after World War II. Their swelling ranks brought the American-born Chinese population in the city to a slight majority (54 percent) over foreign-born Chinese.[12] Taking advantage of better educational and job opportunities in the postwar American prosperity, these Chinese Americans, often referred to as ABCs, were able to break the language and economic barriers that had constricted their parents' generation. They helped transform the Chinese American community through active participation in mainstream politics and the civil rights movement.

The above demographic changes ushered in a phase of transition and adjustment in Chicagoland's Chinese American community. It was no longer one whose social, political, and economic functions primarily congregated in an urban center, Chinatown. Breaking the confines of traditional ethnic employment patterns, more Chinese Americans became white-collar workers and professionals such as lawyers, doctors, and engineers. This trend was particularly noticeable in the suburbs—an indication of rising class differences in a linguistically and culturally diversified community.

The onset of the Cold War on the international level and U.S. domestic politics during the Cold War had a divisive effect on Chinese American communities throughout the nation. The Chinese American communities that had rallied in a united front against fascism and militarism barely survived the internal tensions in their attempt to cope with the realities of the civil war between the Chinese Communists and Nationalists (Guomindang) and the eventual Communist takeover of China in 1949. Violent scuffles erupted on a regular basis between supporters or sympathizers of the newly founded People's Republic of China and loyalists to the Nationalist government in Taiwan. However, most of the incidents occurred at the instigation of the traditional community power brokers who were pro-Guomindang. While San Francisco and New York were the eyes of this anti-Communist and antiliberal storm, Chicago's Chinese American community, centered on Chinatown—with its traditional institutions transplanted from the West Coast—also suffered from its ripple effects. Family associations and other community organizations were forced to take a clear stand. A lack of vocal opposition and an independent local press that would challenge the traditional power structure in Chinatown ensured a seemingly monolithic anti-Communist bloc. The few dissenting voices came mostly from local university campuses. Home-country politics had shattered the sense of common struggle and solidarity forged during World War II.

Meanwhile, the Federal Bureau of Investigation (FBI) and the Immigration and Naturalization Service (INS) joined forces to closely scrutinize and investigate

Chinese immigrants suspected of subversive activities, affiliations with black-listed organizations, or fraudulent entry. Armed with the Internal Security Act of 1950, the INS aggressively pursued those suspected of immigration fraud through informants, raids, and grand jury investigations.[13] The result was a prevailing sense of disruption, frustration, and desperation, and the erosion of the long-established immigrant network that would have otherwise been difficult to penetrate. Xiaojian Zhao, in her study of the Chinese immigrant experience from 1940 to 1965, attributes the success of the INS in breaking up this community network of illegal immigration to the "new dynamic" within the Chinese American communities, which were characterized by intense political rivalries. This in turn "sent an open invitation to federal authorities to intervene in what had previously been seen as internal affairs."[14] From 1956 to 1966, the deeply divided Chinese American communities nationwide became main targets of the INS's new voluntary "Confession Program," intensifying the already prevalent fear of persecution. Using the promise of relief and adjustment of status, the INS managed to induce, press, and sometimes force many "paper sons" and "paper daughters" to confess. Although the majority of those who confessed were allowed to stay, there were a few cases in which the fraudulent entrants admitted guilt but were still deported. Chinese Chicagoans had their good share of "paper sons." Many first generation immigrants, like Billy Moy, a prominent community leader in Chinatown, made the agonizing decision to confess and, to their great relief, were told they could stay. The INS glowed over its achievement in the Confession Program, boasting a total of 22,083 persons exposed nationwide and reduced chances for possible fraudulent entries by half of that number.[15]

Tensions and conflicts within the Chinese American community flared up on the political, cultural, and social fronts. These conflicts were largely framed by the political backgrounds and historical experiences of the newcomers, the anti-Communist stand of the dominant ethnic institutions, and, most important of all, the Cold War politics in the United States. The tensions between Taiwanese speakers and Mandarin-speaking refugees and their descendants from mainland China, who tended to function in mutually exclusive social groupings, are a case in point.[16] Indeed, past scholarship had mostly failed to discuss the often uneasy relationship between the two groups of newcomers after World War II, creating an overarching dichotomy between the anti-Communist majority and the pro–People's Republic of China minority in the Chinese American community. A careful study of the Taiwanese, a little-known group among the majority mainlanders, sheds light on the continued strained coexistence among the various subgroups of Chinese immigrants since World War II. This small number of Taiwanese who spoke a dialect of Fujianese had a different historical experience from the mainlanders who were forced to flee to Taiwan toward the end of the Chinese civil war. These Taiwanese were descendants of emigrants from coastal southern China in the 1600s and victims of Japanese colonialism from 1895 to

1945 and the Nationalist government's repression and discrimination after 1947. They were mostly young men who came to the United States in the 1950s after completing the required military service as students. Chicago, a growing metropolis, beckoned them with educational and employment opportunities. They came with borrowed money and a strong desire to get a good education but little hope of returning to a Taiwan that was under martial law. They were soon dismayed by the lack of freedom in the United States and disturbed that their every move was closely monitored by both the FBI and Nationalist government spies on campuses. Despite their uncertain future, they hoped to remain in the United States as immigrants after completing their education. Indeed, most of them were able to fulfill their desires after 1965 with the liberalization of immigration and naturalization laws.[17]

Liao Shuzhong, professor of biochemistry at the University of Chicago, had been a staunch champion of democracy and a vocal critic of the Nationalist government. Born and raised in Taiwan of a middle-class family, he came to the Illinois Institute of Technology (IIT) at Chicago in 1956 at the age of twenty-five. He was one of the five to six Taiwanese students on scholarship at IIT. A year later, he was enrolled in a doctoral program at the University of Chicago by what he called "sheer coincidence." "In 1947 at the beginning of a large-scale crackdown on Taiwanese rebellion against the Nationalist government," recalled Liao with great emotion, "I was a fourteen-year-old high school student. I witnessed with my own eyes the execution of Taiwanese rebel leaders by the Nationalists. I began to yearn for democracy and human rights. I wanted to gain a deeper understanding of democracy by studying in America."[18] Because of his anti-government stand, Liao was blacklisted for forty years and banned from returning to Taiwan until the late 1990s.

While Chicago's Chinatown was still considered by many as the most important bond tying the Chinese American community together, it was increasingly challenged as the sole face of that community. Nothing is more telling than the gradual erosion of the traditional power structure within Chinatown. From the beginning of its existence, the new Chinatown was dominated at a grassroots level by seven family associations with a total membership of 1,985. The Moy Family Association, then known as Lee Nam Tong, was the largest and oldest. After 1945, the number of family associations doubled—a fact that portended the declining homogeneity of the Chinatown population. By 1946, Chinatown was home to a total of thirty-seven associations of various kinds. Two associations even set up their headquarters outside Chinatown.[19]

Situated above the family associations were the two tongs, or regional associations, which protected the economic and business interests of their members— Hip Sing Tong and On Leong Tong. These two frequently warring tongs were both local offshoots of the national organizations of the same names that recruited their membership based on shared township or counties from China. Hip Sing

Tong (*xiesheng tang*), a splinter group from the Qing period secret society called Hon Mon, was first established in Vancouver in 1856. The Chicago chapter was initiated in 1900 in the original Chinatown. On Leong Tong (*anliang tang*), first established in San Francisco in 1893, branched out to the original Chinatown in 1907. In its competition for territorial rights, On Leong Tong gained the upper hand. It did not hesitate to show off its hegemony in the newly emerging Chinatown by building its grand, pagoda-style headquarters, which became the talk of the entire city in the 1920s. In an attempt to shed its traditional image and consolidate its influence among the changing Chinatown population, the tong leaders decided to change its charter and renamed it On Leong Merchants' Association (*anliang gonghui*) in 1949. Known as the City Hall of Chinatown in the 1940s, this association settled disputes among members of family associations, afforded protection to its member merchants from external threat and competition, and provided potential candidates for the higher-level community-wide organization, the CCBA. In 1960, the On Leong Merchants' Association decided to collaborate with its rival, the Hip Sing Merchants' Association (as it was known by then), when both faced the influx and challenges of newer immigrants from diverse regions of China.[20] Together with family associations, the tongs formed the grassroots level of a power hierarchy in Chinatown. By providing such basic social services as lodging, jobs, debt relief, medical care, funeral expenses, and elderly care, they were able to control the ebb and flow of Chinese immigrants.

The CCBA, also known as the Chinese Six Companies, originated in San Francisco in 1869. The Chicago chapter, created in 1906, was housed in the original Chinatown on Clark and Van Buren. Its initial mission was to offer mutual help and protection for the small number of Chinese merchants doing business in the area. Its headquarters have since moved twice—first in 1912 to 206 Twenty-second Place in the new Chinatown and again in 1958 to its present site at 250 Twenty-second Place—to reposition itself in the ever-changing community. For decades, the CCBA of Chicago enjoyed growing clout and a virtually unchallenged leadership position as the legal and political representative of Chinese in Chicagoland, a community-wide social service agency, and an umbrella organization of other community networks. Its members consisted of mostly local family associations, the two tongs, trade associations, and an assortment of other organizations such as the Nationalist Party's Midwest branch, the Chinese Women's Club of Chicago (1938), and the Chinese American Civic Council (1955).[21] Its presidents, quite often nominated from the leaders of the two tongs, were once considered the most powerful persons in Chinatown. Its wide membership base and its unofficial but popularly accepted position as the leading authority of the community had an integrating effect on a community that had been increasingly fragmented by home-country politics, rival kinship ties, and competing commercial interests. Before World War II, the CCBA, including its Chicago chapter, formed a close alliance with the Nationalist government, which had set up party headquarters in major Chinese American communities throughout the United States to gain control of these communities. CCBA leaders often traded loyalty to the Nationalist government (through membership in the party's local headquarters) in return for the latter's support for local merchant elite's control of the communities.[22]

As the political wind shifted in China, groups representing divergent political views and different class or trade interests began to challenge the CCBA's position as the undisputed spokesperson for the community. Second generation Chinese Americans showed an eagerness to embrace mainstream American politics and culture and did not hesitate to seek advice and information from professionals or the American press. The increasing number of women and families meant that new arrivals no longer had to depend on clans or local associations for initial adjustment. At a time of rapid demographic and social changes, the traditional power structure in Chinatown proved unable to adapt to the needs of new immigrants, new generations of Chinese Americans, and the more vocal classes of professionals, intellectuals, and workers. The CCBA, aligned with the Nationalist government in Taiwan, collaborated with the latter to crack down on dissident voices in the community.[23] Often accused of political horse-trading and corruption, the CCBA began to lose its leadership position among Chinese Americans. This process was to accelerate in the post-1965 era.

Indeed, the Chinese American communities had been confronted with many centrifugal forces such as new immigration, dispersal of population, and the changing boundaries of the communities. However, we also need to recognize the presence of strong common links that tended to tie the Chinese immigrants and their descendants into a unified ethnic group, forces such as a shared ethnic identity that was based on a common cultural sentiment and moral consensus and reinforced by pressures from the larger society. These bonds may have been strong enough to have held the community together before the 1960s. It would be a different story in the post-1965 era. The Chinese American community in the traditional sense, with Chinatown as the urban core and the traditional institutions as the power brokers, would soon be no more. Virtually autonomous subcommunities would emerge, posing serious challenges to this shared sense of common ethnicity and culture.

Fragmentation and Compromises since 1965

The 1965 Immigration and Naturalization Reform Act unleashed an unprecedented wave of immigration from the third world to the United States. For the Chinese, the act meant an increased annual immigration quota from mainland China, Taiwan, and Hong Kong from 105 to 20,000 and priority considerations to family reunion and occupational skills.[24] Riding on the rising tide of immigration from the third world, a second wave of Chinese immigrants came to

American shores in the 1970s and 1980s. Mainland Chinese immigrants had benefited from the normalization of relations between the United States and the People's Republic of China since 1972 and came to the United States through kin sponsorship. Some came by illegal avenues. After 1982, mainland Chinese immigrants began to outnumber those from Taiwan and Hong Kong combined because the United States granted a separate quota of 20,000 for the People's Republic of China and because of the latter's new "open door" policy and economic reform. Students made up the majority of those newcomers in the 1980s and 1990s. Many eventually acquired permanent residency or citizenship.

Concurrently, immigration from Taiwan to major U.S. cities continued on a large scale. These newcomers consisted of three categories: students, who made up the majority; professionals with highly demanded skills; and a third group consisting of entrepreneurs, businessmen, and unskilled workers. The first group sought college education and better employment opportunities in the United States because of overcrowding in Taiwan universities and underemployment for college graduates. Many hoped to use education as a springboard to achieve their dream of getting a good job, owning a car and a house, and eventually acquiring citizenship in the United States. They followed the time-tested path of graduate student–employment–green card–citizenship. The economic motivation behind the new Taiwan students' exodus was a far cry from the idealism of the earlier generation of Taiwan students and political dissidents. As Liao Shuzhong lamented: "Our generation was truly devoted to science and humanity. Today's young people are too practical. They are only concerned about making a good living."[25] The normalization of U.S.-China relations and the de-recognition of the Republic of China also triggered widespread anxiety and fear of Communist takeover among Taiwan residents—another factor that spurred the Taiwan population to vie for the 20,000 annual quota of immigration to the United States. Altogether, 75,400 of the 442,000 foreign-born Chinese population in the United States in 1980s came from Taiwan.[26] By 1990, a revised immigration act further privileged immigration of persons with special skills and potential job-generating investors to the United States. Cushioned by a strong economy, Taiwan businessmen and entrepreneurs swelled the ranks of visa applicants to the United States. Chicagoland's mostly suburban-based high-tech industries and research universities had since become a magnet for these newcomers. It was these American-educated, highly skilled student-turned-immigrants and well-to-do businessmen from Taiwan who spearheaded an even larger suburban movement among the Chinese population in the 1980s and 1990s.[27]

Immigration from the then British Crown Colony of Hong Kong rivaled that from Taiwan by the 1980s, numbering 80,400. These immigrants came to the United States in search for better economic opportunities and to establish permanent residency here before the colony's reversion to the People's Republic of China in 1997. In contrast to the immigrants from Taiwan, most of those from

Hong Kong were of working-class backgrounds and hence tended to settle down in Chicago's Chinatown. Between 100 and 200 families every year came to settle in Chinatown since the 1980s.[28]

The conflicts in Vietnam that culminated in the fall of Saigon on April 30, 1975, and the subsequent Vietnamese nationalization campaign brought in a new group of immigrants from Southeast Asia to major U.S. cities such as Chicago— ethnic Chinese. By 1990, 750,000 to 800,000 ethnic Chinese left Vietnam.[29] In North America, Chicago became a major point of settlement for these involuntary refugee-immigrants. Most had originally migrated from China's Fujian and Guandong provinces in the south at various times in history and spoke both their original local dialects, such as Cantonese, and Mandarin Chinese.

Post-1965 immigration brought the total number of Chinese population in the United States to 1.6 million by 1990, making it the largest Asian American group in the country. Immigration raised Chicagoland's Chinese population to 24,755 in 1980 and 43,000 in 1990. While the city lost 10 percent of its population between 1970 and 1980, the Chinese population continued to grow (from 9,400 in 1970 to 13,600 in 1980), albeit at a much slower rate than that of the suburbs as a result of suburbanization. By 1990, there were 22,300 Chinese immigrants, or about 6.2 percent of the total population, living in the city proper and a nearly equal number living in the suburbs. Illinois claimed the sixth-largest Chinese population in the nation, of which 86 percent were concentrated in the Chicago area. At the beginning of the new millennium, Chicagoland boasted a total Chinese population of 100,000.[30]

What impact did the new immigrants have on a community that had already experienced diversification and changes? How did the local Chinese American community respond to these newcomers? These questions can best be illuminated from the following perspectives: the growth of multiple community cores and institutions around which various groups of certain social, economic, and cultural backgrounds congregated; the transformation in the physical environment of the Chinese American community; the experiences of American-born Chinese Americans; and, finally, issues and forces that tended to divide or unite the communities across class, cultural, geographical, generational, and gender lines.

Post-1965 Chinese immigration to Chicagoland may share many characteristics with that to other major cities. Community formation in Chicagoland hitherto followed a distinctive path. New immigration had transformed this relatively compact urban community from one whose original cultural, economic, and political core was based in Chinatown into multiple communities that scattered throughout Chicagoland. This centrifugal process unfolded when a separate urban center dominated by Southeast Asians and ethnic Chinese began to take shape in the city's North Side. When these newcomers first set foot in Chicago in the mid-1970s, Chinatown, the traditional point of entry for previous Chinese immigrants, was already in dire shortage of housing, social services, and employment opportunities. They readily found refuge in an emerging ethnic neighborhood situated along Argyle Street between Broadway and Sheridan Road in the city's racially diverse Uptown area. The foundation of this new promising neighborhood was laid down by the Hip Sing Merchants' Association, which had relocated its headquarters from the original Chinatown on Clark Street to this location in 1975 when the city decided to raze the old buildings to make room for the Metropolitan Correction Center. A sizable Chinese American community in the Uptown area had already begun to take shape by the 1970s. There, established Chinese residents crossed cultural, language, and ancestral boundaries to sponsor the newcomers and provide aid to those in need. Together, they helped remake Argyle Street into a viable Asian business neighborhood. Popularly known as North Chinatown, where about 90 percent of the population was ethnic Chinese in the 1980s, this community distinguishes itself from South Chinatown by virtue of its relative demographic diversity. The Uptown area had historically been the preferred site for successive waves of migrants, such as impoverished whites from the South and relocated Japanese Americans from the West Coast. It was the more recent influx of Southeast Asian refugees from Vietnam, Laos, and Cambodia that redefined the area.[31] North Chinatown competes and at times cooperates with its larger, older counterpart in the south.[32]

Recent immigration also accelerated the dispersal of the Chinese population beyond the boundaries of the city proper to other areas of Cook County and the suburbs. For instance, Skokie Village, north of Chicago proper, recorded 721 Chinese residents in 1980, the largest concentration in the area. Nine other cities, towns, and villages in Cook County each had 100 or more Chinese residents. In 1990, twenty-one cities, towns, and villages in Cook County beyond the city proper had a sizable Chinese population, most of whom concentrated in Skokie and Evanston. The western suburb of Naperville, DuPage County, had over 1,000 Chinese residents. Lake, Kane, McHenry, and Will counties also reported notable increases in their Chinese population in ten years.[33] These suburban Chinese residents were mostly American-educated professionals from Taiwan and mainland China who found employment in such high-tech industries or research institutions as Argonne National Laboratory, Motorola, Abbott Laboratories, and Northwestern University based in the western, northwestern, and northern suburbs. Ethnic shops and supermarkets began to rise up in or near these areas to cater specifically to this growing Chinese population. The largest of these, DiHo Supermarket Complex in Westmont, became a magnet for nearby Chinese residents.[34] Here, mainland Chinese and Taiwan residents followed a discernable pattern in their social interactions. They might intermingle at work but for the most part kept their distance from each other outside work despite their shared interest in Chinese culture and language. Neither group's interest in the traditional Chinatown in the city of Chicago went beyond an occasional foray to dine and shop there. With the exception of those who own businesses in the city, most

Chinese suburbanites rarely participate in the social structures of the two Chinatowns. Fundamentally, class was a major factor that kept a polite distance between suburban Chinese and residents in the two Chinatowns.

Amid the competition and change, South Chinatown never lost its relevance. On the contrary, it was being transformed and reinvented. Since the 1970s, it has functioned as a way station for the primarily working-class, unskilled, Cantonese-speaking Chinese immigrants from China, Hong Kong, and Southeast Asian countries. The Chinese American community in and around Chinatown readily embraced the newcomers and the great potentials for growth by investing in new housing projects and businesses. The not-for-profit Chinatown Redevelopment Assistance Inc. (originally known as Neighborhood Redevelopment Assistance, Inc. when it was founded in 1959) was a pioneer in developing Chinatown's housing market. With an ambitious revitalization plan and supported by both government and private funds, the organization aggressively acquired land and built townhouses and condominiums, including a housing project for the elderly, in the 1960s and 1970s. In the process, it succeeded in attracting an increasing number of other real estate companies, such as Cacciaitore & Co. and Texwood Development Corp., to invest in Chinatown.[35]

Thanks to the ambitious "Santa Fe Project" envisioned by the Chinese American Development Corporation (CADC), established in 1984, Chinatown continued to expand spatially in the 1990s. This project aimed at expanding the Chinatown boundaries farther north and northwest of Archer Avenue to the abandoned thirty-two-acre railroad and industrial areas owned by the Santa Fe Railroad. Above all, the project developers envisioned a cultural community for those who spoke little English but would find "a place where they can work, raise their families, buy groceries and enjoy a cup of tea with friends, all within walking distance from their homes" and where those Chinese Americans would consider Chinatown "the preferred place to do business and to raise their children."[36] Within fifteen years, CADC was able to accomplish its main goals, with the help of the community and the city. On a thirty-two-acre area along the north side of Archer Avenue emerged Chinatown Square, a complex consisting of fifty stores and restaurants. To its west rose a fourteen-acre Santa Fe Garden residential area. To the east lay the Chinatown Parking Lot. On parts of the old dilapidated industrial sites rose up some Chinese-owned printing shops, garment factories, and ethnic foods and specialty supplies plants.[37] So successful was the CADC redevelopment project that young Chinese American professionals like May Gohres, who grew up in Chinatown but did not return after college, changed their attitude in adulthood. She and her husband, Stephen Gohres, bought a new house in Chinatown and, with their two children, settled down there to take advantage of the new cultural ambiance.[38]

According to the 1990 census, the physical boundary of Chinatown grew from a seven-block area in the 1960s to an almost one-square-mile area bordered by Eighteenth Street on the north, Federal Street on the east, Thirty-first Street on the south, and Halsted Street on the west. At the dawn of the new millennium, a new concept of the Chinatown community emerged that included Chinese residents in the Bridgeport area to the south, which would boost Chinatown's total population to 18,000.[39] The continued success of CADC demonstrated the potential of a community that was able to overcome internal conflict of interests and mobilize community and outside resources for its revitalization. Chinatown is now a bustling cultural, residential, tourist, and business center complete with a newly expanded public library, a post office, a Christian church, two religious schools, a few Chinese schools, several social service agencies, a number of local Chinese presses, a public park, and, more recently, its very own Chinese-American Museum of Chicago.[40]

New immigration after 1965 has fundamentally altered the power structure of the old Chinatown-based Chinese American community and given rise to new ethnic organizations in emerging Chinese American communities. In face of a rapidly growing and increasingly heterogeneous population, traditional ethnic organizations such as clan-based family associations, the two merchant associations, and the CCBA were ill prepared to meet the growing and varying demands for social services, housing, and education. They were often bypassed by new immigrants from mainland China who felt little affinity to Chinatown's traditional social structures.[41] The power of the old merchant class in Chinatown represented by the On Leong Merchants' Association had declined precipitously since the 1980s due to government crackdowns on gambling and other illegal businesses connected to the association's members. A new, more inclusive business organization, the Chicago Chinatown Chamber of Commerce (CCCC), came into being in 1983, functioning as the representative and promoter of Chinatown's new business community. In conjunction with other organizations and City Hall, the CCCC sponsored popular events such as the annual Dragon Boat Race, the New Year Parade, and Chinatown Summer Fair. The number of family associations had also grown to fifteen by 2000.[42]

In North Chinatown, ethnic Chinese joined hands with other Southeast Asian immigrants of different ethnic backgrounds to improve their neighborhood. The Argyle Fest was an annual ethnic fair involving the collaborative efforts of the Chinese Mutual Aid Association, the Vietnamese Association of Illinois, the New Chinatown Chinese Council, and the Asian American Small Businessmen's Association. It has attracted tens of thousands of people to the neighborhood since its inception in 1985.[43]

In suburban areas, Chinese professionals began to form their own associations based on either a shared region of origin or place of residency. The Northern Illinois Chinese Association (later known as the Naperville Chinese American Association) is one such an example.[44] Social activities were organized around the Chinese schools that members of each group set up for their children. They might work together, as was the case in Naperville, to advocate their common agenda to local governments, but for the most part they voluntarily distanced themselves in social functions.[45]

Two social service agencies that emerged in Chicago played a vital role in assisting recent immigrants to settle and adjust—the Chinese American Service League (CASL) and the Chinese Mutual Aid Association (CMAA). Across community boundaries, a new generation of Chinese American community activists rose up to address the new demands and challenges by seeking help from the government. The result was a new type of social service organization that was free from the entanglements in homeland politics and international relations. The CASL came into existence in 1978 when community volunteers, many of whom were recent immigrants, joined hands with United Way of Chicago and the Chicago Community Trust. Though headquartered in South Chinatown, the CASL was committed to assisting all Chinese immigrants in the Greater Chicago area "in attaining self-sufficiency through programs that ensure economic opportunities, ease cultural transitions, and enhance the physical and mental health of individuals and families of all ages and backgrounds."[46] By 2000, it had evolved into the Midwest's largest social service agency, with 190 professional and support staff, $5.2 million in programming, and five facilities servicing 14,000 residents. In addition, the CASL functioned as a cultural center offering classes such as Chinese folk dance, painting, calligraphy, and language. Some of the CASL's accomplishments in the last two decades include its successful mobilization of community support to bring in a new public library (ten times the size of the old one) to Chinatown (1990), completion of a ninety-one-unit Senior Housing Building in the Chinatown Square Development (1998), and its award-winning youth program and senior service center (2004) in the expanded Chinatown.[47]

The CMAA started as a volunteer group by a few sympathetic and involved ethnic Chinese immigrants from Southeast Asia in the late 1970s. In 1981, the CMAA formally registered as a not-for-profit social service organization based in North Chinatown. Its mission was to serve the needs of local immigrant residents in tandem with larger relief organizations such as Catholic Charities and Travelers and Immigration Aid of Chicago. The CMAA's founders believed that they understood their own people's culture and needs better than anyone else. Over the years, the CMAA developed a close partnership with sister organizations such as the CASL and traditional ethnic organizations such as the CCBA, the Vietnamese Association of Illinois, and the Lao American Community Services to provide a wide range of social services in twenty different dialects or languages to the diverse immigrant families in the Uptown area. Under the management of a new cohort of Chinese Americans who were born and educated in the United States, the CMAA was able to weather the continuous demographic changes in the area and opened its door to anyone who needed help, regardless of ethnicity or race. Seeing a higher rate of depression and health care needs among elderly

Chinese immigrants in the suburbs, the CMAA opened a suburban office in Westmont to provide medical workshops, transportation to and from medical facilities, and English and citizenship classes to mostly non-English-speaking and aging parents of middle-class Chinese immigrants.[48]

Compared to the traditional ethnic organizations such as the CCBA, which had no fund-raising staff and was mostly privately financed, both the CASL and CMAA had professional fund-raisers who helped them garner up to half of their funding from federal, state, and city government and the other half from private and corporate donations. These newer organizations also tried to steer away from ethnic politics and homeland issues and focus exclusively on social service and immigrant rights advocacy. Staffed by young, energetic, and forward-looking American-born Chinese Americans, supported by locally prominent boards of directors of all ethnic backgrounds, particularly well-established Chinese American professionals and community leaders, these broad-based social service organizations had an integrating impact on the fragmented Chinese American communities and bridged the gap between Chinese American communities and other Asian American communities and the American society as a whole.

While new ethnic organizations and social service agencies were eroding the dominant position of the CCBA, the latter was forced to make changes as well—to become more inclusive and responsive. Since the 1960s, the CCBA has substantially expanded its services to include a senior dining program, citizenship and language classes, free medical services, a resource library, insurance, tax preparation, real estate investment, and travel agencies. Attempts were also made by traditional ethnic associations under the auspices of the CCBA to reach out to newer community organizations despite language and cultural barriers. In 2000, the CCBA boasted a total of thirty-one Chicago-area member organizations, including such newer ethnic organizations or community service agencies as the Taiwan Benevolent Association of Chicago (1979), the Burmese Chinese Association (1975), the Chinese Mutual Aid Association (1981), the Chicago Chinatown Chamber of Commerce (1983), the Cantonese Association of Chicago (1991), and the Association of Friends of Hong Kong and Macao (1992).[49] The enlarged membership list reflected the demographic changes in Chicagoland but notably left out a very significant part of the Chinese American communities—recent immigrants from mainland China and their corresponding organizations. The CCBA's outreach to suburban Chinese American communities also met with limited success. Consequently, it remains today a city-based umbrella organization whose social service functions are frequently eclipsed by its own members such as the CASL and CMAA.

Perhaps no issue reflects the divided state of Chicagoland's Chinese American communities better than their varying level of involvement in and stand on homeland politics and China-related issues.[50] In the past three decades, intercommunity relations have largely been defined by the changing relations between the United States, China, and Taiwan. Recent immigrants, especially those from mainland China and Taiwan, brought their political biases and a lack of understanding with them to the United States. Interactions between the two groups were often heavily influenced by their preconceived ideas about each other. In the 1970s, Taiwan immigrants found themselves caught in a state of insecurity and ultimately "statelessness" as a result of the declining international position of the Republic of China in Taiwan. The sense of uncertainty largely grew from a fear that mainland China would invade Taiwan after the People's Republic of China normalized diplomatic relations with the United States in 1972. By 1978, de-recognition of Taiwan left many Taiwanese nationals who were yet to obtain permanent residency or U.S. citizenship stateless. Most were resentful of their sudden loss of status and continued to identify themselves with the Republic of China. In the early 1980s, Taiwan went through a process of political liberalization that culminated in political democratization in the 1990s. Many Taiwan immigrants who had the privilege of dual citizenship participated in the first democratic presidential election in Taiwan in 1996.[51]

Concurrently, mainland China's economic reform and ascending international position buoyed pride and confidence among the large number of new immigrants from China. When tensions between Taiwan and China eased, relations between the two immigrant groups in the United States tended to improve. In times of crisis, however, disagreement and debate came out in the open. Pro-Taiwan independence groups were often pitched against pro-unification groups, which formed an unlikely alliance between the CCBA and some mainland Chinese immigrant groups such as the Chinese American Coalition of the Greater Chicago. The difference was that the CCBA, which was dominated by the old-timers from the 1940s and 1950s, still envisioned a rather untenable goal of national unification under the Republic of China, while the latter pushed for reunification under the People's Republic of China. The CCBA leadership had publicly maintained the traditional pro-Guomindang stand vis-à-vis both mainland China and the Taiwan independence movement, which was encouraged by Guomindang's archrival in Taiwan since 1991, the Democratic Progressive Party (*mingindang*). After Beijing's crackdown on student demonstrations in 1989, the CCBA voiced its unequivocal support for mainland Chinese students' democratic movement while denouncing the activities and pro-independence rhetoric of visiting Democratic Progressive Party leaders.[52] Today, the CCBA continues its tradition of sponsoring the annual Double Ten parade to celebrate the founding of the Republic of China on October 10, 1911, and the Chinese New Year celebration in February.

Tensions within and between communities are also reflected in cultural differences, which resulted in voluntary mutual exclusion in social functions. According to John Rohsenow, the "tripartite division" of the Chinese American communities in Chicagoland has created a corresponding linguistic and cultural divide among the Chinese population. As the core of South Chinatown continues to attract mostly uneducated, working-class immigrants from various regions in China and other countries and at the same time loses better-educated second generation residents, half of the Chinatown residents now speak standardized Cantonese in place of the Taishan dialect, and the other half speak Mandarin and various other dialects. In North Chinatown, most of the ethnic Chinese speak some variations of Fujianese, Cantonese, Mandarin, or a language from their country of origin. In suburban communities, Chinese residents (with the exception of their recently arrived elderly parents) are mostly proficient in English and speak Mandarin, which is the standard dialect in both Taiwan and mainland China. However, the two immigrant groups in various suburbs set up their separate Chinese schools, supported respectively by the Taiwan government or the People's Republic of China.[53]

In the city, Chinese-language or Chinese-heritage schools had existed long before new immigrants began to arrive. These schools were either run by the CCBA or Christian churches in Chinatown. Since the 1980s, both the CASL and CMAA offered Chinese-language classes as part of their social service programs. Politics had little to do with their choices of teaching one Chinese-language system or the other. It was a different story in the suburban communities. The rise of two separate Chinese-language school systems in suburban Chicago and throughout the United States was clearly a legacy of homeland politics. In the 1950s, the People's Republic of China adopted simplified Chinese characters while the Republic of China in Taiwan adhered to what it believed to be the true tradition of Chinese culture—classic Chinese characters. The Chinese School Association in the United States (CSAUS) was founded in 1994 with the intention of spreading the education of simplified Chinese and promoting U.S.-China cultural exchanges. The Xilin Association of Chinese Schools (1989) represented the local attempt to achieve the same goals. Its seven affiliated schools throughout Chicago's suburban areas are dominated by mainland Chinese immigrants and funded to some extent by Beijing. In addition, the association operates an art and senior center to extend its reach in the suburban communities. On the other hand, the Cooperative Chinese Language School, founded in 1971 in the western suburbs, remains a cultural and social anchor for immigrants from Taiwan.[54] Both sides attract some students from Chinese American families or non-Chinese families. The Taiwan government also operates the Chinese Cultural Center in Westmont through its Overseas Chinese Affairs Commission to sustain its influence among suburban Chinese Americans. Added to this mutual cultural exclusion was the increasingly vocal rhetoric of American-born Taiwanese students and professionals who challenged the Chinese cultural chauvinism promoted by both sides. They were attempting to construct a new identity for themselves—Taiwanese Americans, not Chinese Americans.[55] The linguistic divide, exasperated by homeland politics, tends to further fragment the already diverse and loosely formed Chinese American communities in Chicagoland.

While first generation Chinese immigrants today are preoccupied with China-related issues, American-born Chinese Americans (ABCs) as a group, as Nancy Yao points out, tend to be more concerned with domestic issues that have a direct impact on the community than with international relations, despite the group's "unique, advantaged cultural position to contribute to improved understanding of China by the American public and its important role as a link between Chinese immigrant communities and mainstream society in terms of U.S.-China relations."[56] However, interest and actual participation in the discourse on U.S.-China relations are limited to a small number of well-informed community activists. Yao attributes the limited organizational involvement of ABCs in foreign policy issues to their "conflicting identity, divided political loyalties, and widespread apathy."[57] This observation seems to be borne out by Chinese Chicagoans' experience. Most of Chicago's American-born Chinese population, particularly those who grew up in the suburbs, are more concerned about issues of economic and political opportunities for Asian Americans as a whole than they are about the concerns of a specific ethnic group. Homeland politics of their parents' generation are nondistinct issues to them. Prominent local ABC activists such as Victoria Chou, dean of the College of Education, University of Illinois at Chicago, and Philip Wong, legal counsel and a director for the CASL and various other Asian American organizations, have worked hard to promote a range of causes in conjunction with fellow Asian Americans and non–Asian Americans. Through such pan-Asian organizations as the Chicago-based Asian American Institute, in which both Chou and Wong serve on the board of directors, Chinese American community leaders strive to empower the Asian American community in Illinois through advocacy against discrimination and support for research, voter education, and coalition building.[58] In this sense, they serve as ambassadors between the immigrant communities and the mainstream society. Nevertheless, the divergence in needs, interests, agendas, and loyalty among the immigrant generation, between native-born and American-born Chinese, and among Chinese Americans of different classes, professions, genders, and religions also works together to deprive the Chinese American communities a unified voice.

Conclusion

Chicagoland's Chinese American communities have come a long way in their struggle for survival, economic success, acceptance, and equality in a multiethnic metropolis. Their experience since 1945 tells a complex story of an ethnic group thriving in a new frontier of immigration. It is a history of immigration, adaptation, expansion, diversification, conflicts, cooperation, and fragmentation. It reminds us of the seemingly insurmountable challenges that have confronted and will continue to confront all Chinese American communities throughout the United States. The experience of Chinese Chicagoans attests to the crippling impact of homeland politics on the first generation immigrants and their uphill struggle to bridge cultural, class, political, and geographical differences to forge a unified voice. The second generation's apathy toward the immigrant generation's agenda and their limited participation in political actions are a far cry from the political activism of their Chinese American counterparts in California and New York. This lack of cohesion among Chicagoland's Chinese American communities renders the new generation's drive for pan-Asian solidarity a daunting task. As long as China remains undemocratized and the Taiwan issue unresolved, and new immigrants with their own biases and cultural preferences continue to arrive, Chicagoland's Chinese American communities will continue to evolve, change, and divide. Despite all these centrifugal forces, there is one ultimate factor that will eventually bind them together—growing loyalty to the new land that they bet their future on.

NOTES

1. Lucy M. Cohen, *Chinese in the Post–Civil War South: A People without a History* (Baton Rouge: Louisiana State University Press, 1984); Wei Li, "Spatial Transformation of an Urban Ethnic Community from Chinatown to Chinese Ethnoburb in Los Angeles" (Ph.D. diss., University of Southern California, 1997); Ying Zeng, "The Diverse Nature of San Diego's Chinese American Communities," in *The Chinese in America: A History from Gold Mountain to the New Millennium*, ed. Susie Lan Cassel, 434–448 (Walnut Creek, Calif.: AltaMira Press, 2002); Huping Ling, *Chinese St. Louis: From Enclave to Cultural Community* (Philadelphia: Temple University Press, 2004).

2. The Chinese experience in Chicago in the recent decades bears many similarities to that of Chicago Polonia since the 1970s. For a comprehensive study of Chicago's Polish community, see Mary Patrice Erdamans, *Opposite Poles: Immigrants and Ethnics in Polish Chicago, 1976–1990* (University Park: Pennsylvania State University Press, 1998).

3. An unofficial estimate by a joint survey conducted by the Chinese Consolidated Benevolent Association and other local organizations put the number of Chinese residents in 1926 at between 4,500 and 5,000. Harry Ying Cheng Kiang, *Chicago's Chinatown* (Lincolnwood, Ill.: Institute of China Studies, 1992), 5, 30; Tin-chiu Fan, "Chinese Residents in Chicago" (Ph.D. diss., University of Chicago, 1926), 22–24; Susan Lee Moy, "The Chinese in Chicago: The First One Hundred Years," in *Ethnic Chicago: A Multicultural Portrait*, 4th ed., ed. Melvin G. Holli and Peter d'A. Jones, 378–408 (Grand Rapids, Mich.: William B. Eerdmann, 1995).

4. Xiaolan Bao, "Revisiting New York's Chinatown, 1900–1930," in *Remapping Asian American History*, ed. Sucheng Chan, 31–48 (Walnut Creek, Calif.: AltaMira Press, 2003); Barbara M. Posadas and Roland L. Guyotte, "Unintentional Immigrants: Chicago's Filipino Students Become Settlers, 1900–1941," *Journal of American Ethnic History* 9, no. 2 (Spring 1990): 26–48; Barbara M. Posadas, "Cross Boundaries in Interracial Chicago: Filipino American Families since 1925," *Amerasia* 8, no. 2 (1981): 31–52.

5. John Hayakawa Torok, "'Interest Convergence' and the Liberalization of Discriminatory Immigration and Naturalization Laws Affecting Asians, 1943–1965," in *Chinese America: History and Perspectives, 1995*, ed. Marlon K. Hom et al., 1–28 (San Francisco: Chinese Historical Society of America, 1995).

6. David M. Reimers, *Still the Golden Door: The Third World Comes to America*, 2nd ed. (New York: Columbia University Press, 1985), 26.

7. Census reports as cited in Kiang, *Chicago's Chinatown*, 29–30.

8. Minglan Cheung Keener, "Chicago's Chinatown—A Case Study of an Ethnic Neighborhood" (master's thesis, University of Illinois at Urbana–Champaign, 1994), 20.

9. Ibid.

10. According to Tables IV and V, cited in Fan, "Chinese Residents in Chicago," 25–26.

11. Chicago Chinatown Chamber of Commerce (CCCC), "History of Chicago's Chinatown," www.chicagochinatown.org, accessed September 8, 2002.

12. Kiang, *Chicago's Chinatown*, 4, 31.

13. For the role played by local leaders of the Guomindang Party and the Six Companies in the anti-Communist campaign, see Victor G. Nee and Brett de Barry Nee, *Longtime Californ': A Documentary Study of an American Chinatown* (New York: Pantheon Books, 1973), 217–221.

14. Xiaojian Zhao, *Remaking Chinese America: Immigration, Family, and Community, 1940–1965* (New Brunswick, N.J.: Rutgers University Press, 2002), 165.

15. Billy Moy, executive director of the Chinese Consolidated Benevolent Association, interview by author, October 15, 2002; News Release, Department of Justice, December 31, 1972, as cited in Zhao, *Remaking Chinese America*, 183.

16. John Rohsenow, "Chinese Language Use in Chicagoland," in *Ethnolinguistic Chicago: Language and Literacy in the City's Neighborhoods*, ed. Marcia Farr, 321–355 (Mahwah, N.J.: Lawrence Erlbaum, 2004).

17. Ling Z. Arenson, "Taiwan xinyimin zai meiguo de wenhua rentong" [Taiwanese Americans: The Construction of a New Group Identity in the U.S.], in *Modernity and Culture Identity in Taiwan*, ed. Lu Hanchao, 208–237 (River Edge, N.J.: Global, 2001).

18. Liao Shuzhong, interview by author, September 29, 2000.

19. Keener, "Chicago's Chinatown," 15.

20. Hsiu-Wen Chiou Yin, "Yi mo xian ru, zhou guo bai nian—zhonghua huiguan qiaotuan jianshao" [Survival and Cooperation in a Century—An Introduction to Member Organizations under CCBAC], in *A Century of Chicago Chinatown*, comp. Chinese Consolidated Benevolent Association of Chicago (CCBAC), 68 (Chicago: CCBAC, 2000).

21. Liu Tongtien, "A Brief History of Chicago's Chinatown," in ibid., 20–21.

22. Bernard Wong, *Patronage, Brokerage, Entrepreneurship and the Chinese Community of New York* (New York: AMS Press, 1988), 82–86.

23. For a detailed discussion of the transformation of community institutions from the 1940s to 1950s, see Zhao, *Remaking Chinese America*, 94–125.

24. Immigration and Nationality Act of October 3, 1965, 79 Stat. 911, reprinted in Michael Lemay and Elliot Robert Barkan, eds., *U.S. Immigration and Naturalization Laws and Issues: A Documentary History* (Westport. Conn.: Greenwood Press, 1999), 257–259.

25. Liao, interview.

26. Kiang, *Chicago's Chinatown*, 2.

27. Arenson, "Taiwan xinyimin zai meiguo de wenhua rentong," 214–217.

28. Kiang, *Chicago's Chinatown*, 2.

29. Tran Khanh, "Ethnic Chinese in Vietnam and Their Identity," in *Ethnic Chinese as Southeast Asians*, ed. Leo Suryadinata, 267–295 (Singapore: Institute of Southeast Asian Studies/New York: St. Martin's Press, 1997).

30. Kiang, *Chicago's Chinatown*, 29, 36; U.S. Census Bureau and U.S. Department of Commerce, *We the Americans: Asians* (Washington, D.C.: Government Printing Office, 1993), 2.

31. Elizabeth Warren, *Chicago's Uptown: Public Policy, Neighborhood Decay, and Citizen Action in an Urban Community*, Urban Insight Series No. 3 (Chicago: Loyola University, 1979), 3–4.

32. Yin, "Yi mo xian ru, zhou guo bai nian," 70; Moy "Chinese in Chicago," 384.

33. Rohsenow, "Chinese Language Use in Chicagoland," 7.

34. Hsiu-Wen Chiou Yin, "Xinlaizhe yu huafu" [Newcomers and Chinatown], in CCBAC, *Century of Chicago Chinatown*, 51–52.

35. Keener, "Chicago's Chinatown," 25–27; Kiang, *Chicago's Chinatown*, 6.
36. Keener, "Chicago's Chinatown," 26; Project proposal as cited in ibid., 28; Philip Wong, interview by author, September 25, 2002.
37. Kiang, *Chicago's Chinatown*, 8.
38. Jane Adler, "Family Ties: Former Residents of Chinatown Find Roots Pulling Them Home," *Chicago Tribune*, October 8, 2000.
39. Ibid.; CCCC, "History of Chicago's Chinatown."
40. Chinese-American Museum of Chicago, http://camoc.homestead.com/Index.html, accessed May 25, 2005.
41. Rohsenow, "Chinese Language Use," 6.
42. CCCC, "Culture of Chicago's Chinatown," www.chicagochinatown.org, accessed September 8, 2002.
43. Richard Lindberg, *Passport's Guide to Ethnic Chicago: A Complete Guide to the Many Faces and Cultures of Chicago*, 2nd ed. (Lincolnwood, Ill.: Passport Books, 1997), 282.
44. Yin, "Xinlaizhe yu huafu," 51–52.
45. Ibid.
46. Chinese American Service League, History, www.caslservice.org, accessed January 15, 2006.
47. Ibid.
48. Steven Brunton, development manager of CMAA, interview by author, September 3, 2002.
49. Yin, "Yi mo xian ru, zhou guo bai nian," 60.
50. Chicagoland's Chinese American communities share many similar experiences with other cities on these issues. See Ying Zeng, "The Diverse Nature of San Diego's Chinese American Communities," in Cassel, *Chinese in America*, 434–448.
51. Arenson, "Taiwan xinyimin zai meiguo de wenhua rentong," 216–231. The Society of Taiwanese Americans–Chicago is a popular organization among young Taiwanese professionals in Chicagoland. See SOTA, Mission, http//members.aol.com/sotaill/mission.html, accessed October 14, 2002.
52. CCBA of Chicago to Chairman Guan Qilian, CCBA, San Francisco, August 14, 2000, CCBA Archives.
53. Rohsenow, "Chinese Language Use," 5–7.
54. See the Chinese School Association in the United States Web site at http://csaus.org and the CCLS Web site at www.asiannet.com/ccls, both accessed October 9, 2002.
55. American-born Taiwanese in the Chicago area have been closely tied to such nationwide organizations as the Taiwanese American Professionals (TAP), the Taiwanese American Citizens League (TACL), and the Intercollegiate Taiwanese American Student Association (ITASA). All proclaim to promote Taiwanese culture, heritage, and identity. For their mission statements and links with other organizations, refer to the respective Web sites at http://tap.tacl.org, www.itasa.org, and www.tacl.org.
56. Nancy Yao, "From Apathy to Inquiry and Activism: The Changing Role of American-Born Chinese in U.S.-China Relations," in *The Expanding Roles of Chinese Americans in U.S.-China Relations: Transnational Networks and Trans-Pacific Interactions*, ed. Peter H. Keohn and Xiao-huang Yin, 85–96 (Armonk, N.Y.: M. E. Sharpe, 2002).
57. Ibid.
58. Asian American Institute, Programs, 2005, http://aaichicago.org/index.html, accessed January 15, 2006.

4

Transforming an Ethnic Community

Little Saigon, Orange County

LINDA TRINH VÕ

In 1975, few Vietnamese lived in the United States; however, by 2005 over 1.2 million Vietnamese Americans commemorated the thirty-year anniversary of the end of the Vietnam War, referred to as the American War by the Vietnamese.[1] In the intervening years, numerous refugee and immigrant waves settled in the Little Saigon area of Orange County, California, known as the capital of Vietnamese America. This vibrant area boasts thousands of Vietnamese businesses that cater to almost 300,000 Vietnamese in Southern California—the largest population of Vietnamese outside of Vietnam—who gather for shopping, entertainment, dining, and professional services.[2]

Rather than focusing on the origins of the community[3] and the initial spatial establishment of the community,[4] which other scholars have discussed, this chapter analyzes the continual development and transformation of the Little Saigon community after thirty years. I focus on the primary factors that define this ethnic community: spatial expansion, economic growth, and political developments.[5] While many outsiders see this as a monolithic community of downtrodden refugees, this hardly captures the diversity of the community, the range of their activities, or their transformation from a refugee to an immigrant community. Another perception is that this community remains mired in anti-Communist politics, and although homeland issues continue to shape their activities, this only defines certain aspects of community life. With a new generation coming of age who were born at the war's end or in the postwar era, there are a multitude of voices that are shaping this community. Additionally, scholars who examine Vietnamese Americans from merely an assimilationist framework, or "melting pot" model, overlook larger structural forces and transnational aspects that encourage Vietnamese Americans to retain their ethnic identities and to sustain ethnic communities.[6]

This community differs from other Asian American communities, which are largely immigrant based, whereas Vietnamese "refugees" forced into exile created Little Saigon.[7] Similar to Cuban and Jewish refugees who preceded them, they escaped with literally the clothes on their backs, and this was instrumental in motivating them to rebuild new lives. In 1975, when approximately 120,000 refugees escaped in the first wave, they were unsure about their fate or the future of their country, but as the new Communist government became entrenched and those like them who remained behind were persecuted, they overcame their shock and went about the business of restarting their lives. The U.S. government's efforts to disperse the refugees to avoid overburdening local municipalities and also to hasten their assimilation countered the refugees' own desires to be located near coethnics.[8] More important, in a process of secondary migration, they flocked to areas where they could find educational and occupational opportunities. From these concentrations they created Vietnamese American communities, which are now known as "Little Saigons," across the country.[9] The fact that ethnic concentrations have allowed them to thrive economically and politically presents important lessons on the limits of managing and controlling displaced persons. It suggests we need to rethink our policies on how best to support refugees during their resettlement process. They now resemble other immigrant communities in terms of the dilemmas they face, such as contending with the internal diversity of their population, negotiating their expansion within the existing community, and figuring out how to engage in civic matters.[10]

Little Saigon, Orange County

In the mid-1970s, when the first group of Vietnamese refugees arrived, the area that would become Little Saigon was a bedroom community populated mainly by elderly whites and was known for its aging tract houses, trailer parks, small farms, auto yards, and open lots. The area experienced a population growth in the post–World War II era when service personnel stationed in local military bases decided to settle permanently; however, younger generations abandoned this suburb for better opportunities elsewhere.[11] Many of the early Vietnamese came through "Operation New Arrival" and were processed in the resettlement center at El Toro Marine Corps Air Station in Orange County, while others came from nearby Camp Pendleton, a marine base in northern San Diego County, where the first wave of refugees were temporarily housed in 1975. Attracted by the warm weather and educational and occupational opportunities, along with affordable housing and commercial space, second and third waves of refugees joined this first group, quickly enlarging the population and revitalizing the area.[12]

In 1988, after being lobbied by Vietnamese American community leaders, the Westminster City Council designated the 1.5-mile stretch of Bolsa Avenue, from Magnolia to Brookhurst, as the Little Saigon Tourist Commercial District, which is noted on freeway exit signs. On the main streets leading into the area, there is official signage welcoming visitors to Little Saigon in three cities: Westminster,

Garden Grove, and Santa Ana. Cluster Vietnamese businesses are spilling into Fountain Valley, Huntington Beach, Midway City, and Stanton, so its boundaries are porous. Encompassing over four square miles in the main section and spread out in an array of suburban-like mini-malls, this area is enclosed by McFadden Avenue to Trask Avenue and Beach Boulevard to Euclid Avenue.[13] Ironically, while there continues to be resistance to the "Vietnamization" of the area, mainstream city leaders recognize the growing clout of this ethnic community and have fought over the right to claim ownership of Little Saigon.[14]

The number of Vietnamese residents has increased rapidly in Westminster, and to a lesser extent in Garden Grove and Santa Ana, changing the demographics and aesthetic of the neighborhood. Vietnamese reside in homes, trailer parks, and apartments, remnants from the earlier period, as well as in the newly developed gated communities, indicative of the socioeconomic diversity of the population. In 1990, the average price of a detached single-family stucco ranch house built in the 1960s or 1970s, averaging 1,200 to 1,500 square feet, was $186,000, and in 2005 it was $523,500.[15] As they became more economically stable, many families expanded and remodeled their homes, and the majority of real estate sales in this part of Westminster are to Vietnamese households. In addition to adding Asian architectural features to their homes, Vietnamese residents have transformed their gardens with familiar plants such as banana, guava, and dragon fruit, as well as with lemon grass and a variety of *rau*, herbs that commonly accompany Vietnamese cuisine. Plans have also been approved to build the first senior citizen housing complex in the heart of the community on Bolsa Avenue.[16]

Little Saigon has become the largest Asian business district in the county and rivals those in nearby Los Angeles. Vietnamese from surrounding Los Angeles, San Bernardino, Riverside, and San Diego counties flock to this area for their shopping and social needs, but it also attracts a fair number of regular out-of-state visitors, who come to socialize with relatives and friends as well as to buy ethnic goods. While in flight from Hawaii, commercials on television monitors encourage airline passengers to visit Little Saigon. Mainstream tourist guidebooks and travel or food sections of local periodicals on Southern California direct visitors to this ethnic "treasure," where they can shop and eat in Little Saigon. The area cannot be defined solely as an "ethnic enclave" that caters just to Vietnamese "refugees," but attracts other Asian ethnics and non-Asians interested in finding a bargain meal and affordable groceries or those interested in exploring an ethnic community.

Demographic Transformations

In Orange County in 2000, Asian Americans comprised 14 percent of the population, with Asians and Latinos combined making up almost half of the county, so the Vietnamese are part of the major transformation shifts in the region.

According to the U.S. census, the Vietnamese are the largest group, with 135,548, an increase of 89 percent from 1990 when they numbered 71,822, and now the Vietnamese are more than twice the next largest group, the Chinese. This is in contrast to statewide levels, with the number of Vietnamese at 12 percent and the Chinese population at 27 percent. There are 27,109 Vietnamese living in Westminster, comprising 31 percent of the city's population, and 35,406 in Garden Grove, comprising 21 percent of the city's population. More recently, this increase is a result mainly of higher birth rates and Vietnamese migrating from other parts of the United States, not from new immigration. The population includes groups who came through different programs for war brides, refugees, immigrants, former political prisoners, and Amerasians (multiracial Vietnamese).[17] Local schools have been transformed by the rising Asian American enrollment, mainly Vietnamese, which has increased to almost 30 percent in the Garden Grove Unified School District, with high schools such as Bolsa Grande being 50 percent Asian American and La Qunita being 70 percent Asian American, while others are majority Latino.[18]

Reshaping Economic Opportunities

In the late 1970s, the Vietnamese community in Orange County started with just four businesses: a pharmacy, a grocery store, an insurance company, and a restaurant. And while it has been labeled an ethnic enclave similar to densely populated urban immigrant neighborhoods—it does have many similar features—it is located in a sprawling suburb and joined by mini-mall structures. Frank Jao of Bridgecreek Development Group Inc. is credited with the creation of Little Saigon, and he, along with his international business associates, continues to invest in its economic expansion. He transformed many of these low-end shopping centers into profitable spaces, of which Asian Garden Mall, with its 150,000-square-foot site filled with shops, cafés, and jewelry stores, is the most well known community landmark. Many centers are named after the street locations, while others are given more ethnic names, such as Le Loi Center, Asian Village Mall, Cathay Bank Center, Pearl of the Orient Mall, Little Saigon Village, and Saigon Plaza.

While some structures are quite modern, others are still dilapidated storefronts. The area has an eclectic architecture, with remnants of earlier bland designs intermixed with Vietnamese and Chinese design elements. Over the years, controversy has arisen over the perception that Vietnamese of ethnic Chinese descent are dominating Little Saigon, bringing in networks of overseas Chinese investors and pushing for Chinese architectural designs. This was exemplified by the conflict over the Harmony Bridge Project to build a pedestrian bridge over the main street, which was eventually scrapped, and the failure of the Saigon Market, with its prominent Chinese statutes on display. Traditional structures coexist with European and contemporary structures, some multileveled ones, which have been remodeled or are new projects. New landscaping in street dividers, bus stop stands with an Asian flair, and other infrastructure improvements are part of the ongoing projects to revitalize the area and create a more welcoming ambience for visitors.

An increase in the number of Asian residents may be acceptable because they can blend into a residential neighborhood; however, an Asian commercial presence that transforms the physical composition of landmark buildings, replaced by ethnic signs and businesses, can be met with discomfort from long-time residents. The Vietnamese American community has faced antagonism that has resulted in defacement of their businesses and racial slurs from white residents, especially in the early years of their expansion, when longtime white residents called for controlled growth of this ethnic community. For the most part, other Asian, Latino (mainly Mexican), Middle Eastern, and mainstream American businesses peacefully coexist side-by-side with the Vietnamese establishments. Businesses such as markets, cafés, restaurants, and bakeries, and shops that sell goods such as jewelry, clothing and accessories, herbal remedies, or various knickknacks are ubiquitous, so competition is fierce. Buyers can still bargain with vendors, and prices are extremely cutthroat, so business owners make a profit in volume sales. Every year, some of the formerly popular businesses, especially the mom-and-pop ventures, disappear to be replaced by newer models, with a number of mini-malls experiencing several reincarnations already. Visitors can purchase furniture and appliances or have their cars serviced by Vietnamese-owned businesses. While the businesses were started by the first generation, a second generation is inheriting their parents' businesses, and some are opening businesses of their own in the community. Their socialization, sensibilities, and aesthetics are altering the character and management of businesses, especially their ability to attract non-Vietnamese clientele to sustain a livelihood. Vietnamese American economic leaders, from politicians to Chamber of Commerce officials, continue to encourage store owners to improve their storefront displays and interpersonal services to increase business.

As a self-sufficient community, service needs can all be fulfilled in Little Saigon, such as real estate, insurance, legal, finance, and tax services. Although mainstream and other Asian American–owned banks are located in the district, the First Vietnamese American Bank opened its doors in 2005, which is the third attempt to establish a Vietnamese American–owned bank.[19] All kinds of medical services are available, from plastic surgery to dental care. From birth to death, Vietnamese Americans can rely on coethnic-owned businesses, such as Vietnamese American funeral homes offering burial services and space in ethnic areas of local cemeteries. There are industries in which the Vietnamese have found an economic niche. For example, Vietnamese American–owned beauty schools are noticeable, along with shops where beauty products can be purchased in massive quantities; however, hair or nail salon shops are rare. Instead, these ubiquitous shops are located throughout the county (and Southern California), with estimates indicating that the majority are owned or operated by Vietnamese Americans, and they cater to a racially diverse clientele.

Vietnamese American presence has changed mainstream businesses, which recognize the potential profits of catering to this population. For example, banks such as Wells Fargo Bank and Bank of America have bilingual tellers, but also include Vietnamese language in their automated teller machines. Local car dealerships, from Toyota to Mercedes-Benz, have Vietnamese sales crews and market heavily in the community. In addition, other mainstream financial, insurance, communication, and medical companies have targeted this group, hiring bilingual representatives. Even American Indian–owned casinos throughout Southern California have lavish marketing campaigns in the community, such as hosting concerts by Vietnamese singers to entice the Vietnamese to come gamble in the nearby reservation casinos.

Culturally, the area boasts a thriving center for the media, art, and entertainment industries, becoming an integral part of the local economy. Music concerts, art shows, beauty pageants, theatrical performances, book readings, and fund-raising events are commonplace. There are three daily papers, most notably the *Nguoi Viet Daily News*, the oldest and largest newspaper, and *Viet Bao*, in addition to a host of other print publications, with an estimated forty weeklies and monthlies. In addition to Little Saigon Radio on 1480 AM and the Vietnamese California Radio (VNCR) on 106.3 FM, there are television stations, such as Little Saigon TV, SBTN, Saigon TV, VATV, and VHN-TV, which provide news and entertainment. Trendy nightclubs are venues for concerts, and stores selling movies, Paris By Night entertainment videos, and music CDs, many selling for as low as $1, are ubiquitous. Traditional organizations, such as Loc Hong, preserve cultural practices by promoting lessons on traditional instruments, dance, and songs to the next generation. Many of the songs include nationalist prewar songs or wartime songs of nostalgia, loss, and love.[20] In contrast, Club O'Noodles, a theatrical group originally started by college students at California State University, Northridge, was revitalized in the early 2000s locally with some of the original cofounders and performers. They infuse drama and comedy in their bilingual performances, which critique controversial issues related to gender, race, sexuality, class, and internal community politics.

Previously, when U.S. trade with Vietnam was banned, products from Vietnam arrived via another country. Now the "Made in Vietnam" label can be found on clothes, household goods, and other items that are sold in mainstream stores as well as in shops in Little Saigon. Unlike other Asian ethnic communities, which welcome and in some cases rely on real estate and financial investments from their home countries, anti-Communist Vietnamese Americans publicly condemn investments from their homeland government. Yet on a more personal level, community members welcome new products from Vietnam that can be readily purchased, rekindling the nostalgia for homeland foods and goods. For entrepreneurs, the profits derived from their businesses override political ideologies. In Little Saigon, travel agencies, money transferring businesses, and shops that sell goods that will be resold on the black market in Vietnam rely on homeland connections for their livelihoods.

Money from the profits and earnings that could be reinvested in Little Saigon is used to support family members back home, which is then directly or indirectly invested in the Vietnamese transnational capital circuits. As mainly a refugee population forced to flee their homeland, most of the first generation still have familial connections in Vietnam. The Vietnamese government welcomes capitalist investment, given that the per capita income is equivalent to US$200–300.[21] The remittances sent home are estimated to be in the multimillions, which is in addition to the millions that overseas Vietnamese, known as Viet Kieu in Vietnam, spend while visiting Vietnam, especially during Tet, the Vietnamese New Year. The end of the Cold War and the collapse of the former Soviet Union have affected postwar Communist Vietnam, with the country looking to Western nations for economic investments. Vietnam's 1986 *doi moi* policy, which allowed for free market enterprises; the end of the U.S. trade embargo against Vietnam in 1994; and President Clinton's historic visit to Vietnam in 2000 created more conducive conditions for normalizing trade and establishing diplomatic relations with the United States. The Viet Kieu are capitalizing on the potential to profit from a burgeoning economy in a country with a population of 80 million who, for the most part, have moved beyond the wartime animosities and welcome U.S. products and trade relations. With relatively modest capital, these Viet Kieu can utilize their material and cultural capital, namely their ethnic and bilingual skills, along with their nongovernmental organizational endeavors, to establish transnational business enterprises to rebuild the country. However, Vietnamese Americans are fearful of backlash by coethnics, so are guarded about discussing these transnational business connections, which are still risky ventures with a socialist-controlled government. The potential for profits, along with ethnic pride in their former homeland, ensures that Little Saigon's transnational economic connections will most likely increase.

However, the rosy picture of Little Saigon's economic success also reveals the socioeconomic challenges confronting the community. It faces similar economic problems encountered by other Asian ethnic enclaves, in which the high percentage of small businesses is an indicator of Vietnamese Americans being locked out of the mainstream economy because of linguistic or discriminatory barriers. With the fierce competition, turnover is high, and many only manage to eke out a meager living, hoping for better options for their Americanized children. Refugees and immigrants with limited education, job skills, and English fluency live in poverty, have inadequate access to health care, and depend on welfare services. Newcomers without other employment options subsist on low-paying service-sector jobs or industrial jobs and compete with a ready supply of Latino workers, especially in the restaurants and markets in Little Saigon. Vietnamese workers are paid under the table to supplement their welfare checks, providing opportunities for coethnic exploitation. Union involvement is basically nonexistent in the community, which reflects the conservatism of the county, but it is difficult to organize Vietnamese workers because they associate unions with "Communism."[22] Additionally, because of the negative publicity regarding coethnic crimes, such as gang shootings and home invasion robberies, which tarnishes the image of Little Saigon, ethnic business leaders have tried to portray the district as a safe and welcoming community to all.

Redefining Political Engagement

Like other immigrant groups who have gained relative economic stability, Vietnamese Americans are attempting to use their economic clout to flex some political power. While the media often focus on the staunchly anti-Communist aspects of the community, the community's political opinions and activities are much more diverse than depicted by the media or by politicians. The local community is not only engaged in fighting for "freedom, democracy, and human rights" in Vietnam but also is emerging on the local political scene. They have formed literally hundreds of professional, cultural, religious, political, and other nonprofit organizations, clubs, and associations. As a refugee community forced into exile from a country that endured unimaginable hardships, they have a rich history of political involvement. This history permeates every aspect of community life; however, it is tempered by the opportunities to engage in civic life in this country and by the emergence of a new generation of leaders.

Vietnamese Americans, both first generation and younger generations, have made impressive inroads into elected office, with a number of candidates running for office during elections. By early 2007, there were ten in elected positions, more than any other Asian ethnic group in the county. Tony Lam, who won a seat on the Westminster City Council in 1992, was the first Vietnamese American politician in the country and served two terms. In 2002, he was succeeded by Andy Quach, who made an unsuccessful bid for mayor of Westminster. Three of the five-member Garden Grove Unified School District Board of Education members are Vietnamese, with Lan Nguyen winning his seat in 2002 and Trung Nguyen and KimOanh Nguyen-Lam winning theirs in 2004. Van Tran, who won his seat on the Garden Grove City Council in 2000, moved on to win a State Assembly position and has ambitions for higher office.[23] He was followed by Janet Nguyen in 2004, the first woman in nearly thirty-five years and the youngest person elected to the Garden Grove City Council. In early 2007, Trung Nguyen and Janet Nguyen, both Republicans, ran for the hotly contested Orange County Supervisor position in a district with high concentrations of

Vietnamese, and easily trounced the front-runner, a seasoned Anglo Democrat who made limited efforts to reach out to Vietnamese constituents, who rallied behind the Vietnamese politicians. Initially, Trung Nguyen won by seven votes, but when the election recounts were taken to court, Janet Nguyen won by a mere three votes, making this the closest election in the county's history. This supervisor election gained national attention because of the dispute and because she was the youngest and first Asian American in this position, and the election marked the "coming of age" of Vietnamese American politics, highlighting that politicians cannot ignore the Vietnamese electorate. In addition to these elections, mainstream politicians have hired Vietnamese American field representatives and also appointed them to city positions and boards to appease these new voters.

Although local politics is supposedly nonpartisan, the major elected officials, except Nguyen-Lam, who is a Democrat, are Republicans. It seems ironic that a community with lower socioeconomic status (SES) and that continues to face racial discrimination and marginalization is aligned with a conservative party not known for supporting social programs or other policies that address inequalities. There are several internal and external reasons for this. Primarily, the Republican Party's anti-Communist and probusiness stance and its more conservative social policies make it favorable to the community.[24] Vietnamese American politicians have had to pass the litmus test, promoting their anti-Communist platforms in order to garner votes and funds from the community, so aligning themselves with this party is symbolic of their ideological stance. Unlike local Democratic entities, the Republican Party recognizes the political potential of this ethnic community and has provided endorsements and some financial backing of Vietnamese politicians, which further boost the party's popularity. As newcomers to the electoral process, the Vietnamese will donate to and vote for Vietnamese politicians irrespective of their partisan allegiances, because of feelings of ethnic affinity and pride. With more Vietnamese individuals running for office and vying for votes from the community, there is an opportunity for the community to scrutinize their political viewpoints and records to ensure those claiming to represent them are legislating policies that are actually in the interest of the community. Although the Democratic base is increasing among some first generation voters and with the younger generation, the politically active and economically powerful elements of the community are still Republican.[25]

The mainstream media attention that the Vietnamese garner usually is related to the numerous anti-Communist demonstrations and protests, and this issue has been a divisive one for the community. In 1999, approximately 15,000 protesters descended on a mini-mall Little Saigon for fifty-three days to demonstrate against Truong Van Tran, the Hi-Tek video store owner who displayed a flag of the socialist Republic of Vietnam and a picture of former Communist leader Ho Chi Minh. The fear of being labeled a "Communist" is a real threat that has palpable consequences. Entertainers, politicians, newspaper publishers, and other notable leaders, even when the accusations are baseless, have been the targets of violence, protest, boycotts, and smear campaigns. Little Saigon is unique because of the high number of former military and political leaders—survivors of the infamous "reeducation" camps, which were Communist prisons—who immigrated through the Humanitarian Operation Program and who have relocated to the area. They have been instrumental in the building of the Vietnam War Memorial in Westminster, which commemorates both the South Vietnamese and Americans who served in the war.[26] Although some community members state that the vociferous anti-Communists are small in number and declining in power, they still pose a looming threat to anyone who is suspected of harboring or displaying what they interpret to be pro-Communist rhetoric or actions.

Privately, members of the community do not support the Communist regime, but they want to reconnect with their loved ones, or the lure of lucrative economic opportunities overrides political sentiments. Times are definitely changing, with those who experienced the most horrific escapes, even former political prisoners, returning to visit their homeland. Key local community members have made well-publicized visits to their homeland, such as Nguyen Cao Ky, the former wartime prime minister and vice president of South Vietnam who made his first visit in 2004, and Kieu Chinh, the most well known Vietnamese actress, who has set up a charity to build schools there. Major political delegates from Vietnam have quietly visited the community, and in 2005 the prime minister from Vietnam visited the United States, the first one to do so since the end of the war.[27] During the fall of 2005, the U.S. ambassador to Vietnam, Michael Marine, visited the area to nurture diplomatic relations and faced repeated questions regarding corruption and repression by the government in Vietnam and human trafficking.[28] Vietnamese Americans work with nongovernmental organizations (NGOs) and charity organizations, such as medical or educational ones, to help rebuild Vietnam, as well as with organizations such as the Vietnam Education Foundation, which sponsors college students from Vietnam to study in the United States, in the hopes that they will return and improve their country. Organizations such as the Vietnamese Alliance to Combat Trafficking (Viet Act), started by a young generation of Vietnamese Americans in Little Saigon, have raised awareness on the human trafficking of Vietnamese women as "brides" and as slave laborers in Taiwan, so multiple Vietnamese American generations are involved in building these transnational connections.

However, there is a political disconnect between generations, and this can be illustrated by a 2004 controversy that arose over the *Vietnamese American Xposure* (VAX) show, a thirty-minute MTV-style English-language entertainment show geared toward the 1.5 and second generation youth. This production included stories about social and cultural issues, but also integrated serious political issues facing the community. The hosts were interviewing two Asian American filmmakers about their documentary *Saigon, U.S.A.* and showed clips that included a protest against the video store owner who displayed a Vietnamese Communist flag and a picture of Ho Chi Minh.[29] It was aired on a station that usually has Vietnamese-language programming, so the core audience, not understanding the context or the language, immediately threatened to boycott the station for showing these "pro-Communist" images. The VAX creators held a community forum to explain that their intent was to inform youth about the documentary and to instill ethnic pride, since the documentary revolves around interviews with community leaders regarding the formation of Little Saigon. The protesters, mainly ex-Vietnamese military personnel, some wearing military regalia, scolded them in Vietnamese for their lack of fluency in Vietnamese and their lack of respect for their elders by not singing the South Vietnamese anthem when the former South Vietnamese flag was displayed at the beginning of the forum.[30] Although the volunteer staff had already completed additional pilots, their airtime was canceled, and they have yet to find another willing station sponsor. At this meeting, those who spoke publicly and those I talked to privately verbalized their dismay at the misunderstanding and the censorship, noting how this could dampen future creative expression by younger generations.[31]

One of the most impressive cultural organizations is the Vietnamese American Arts and Letters Association (VAALA), which has been able to navigate the political terrain. They have organized art shows, theatrical performances, spoken word performances, concerts, and a book fair. VAALA is also the sponsoring organization for the biennial Vietnamese International Film Festival (ViFF), the largest artistic cultural event in the community, which includes all genres, such as documentary, animation, and feature-length films, submitted from the Vietnamese diaspora.[32] They have shown films made by local Vietnamese American 1.5 generation and second generation in Vietnamese with English subtitles, highlighting themes related to the war and postwar Vietnam, refugee experiences, and legendary tales.[33] Some are transnational productions and were filmed on location in Vietnam and have received laudatory praise from multigenerational Vietnamese American audiences. Additionally, films made by filmmakers from Vietnam were shown at ViFF, such as *The Deserted Valley*, *Living in Fear*, and *The White Silk Dress*, followed by question-and-answer sessions with the filmmakers, without any protests. This is in contrast to the well-publicized community protest by more than 300 people against the Bowers Museum of Cultural Art in Santa Ana in 1999 when it exhibited artwork from artists in Vietnam, with complaints that Communist symbols were infused in the artwork.[34] The Vietnamese suffered from foreign invasions, the civil war, and the aftermath of the war, all of which created internal chasms within families and within the nation, and the struggles to survive escape and re-create their lives left deep scars. Not surprisingly, these divisions will continue to politicize the first generation, but it will also affect the younger generation, even those who want to avoid anything "political" and to establish their own agenda.[35]

Some have complained that a disproportionate focus on homeland issues has led to negligence in addressing local social problems facing the community. At Vietnamese American events, it has become customary for local and state politicians to highlight in their speeches the need to bring "independence, democracy, and freedom" to Vietnam, often to loud cheers, most notoriously at the annual local Tet festival, rather than identifying local issues that need to be addressed. The community faces pressing social problems that are masked by the image of them as "model minority" refugees who have pulled themselves up by their own "bootstraps." For example, there is continual effort by community-based organizations to push for the hiring of bilingual health educators who can work on preventive health care services and establish health care awareness programs, and some have formed the Vietnamese American Human Services Association. Since 1979, the Vietnamese Community of Orange County has provided health care and support services for refugees and their families, along with organizations such as St. Anselm's Cross-Cultural Community Center, founded in 1976, and the Orange County Asian and Pacific Islander Community Alliance (OCAPICA). Project MotiVATe (formerly Camp for Youth), run by younger generation Vietnamese Americans, is a mentoring and tutoring program that attempts to address high school dropout rates and juvenile delinquency problems facing Vietnamese American teenagers.[36] At this stage, the community still faces challenges regarding how to balance their limited energy and resources to address homeland issues, as well as advocating for the educational, social, health care, and economic needs of the Vietnamese in Orange County. It is an intricate balance to promote a "model minority" success story of a thriving community that appeals to tourists, while at the same time addressing the social problems that continue to plague the community.

Conclusion

Although it started as a community that catered to the refugee population, Little Saigon, similar to other immigrant communities, now faces dilemmas about its livelihood and survival. Many first generation are nostalgic for their homeland and enjoy visiting it, but recognize that the Vietnam of today is not the one they left behind, and they have readjusted to their life in America, where their children and grandchildren have established roots. With only a few new immigrants expanding the population, the community is making the transition to being a predominantly second generation population, with some having strong ethnic identities and community affinities and others feeling detached. Many of the first generation leaders are retirement age, and with a new generation coming of age who are removed from the trauma of war and relocation, the leadership of the community is changing. There are over twenty Vietnamese American high school associations, and most college campuses in Southern California have Vietnamese student associations or similar organizations. The Union of Vietnamese Student Associations of Southern California (UVSA), a nonprofit organization started in 1982 by college students and alumni, has worked to bridge the cultural and social divide between generations. They are known for organizing the annual Tet Lunar Festival in Garden Grove, which raises hundreds of thousands of dollars each year that are redistributed to community organizations. With an aging first generation, the younger generation will become the future leaders; however, the first generation places priority on customs of deference for elders, so transferring power is difficult, and traditional male leaders are uneasy with supporting female leaders, which has stifled the potential of the next generation.[37] Change is occurring, however, as when the Vietnamese American Community of Southern California (VACSC), a nonprofit, nonpartisan organization established in 1990 with the objective of preserving cultural heritage, uniting and representing the population, and advocating for a free Vietnam, elected Phu Nguyen, a member of the younger generation, as president.[38] Ysa Le, executive director of VAALA, and Anh Do, reporter and editor for *Nguoi Viet* newspaper, both are 1.5 generation women who have taken responsibility for inheriting their father's leadership role, providing new opportunities for future women leaders in the community.

In the coming years, there are three major concerns that Little Saigon will face, all of which are related to the expansion and longevity of the community. With exorbitant housing prices—among the highest in the country, with the median price of a home at $270,000—and manufacturing jobs declining, Vietnamese Americans have left the Golden State seeking more affordable housing and improved job opportunities elsewhere.[39] With few new Vietnamese immigrants entering the United States and socioeconomically mobile Vietnamese Americans choosing to leave this enclave, business owners are concerned about sustaining their clientele, especially beyond the first generation. Although Vietnamese are moving outside of the core of Little Saigon, many remain in Southern California and return for shopping, entertainment, religious services, and professional needs, which is quite evident from weekend traffic jams.

There is also concern about the growing entrepreneurial competition from satellite Vietnamese areas in the San Gabriel Valley and downtown Chinatown areas, both located in nearby Los Angeles County. Furthermore, other Asian ethnic businesses, such as markets and restaurants, have opened up in neighborhoods throughout Southern California, making the excursion to Little Saigon unnecessary.[40] Some community leaders are trying to capitalize on Little Saigon's location near Disneyland and Knott's Berry Farm amusement parks, as well as its proximity to beach cities, to attract Asian and non-Asian tourists. Debates continue on how to preserve it as a culturally comfortable and appealing space for the Vietnamese American population, including the younger generation, while enhancing it as a mainstream tourist site. Additionally, sharing the trauma of war, escape, and resettlement, as well as anti-Communist sentiments, bonds the first generation and builds community; however, unlike their parents, the younger generations may not have these same attachments to the "safe haven" that has become Little Saigon.[41]

Furthermore, like other immigrant communities, Vietnamese Americans will be forced to navigate the diverse ethnic and racial terrain of the county and figure out how to build effective coalitions.[42] Little Saigon has expanded into neighboring areas, such as the Korean business district in Garden Grove and the Latino concentrations in Santa Ana, which has created animosity. For example, there was a plan to build a Vietnamese cultural center in the Korean area, which was halted when the Korean community protested, and there were complaints from the Latino community when a "Welcome to Little Saigon" sign was approved for posting in Santa Ana. Although Orange County is generally perceived to be racially white, the Asian population is around 14 percent, and the Latino population is approximately 30 percent, and both groups will continue to increase in the foreseeable future. This will transform the economic, political, and cultural character of the county. The Vietnamese, as an extremely diverse community, are still in the preliminary stages of figuring out how to build crucial alliances among themselves as well as with their neighbors.

NOTES

1. Scott Martelle and Mai Tran, "25 Years After the Fall of Saigon, a Vietnamese Enclave Thrives," *Los Angeles Times*, April 28, 2000.

2. The estimate on the number of Vietnamese-owned businesses varies significantly from 2,000 to 5,000 depending on the source. It is commonplace for one site to operate multiple businesses, in order for business owners to maximize their profits in such a competitive environment, which increases the count significantly, but not the spatial factor. The population estimate is based on 2000 U.S. census data of Orange, Los Angeles, Riverside, San Bernardino, San Diego, and Ventura counties.

3. C. Beth Baldwin, *Capturing the Change: The Impact of Indochinese Refugees in Orange County; Challenges and Opportunities* (Santa Ana, Calif.: Immigrant and Refugee Planning Center, 1982); Jacqueline Desbarats and Linda Holland, "Indochinese Settlement Patterns in Orange County," *Amerasia Journal* 10, no. 1 (Spring/Summer 1983): 23–46; Steven R. DeWilde, "Vietnamese Settlement Patterns in Orange County's Little Saigon" (master's thesis, California State University, Long Beach, 1996); Hien Duc Do, "The Formation of a New Refugee Community: The Vietnamese Community in Orange County, California" (master's thesis, University of California, Santa Barbara, 1988).

4. Karin Aguilar-San Juan, "Creating Ethnic Places: Vietnamese American Community-Building in Orange County and Boston" (Ph.D. diss., Brown University, 2002); Robert Daniel Michaels, "The Structure and Spatial Morphology of the Ethnic Commercial Enclaves of Little Saigon and Koreatown in Orange County, California: A Comparative Study" (master's thesis, California State University, Long Beach, 2000); Sanjoy

Mazumdar, Shampa Mazumdar, Faye Docuyanan, and Colette Marie McLaughlin, "Creating a Sense of Place: The Vietnamese-Americans and Little Saigon," *Journal of Environmental Psychology* 20 (2000): 319–333; Colette Marie McLaughlin and Paul Jesilow, "Conveying a Sense of Community along Bolsa Avenue: Little Saigon as a Model of Ethnic Commercial Belts," *International Migration* 36, no. 1 (1998): 49–63.

5. Since 2000, I have attended numerous community events, informally interviewed community leaders, helped to organize community events, and been on boards of community organizations, giving me an opportunity to understand the transformations occurring in Little Saigon and the surrounding community.

6. Min Zhou and Carl L. Bankston III, *Growing Up American: How Vietnamese Children Adapt to Life in the United States* (New York: Russell Sage Foundation Press, 1998).

7. Although some groups or waves from Vietnam were classified as "immigrants" for political purposes, they were treated as "refugees" and provided the services accorded to them.

8. Linda Trinh Võ, "The Vietnamese American Experience: From Dispersion to the Development of Post-Refugee Communities," in *Asian American Studies: A Reader*, ed. Jean Yu-Wen Shen Wu and Min Song, 290–305 (New Brunswick, N.J.: Rutgers University Press, 2000).

9. There are large Vietnamese American communities in Northern California as well as in Houston, Texas, but other concentrations exist in Boston, Chicago, Seattle, Louisiana, Virginia, and elsewhere.

10. Timothy P. Fong, *The First Suburban Chinatown: The Making of Monterey Park, California* (Philadelphia: Temple University Press, 1994); John Horton, *The Politics of Diversity: Immigration, Resistance, and Change in Monterey Park, California* (Philadelphia: Temple University Press, 1995); Jan Lin, *Reconstructing Chinatown: Ethnic Enclave, Global Change* (Minneapolis: University of Minnesota Press, 1998); Min Zhou, *Chinatown: The Socioeconomic Potential of an Urban Enclave* (Philadelphia: Temple University Press, 1992).

11. Rob Kling, Spencer Olin, and Mark Poster, eds., *Postsuburban California: The Transformation of Orange County since World War II* (1991; reprint, Berkeley: University of California Press, 1995).

12. Elisabeth Orr, "Living Along the Fault Line: Community, Suburbia and Multi-Ethnicity in Garden Grove and Westminster, CA 1900–1995" (Ph.D. diss., Indiana University, 1999); Linda Trinh Võ and Mary Danico, "The Formation of Post-Suburban Communities: Little Saigon and Koreatown, Orange County," *International Journal of Sociology and Social Policy* 24, nos. 7-8 (2004): 15–45.

13. This is just a general outline since there are Vietnamese businesses outside this area and Vietnamese do not own all the businesses in the district; however, they are highly visible in this vicinity.

14. Phil Willon and Mai Tran, "2 Cities Vie for Commerce of 1 Ethnicity," *Los Angeles Times* (Orange County Edition), November 30, 2002.

15. Merrill Balassone, "The Heart of Little Saigon Beats Strong," *Los Angeles Times*, October 23, 2005.

16. This is not low-income housing, but will be sold at market value. In my discussions with the developers of the complex, they informed me they expect that the children who have the financial means to do so will assist their parents with the purchase of these residences.

17. Linda Trinh Võ, "Managing Survival: Economic Realities for Vietnamese American Women," in *Asian/Pacific Islander American Women: A Historical Anthology*, ed. Shirley Hune and Gail Nomura, 237–252 (New York: New York University Press, 2003).

18. Garden Grove Unified School District includes seventy schools and serves students from the cities of Garden Grove, Westminster, and Santa Ana. CCD Public School Data 2003–2004 and 2005–2006 School Accountability Report Card at www.ggusd.us, accessed April 30, 2007.

19. The former CEO and president of the bank informed the author of the other efforts during a conversation.

20. Adelaida Reyes, *Songs of the Caged, Songs of the Free: Music and the Vietnamese Refugee Experience* (Philadelphia: Temple University Press, 1999).

21. UNICEF, "Vietnam Children and Women: A Situation Analysis," 11, United Nations Children's Fund, 1994; Andrew Pierre, "Inside Vietnam Today," *Foreign Affairs* (November/December 2000): 69–86.

22. Thanks to discussions with Quynh Nguyen, formerly the organizing director of the Asian Pacific American Labor Alliance in Los Angeles (November 19, 2002), and An Le, formerly with the Korean Immigrant Workers Advocates in Los Angeles (January 20, 2006), who informed my views on the challenges of union organizing in Little Saigon.

23. The Sixty-eighth Assembly District at the time of his election had voter registration rates at 45 percent Republican and 33 percent Democrat. Half of this district is made up of Costa Mesa and Garden Grove and also includes sections of Westminster, Fountain Valley, Anaheim, and Stanton.

24. It seems that the high concentration of Vietnamese Catholics reinforces conservative perspectives on hot button issues such as abortion and gay rights, which are aligned with the Republican Party.

25. Christian Collet and Nadine Selden, "Separate Ways ... Worlds Apart?: The 'Generation Gap' in Vietnamese America as Seen through the *San Jose Mercury News* Poll," *Amerasia Journal* 29, no. 1 (2003): 199–219.

26. This is rare since of the numerous Vietnam War memorials across the country, only a few honor Vietnamese military personnel. Another exception is the one in Boston, which notes the loss of South Vietnamese soldiers on a plaque.

27. Anti-Communist protestors quelled plans for a public tour of Little Saigon, and local police said they could not ensure his safety.

28. I attended two community meetings during his visit, one open event at the University of California, Irvine, which I moderated, and another with invited Vietnamese community leaders in Irvine on October 27, 2005.

29. Produced and directed by Lindsey Jang and Robert C. Winn, 2003.

30. At the November 4, 2004, forum, in fluent Vietnamese, a number of the staff defended their decision and explained that it was not their intent to support Communism, rather to educate the public about a film made about Little Saigon. Tim Bui and Tony Bui, filmmakers of *Three Seasons* fame, attended and spoke up in English with some Vietnamese on behalf of VAX. Like many Vietnamese Americans, including a number of the staff, they can speak some Vietnamese, but are not fluent, especially at the level to convey complex ideas; however, they are making vital contributions to the community, whereas many who are fully fluent do not participate in the community. This deals with larger debates about "ethnic authenticity" and "essentialized identities" and what this means for who can "speak" on behalf of the community.

31. I consulted with them before they went into production, provided information for their accompanying Web site, and attended their celebratory gala event and the community forum. The volunteer staff continues to contribute their talents to other cultural productions.

32. I have been involved with ViFF in 2003 (its first year), 2005, and 2007, and showings are held mainly in Little Saigon, the University of California, Los Angeles, and the University of California, Irvine.

33. Tony Bui and Tim Bui, *Three Seasons* and *Green Dragon*; Ham Tran, *Journey from the Fall*; Nghiem-Minh Nguyen-Vo, *Buffalo Boy*; Charlie Nguyen, *Thoi Hung Vuong 18*, *Chances Are*, and *The Rebel*; and Victor Vu, *First Morning* and *Spirits*.

34. Janet Dang, "Protesters Call Vietnamese Art Propaganda," *Asian Week* 20, no. 46 (July 15, 1999). The exhibit, titled "A Winding River: Journey of Contemporary Art in Vietnam," was organized by the Meridian International Center, a nonprofit group in Washington, D.C., and features about seventy-five works by Vietnamese artists from the 1920s onward.

35. I often hear at all kinds of organizing meetings and in personal conversations that it's important to avoid anything that can be interpreted as "political," meaning they want to make sure it's dissociated with the "Communism" controversy, which means that there continues to be a heightened level of self-censorship in the community.

36. They were previously sponsored by the Union of Vietnamese Students Association of Southern California, but switched sponsors to the Orange County Asian and Pacific Islander Community Alliance (OCAPICA), which includes health care, education, and advocacy programs that serve Vietnamese Americans. I serve as a board member of both OCAPICA and Project MotiVATe.

37. I make this assessment after numerous conversations with first, 1.5, and second generation community leaders as well as through my observations of community networks. Many of the newer or emerging leaders in the community are women, and they have met indirect and direct resistance from the male leadership, or their authority has been undermined—from simply spreading gossip about them to not providing them with crucial political support. I discuss some of the gender and generational issues in Linda Trinh Võ, "What a Difference a Generation Makes: Negotiating Vietnamese American Womanhood in the Diaspora," in *Le Vietnam au Feminine/Vietnam: Women's Realities*, ed. Gisèle Bousquet and Nora Taylor, 323–336 (Paris: Les Indes Savantes Publisher, 2005).

38. One of their main missions is "To advocate for human rights and democracy in Vietnam in order for Vietnamese nationals to live in a country based on freedom, peace and justice." http://www.namcali.org/aboutus.aspx, accessed February 20, 2006.

39. This is according to the U.S. census, which reports the median price for a home in the United States is $119,600.

40. Linda Burum, "Suddenly Saigon," *Los Angeles Times*, September 22, 2005.

41. Thanks to Andrew Lam, Mariam Beevi-Lam, Viet Le, and Hong-An Truong for our lively discussion in Little Saigon, Orange County, on March 2, 2006, which helped shaped this section.

42. Leland Saito, *Race and Politics: Asian Americans, Latinos, and Whites in a Los Angeles Suburb* (Chicago: University of Illinois Press, 1998).

5

Building a Community Center

Filipinas/os in San Francisco's Excelsior Neighborhood

ALLYSON TINTIANGCO-CUBALES

I stood at the corner of Mission and Geneva around 4:30 on a Tuesday afternoon. I was told by several locals that this was the most dangerous intersection in San Francisco. There sits a bus stop right in front of Popeye's Chicken. Various types of people stand underneath graffiti-tagged billboards advertising Courvoisier cognac and Wal-Mart in Tagalog.[1] Chillin' at the bus stop is a *barkada*, or a group of young Filipina/o friends. They are *tsismising*, gossiping in Tagalog, about some guy who thinks he's better than them because he was born in the United States. Next to them stands three older Pinoys in their late sixties; they are conversing in Kapampangan.[2] There are also several women with children. I overhear a *lola*, a Filipina grandmother, asking a young mother in Tagalog who takes care of her daughter when she is at work. In English, the young mother responded that she doesn't work right now. The *lola* offered to help her find a job. Another woman in her forties stands by herself in a burgundy-colored polyester skirt suit with sun-tan-colored nylons, white ankle socks, and sneakers. She carries her imitation Louis Vuitton briefcase in one hand and a worn-out Christmas gift-bag in the other, presumably containing the remains of her lunch.

The bus stop crowd looks like an intergenerational Filipina/o family party in which all the characters are present, yet they are grouped by age, gender, and language. They are all Filipina/o, they share the same bus stop, they coexist in the same space, they all live in the neighborhood together, but they maintain separation. This mini-ethnography of the bus stop is a microcosm of the Filipinas/os in the Excelsior neighborhood of San Francisco.

This chapter is about a community of Filipinas/os who live in and around the Excelsior District, a working-class neighborhood in San Francisco that borders Daly City. According to the 2000 census, San Francisco is home to over 40,000 Filipinas/os.[3] Today, the greatest concentration of Filipinas/os in San Francisco live in the southeastern neighborhoods of the city, particularly in the Excelsior/Outer Mission, Visitation Valley, and Portola neighborhoods. This chapter looks at the experiences and needs of these Filipinas/os and describes the development of the Filipino Community Center (FCC), which caters to this community's needs.

In the first section, I begin by engaging in the discourse on "ethnic community" within Asian Pacific American and ethnic studies. The second section examines the long and diverse histories, identities, and transformations of Filipinas/os in San Francisco to help establish their roots. The third section explores some of the major issues, circumstances, and tensions between Filipinas/os in this neighborhood. The final section presents the needs and experiences of Filipinas/os in the community, along with strategies that can be used to build and sustain the services provided by the FCC.

Ethnic Enclave or Community: Locating Filipinas/os in the Excelsior Neighborhood

In regards to understanding the experiences of Filipinas/os in the Excelsior, there is a great need to rearticulate the meaning of the term "community." Scholars in Asian Pacific American studies and in ethnic studies have developed a wide field of scholarship around defining the meaning of, and concept of, "community" as a place of contention, change, development, and multiplicity. Over the past two decades, many scholars have conducted research on Asian Pacific American communities with or without geographical boundaries.[4] They have theorized ways to understand how race, ethnicity, class, geography, generation, and culture affect how one person or a group of people negotiate meanings of "community."

Are the Filipinas/os in the Excelsior part of a community, or are they an ethnic enclave? In "Asian Americans in Enclaves—They Are Not One Community: New Modes of Asian American Settlement," Chung chooses to use the term "ethnic enclave" instead of community "because it does not presume any internal cohesiveness." Chung refers to these enclaves as "ethnic" because the title provides a cross between race and culture, while also acknowledging an "externally imposed ethnic identity (that) does not assume cultural and emotional homogeneity."[5]

Although Chung makes a strong argument for the usage of "ethnic enclave" versus that of "community" for Asian Americans, this conceptual framework may have little relevance for Filipinas/os in the Excelsior. For them, it may not be a question to use one or the other. The fact that the highest concentration of Filipinas/os in San Francisco live in the Excelsior neighborhood could constitute it as an ethnic enclave, but as Chung points out, this in and of itself does not mean that it is a "community." However, despite the assumptions of cohesiveness and homogeneity that are associated with the term "community," it is also a construct that allows members to imagine a sense of belonging and possibility that is often needed to pursue social change.

Because of its ability to be both broad in describing the Filipinas/os across the nation and in diaspora and as specific as an association with an ethnic enclave, the term "community" has its complications as well as its benefits. It can include both the needs of the population living in their geographical location as well as issues that Filipinas/os face outside their neighborhood. It is important to describe the characteristics that make up a community with a developing history, and it is important to connect this with their relationships to Filipinas/os in other geographical locations. Moreover, it is necessary to chart their relationships to Filipinas/os outside of American ethnic enclaves to include Filipinas/os in diaspora.

Relationships among Filipinas/os in Excelsior and with Filipinas/os outside of their geographic boundaries contribute greatly to how they conceptualize community. Huping Ling proposes a "cultural community" as a new framework to understand the complexities of the Chinese American community in St. Louis. She points out that the focus on geographic boundaries can alienate those who do not live in ethnic enclaves but see themselves as part of a larger "cultural community." But her main point is to explore how the "cultural community does not always have particular physical boundaries, but is socially defined by the common cultural practices and beliefs of its members."[6]

Ling proposes that a "cultural community" model allows for a better understanding of the complexity of the contemporary Chinese American community, cultural identity, and acculturation. The "cultural community" model that Ling presents has a possible application for Filipina/o Americans and their relationship to each other. But it is important to note the danger in associating "common cultural practices and beliefs" with the notion of being Filipina/o.

In the attempt to develop a Filipina/o American community, there is a need to be careful when creating standards based on notions of static, "traditional" culture to measure "Filipina/o-ness." Filipinas/os are a people from a vast number of regions in the Philippines, with over 7,000 islands, and come to the United States with diverse languages, cultures, and identities. It is also dangerous to essentialize a static notion of culture in the Filipina/o American community because to do so denies multiplicity and hinders the possibilities of cultural production.

By no means does this caution mean that Filipinas/os and Filipina/o Americans do not pursue common practices or beliefs that are associated with culture and traditions, because many would argue that Filipinas/os embrace a set of core values. According to Danilo Begonia, these core values were identified by the late Virgilio Enriquez, the eminent Filipino American psychologist. These include *Kapwa* (identity based on shared inner-self), pivotal interpersonal values such as *Pakiramdam* (shared inner perception), linking sociopersonal values such as *Kagandahang-Loob* (shared humanity) and associated societal values such as *Karangalan* (dignity), *Katurungan* (justice), and *Kalayaan* (freedom). These values "constitute the center of gravity of Filipina/o life," Begonia writes. "These are the basic organizing principles that govern the way Filipinas/os feel and act, and anchor the interpretation of their existence and their relationship to others."[7]

Allowing for the pursuit of these core values presents a dynamic notion of culture. Rather than using these values to measure Filipina/o-ness, they can be used as "organizing principles." The development of these principles was not meant to limit the dynamic nature of Filipina/o culture. Regardless of cultural diversity, Filipinas/os do share some common experiences that are rooted in the history of colonialism in the Philippines, immigration patterns, and Filipina/o racialization in American society. Root states that "the traumas associated with colonization that lasted almost 400 years scarred us all, regardless of our nativity, language, class, or gender."[8] All of these contexts have shaped and affected Filipina/o cultures, identities, and communities.

Drawing from both the ethnic enclave and cultural community models, there is a need to begin viewing the Filipinas/os in the Excelsior as an "ethnic community"—"ethnic" because, like an ethnic enclave, it allows for a cross between race and culture. In this particular model, ethnicity is based on race being a sociohistorical construction that is externally imposed in combination with a culture that is not assumed to be static. "Community" is also an important element in describing the Excelsior, not to assume cohesiveness and not merely because of geographic boundaries but rather because it allows for a possibility that there can be a sense of belonging that will be needed for Filipinas/os in the Excelsior to pursue social change. Understanding Filipinas/os in the Excelsior as an "ethnic community" presents a model that can incorporate a larger people's history and contemporary situations to contextualize this particular enclave's needs.

Community needs are often rooted in the context in which a community is formed. Võ and Bonus present three themes that explore the following formations of Asian American communities. They write that "Asian American social spaces and practices have been in transition; internal group compositions and identities have been undergoing transformations; and group initiatives have been positing alternative constructions of cultural representations and political interests." They also point out that these themes are "more fluid and intersecting than they appear to be."[9] Interestingly, the "ethnic community" of Filipinas/os in the Excelsior reveals how these multiple contexts can intersect.

Development of the FCC in an ethnic community with "multiple contexts" will further benefit from the work of Kil Huh and Lisa Hasegawa and their two-prong approach to community development. They propose a social action approach that focuses on community organizing and empowerment while also ensuring that local development focuses on programs and services. Huh and Hasegawa borrow from Robert Putnam's distinctions of social capital as being either for bonding or bridging. Bonding refers to the exclusive capital that is used within a community to mobilize solidarity, and the bridging social capital deals with a more inclusive strategy to connect to those outside of their particular community. For both geographical and ethnic communities, the relationship between bonding and bridging social capital is clearly symbiotic. For Filipinas/os in the Excelsior and in San Francisco, because of their history, both types of social capital are key to community development. While the FCC is a place in which organizing and services can be built, their success will rely heavily in developing ways in which bonding and bridging social capital can be fostered.[10]

Interdisciplinary Methodology

The research project that led to the completion of this chapter began with a needs assessment conducted by the board of the FCC.[11] Prior to the needs assessment, I was already collecting interviews and stories from residents and students in the neighborhood. As part of the FCC research team, we developed a triangulated study to uncover the needs of the Filipina/o community in the area. The data was gathered from Filipina/o residents through the following methods: a "community friendly" survey of more than 200 residents regarding their familiarity with local services; a town hall meeting at Corpus Christi Church Hall on June 13, 2004, of over 100 Filipinas/os, where they were asked about their issues and concerns; and focus groups of different sectors in the community. While conducting the needs assessment, the research committee reviewed existing research and studies about the Excelsior neighborhood, and assessed existing service providers in the district and surrounding areas.

Community in Transition:
Traversing the Landscape of Filipinas/os in San Francisco

"For Filipinas/os in San Francisco, neighborhood is part of who we are."
—Olivia Malabuyo, San Francisco native

The ethnic community of Filipinas/os in the Excelsior neighborhood has been shaped by multiple waves of immigration. On the surface, the community often seems as though it is comprised mostly of new immigrants, many of whom have arrived in the last decade. The reality is that the story of Filipinas/os in this neighborhood and in San Francisco in general starts much earlier. For Filipinas/os, the story of their immigration to the United States and their labor begins with imperialism and the American colonial project in the Philippines.

The historical relationship between San Francisco and the Philippines is long and complex. In *Imperial San Francisco: Urban Power, Earthly Ruin*, Gray Brechin writes that San Francisco capitalists sought both the rich topsoil in the Philippines and the cheap labor that could be imported to better pursue business ventures. In fact, the brutal Philippine-American War, which wrested control of the Philippines from Filipina/o nationalists intent on independence, was launched from the Presidio, and several "heroic" veterans of the war, including

Frederick Funston, settled in San Francisco after the war. Filipinas/os were being "pulled" to fuel the American economy and were simultaneously being "pushed" by the poverty that came as a result of the colonial drain of both natural and human resources.[12] This is the underlying context in which immigrants describe their pursuit of a "better life" in the United States.

Early Immigration

Filipinas/os are the oldest Asian American group in the United States, and they trace their presence in California to the landing of a Spanish galleon in present-day Morro Bay, California, on October 18, 1587. Historians have found that beginning as early as 1763, Filipinas/os, dubbed "Manilamen," began establishing shrimping villages on the bayous and marshes near New Orleans in Louisiana. By 1788, Filipinas/os, also as crew members on Spanish galleons, were starting to arrive in Alaska. By the early twentieth century, Filipinas/os, who nicknamed themselves "Alaskeros," began working in local Alaskan salmon canneries. Although these arrivals mark the beginning of the story of Filipina/o settlement in the United States, it was not until the twentieth century that larger populations of Filipinas/os arrived and settled.[13]

The vast majority of Filipinas/os in the United States trace their ancestry to immigrants who came in the twentieth century, as the Philippines became a colony of the United States in 1898 following the Philippine-American War. In the years immediately following annexation, the U.S. government funded programs in which the children of elite and middle-class families could study at universities in the United States, with the intention that they return to the Philippines to assist in the development of the country. These students were nicknamed "*pensionados.*" Those who followed the *pensionados* came, according to former Excelsior resident Daniel Phil Gonzales, now a professor of Asian American studies at San Francisco State University, in three successive waves. According to Gonzales, these three waves include those who came from the 1920s to the 1940s, those who arrived after the passage of the McCarran-Walter Act and arrived from 1955 to 1965, and those who came after the 1965 Immigration Act abolished preferences based on national origin.[14] In addition, a new and emerging population of Filipinas/os consists of those who arrived after the Immigration Act of 1990, which allowed for the increase of legal immigrants into the United States.

Many of the first Filipina/o families who settled in San Francisco came from Hawaii.[15] This pattern is evident in the family of Excelsior resident Jesse Racines, whose family first came to Hawaii in the 1930s, and later moved to San Francisco.[16] In 1906, recruiters from the Hawaiian Sugar Plantation Association (HSPA) brought the first Filipina/o laborers, called *sakadas*, to Hawaii. Thousands of men and families followed these first workers. By the 1920s, a new immigrant group of Filipinas/os—most of them single men—were bypassing Hawaii and streaming into the West Coast ports of Seattle, San Francisco, and Los Angeles, drawn by their

American teachers' glowing descriptions of the United States and pushed by the poverty of American colonial economy. Most of these immigrants became agricultural laborers or workers in the service economies of the urban centers of the West Coast. By the 1920s and 1930s, many of the *sakadas* began leaving Hawaii for the mainland. This migration pattern was not uncommon among Filipina/o families, many of whom made their start in Hawaii but left for the mainland upon learning that California wages and working conditions were better.[17]

San Francisco's Manilatown

Many of the Filipina/o immigrants who arrived before World War II worked in the fields near Stockton, Salinas, Delano, and Watsonville, but they also found work in cities like San Francisco. In the off-season, or year-round, many of them found temporary or permanent work as busboys, bellhops, elevator "boys," cooks, waiters, servants, house cleaners, or chauffeurs. Some who settled in San Francisco were entrepreneurs who served the ethnic community, such as barbers, grocers, and restaurateurs. These urban immigrants settled in several blocks in the "heart" of San Francisco, adjacent to Chinatown, in a neighborhood they called "Manilatown."

In addition, Manilatown was home to several residential hotels, where many Filipinas/os lived. The most famous of these was the International Hotel (I-Hotel), not only because of the large numbers of Filipinas/os who lived there but also because the decade-long struggle waged in the 1960s and 1970s against the eviction of its residents and its demolition to make room for urban redevelopment "symbolized the Filipina/o American struggle for identity, self-determination, and civil rights."[18] The campaign to save the hotel not only symbolized the Filipina/o American struggle, but it also represented a roadblock to the desires of San Francisco capitalists for the expansion of the Financial District and the destruction of working-class, "blighted" districts in downtown. Manilatown fell victim to urban renewal projects and the larger campaign to rid downtown of "blight."

By 1968, the I-Hotel, which was the last standing edifice that marked the Filipina/o community in Manilatown, and hundreds of single, elderly Filipinas/os, called *Manongs* (older brother or older male) by the younger generation, had been displaced from Manilatown; the hotel was sold to a developer with little sensitivity to the residents. These residents were served eviction notices so that the building could be demolished for a parking lot. From 1968 to 1977, the attempt to demolish the I-Hotel was met by great protests from a broad coalition of students, activists, and tenants. After successfully delaying the demolition for almost a decade, the battle hit a low point when the tenants were eventually evicted in 1977 and the building was demolished. However, the fight was not over. The struggle continued for two more decades. Activists successfully managed to stop any building of a parking lot. After decades of waiting and negotiations, a new I-Hotel with affordable housing was completed in 2005. On the bottom floor, the Manilatown Center was built to commemorate and encourage activism and education and support the rebirth of the historic community.

South of Market

There are direct connections between the history of Manilatown and the settlement of Filipinas/os in the South of Market and Excelsior neighborhoods of San Francisco and in Daly City. In the 1940s and 1950s, Filipina/o seasonal workers and some Filipina/o families began to stay in the South of Market district, nicknamed the "SoMa." After World War II, the SoMa housed mostly workers in the war industry and military personnel.[19] Although in 1950 about 72 percent of the SoMa residents were single men, the SoMa was becoming home to Filipina/o families and a generation of San Francisco–born Filipinas/os. The population of Filipinas/os—mostly single men before World War II—was beginning to transform.

The Gonzales family's experiences mirror those of many families. Dan Gonzales was born in San Francisco in 1948, and his family lived on Harriet Street in the SoMa. Gonzales's father came in 1929, paying his own way with the help of his family and his province. He made his start here by working in the fields, then in a hotel restaurant, and eventually he served in the military. He was part of the all-Filipino U.S. Army unit, the First Filipino Regiment, and was sent to the Philippines to "liberate" Samar from the Japanese. This was where he met his wife. Prior to their wedding in the Philippines, he returned to San Francisco to work and save up for their future. In 1947, immediately after they married, they settled in San Francisco's SoMa District.[20]

But like Manilatown, the SoMa was dramatically affected by urban renewal projects that were immensely popular after World War II. Sobredo points out that as "early as 1946, corporate organizations proposed ambitious urban development projects."[21] Along with other communities in San Francisco, like the Western Addition, which was mostly Japanese American and African American, thousands of SoMa residents, many of whom were Filipinas/os, were being displaced by urban renewal projects. These residents then began to move toward the borders of the city, like the Excelsior neighborhood, and into Daly City.

Many Filipinas/os in San Francisco trace their roots to the SoMa District. Olivia Malabuyo, a thirty-year-old woman who has lived in both the SoMa and Excelsior, shared, "Despite where I live in San Francisco, I will always trace my roots to the SoMa."[22] Similar to Chung's concept of Chinatown as the "hub," MC Canlas names SoMa Pilipinas in the SoMa in San Francisco as being the "center" or the "plaza" for Filipinas/os.[23] SoMa Pilipinas, like Manilatown, was greatly affected by gentrification. In the last decade, Filipinas/os in the SoMa have fought to keep their place there.

The main street traversing between the SoMa and the Excelsior is Mission Street. Many Filipina/o families who live in San Francisco, in Daly City, and in surrounding suburbs have roots in the SoMa. As in Chinatown, there is a long history of organizing, activism, and social services that are rooted in SoMa Pilipinas, but unlike Chinatown, there is not a concentration of Filipina/o businesses in the SoMa that attract Filipinas/os who live outside of the neighborhood to return there, nor is there the same kind of tourism associated with Chinatown. In fact, the highest concentrations of Filipina/o businesses in San Francisco are in or very close to the Excelsior neighborhood.

The Excelsior

"The Excelsior District and its exact location is little known to the average San Franciscan."
—Walter G. Jebe Sr., San Francisco's Excelsior District

Most of the community studies conducted on Filipinas/os in the San Francisco Bay Area have focused primarily on those in the SoMa District of San Francisco and the suburb of Daly City. While there are approximately 2,200 Filipinas/os residing in the Tenderloin, and approximately 3,000 in the SoMa, the Excelsior District has over 12,000 Filipinas/os, making it home to 30 percent of Filipinas/os in San Francisco. The Excelsior District also has a high concentration of Filipina/o youth and seniors.

In Filipina/o American San Francisco history, there is an undeniable relationship between the SoMa District, the Excelsior, and Daly City. A couple of years after Dan Gonzales's family made their start in the SoMa, his father was offered housing in the Crocker Amazon projects in the Excelsior neighborhood. After three years they actually moved back to the SoMa, and they later settled on Geneva Avenue in the Excelsior. Gonzales describes this back and forth as migration that was unique to his family's situation. But common to the Gonzales's family experience and that of Filipinas/os in San Francisco is the need to pursue affordable housing opportunities.[24]

According to Gonzales, the Excelsior neighborhood was not the first place of residence for many Filipinas/os who came to San Francisco prior to 1965. Many were members of the families of migrant workers or those who came after World War II. They often began their lives in the United States in Hawaii or in the SoMa. As they were able to establish themselves, many purchased homes in the Excelsior neighborhood. Filipinas/os were attracted to the neighborhood because homes were affordable in the mostly residential neighborhood, and because it was far from the hustle and bustle of San Francisco's downtown. Possibly, those who moved to the Excelsior were forced to move because of gentrification and the expansion of the businesses downtown.[25] Filipinas/os also chose the Excelsior because although it was on the borders of San Francisco, the neighborhood was close to public transportation for the commute to downtown, where many blue- and white-collar jobs were located.

Prior to the influx of Filipinas/os, there were strong Irish and Italian communities that made Excelsior their home.[26] Bill Sorro, who went to Balboa High School in the Excelsior in the 1950s, remembers being tormented by some of the white boys at schools. Sorro was met with violent reminders that they deemed him inferior because he was Filipina/o, and because he was poor. This racial tension not only occurred between the whites and Filipinas/os, it was between whites and all nonwhites. Although these situations provided a difficult coming of age for Sorro, he roots his politicization and activism in his personal struggles with racism.[27]

Filipina/o families were living in the Excelsior as early as the 1950s, including the Racines and Gonzales families.[28] The small number of Filipina/o families mushroomed dramatically after 1965, when U.S. immigration policy abandoned racist national-origin preferences to embrace twin goals: family reunification for U.S. citizens with noncitizen family members who lived outside of the United States, and encouraging the entry of highly educated and trained professionals from Asia and Latin America. Because so many highly educated professionals left Asia for the United States after 1965, many Asian American scholars call this period the "brain drain." The new immigration law brought dramatic demographic changes in the Excelsior community, as more and more Filipina/o families began to settle in the Excelsior. This movement was facilitated by a phenomenon that scholars call "chain migration," in which newly immigrated family members who are sponsored by U.S. citizens in turn sponsor even more family members, and the cycle continues. Many Filipina/o families are in the Excelsior as a result of family reunification.

The fact that the highest concentration of Filipina/o businesses in San Francisco is now in the Excelsior is a direct legacy of the post-1965 influx of people and capital into the community. In the Excelsior neighborhood, Filipina/o businesses are numerous on Mission Street. Behind ornate wrought-iron gates that lace the entrances to most of the businesses, businesses like Kadok's and Buena Suerte, restaurants, and the *balikbayan* box delivery service LBC stand out among the other businesses. In the neighborhood, you can find everything from Filipina/o food and groceries to services such as Filipina/o-owned insurance brokers and realtors, to businesses that encourage transnational ties by facilitating the remittance of goods and money to family in the Philippines.[29] These businesses help sustain the community. They become hangouts, and, as MC Canlas describes, they are "centers of gravity."[30] Similar to the barbershops in the old Manilatown, these businesses not only sell products to Filipinas/os, but they also become places where information is disseminated.

Along with businesses, the Excelsior also contains several other centers of gravity. Some of the major centers have been the bowling alleys and theaters.[31] Dan Gonzales and Bill Sorro remember the times in the 1960s when they used to hang out with their "boys" at the bowling alley near the Cow Palace. Both mentioned stories of fights between Filipinas/os and other ethnic groups that would break out at the bowling alleys.[32] Christine Capacillo, a twenty-eight-year-old Filipina who was raised in the Excelsior, recalled that in the 1980s and 1990s, members of her family would also hang out at the nearby bowling alley. She also spoke of fights, but those were primarily between Filipinas/os.[33] Some attribute the closing of the bowling alleys to the fights and the gang activity that was rising in the 1980s and 1990s. Others attribute it to gentrification. A new housing development took the place of the bowling alley in the mid-1990s, and more of the young folks began to hang out at restaurants and parking lots on Mission Street.[34]

Along with the bowling alleys, theaters also drew in Filipina/o families. In the late 1970s and 1980s, there were several theaters in the neighborhood that featured Filipina/o films. These theaters not only provided entertainment for Filipinas/os in the neighborhood, but they also drew in people from other parts of the city, from Daly City, and from other areas in the Bay Area. The theaters greatly influenced the connection between Filipinas/os in the United States, even those who were American-born, to the Philippines. Along with the feelings of nostalgia that these theaters created for Filipina/o immigrants, they also provided a sense of belonging to a larger community outside of their families and small neighborhoods. Novelist Tess Uriza Holthe, who was born and raised near the Excelsior, remembers fondly her experience at the Apollo Theatre. "Oh, we went to the Apollo Theatre on Geneva all the time," she said. "I can still see those double doors and the popcorn stand and feel the texture of the darkened lobby and the balconies. I think it made a big difference to see beautiful, strong Filipinas/os on screen as the heroes and heroines, because otherwise, I think there would be that disconnect where we only existed within our small communities but not in the worlds portrayed on the big screen, where exciting things happened."[35]

In the 1980s and 1990s, rents rose for businesses in the area, and theaters and bowling alleys closed down. However, certain neighborhood institutions, like churches and schools, remained strong centers of gravity. More recently, Filipinas/os in the Excelsior gravitate toward Catholic parishes, such as Corpus Christi and Church of the Epiphany. At many of the masses on Sundays, a large majority of the parishioners are Filipina/o. The church, along with being a place of worship and prayer, is also a place for Filipina/o families to congregate and share information. While churches are physical centers of gravity, the Catholic religion for Filipinas/os has also provided a spiritual sense of community through prayer groups. Christine Capacillo described her family's involvement, especially her grandmother's, with a Santo Nino group, a prayer group that would share a devotion to the infant Jesus and share a community statue of the saint. Every week, the Santo Nino would travel from Filipina/o home to Filipina/o home in the neighborhood.[36] At the beginning of each stay at one's home, the host family would welcome Santo Nino with a prayer and a party.

These celebrations were times when Filipinas/os would share stories, make friends, and exchange resources and strategies that would help them survive in the United States.

Like the churches and prayer groups, schools also provided spaces where Filipinas/os would come together. Valentino Tintiangco-Cubales, a teacher, coach, athletic director, and nearby resident, describes the "spirit" of Balboa: "There is something about Balboa that brings them back. Good or bad. Love or hate. There is something really spiritual about Balboa. . . . It may be because it was one of the first buildings in the Excelsior District."[37] One of the oldest institutions in the Excelsior neighborhood, Balboa High School was established in 1928. Unlike many urban high schools, Balboa is tucked away in the middle of a residential neighborhood. Its central location caters to young San Franciscans from the low-income areas of the Excelsior, Outer Mission, Crocker Amazon, Visitation Valley, and the Sunnydale housing project. Some students, many Filipinas/os, travel from as far as the working-class streets of the SoMa, and take as many as three or four buses just to get to school. This high school prides itself on the ability to serve diverse populations and students who live in these working-class neighborhoods. Despite the school's long history of struggle, survival, and success, its reputation has been tainted by negative media portrayals, gang violence, multiple attempts of teacher reconstitution, low test scores, lack of district funding, poor faculty retention, and high student dropout rates.

Although Balboa High School has had its share of struggles, it has also been a center for the development of the Filipina/o American community in and around the Excelsior. As one of the first Filipinas/os to play high school and college football in San Francisco, Excelsior resident Jesse Racines had his start at Balboa in the mid-1950s.[38] He gained fame for his sports ability and is a great pride both for the school and for Filipinas/os who went to school with him. Sorro mentioned that the handful of Filipina/o students at Balboa felt great pride when they would watch their "brother" on the football field.[39] Sports for Racines allowed him more acceptance than other Filipinas/os at Balboa. Informal sports clubs also provided Filipinas/os a reason to get together and create teams. Some members of the community remembered Filipina/o basketball clubs where they would play games on the weekends in Balboa's gym in the 1980s.[40]

As the number of Filipina/o families grew in the neighborhood, the Filipina/o student population at Balboa increased as well. Divino Antonio, a longtime resident, former student, and current coach at Balboa High School, mentioned that by the time he came to the Excelsior in the 1970s, there were already many Filipinas/os living in the district. But he also said that from the time he was a student at Balboa until now, the Filipina/o population has skyrocketed.[41] By the early 1990s, Filipinas/os comprised almost 28.7 percent of the school's population, second only to Latinas/os, who made up 29.7 percent.[42] This rise in population sparked the need to create ethnic and cultural services for the students at the school. This came with the birth of the Filipina/o Parent Center in the 1990s and the Pin@y Educational Partnerships, created in 2001.

This rise in student population correlates with a rise in the number of Filipina/o families who are living in the Excelsior. Although there are remnants of families who came prior to 1965, there are two main populations of Filipinas/os who are now living in the Excelsior: Filipinas/os who came to the United States as a result of the Immigration Act of 1965, including the family members they sponsored and their American-born children, and Filipinas/os who came after the Immigration Reform Act of 1990, many of whom came only in the last few years. This latter population is often referred to as the "new immigrants." From an outside perspective, these two groups are often considered homogeneous. However, there are great animosities between the two groups, and they experience immense tension with each other.

Identities and Tensions of Post-1965 Filipinas/os in the Excelsior

In *Homebound*, Yen Li Espiritu points out that Filipina/o immigrant parents came to the United States to provide for a better life for their children.[43] All of the families in this study, at some point, came to the United States to live better lives. In this pursuit, they have found themselves confronted with often unbearable conditions such as poverty, occupational downgrading, overcrowding, and tensions within their ethnic community.

Working Multiple Jobs for Low Pay

Christine Capacillo describes her mother as a survivor and a guru on how to get through the system. In 1971, a fifteen-year-old Filipina, nicknamed "Ate Baby" by her family, left Zampaloc, Philippines, for San Francisco with her younger sister and her mother. She gave birth to a daughter, got married, and dropped out of high school, all before she was seventeen years old. Like many immigrants before them, Ate Baby and her family came to pursue the American Dream, but the pursuit was not without struggle. She worked at the downtown Woolworth's on Market Street; then, by lying about her age, she was able to get a job at the Holiday Inn, then in the Silicon Valley. Finding a good job was not easy because not only was she a high school dropout, but she was also a new immigrant. There were times when she had to work more than one job at a time or sell her things at a local pawnshop.

Filipina/o employment has also been affected negatively by the souring California economy. While most Filipinas/os come to this country expecting to find more and better economic opportunities for themselves and their families, globalization, as well as domestic policies such as the Homeland Security Act and the Aviation and Transportation Security Act, are reducing the number of opportunities for Filipinas/os, according to a report by San Francisco's FCC. For example, the Filipina/o American community was particularly affected throughout the Bay Area when hundreds of airport security screeners, the majority of whom were Filipina/o, were fired in the wake of 9/11.

In some families, only one parent is working and in other situations is forced to work more than one job. These parents find work mainly in the service sector, and are the city's janitors, housekeepers, clerks, and cooks. Many of these parents face occupational downgrading. They sometimes have college educations from the Philippines, but are often in positions that are not commensurate with their degrees and credentials. Reasons for this include the lack of matriculation between foreign universities and the curriculum at American institutions, language difficulties, and racism.

Family Consolidation

As discussed previously, the number of Filipina/o families in the United States began to grow in record numbers after 1965, and many immigrants who came to the United States were sponsored by their predecessors. Many of these immigrants, even if they were educated in the Philippines, find themselves in service sector jobs in the United States. In the 1970s, Ate Baby and her family moved from the SoMa to the Excelsior neighborhood. She never owned a house, nor did she live alone with her nuclear family unit; instead, Ate Baby and her immediate family lived with her extended family and shared living expenses. Housing is extremely expensive, and many families cannot afford to live alone, so they are forced to live together out of necessity. But what happens when, as a result of the high price of housing in San Francisco and other urban areas, houses are shared among many members of an extended family, and rooms are full to bursting?

In this essay, "family consolidation" refers to more than one nuclear family living in a single-family home. This phenomenon often results in overcrowding for low-income Filipina/o American households. Family consolidation is rooted in the history and process of chain migration. Although this may not seem uncommon to the Filipina/o American experience, its effects on the family and the individual have yet to be studied. This essay is an attempt at beginning a discussion about how this phenomenon is an important component in the Filipina/o ethnic community in the Excelsior neighborhood.

The multiple-family household that results from chain migration can mean that anywhere from five to fifteen people live in two- to four-bedroom houses. Many families have converted the garages and living rooms into sleeping quarters. The needs assessment conducted by the FCC found that a significant majority of Filipina/o households in the Excelsior had more than four members. Many had five or six members, and some had up to ten living in single-family homes. In a survey of Filipina/o youth at Balboa High School, the number of members living in their households ranged from five to thirteen. Many students named grandparents, aunts, uncles, and cousins, along with parents and siblings, as being part of their households.

This concept of family consolidation can be seen as a coping mechanism for Filipina/o American immigrant families. It can also be viewed as being "culturally specific," with roots in the Filipina/o practice of a "tribal system" versus a nuclear family system where "the whole tribe or community is the family."[44] Although it is important to contextualize family consolidation as a "cultural" means to address the economic hardships faced by immigrant families, an analysis of the economic conditions that force these families to live together cannot be overlooked. The focus on cultural explanations for multiple Filipina/o families in a single-family home can easily put the blame of overcrowding in the households on Filipina/o cultural practices. In this "cultural deficiency" discussion, the economic root of the problem gets lost. Moreover, "culture" cannot alone explain how overcrowding may affect the lives of those who live in these consolidated households, because it reduces family consolidation to a cultural practice. There is a great need to look at how socioeconomic class is a major factor that forces Filipinas/os to turn to the practice of family consolidation.

When asked about their home lives, Balboa students were generally open about their living conditions, and told us that sharing crowded quarters often caused them stress and created a lack of space that they needed for studying and doing homework. In most cases, there were more than ten persons living in their household. In *Where We Stand: Class Matters*, bell hooks writes, "Living with many bodies in a small space, one is raised with notions of property and privacy quite different from those of people who have always had room."[45] Along with the pressures and tensions surrounding overcrowding as a result of family consolidation, Filipinas/os in the Excelsior neighborhood must also deal with issues of severe family conflict that result from perceptions about Filipina/o identities, which can often threaten household peace in the crowded homes of their Filipina/o ethnic community.

There are severe issues of family conflict that can arise from crowding and resentment when too many people live in one house. Some of the American-born students or those who immigrated as children find their immediate families "hosting" some of their more recently arrived relatives. Immigrant students find themselves in situations in which their immediate family is staying temporarily with relatives until they are able to rent or purchase a home of their own. One student described her home life as a "war zone."[46]

Filipinas/os versus Filipina/o Americans

The tensions between Filipina/o American and Filipina/o new immigrants in the Excelsior go beyond the overcrowding associated with the consolidated family household. The FCC needs assessment showed that the majority of respondents living in the Excelsior are older immigrants, many of whom have lived in the United States between ten and twenty years. The second largest group is comprised of newer immigrants who have lived in the United States less than five years.[47]

The new immigrant population is growing dramatically. Raymond Castillo, a volunteer at the FCC, describes the conflict between Filipina/o Americans and newly arrived immigrants as something that keeps the community divided.[48] A sixteen-year-old Filipina was born in the Philippines but came here when she was three years old. She identifies as being Filipina American, and she does not hang out with recent immigrants. Most of her friends are also American-born Filipinas/os, African Americans, and Samoans. She recognizes that there is a great divide in the Filipina/o community at her high school. She also notices that each group thinks that it is better than the other.[49]

These issues between Filipina/o Americans and new immigrants have erupted in events of violence. In 1996, there was a fight between the two groups in front of Balboa High School. This fight not only involved students but also their adult relatives.[50] The issues between these two groups go beyond the tension between young people.

Ate Baby often opened up her home to Filipinas/os, both new immigrants and those who considered themselves more Americanized. She was great at being a bridge between the two. She spoke Tagalog and Kapampangan, and she knew the streets.[51] Dan Gonzales reminisced about his parents developing negative opinions about new immigrants in the 1960s. He described that the more "Americanized" Filipinas/os, even if they were born in the Philippines, have a tendency to disassociate with Filipinas/os who just arrived from the Philippines.[52] They often make fun of new immigrants' accents and ways of dress to present themselves as being more "American." Filipina/o Americans have popularized the acronym "FOB" to mean "fresh off the boat." "FOB" has been used to refer negatively to Filipina/o immigrants.

These issues between Filipina/o Americans and new immigrants come from the need to prove one's "Americanness." New immigrants are not the only target of this tension. It is also rooted in how some Filipinas/os tend to measure "Filipina/o-ness" and Filipina/o culture. New immigrants also judge Filipina/o Americans, deeming them not being Filipina/o enough, and often referencing their inability to speak Tagalog or any Philippine language. As the demographics shift, the tension between Filipina/o Americans and newer immigrants continues to rise. This tension poses a great challenge to those who are trying to serve and organize the Filipinas/os in the Excelsior.

Community of Alternatives:
Building the FCC and an Ethnic Community

Given the diversity among Filipinas/os in the Excelsior, which often results in a divide, how do their needs get addressed? Understanding the history of Filipinas/os in San Francisco and the issues of underemployment, family consolidation, and the tension between Filipina/o Americans and new Filipina/o immigrants is essential in the development of an ethnic community and to the building of a community center. This section assesses the current needs of the community by drawing on the FCC Needs Assessment report, conducted in 2004, and it describes the emergence and significance of the FCC in the lives of Excelsior Filipina/o residents.

The problems of working-class immigrant Filipinas/os in the Excelsior, including employment issues, overcrowding due to family consolidation, and the tensions between Filipina/o Americans and newly arrived immigrants, provide the backdrop to the many needs that Filipinas/os have in the Excelsior. It is clear that there was a need for resources and services that catered to Filipinas/os in the Excelsior. At the beginning of 2004, Rachel Redondiez, a community organizer and resident in the Excelsior, and her husband, Jason Ildefonso, along with Artnelson Concordia and Joanna Maderazo-Robledo, both teachers in the neighborhood, came together and recruited residents and service providers in the area to build a community center to address the needs of Filipinas/os in and around the Excelsior neighborhood.[53] They were able to gather a core group of people to serve as a working board for the FCC. As part of this core group, I was able to bring in my involvement with Pin@y Educational Partnerships, a service learning project that has college students teach Filipina/o American studies to youth in the Excelsior.[54] I was also able to lend my research background to help with the needs assessment to establish the FCC.

With minimal seed money from the city and no physical space, the FCC board focused on conducting a needs assessment project that consisted of a survey, a town hall meeting, and focus groups. In the FCC's needs assessment of the Filipina/o community in the Excelsior, an overwhelming majority of respondents were concerned about job opportunities. Many were also concerned about affordable health care and housing, especially for Filipina/o elderly. There were also concerns about college preparation, financial aid, and academic tutoring for the youth. The importance of these needs and many others was reinforced in the town hall meeting and in the focus groups that followed. At the town hall meeting, the following problems were prevalent in the discussions: no central space, lack of bilingual/culturally appropriate services and programs, violence/safety, housing, employment, child care, health problems, and immigration needs.

In the FCC's needs assessment, one major finding justified the need of FCC's existence. Almost 80 percent of the Filipinas/os in the neighborhood do not know where to go when family members or they themselves need services and resources. This could mean that there are not enough services in or near the Excelsior to address their particular needs. It could also be an indicator that Filipinas/os are not aware of the existing resources. It may also point to a certain need for a central space where families and individuals can go for information and referrals.[55]

All sectors that were part of the needs assessment—seniors, workers, women and young girls, young men, and parents—identified the need for a central space. For seniors and workers, a central space was about the need for dissemination of information. Women and young girls spoke of the need to have a space for a youth/teen center that included child care, cultural activities, leadership training, college support, and substance abuse prevention. The young men would like a "safe" space for support groups, performing and visual arts, academic tutoring, and sports activities. The parents presented a great need for this center to be more than a place to receive information, and they wanted a center that will "revive the *bayanihan* (sense of community) spirit."[56]

The needs assessment clearly measured the need for services for Filipinas/os in the Excelsior community and a need to develop a "*bayanihan* spirit" within this ethnic community. After getting a sense of the concrete needs of the community, the FCC board was able to rent a space from the Ocean Presbyterian Church. In December 2004, the FCC opened its doors on 35 San Juan Avenue in the Excelsior neighborhood. From the beginning, the FCC knew that if the goal was to achieve this "*bayanihan* spirit," the center must deal directly with the tension between Filipina/o Americans and new immigrants. The challenge for the FCC is to find ways to build an ethnic community, despite the diversity and divisions among the Filipinas/os.

Terrence Valen, the organizational director of the FCC, has presented his vision of developing an "intentional" community from a "coincidental" community. By "coincidental," Valen understands that Filipinas/os came to the United States to find opportunities and also that many of them ended up in the Excelsior for affordable housing. This feeling of coincidence also contributes to the disconnection between Filipina/o Americans and new immigrants. There is a lack of common purpose if each group feels it is in opposition to the other. Valen's aim at the FCC is to go beyond the Filipina/o presence in the neighborhood as being just of coincidence, but rather that the Filipina/o community has an "intentional" purpose to improve their lives.[57]

To create this intentional community, the FCC's goal is to access social support networks, centers of gravity for Filipinas/os in the Excelsior, and social capital that has already been present among the Filipinas/os in the neighborhood. The FCC does not aim to replace schools, churches, restaurants, and other social services that are centers of gravity for Filipinas/os in the Excelsior; instead, it plans to work with neighborhood institutions and organizations to build an intentional community. It also hopes to access and learn from informal modes of social capital, such as social ties with families and individuals who have been serving the community through their own means.

To build social capital, like Ate Baby has done among her networks, the FCC will need to provide a "bond" between Filipina/o Americans and new Filipina/o immigrants and also a "bridge" to those outside of the ethnic community to ensure that they gain access to the resources they require to meet their needs. Like Ate Baby, the FCC must be an "intentional" place that tries to help people "through the system." As mentioned in the previous section, three main problems plague this ethnic community as a result of new immigration after

1965: underemployment or low-paying jobs, overcrowding due to family consolidation, and tensions between Filipina/o Americans and new Filipina/o immigrants and between "old" and "new" immigrants. Through organizing and
programming, the FCC may be able to develop this dual-faceted "bonding" and
"bridging" social capital to provide information about acquiring jobs and training while also providing a space for workers to organize around their specific
issues and offering support services for overcrowding and educational forums to
address the tensions between Filipina/o Americans and new immigrants.

Also learning from the history of Filipinas/os in San Francisco, including the
organizing around the struggles for the I-Hotel and the SoMa, Filipinas/os in the
Excelsior need to develop relationships with Filipinas/os in other communities and
also create coalitions among other ethnic groups in the neighborhood and
throughout the city. Drawing from Robert Putnam's work on American communities, the FCC should practice both the bonding and bridging of social capital to
ensure that the Filipina/o ethnic community of the Excelsior itself is strong enough
to bridge to other communities, especially with other Filipinas/os in San Francisco,
in California, and throughout the nation and globe. It is also key for the FCC to be
a bridge to other resources and services in and outside of the Excelsior neighborhood. All of these efforts by the FCC to create a community must be intentional.

By building an intentional bond and bridge for the Filipina/o community in
the Excelsior, the FCC has also developed core strategies of organizing, educating, advocating, and serving the community. Artnelson Concordia, a teacher at
Balboa High School and an FCC board member, shared the multitude of reasons
why he helped create the FCC. First and foremost, he pointed out the purpose of
the FCC as being to serve and address the needs of the community. Along with
service, the FCC should help organize the community to help advocate and
access resources for more services. And last, the FCC should be a center and
space for Filipinas/os to feel welcome.

The FCC's mission is to provide a safe space where Filipina/o families can
access services, meet, and hold activities and to improve their collective capacity to
address their immediate and long-term needs, with a commitment to low-income
and underserved Filipinas/os, through organizing, advocacy, and service.[58] While
upholding this mission, the FCC has had a strong beginning, and in a short time it
has been able to do amazing work with the community. Between the opening and
the first-year anniversary, the FCC has become a "center of gravity" for Filipinas/os
in the Excelsior. The youth, most of whom are newly arrived immigrants, have grav-
itated toward the space and have established the FCC as their home base after
school. The FCC has sponsored and housed many community events, including
youth performances and hip-hop shows, along with supporting campaigns against
domestic violence. The FCC has also been able to support other organizations, like
the Manilatown Heritage Foundation, by helping recruit seniors to live in the new
I-Hotel. Since Pin@y Educational Partnerships was established as a program of the

FCC, it has been able to expand from offering services at Balboa High School to Burton High School and Longfellow Elementary School. The FCC has a long list of accomplishments in such a short time.

In line with the work of Huh and Hasegawa, the FCC upholds their vision by setting core strategies that aim to build social action and provide social services for Filipinas/os in the Excelsior. The FCC aims to be a place where organizations and community campaigns can be built and supported. It is also a place where members of the community can seek out services or references to other agencies that can serve their needs. To support organizing and serving the community, the FCC aims to provide education, training, and advocacy for the community to participate in sustaining themselves. The FCC is not only about social action and social services as isolated strategies. Valen points out how the development of social action through organizing will help maintain and support the social services needed in the community. He believes that there will always be the need for more services for Filipinas/os in the Excelsior, and the way to make sure they are provided is to build the capacity of this ethnic community and the "*bayanihan* spirit" through community organizing.

Through the use of both organizing for social action and providing services, the FCC in the Excelsior aims to create an intentional community. This community intends to improve their lives, the lives of the families, and the neighborhood in which they live. The FCC is already becoming a "center of gravity" for Filipinas/os in the Excelsior neighborhood.

NOTES

This chapter would have not been possible with out the patience and dedication of my family and community. I especially would like to thank Terrance Valen, Christine Capacillo, Olivia Malabuyo, Dan Gonzales, Bill Sorro, Jesse Racines, Rachel Redondiez, Raymond Castillo, Dino Antonio, MC Canlas, Roy Recio, Artnelson Concordia, Rudy Corpuz, and all the community members and youth who were willing to share their stories, experiences, and insights for this project. I would like to acknowledge the board of the FCC along with the teachers and students in the Pin@y Educational Partnerships program, and Claudine delRosario-Concordia for helping complete the needs assessment for the FCC. If it wasn't for the patience of Huping Ling, the editor of this book, I think I would have given up on completing this chapter long ago. I want to thank Dawn Mabalon for her historical expertise and editing skills, and for believing that I could finish this chapter, and my mother for taking care of my flu-ridden daughter and for taking care of me while I wrote this chapter. And last but not least, I would like to dedicate this chapter to my inspiration, my husband, Valentino Tintiangco-Cubales, for dedicating his life's work to the youth in the Excelsior as a teacher, coach, and athletic director at Balboa High School.

I. This is interesting because there is no Wal-Mart for nearly forty miles. It is also interesting that Wal-Mart is capitalizing on the Filipina/o community in the Excelsior by advertising in Tagalog, the national language of the Philippines. A Filipina/o family is also used to make a connection to the target demographic of the billboard.

2. *Kapampangan*, spoken mostly in the Pampanga region, is one of the major languages spoken in the Philippines. There are more than eighty languages spoken in the Philippines.

3. See Eric Lai and Dennis Arguelles, *The New Face of Asian Pacific America* (Los Angeles: UCLA Asian American Studies Center Press, 2003), for more details on Filipina/o and Asian American demographics.

4. See Huping Ling, *Chinese in St. Louis: From Enclave to Cultural Community* (Philadelphia: Temple University Press, 2004). For other works on the Asian American community, see Linda Trinh Võ and Rick Bonus, eds., *Contemporary Asian American Communities: Intersections and Divergences* (Philadelphia: Temple University Press, 2002); Timothy Fong and Larry H. Shinagawa, *Asian Americans: Experiences and Perspectives* (Upper Saddle River, N.J.: Prentice Hall, 2000).

5. Tom Chung, "Asian Americans in Enclaves—They Are Not One Community: New Modes of Asian American Settlement," in Fong and Shinagawa, *Asian Americans*, 100.

6. Ling, *Chinese in St. Louis*.

7. Danilo Begonia, "Matrix," 2000 (essay on Carlos Villa), on Mary and Carter Thatcher Gallery Web site: http://www.usfca.edu/library/thacher/villa/begoniaessay.html.

8. Maria P. P. Root, *Filipina/o Americans: Transformation and Identity* (Thousand Oaks, Calif.: Sage, 1997).

9. Võ and Bonus, *Contemporary Asian American Communities*, 3.

10. See Kil Huh and Lisa Hasegawa, "An Agenda for AAPI Community Economic Development," *AAPI Nexus* 1, no. 1 (Summer/Fall 2003): 47–65.

11. Filipina/o Community Center, *A Community Needs Assessment* (2005). An unpublished report seeking to demonstrate the critical need for Filipina/o-specific outreach, services, and resources in San Francisco's District 11.

12. Gray Brechin, *Imperial San Francisco: Urban Power, Earthly Ruin* (Berkeley: University of California Press, 1999).

13. Fred Cordova, *Filipina/os: Forgotten Asian Americans* (Dubuque, Iowa: Kendall, 1983).

14. Daniel Phil Gonzales, interview by author, January 25, 2006.

15. Bill Sorro, interview by author, January 25, 2006; Gonzales, interview.

16. Jesse Racines, interview by author, January 25, 2006. Hawaii still continues to be a first home for immigrants, as in the case of Raymond Castillo, whose family first immigrated to Hawaii in the 1990s and later moved to the Excelsior. Raymond Castillo, interview by author, February 9, 2006.

17. See Angeles Monrayo-Raymundo and Rizalene Raymundo, *Tomorrow's Memories: From the Diaries of Angeles Monrayo-Raymundo, January 10, 1924–November 17, 1928* (Honolulu: University of Hawaii Press, 1998).

18. James Sobredo, "From Manila Bay to Daly City: Filipinos in San Francisco," in *Reclaiming San Francisco: History, Politics, Culture*, ed. James Brooks, Chris Carlsson, and Nancy J. Peters, 279 (San Francisco: City Lights Books, 1998).

19. Chester Hartman, *City for Sale: The Transformation of San Francisco* (Berkeley: University of California Press, 2002), 59.

20. Gonzales, interview.

21. Sobredo, "From Manila Bay to Daly City," 279.

22. Olivia Malabuyo, interview by author, December 21, 2005.

23. MC Canlas, interview by author, January 5, 2006.

24. Gonzales, interview.

25. Ibid.

26. Walter G. Jebe Sr., *Images of America: San Francisco's Excelsior District* (Charleston, S.C.: Arcadia, 2004).

27. Sorro, interview.
28. Racines, interview; Gonzales, interview.
29. Interestingly, some businesses have changed owners. Some of the once Filipina/o-owned businesses have been bought by others, some who are Chinese or Vietnamese, but they still cater to Filipina/o customers.
30. Canlas, interview.
31. Ibid.
32. Sorro, interview; Gonzales, interview.
33. Christine Capacillo, interview by author, January 5, 2006.
34. Canlas, interview.
35. Tess Uriza Holthe, interview by author, January 6, 2006.
36. Capacillo, interview.
37. Valentino Tintiangco-Cubales, interview by author, January 6, 2006.
38. Racines, interview.
39. Sorro, interview.
40. Canlas, interview.
41. Divino V. Antonio, interview by author, January 25, 2006.
42. See California Department of Education, Dataquest Web site: http://data1.cde.ca.gov/dataquest/.
43. See Yen Li Espiritu, *Homebound: Filipino American Lives Across Cultures, Communities, and Countries* (Berkeley: University of California Press, 2003).
44. Emily Gaborne Dearing, "The Family Tree: Discovering Oneself," in *Filipina/o Americans: Transformation and Identity*, ed. Maria P. P. Root, 287–298 (Thousand Oaks, Calif.: Sage, 1997).
45. bell hooks, *In Where We Stand: Class Matters* (New York: Routledge, 2000).
46. Balboa High School Student 1, interview by author, February 5, 2002.
47. FCC, *Needs Assessment.*
48. Castillo, interview.
49. Balboa High School Student 4, interview by author, February 5, 2002.
50. Tintiangco-Cubales, interview.
51. Capacillo, interview.
52. Ibid.
53. Hennijay Espinosa, "Filipina/o Community Center: Working for a United and Empowered People," *Manila Bulletin USA*, January 19–25, 2006.
54. I founded Pin@y Educational Partnerships (PEP) in the fall of 2001. PEP is a teaching/service-learning and community-based research program that aims to create educational partnerships between San Francisco State University college students, the community, and youth to develop projects that work toward social justice. Through teaching/service-learning projects, youth campaigns, and educational research, PEP aims to provide opportunities for college, high school, middle school, and elementary school students to teach and learn from each other about the experiences of Filipinas/os while also addressing and organizing around community issues.
55. FCC, *Needs Assessment.*
56. Ibid.
57. Terrance Valen, interview by author, December 10, 2005. See also the FCC Web site: www.filipinocc.org.
58. See the FCC Web site: www.filipinocc.org.

PART THREE

Asian Communities
in America

With Cultural/Social Boundaries

6

Cultural Community

A New Model for Asian American Community

HUPING LING

In 1857, Alla Lee, a twenty-four-year-old native of Ningbo, China, seeking a better life, came to St. Louis, where he opened a small shop on North Tenth Street selling tea and coffee. As the first and probably the only Chinese there for a while, Alla Lee mingled mostly with immigrants from Northern Ireland and married an Irish woman.[1] A decade later, Alla Lee was joined by several hundred of his compatriots from San Francisco and New York who were seeking jobs in mines and factories in and around St. Louis. Most of the Chinese workers lived in boardinghouses located near a small street called Hop Alley. In time, Chinese hand laundries, merchandise stores, herb shops, restaurants, and clan association headquarters sprang up in and around that street; thus Hop Alley became synonymous with Chinatown.

Local records indicate that Chinese businesses, especially hand laundries, drew a wide clientele, and thus the businesses run by Chinese immigrants contributed disproportionately to the city's economy. They provided 60 percent of the services for the city during the late nineteenth and early twentieth centuries, although Chinese comprised less than 0.1 percent of the total population.[2] While the city's residents readily patronized their businesses, they did not welcome the Chinese themselves, regarding them as "peculiar" creatures. Hop Alley was seen as an exotic place where criminal activities such as the manufacturing, smuggling, and smoking of opium, tong fighting, and murder existed. Despite frequent police raids and bias among other residents, Hop Alley survived with remarkable resilience and energy until 1966, when urban renewal bulldozers completely leveled the area to make a parking lot for Busch Stadium.

While the old Chinese settlement around Hop Alley was disappearing, a new suburban Chinese American community had been quietly, yet rapidly, emerging since the 1960s. In the next few decades, the ethnographic distribution changed considerably with more Chinese residing in St. Louis County, which constitutes the suburban municipalities in the south and west areas outside of St. Louis City. The U.S. censuses indicate that the number of suburban

Chinese Americans increased from 106 (30 percent of the total Chinese population in the St. Louis area) in 1960 to 461 (80 percent of the total) in 1970, to 1,894 (78 percent of the total) in 1980, and to 3,873 (83 percent of the total) in 1990.[3] Since 1990, the Chinese population in the Greater St. Louis area has increased rapidly to 9,120 according to the U.S. census of 2000.[4] Various unofficial estimates, however, show the figure to be between 15,000 and 20,000, with an overwhelming majority scattered in suburban communities and constituting 1 percent of the total suburban population of the St. Louis metropolitan area.[5]

Although the Chinese population in St. Louis has increased substantially, one cannot easily spot either a commercial or residential Chinese district. Signs of Chinese American presence, however, are clear. More than half of the city's modern buildings and structures have involved the engineering design of a Chinese American consulting firm, William Tao & Associates. Two weekly Chinese-language newspapers vie to serve the community. Three Chinese-language schools offer classes of Chinese language, arts, and culture to St. Louis Chinese American youth. A dozen Chinese religious institutions are attracting significant numbers of members. More than forty community organizations independently or jointly sponsor a wide array of community activities, ranging from cultural gatherings of hundreds to the annual Chinese Culture Days held in the Missouri Botanical Gardens with more than 10,000 visitors. More than 300 Chinese restaurants cater to the St. Louisans who are fond of ethnic cuisine.

How does one understand this phenomenon of a not quite visible yet very active and productive Chinese American community? How did it evolve, and is it unique? In this chapter, I propose a model of "cultural community" to define the Chinese American community in St. Louis since the 1960s. I also demonstrate the significance and applicability of the St. Louis model to our understanding of the multiethnic and multicultural American society.

Defining Cultural Community and Its Significance

Resting on the framework of social space, this study proposes a new model of the Chinese American community in St. Louis as a "cultural community." A cultural community does not always have particular physical boundaries, but is socially defined by the common cultural practices and beliefs of its members. A cultural community is constituted by the Chinese-language schools, Chinese religious institutions, Chinese American community organizations, Chinese American cultural agencies, Chinese American political coalitions or ad hoc committees, and the wide range of cultural celebrations and activities facilitated by the aforementioned agencies and groups. The St. Louis Chinese community since the 1960s is a typical cultural community. Its members dwell throughout the city and its suburban municipalities, and there are no substantial business and residential concentrations or clusters to constitute a "Chinatown" or even a

FIGURE 6.1 The annual Chinese Culture Days has evolved over the years into a huge annual Chinese cultural display attracting thousands of St. Louisans.

Photograph by Huping Ling

FIGURE 6.2 A mock Chinese wedding demonstrated at the Chinese Cultural Days, Missouri Botanic Gardens, June 5, 1999.

Photograph by Huping Ling

"suburban Chinatown." Nevertheless, Chinese St. Louisans have formed their community through various cultural activities organized by community organizations and cultural institutions of Chinese-language schools, churches, and other cultural agencies. They have preserved their cultural heritage and achieved ethnic solidarity without a recognizable physical community. Such a community therefore is better understood as a cultural community.

A cultural community can also be identified by its economy, demography, and geography. Economically, the overwhelming majority population of a cultural community is professionally integrated into the larger society; therefore, the ethnic economy of the community does not significantly affect the well-being of its members and the community as a whole. Demographically, a cultural community contains a substantial percentage of professionals and self-employed entrepreneurs whose economic well-being is more dependent on the larger economy than on an ethnic economy. The former are mostly employed by the employers of the larger society, and the latter, though self-employed, also depend on the general population for their economic success. The working-class members, in terms of population, only constitute a minor part of the Chinese American community. Geographically, a cultural community is more likely to be found in hinterland and remote areas where the transnational economy has limited penetration.

Unlike the Chinese suburban communities in Flushing, New York; Monterey Park, California; and Vancouver and Toronto, Canada, where Chinese Americans/ Canadians invest substantially in banking, manufacturing, real estate, and service industries, Chinese Americans in St. Louis are primarily professionals employed mostly by mainstream companies and agencies.[6] Therefore, economic interest and economic networking are less likely the dominant motives for the formation of the St. Louis Chinese community. In St. Louis, Chinese congregate more frequently in cultural institutions of Chinese-language schools, Chinese Christian churches and Buddhist temples, and cultural activities organized by various community organizations.

Moreover, this community does not have clearly defined physical boundaries, either in the inner city or in the suburbs. The prevalent terms of Chinese American settlements—"Chinatowns," "urban ghettos," "ethnic enclaves," "suburban Chinatowns," or "ethnoburbs," which focus on physical space of the Chinese American communities—are less adequate in explaining the Chinese American community in St. Louis.[7]

The significance of the cultural community model goes beyond the interpretation of the St. Louis Chinese American community. First, the idea of cultural community could serve as a new model for Chinese American communities, where the Chinese professionally assimilated into the larger society and their economies are not much connected with the Chinese ethnic community. This model could be found in areas where there are no significantly large Chinese populations to constitute physical ethnic concentrations, but the Chinese

American populations are still substantial enough to form social communities even without physical boundaries. The cultural community model could thus provide an alternative theory for understanding the complexity of the contemporary Chinese American community.

Second, the cultural community model helps one better understand the issue of cultural identity. A cultural community is formed not because of an economic need of mutual aid, but because of a psychological need of cultural and ethnic identity. When the Chinese Americans are scattered throughout middle-class or upper-middle-class neighborhoods, it is difficult and less practical to establish a physical Chinese ethnic concentration. But the desire to share, maintain, and preserve Chinese cultural heritage validates the need to form a cultural community in the forms of Chinese-language schools, churches, community organizations, cultural agencies, political long-term or ad hoc committees, and cultural celebrations and social gatherings. On these occasions, the presence of a larger number of Chinese Americans makes cultural and ethnic identity easily recognizable. Cultural identity or ethnic solidarity in turn provides comfort to the Chinese who do not have significant ethnic surroundings in their regular daily lives.

Third, the cultural community model exhibits a certain stage of assimilation and acculturation of ethnic groups in their American experiences. History has indicated that an immigrant or ethnic group's socioeconomic advancement in America generally goes through three stages: physical concentration for economic survival; cultural congregation for ethnic identity; and political participation or coalition for a sense of democracy and justice.[8]

Most immigrant or ethnic groups in their socioeconomic evolution in American society need first to survive. Survival in an alienating and less-welcoming, often hostile, environment would necessarily and inevitably result in a practical strategy of mutual aid, which naturally binds the members of an ethnic group together and forms a physical ethnic community. Such ethnic communities have historically been identified as "ghettos;" "enclaves;" ethnic settlements such as "Germantown," "Jewishtown," and "Chinatown;" or replicas of the ethnic groups' original cultures signified by the name of the capital city of a sending country, such as "Little Tokyo" or "Little Saigon." In this stage, a physical ethnic settlement is essential to facilitate the survival of the ethnic group.

When an ethnic group has professionally and economically integrated into the larger society, its chief concern is no longer mutual aid for survival, and this change accounts for the abandonment of a physical ethnic settlement.[9] The economically integrated yet geographically dispersed ethnic group is now more concerned about how to maintain and preserve its cultural heritage without the physical ethnic settlement. European immigrants up to the 1960s had mostly constituted the earlier and larger ethnic components of America. Most of these groups had by this time moved out of the ethnically distinguished communities and had merged into the mainstream, or "white," society. However, the economically assimilated European ethnic groups, especially the smaller ones such as the Jews, still have relatively pressing needs to preserve a distinctive ethnic and religious heritage to identify themselves. For Jews, these needs therefore have produced a variety of Jewish communities embodied in synagogues, schools, theaters, and cultural and social gatherings.[10] Asian immigrants have also demonstrated similar patterns of preservation of ethnic identity. Scholars have documented the importance of cultural institutions such as Christian churches and community organizations in stabilizing the Korean American communities in New York.[11] Similarly, Chinese Americans in St. Louis since the 1960s have formed a cultural community. In this stage, cultural and social space, rather than physical space, constitutes the ethnic community.

When an ethnic group is economically secure, it also actively participates in mainstream electoral and coalition politics, and in currently controversial issues to preserve democracy and social justice. The establishment of the Organization of Chinese Americans in 1973 and its continuing battles against discrimination and social injustice against Chinese Americans are the most illustrative examples. The "Committee of 100," formed after the Tiananmen incident in 1989 and consisting of 100 prominent Chinese Americans, has served as an active lobby to promote a positive relation between the United States and China.[12] Since the 1990s, Asian Americans have been more involved in local and national politics in order to protect their civil rights and freedom. In this stage, the political manifestation of an ethnic community is more visible.

Literature Review: Chinese Community of St. Louis in the Contexts of Chinese Urban Communities and Urban Studies

Chinese immigration to the United States has largely been an urban phenomenon since the early twentieth century. Table 6.1 shows that in the 1930 census, 64 percent of the 74,954 Chinese resided in urban centers. A decade later, the Chinese population totaled 77,504, and 71 percent lived in major American cities. By the 1950 census, more than 90 percent of the Chinese population resided in cities,[13] and the trend continues upward. The urban presence of Chinese Americans undoubtedly warrants urban study as a significant focus within Chinese American studies.

Like other immigrant groups, Chinese immigrants predominantly settled in entry ports and major urban centers, where they established their communities known as Chinatowns. Scholars have attempted to define Chinatown in terms of its socioeconomic and cultural functions. Historian Mary Coolidge in 1909 described San Francisco Chinatown as a "quarter" in the city formed by the Chinese to "protect themselves and to make themselves at home."[14] Sociologist Rose Hum Lee provided a similar description of Chinatown as an area organized by Chinese "sojourners for mutual aid and protection as well as to retain their

TABLE 6.1

Percentage of Chinese Population in the U.S. by Urban and Rural Residence, 1930–2000

Year	Total	Urban	Rural	Percentage of Urban
1930	74,954	47,970	26,984	64
1940	77,504	55,028	22,476	71
1950	117,140	109,036	8,104	90.5
1960	236,048	225,527	10,557	95.5
1970	431,583	417,032	14,551	96.6
1980	812,178	787,548	24,630	97.0
1990	1,645,472	1,605,841	39,631	97.6
2000	2,432,585	2,375,871	56,714	97.7

Source: Figures of 1930 and 1940 are computed according to Shih-shan Henry Tsai, *The Chinese Experience in America* (Bloomington and Indianapolis: Indiana University Press, 1986), 105. The rest of the table is tabulated according to the U.S. Census, 1940–2000.

cultural heritage,"[15] and Chinatowns are "ghetto-like formations resulting from the migration and settlement of persons with culture, religion, language, ideology, or race different from those of members of the dominant groups."[16] Examining Chinatown from the condition of racial discourse, anthropologist Bernard P. Wong views it as a racially closed community, while geographer Kay Anderson interprets it as "a European creation."[17] By far, probably the most comprehensive scholarly conceptualization of Chinatown has been made by geographer David Lai: "Chinatown in North America is characterized by a concentration of Chinese people and economic activities in one or more city blocks which forms a unique component of the urban fabric. It is basically an idiosyncratic oriental community amidst an occidental urban environment."[18] Lai's definition of Chinatown explains well the Chinese settlement in downtown St. Louis prior to its demolition in 1966 but shows an inability to elucidate the Chinese American community in the area since the 1960s.

Typology of Chinatowns

By 1940, according to Rose Hum Lee, Chinese Americans had established Chinatowns across the country in twenty-eight cities; those in San Francisco,

New York, and Los Angeles were the largest, in that order. Of the country's 77,504 Chinese, 69 percent, or 53,497 people, congregated in these Chinatowns. Although Lee omitted St. Louis from this list of Chinatowns, a separate study by her suggests that St. Louis, with a Chinese population of 236 in 1940, should be ranked twenty-second between Newark (259) and New Orleans (230).[19] To situate the St. Louis Chinese American community in the context of Chinese American urban history, and to help readers understand the larger phenomenon of the Chinese American urban development in North America, I have categorized the studies of Chinatowns by geographical division and characteristic divisions.

Geographical Divisions. Although Chinese American settlement has been an urban phenomenon, the studies of Chinatowns in America have long been limited to the three major Chinese urban communities of San Francisco, New York, and Los Angeles and their social structures. The following works are representative of the many studies of San Francisco Chinatown. Based on oral history interviews of San Francisco Chinatown residents, Victor G. Nee and Brett de Bary Nee's *Longtime Californ': A Documentary Study of an American Chinatown* explores the forces that created Chinatown and continued to perpetuate its existence and the sources of its cohesiveness and resilience as an ethnic community.[20] Thomas W. Chinn's *Bridging the Pacific: San Francisco Chinatown and Its People* chronicles the history of San Francisco Chinatown by examining its social structure and the individuals who helped shape its history.[21] Chalsa M. Loo's *Chinatown: Most Time, Hard Time* is an empirical study that provides "an understanding of the life problems, concerns, perceptions, and needs of a major segment of the Chinese American population."[22] Yong Chen's *Chinese San Francisco, 1850–1943* depicts the cultural and social transformation of the Chinese in San Francisco over a century.[23] Nayan Shah's *Contagious Divides: Epidemics and Race in San Francisco's Chinatown* offers refreshing insights into a complex picture of public health and race in the city.[24]

A rich body of literature on New York Chinatown has also emerged. Bernard P. Wong alone has contributed three books on the subject, in which he analyzes the dynamics of the interpersonal relationships of the Chinese and their contributions to the economic well-being and social life of the community,[25] investigates the adaptation of the Chinese in New York,[26] and examines the formation and manipulation of the patronage and brokerage systems in the economic adaptation of the Chinese in New York.[27] Similarly, two studies by Peter Kwong also examine the internal social structure of New York Chinatown.[28] Underneath the appearance of ethnic cohesion, New York Chinatown is a polarized community including "Uptown Chinese" (professionals and business leaders who are engaged in property speculation) and "Downtown Chinese" (manual and service workers who have to work and rent a tenement apartment in Chinatown).[29] Min Zhou's work continues to examine the socioeconomic life in New York Chinatown, but challenges the earlier notion of Chinatown as an urban ghetto plagued by urban problems and views Chinatown as an immigrant enclave with strong socioeconomic potential.[30]

Scholarship on New York also proposes different models than Chinatown. Hsiang-shui Chen's work on the post-1965 Taiwanese immigrants in the neighborhoods of Flushing and Elmhurst of Queens asserts that these communities are "Chinatowns no more," as their residents scatter and mix with other ethnic groups.[31] Jan Lin's study regards New York Chinatown as a global town.[32] Other scholars also investigate the workforce and unionism within the New York Chinatown community—Chinese hand laundrymen and Chinese women garment workers—as represented by Renqiu Yu and Xiaolan Bao, respectively.[33] More recently, some scholars have utilized a comparative approach in their work.[34]

Chinatowns in Los Angeles have also attracted scholarly attention recently. Timothy P. Fong's *The First Suburban Chinatown* presents the experiences of the multiethnic residents of Monterey Park and their reactions to changes in the community, and analyzes the intraethnic and interethnic political strife within the community.[35] John Horton's work views the multiethnic diversity of Monterey Park as the key to understanding the middle-class city in a world whose economy is undergoing rapid internationalization of capital and labor.[36] Similarly, Yen-Fen Tseng asserts the Chinese ethnic economy in Los Angeles has formed multinuclear concentrations in suburban communities in the San Gabriel Valley. The inflow of capital and entrepreneurs from the Chinese diaspora has made the valley's economy an integral part of the Pacific Rim economy.[37] Leland Saito's study continues to examine Monterey Park, giving special attention to Asian Americans' participation in local political campaigns.[38] Wei Li proposes a new model of ethnic settlement—"ethnoburbs" (ethnic suburbs), suburban ethnic clusters of residential areas and business districts in large metropolitan areas that are intertwined with the global, national, and place-specific conditions.[39]

Characterization Divisions. Studies of Chinatown can also be classified by their examination of social structure, socioeconomic functions, and the ethnic compositions and physical space of Chinatowns. In terms of the social structure of Chinatowns, scholars are debating whether Chinatowns are communities of ethnic cohesion or ethnic class cleavage. While the earlier writing looked at Chinatowns as communities of order and ethnic harmony, more recent studies by Peter Kwong, Chalsa Loo, and Jan Lin view Chinatowns as oppressive and polarized communities where ethnic capitalists and a political elite have exploited those with less education, skills, money, and knowledge of English, but who have also had to meet challenges from this group.

In terms of socioeconomic functions of Chinatowns, writers differ over whether Chinatowns prevent Chinese immigrants from assimilating into American society. While some scholars focus on addressing the social and economic problems of ethnic communities, others view Chinatowns as dynamic ethnic economic successes. The former view, represented by Rose Hum Lee,

Peter Kwong, and Chalsa Loo, finds that the Chinatown masses were trapped in ethnic confinement and thus hampered in upward social mobility and cultural assimilation. Min Zhou's work, on the contrary, emphasizes that the Chinatown enclave economy provided employment opportunities to new immigrants that would help the social and cultural integration of the second and third generations.

In terms of ethnic composition and physical space of Chinatowns, the differences lie in whether Chinatowns are isolated and homogenous Chinese urban ghettos or multiethnic suburban communities. Most works dealing with Chinatowns treat them as urban ghettos or enclaves consisting of primarily Chinese immigrants. Hsiang-shui Chen, Timothy P. Fong, Yen-Fen Tseng, Jan Lin, and Wei Li argue that with the diverse socioeconomic backgrounds of the new immigrants since the mid-1960s, Chinese communities are no longer homogenous and urban-bound, but are mixed with other ethnic groups and are increasingly living in suburbs.

It is generally understood that any population settlement includes two basic elements: physical space and social space. Physical space provides geographical boundaries in which the settlement is defined and its members interact with one another in a variety of economic, social, and cultural activities. While the physical space is easily recognizable, the social space of a community is not necessarily confined by a physical space, and could be within or beyond the physical boundaries of the settlement. Most studies discussed above focus on the physical space of any given Chinese community, whether it is urban or suburban, thus overlooking the social spatial aspect. Prior to the appearance of suburban Chinese communities, there was little problem interpreting Chinatowns within physical spatial boundaries. The traditional Chinatowns in San Francisco, New York City, Chicago, and many other urban centers, including the old Chinatown in St. Louis, unquestionably fit the model of urban ethnic ghetto or enclave. Yet ever since the emergence of suburban Chinese communities, such as Oakland in the San Francisco Bay area, Flushing, and Monterey Park, scholars have faced the challenge of how to interpret them accurately. The suburban Chinatown interpretation by Timothy P. Fong recognizes continuity between the urban ethnic enclave and the suburban Chinese communities. Contrarily, the "ethnoburb" model by Wei Li notes the contrast between the traditional urban Chinese settlement and the ethnoburbs.[40] Yen-Fen Tseng sees that the expansive growth of upper-class professional jobs and service/petty manufacturing jobs at the same time has created dual cities in Los Angeles.[41] Similarly, Jan Lin attributes congestion in the inner city to the emergence of "satellite Chinatowns" in the suburban areas.[42] Yet all of these models primarily focus on the geographical parameters of the new Chinese suburban settlements, and are thus unable to explain an ethnic community without a geographical concentration.

Clearly, without looking at the social space of a Chinese settlement, it is difficult to explain the causes behind the emergence and existence of new suburban

Chinese communities that have been scattered among and blended with other ethnic groups. Since the physical spatial definition alone is not adequate to explain these dispersed suburban settlements, one needs to study the socioeconomic structures of the suburban Chinese communities not only from their physical spatial parameters but also from their social spatial dimensions.

Chinese Americans in St. Louis

What was life really like in Hop Alley? Although the absence of firsthand written records by Chinese residents has produced difficulty for scholars, a critical reading of media reports and use of archival manuscripts and oral history materials enables us to restore a more realistic picture of life in Hop Alley in the late nineteenth and early twentieth centuries.

In 1894, Theodore Dreiser, the author of *Sister Carrie* (1900), who was then a twenty-three-year-old reporter for the daily *St. Louis Republic*, went to Hop Alley to write a sensational and somewhat biased story about the Chinese in St. Louis.[43] Dreiser's lengthy article indicates the economic significance of the early Chinese settlement as a peculiar component of the ethnically diverse city, and reveals a great cultural curiosity (and bias as well) about the Chinese among the general population in St. Louis. Raking through words such as "Celestials," "Mongolians," "Chinaman," and "heathen," popular terms referring to Chinese widely used by writers of the Victorian Age, a great deal of information remains, thus offering a starting point for the following discussion.

Dreiser's report is the first to describe the Chinese laundries in St. Louis. It is, however, questionable whether the Chinese population had reached 1,000 and whether about 500 Chinese were operating laundries. Other sources, fortunately, could easily verify that there were more than 300 Chinese dwelling in the Chinatown area, and most of them were working in Chinese hand laundries in Hop Alley and the peripheral area.[44] Court records further note laundry as the primary trade for the Chinese in St. Louis prior to the 1930s. In the first decades of the twentieth century, St. Louis police raided Chinatown frequently and arrested Chinese laborers without certificates of residence. Most of these Chinese laborers worked in Chinese laundries.[45] In addition to the court records, the census also reveals information, though laconic, about the Chinese laundrymen. The 1890 census recorded a Chinese man named Amon Donn running a Chinese hand laundry in the St. Louis downtown area.[46]

If the above sources still seem to be sporadic or anecdotal about the Chinese hand laundrymen, *Gould's St. Louis Directory* provides systematic and significant data on the Chinese hand laundry business. According to *Gould's St. Louis Directory*, the sixteen years from 1873 to 1889 constituted the initial stage of the Chinese hand laundry business in St. Louis. During this period, Chinese laundries not only increased in number but also gradually spread beyond the boundaries of Hop Alley. From 1873 to 1879, Chinese laundries were unexceptionally located on the Chinatown premises, mainly clustering along Sixth, Seventh, Eighth, Market, Chestnut, Pine, Locust, and Elm streets. After 1880, a few laundries opened in the peripheral area of Chinatown, such as Washington and Chouteau avenues, while the majority still remained in the Chinese district.[47]

Chinese hand laundries started to reappear in *Gould's St. Louis Directory* in 1911, and the laundry business continued to be the primary occupation of the Chinese in St. Louis until the end of the 1930s. These three decades witnessed the heyday of the Chinese hand laundry business in St. Louis. During this period, as indicated by the primary sources, two distinctive features of clan domination and geographical dispersion characterized Chinese hand laundries. Surnames of Kee, Lee, Leong, Sing, Wah, and Wing were the ones that appeared in the directories most frequently.[48] Lee, Lung, Sing, and Wah clans were predominant in the 1910s, and were joined in the 1920s by Kee, Leong, Lum, Wing, and Yee clans. In 1927, *Gould's St. Louis Directory* began to list Chinese hand laundries under a separate heading as Chinese laundries, which comprised more than 60 percent of the total laundries in the city. In the listings, Lee and Sing stood out as two most frequent surnames. The predominance of certain clans in the Chinese laundry business illustrates at least two important implications regarding patterns of immigration and urban ethnic adaptation. First, it reveals that many Chinese laundrymen came to America as links of chain immigration; common surnames well indicate the blood ties or lineage among the laundrymen. Second, it speaks of the necessity of ethnic networking in initiating and operating a business.

Along with clan domination, geographical dispersion was evident among the Chinese hand laundries from the 1910s to the 1930s. Unlike the early stage of the Chinese laundry business when most Chinese laundries were concentrated in the Chinese business district, now the Chinese laundries were scattered throughout the city. The geographical dispersion was partially a result of the self-governance of the Chinese community in order to prevent competition among the Chinese laundries. On Leong Merchants and Laborers Association, the primary Chinese business organization founded in 1909 and the de facto Chinese government in St. Louis, ruled that "there was only one Chinese laundry allowed within the perimeter of a mile," and the violation of the restriction could result in unexpected catastrophe or murder of the offender.[49] Intimidated by the power of On Leong, Chinese laundrymen abided by the rule. More important, the Chinese laundrymen followed the rule of the market—supply and demand—to operate a laundry wherever there was a demand or lack of a Chinese laundry. Since the primary clientele of the Chinese hand laundry were non-Chinese, it was natural for Chinese laundries to spread out in the city to meet the demand.

Although Dreiser's story failed to mention Chinese grocery stores, they had already emerged as another important Chinese business in St. Louis to provide ingredients for Chinese cooking and laundry supplies for hand laundries.

Gould's St. Louis Directory first listed two Chinese grocers in 1888.[50] From the 1890s to 1900s, Chinese grocers slowly but steadily increased, with the total number ranging from four to six.[51] The years between 1912 and 1914 witnessed a sudden increase of Chinese grocers, with a total of a dozen.[52] During the 1920s, the number of Chinese grocers decreased but remained steady, with half a dozen listed regularly.[53]

Different from Chinese hand laundries that primarily served non-Chinese in St. Louis and therefore dispersed across the city, grocery stores catered to the Chinese community and consequently clustered around the Chinese business district, resembling the patterns prevailing in other urban Chinese communities.[54] In the first decade of the 1900s, these grocery stores sold merchandise imported from China, including tea, cigars, cooking ingredients, Chinese cloth with intricately embroidered parts, and supplies for laundries. The Chinese grocery stores also sold locally produced fresh fruits, vegetables, and fish delivered daily by Chinese farmers on the other side of the river in Illinois. Many of the Chinese stores also handled the ordering and shipping of supplies to Chinese laborers in the southern and southwestern states.[55]

Annie Leong's family history offers a good example of how the Chinese grocery stores operated. The Leong family owned a Chinese restaurant downtown and a grocery store in Hop Alley during the 1920s and 1930s. They ordered merchandise for their grocery store from wholesalers in San Francisco, New York, and Chicago. Annie Leong and her brothers spent their time after school working in the family grocery store. Annie Leong recalled her childhood experiences retailing goods: "We got them on credit, and we have thirty days to pay. If you don't have a good credit, you have to pay right away. They gave us wholesale price, and we retail them. The whole family helps to do the business. After the operation whatever is left is our profit."[56]

In addition to grocery businesses, some Chinese merchants in St. Louis operated general merchandise stores. Oriental Tea was such a store in business as early as the 1920s. Bigger than most grocery stores with single ownership, Oriental Tea had several partners to finance and operate the store, and sold supplies to Chinese laundries and restaurants. Richard Ho's father was a partner of Oriental Tea who brought then ten-year-old Richard Ho from Canton, China, to St. Louis in 1928. Richard Ho later worked in the store as a driver of a small panel truck to deliver ordered goods to Chinese laundries and restaurants, and accepted new orders from them for the next round.[57] The operation of the Chinese general merchandise stores in St. Louis well resembled that of their counterparts on the West Coast, as documented in scholarly writings.[58]

Chinese restaurants and chop suey shops had also been part of the businesses in St. Louis Chinatown. The Chinese restaurants in St. Louis were first established to serve Chinese workers, mostly laundrymen who took a half-day off on Sunday afternoon and came to Chinese restaurants to satisfy a week-long craving for good Chinese food. Most of these restaurants were located in the Hop Alley district, as the Chinese laundrymen would normally come there for socialization and recreation on Sunday. Around the turn of the century, some Chinese restaurants not only served dishes for casual eaters but also began to cater banquets for special occasions such as weddings and holiday celebrations. Dishes for these special occasions could range from $2 to $20 a plate, far more expensive than the regular price of 40 to 80 cents.[59] Restaurants with such capacity would be quite lucrative. Some of the Chinese restaurant owners could make a handsome income from the business and could thus take on a more American appearance. One downtown Chinese restaurant owner, described by the media as "a dapper little Chinaman," dressed stylishly with a "mohair suit, lavender silk hose, and tan shoes, diamond stud and Panama hat."[60]

When Chinese food became more popular in the first decades of the twentieth century, more chop suey shops emerged in St. Louis. Both chop suey shops and larger Chinese restaurants not only served Chinese eaters, but also catered to European Americans and African Americans. Annie Leong's parents opened a Chinese restaurant at 714 Market Street in St. Louis in 1924. The restaurant served Cantonese cuisine of shark fins, bird nests, steamed fish, barbecued pork, duck, and rooster to Chinese guests from China and the United States. It also frequently received local European American customers who came from theaters downtown in the late evenings.[61]

In addition to grocery stores and restaurants, Chinese merchants also opened tea shops. The earliest recorded tea shop was run by Alla Lee in 1859 at 106 North Tenth Street.[62] After that, Alla Lee's tea shop and residence changed locations several times, mostly outside Chinatown, yet it was continuously listed in the *St. Louis Directory* until 1880.[63] Alla Lee came to St. Louis in 1857 at the age of twenty-four years and married a young Irish woman named Sarah Graham, who bore several children for him. The income from the tea shop was able to support Lee and his growing family.[64]

The Great Depression engendered a population dispersion and economic reshuffling for the Chinese St. Louisans. The Depression caused at least two demographic changes among the Chinese in St. Louis: the movement of the Chinese population from St. Louis to China and to states outside of Missouri, and the gradual decline of the Chinese hand laundries. During the first decades of the century, the Chinese population in Missouri steadily increased, from 449 in 1900, to 535 in 1910, to 612 in 1920, and to 634 by 1929. Ten years later, however, the figure had dropped to 334, almost a 50 percent decrease of the Chinese population in Missouri.

After World War II, the Chinese population in St. Louis witnessed another transformation. The wartime economic recovery and prosperity continued in the postwar years. Americans enjoyed the greatest economic expansion in the century. Economic expansion in St. Louis attracted newcomers from other parts of the country as well as from overseas. The population in St. Louis jumped from 1,090,278 in 1940 to 1,262,145 in 1950 and 1,263,145 in 1960.[65] As thousands of Americans moved to St. Louis, professionals from China, Taiwan, and Hong Kong also came to the city for a better economic opportunity. The earliest Chinese professionals were engineers, scientists, and physicians.

Meanwhile, the urban renewal movement in St. Louis was threatening the physical existence of the city's Chinatown. Starting in 1955, the Land Clearance for Redevelopment Authority began clearing the land. The 454-acre Mill Creek valley site between Lindell-Olive and Scott avenues was cleared in 1955, and Twentieth Street and Grant Avenue in 1959. Next, the downtown district was to be demolished. A group of downtown businessmen formed the Civic Center Redevelopment Corporation, which contracted with the Land Clearance for Redevelopment Authority to carry out the downtown renewal project. The century-old commercial district, old residences, and industries were to be razed to make space for thirty-four commercial buildings, twenty-six industrial buildings, and extensive parking and loading facilities.[66] The centerpiece of the downtown renewal was Busch Stadium. The Chinatown district was intended to be the parking lot for the stadium.

The Chinese community reacted to the downtown removal with deep sorrow, reluctance to move, but no organized resistance. Many who grew up in the alleys of Chinatown lamented the imminent disappearance of the district. The elderly bachelors who resided in the flats above the Chinese businesses or in the apartment buildings were worried where they should move. On Leong finally bought a building at 1509 Delmar by the end of 1965.[67] On August 1, 1966, the close of Asia Restaurant, long a favorite eating place for many St. Louisans and the last remaining business in Chinatown, quietly announced the end of an old and respected St. Louis neighborhood. Three days later, On Leong moved its headquarters to 1509 Delmar. Two weeks later, the last building in Chinatown was leveled. Hop Alley quietly vanished.

While the St. Louis Chinatown and On Leong were struggling for survival, the city received new arrivals from China. According to the census, by 1960 the Chinese population in St. Louis area totaled 663. A decade later, the Chinese population had more than doubled, reaching 1,451. By 1980, the Chinese population was 2,418, a fourfold increase within two decades.[68]

Beginning in the 1960s, the economy of Chinese St. Louisans also underwent a remarkable transformation. The Chinese hand laundries disappeared one by one, and Chinese restaurants mushroomed throughout the area, especially in shopping malls and plazas. While the occupational shift from hand laundries to restaurants took place, the newly arrived Chinese professionals were mostly recruited by a number of major employers of the region— Washington University, Monsanto Chemical Company (changed to Pharmacia in 2001), McDonnell-Douglas Company (changed to Boeing when purchased by the Boeing Company in 1999), the Ralston-Purina Company, the Emerson Electric Company, and the Anheuser-Busch Company.

The Chinese economy in St. Louis after the 1960s was characterized by the following factors. First, the Chinese restaurant businesses depended on ethnic networking for labor and capital and on mainstream society in the market. On the one hand, Chinese restaurant businesses had to depend on an ethnic networking system in collecting capital, recruiting laborers, and ordering supplies, a characteristic common among overseas Chinese businesses in America, Canada, and Southeast Asia.[69] As a link of the global overseas Chinese businesses, the Chinese restaurant business in St. Louis in the post-1960s was also bound by and benefited from the ethnic networks. Capital to start a restaurant business often came from family savings and loans from relatives. Laborers were recruited mostly from unpaid family members and underpaid relatives or clansmen. Supplies were ordered at wholesale prices from ethnic wholesalers. Ethnic networks thus were indispensable to the operation of the Chinese restaurant businesses in St. Louis.

On the other hand, as a food service industry, the Chinese restaurant businesses had to rely on the consumers they served, including not only Chinese customers but patrons of all ethnic backgrounds as well. The dependence of Chinese restaurants on the mainstream society for their clientele inevitably connected the ethnic Chinese economy with the larger economy. To find a profitable market and to avoid competition with counterparts, Chinese restaurants had to be geographically dispersed, which enabled the survival and possible success of individual Chinese restaurants, but also hindered them from forming ethnic business concentrations in any given geographic locality. The geographical dispersion of Chinese restaurant businesses in St. Louis was partially responsible for the absence of a Chinese business district.

Second, the Chinese professionals enjoyed a complete professional and economic integration with the larger society. Primarily employed in major mainstream enterprises, they were cozily sheltered from risking the ups and downs of running a small business and completely subjugated to the economic force of the larger society for their livelihood and career advancement. Consequently, they were more concerned about the larger economy than the Chinese ethnic economy.

The duality of the Chinese restaurant businesses with ties in both the ethnic business sector and mainstream economy and the economic integration of Chinese professionals affected, if not determined, the formation of a new type of Chinese community in St. Louis, a community without physical boundaries but dominated by the common cultural interests of its members.

Meanwhile, the urban renewal movement repeatedly frustrated the community's attempts to build a physical Chinese commercial district. The urban renewal movement since the 1950s demolished Hop Alley, the historical

Chinatown in St. Louis. The urban renewal projects in the 1970s halted the efforts of the Chinese to build a new Chinatown on Delmar Boulevard. The concerns and fears that future urban renewal development would nullify any Chinatown building effort effectively prevented Chinese St. Louisans from making plans to redevelop a Chinatown. At the same time, the denigrating stereotypical images associated with Chinatowns also discouraged many in the community from pursuing an action to rebuild a Chinatown.[70]

Yet there still was a need for the existence of an ethnic community in order to survive, succeed, and secure the achievements. The survival and security now were not so much focused on economic needs as they used to be, since most Chinese in the region were professionals and enjoyed a middle-class lifestyle, but more on cultural, emotional, and political needs. Culturally, they needed to preserve the Chinese ethnic identity, which they feared they might lose as the population dispersed. The establishment of Chinese-language schools and celebrations of Chinese culture were the direct result of the desire to preserve cultural identity. Although most of the Chinese professionally and economically integrated into the larger society, the feelings of cultural displacement and cultural conflict resulting from an immigrant life caused emotional anxieties that could be better soothed by sharing issues and values with other members of the ethnic community. Moreover, to protect their socioeconomic achievements and to make further progress, the Chinese had to form a single and louder voice; an ethnic community would serve as means of political empowerment. These cultural, emotional, and political needs therefore validated the existence of an ethnic community. Thus, in the place of a physical Chinese community, a Chinese cultural community emerged.

Different from many of the Chinese American communities throughout the country, the cultural community in St. Louis did not have identifiable physical boundaries. Instead, the cultural community was defined within social boundaries of community organizations, Chinese churches, and Chinese-language schools, as well as the dispersed Chinese restaurants, grocery stores, and other service businesses. Although most elements of the cultural community such as Chinese churches and Chinese-language schools did occupy a physical structure where they rendered services to the community, these physical structures did not constitute a physical Chinatown since they were scattered throughout the city. Likewise, the dispersed Chinese businesses also failed to create a physical commercial district. However, the cultural activities organized by the community organizations and that took place in the cultural institutions generated a sense of community and constituted the social/emotional space of the cultural community. Therefore, the cultural community can be understood in two dimensions: physical and social/emotional. The facilities of the cultural institutions or community organizations, either owned or rented, constituted the physical space of the cultural community. The activities that took place in these facilities created the social space of the cultural community. The latter depended on the former but was more significant than the former in creating a cultural community.

Unlike other types of Chinese communities with physical boundaries, the physical space of the cultural community was undefined and often unidentifiable, for the significant part of the community organizational structure possessed no permanent physical space, whereas the social space of the cultural community was visible and easily recognizable when Chinese-language classes were held, religious congregations were convened, and cultural activities took place. Hence, the investigation of the social space of the community in this study is more relevant and feasible than the examination of the physical space. Although it is difficult to gauge the social/emotional dimension of the cultural community, three integral components of the cultural community can define the social boundaries of the cultural community—community organizations, Chinese churches, and Chinese-language schools. They can also help us understand the social/emotional dimension of the cultural community.

The new community organizations in St. Louis included the St. Louis Chinese Society, the St. Louis Chapter of the Organization of Chinese Americans (OCA), the St. Louis Taiwanese Association, the St. Louis Chinese Jaycees, the Chinese Liberty Assembly, and the Chinese Cultural Center (the St. Louis Overseas Chinese Educational Activity Center). The Chinese churches consisted of the St. Louis Gospel Church, the St. Louis Chinese Christian Church, the Taiwanese Presbyterian Church, the St. Louis Chinese Baptist Church, the Lighthouse Chinese Church, the St. Louis Chinese Lutheran Church, the Lutheran Asian Ministry in St. Louis, the Lutheran Hour Ministries, the Light of Christ Chinese Missions in St. Louis, the St. Louis Tabernacle of Joy, the Mid-America Buddhist Association, the St. Louis Tzu-Chi Foundation, the St. Louis Amitabha Buddhist Learning Center, the St. Louis International Buddhist Association, and the St. Louis Falun Dafa. The Chinese-language schools were the St. Louis Chinese Academy and the St. Louis Chinese Language School.

The establishment and development of Chinese community organizations, Chinese churches, and Chinese-language schools between the 1960s and 1980s signified the formation of a Chinese American cultural community in St. Louis. From the very beginning, the cultural community possessed some unique characteristics. First, in examining the physical dimension of the cultural community, the absence of a geographical concentration of physical structures facilitating community activities relating to Chinese American culture was evident. Nearly none of the Chinese community organizations owned or rented a property as headquarters or as a place for their meetings and other activities. Instead, the Chinese community organizations convened in meeting rooms available at institutions of the mainstream society or at homes of board members, and rented spaces from private or public facilities for large-scale cultural activities. The Chinese churches, although most either rented or owned a permanent structure for their congregations, were scattered in suburban municipalities. The Chinese-language schools, similar to the Chinese churches, needed permanent locations for their regular weekend classes, but managed to rent rooms from churches or educational institutions to meet their needs. The absence of a geographical concentration of cultural facilities was partially a result of the residential pattern of Chinese St. Louisans, who spread among suburban middle-class or upper-middle-class neighborhoods, but was partially a preferred choice of the community that shunned the idea of forming an ethnic concentration, in fear of racial profiling from the larger society.[71]

Second, professionals dominated the cultural community. Demographically, the professionals constituted a majority of the population in the cultural community. Politically, the professionals, especially those from Taiwan, had been the key power holders of the cultural community. They established and operated most of the community organizations and institutions. They were primarily responsible for all the cultural activities and events that took place in the community. When examining the motives for the professionals to be involved in the cultural community, it is clear that cultural interests overshadowed economic interests, since the professionals, who had economically integrated into the larger society and therefore had little vested interest in exploiting an ethnic community for economic benefit, still needed an ethnic community for their own cultural welfare and that of their offspring.

Third, a class cleavage or confrontation, present in other types of Chinese American communities, was absent in the cultural community in St. Louis. There the distinction between the community elite and masses was blurred, as both the community leaders and members belonged to the same socioeconomic bracket. Although a working class existed in the cultural community of St. Louis, it was dispersed throughout the city in the kitchens of Chinese restaurants and in the back of Chinese grocery stores, and was unable to develop into a visible and influential social force.

Without physical boundaries, the cultural community still proved to be a functional, cohesive, and tightly knit ethnic community structure. Without physical concentrations, the myriad community organizations and cultural institutions still created a visible and indispensable ethnic community. Through its wide array of activities and events, the cultural community effectively bound its members together and provided them invaluable social/emotional services. The cultural community has exhibited an alternative ethnic community model when a physical ethnic concentration is absent and a physical ethnic community is difficult to construct.

After its building period from the 1960s to 1980s, the Chinese American cultural community in St. Louis entered a stage of rapid development in the 1990s and the early twenty-first century. Demographically, it embraces a more diverse population, including a large number of Chinese students and professionals from mainland China since the late 1980s. The presence of mainland Chinese has resulted in a structural realignment within the cultural community that is embodied in the increasing numbers of business owners and professionals from China, the incorporation of the teaching of simplified Chinese characters in the Chinese-language schools, and the growing influence of the St. Louis Chinese Association—a community organization primarily comprising mainland Chinese.

The rapid growth of the cultural community is also reflected in the development of the Chinese-language media and the diversification of the new ethnic economy. The birth and growth of the Chinese-language press in the community have been monumental in promoting the Chinese ethnic economy, preserving Asian American ethnic heritage, and bridging the cultural community and the larger society. In 1990, the *St. Louis Chinese American News* was established to meet the needs of the community. As the community continued to develop, another Chinese newspaper, the *St. Louis Chinese Journal*, began publishing in 1996. The new ethnic economy of the cultural community is more diversified; it embraces not only a growing and more competitive food service industry but also the rapidly expanding nontraditional service industries of real estate, health, insurance, construction, architecture and design, legal consultation, accounting, auto repair, and computer services.[72]

Meanwhile, the cultural community is also more politicized than ever before. The complexity of the community has divided its members along various lines of linguistics, origins of birth, professional training and occupations, political inclinations, religious beliefs, and cultural interests. While the Chinese St. Louisans are profoundly divided, they are at the same time united under the common interest and commitment to preserving and promoting the ethnic Chinese American culture and to protecting and improving their conditions through socioeconomic integration and political empowerment.

Conclusion

Two factors have chiefly contributed to the emergence of a cultural community—socioeconomic integration and preservation of ethnic identity. Socioeconomic integration would naturally dissolve an ethnic physical community, making way for a different form of community. As demonstrated by American ethnic history in general and Chinese American history in particular, when the overall socioeconomic climate disfavors a minority group, the economic survival of the group demands a self-sufficient physical commercial as well as residential community, in which its members sustain themselves by depending on the internal mutual reliance. When the external environment improves and becomes more receptive of a minority group, the physical boundaries of the minority community begin to break down and to gradually erode away. As shown in the history of the

Chinese St. Louisans, while a physical ethnic community disappeared as its members economically and residentially integrated into the larger society, a cultural community developed in its place. The socioeconomic integration dismantles the physical concentrations of an ethnic group and forges a cultural community. Therefore, the more integrated a minority group is, the more likely the emergence of a cultural community among its members.

However, socioeconomic integration alone is not sufficient to explain the formation of a cultural community. Socioeconomic integration causes the dispersal of an ethnic population, thus resulting in the absence of a physical ethnic community, but it does not necessarily create a different form of ethnic community. Integration has historically led to assimilation of different ethnic groups into the larger or mainstream "white" society. Only when an integrated ethnic group is conscious about preserving its ethnic identity may a cultural community emerge. Fearing possible loss of an ethnic identity because of the integration, an ethnic group would strive to create a community to preserve its identity. If a physical community proves unfeasible, a cultural community or its variants would naturally arise, which is exactly what has happened to Chinese Americans in St. Louis. The dispersion of the Chinese ethnic economy and the integration of the Chinese professionals have been attributed to an absence of physical concentrations of the Chinese community, either commercial or residential. Nevertheless, a strong sense of being Chinese and the keen desire to preserve the Chinese identity have motivated Chinese St. Louisans to build the cultural community's infrastructures of community organizations, Chinese churches, and Chinese-language schools. Consequently, a cultural community is born.

The reconstruction of the history of Chinese St. Louisans is not merely another case study of Chinese American communities. The model of cultural community is not limited to St. Louis. It is applicable to communities where the physical concentrations of the ethnic minority groups are absent. It is applicable to communities where the ethnic minority groups have economically and professionally integrated into the larger society, but culturally remain distinct from the larger society. It is also applicable to communities where the members of ethnic minority groups are overwhelmingly professional.

The cultural community in St. Louis provides an alternative model for understanding the diversity and complexity of the Chinese American communities. When the existing theories of Chinese communities are less adequate in explaining an ethnic community that is geographically dispersed and intermingled with the majority society, yet consciously congregates in cultural events that distinguish itself from the larger society, the model of cultural community stands out as a more appropriate and satisfactory interpretation.

The cultural community as a variant of ethnic community also reflects the social advancement of an ethnic minority group in a classed and racialized society. The transformation of the Chinese community from a Chinatown to a cultural community hails the socioeconomic and political progress Chinese Americans have achieved since the 1960s. In other words, the presence of cultural community indicates the socioeconomic progress of an ethnic minority.

Thus far, the model of cultural community displays a prospective pattern for an ethnic community when it achieves socioeconomic integration, yet is still yearning for its cultural identity. It is certain that as long as America remains a multicultural and multiracial society, one will be able to find various cultural communities. Meanwhile, it is also important to note that a cultural community is not an advocate of cultural separatism, but a celebration of multiculturalism or cultural pluralism in a multicultural and multiracial society.

NOTES

1. *Missouri Republican*, December 31, 1869; *Louisville Courier-Journal*, December 30, 1896; Lucy M. Cohen, *Chinese in the Post–Civil War South: A People without a History* (Baton Rouge: Louisiana State University Press, 1984), 86–87; *Kennedy's St. Louis Directory*, 1859–1863; *Edward's St. Louis Directory*, 1864–1871; *Gould's St. Louis Directory*, 1872–1879; 1860 Census; and C. Fred Blake, "There Ought to Be a Monument to Alla Lee," *Chinese American Forum* 15, no. 3 (January 2000): 23–25.

2. This claim is based on the author's tallies of Chinese laundries and non-Chinese laundries in St. Louis during the last decades of the nineteenth century and the first decades of the twentieth century, census data, and information from news reports.

3. The definition of St. Louis has changed over time. Prior to 1876, St. Louis City was within St. Louis County, and it became an independent city in 1876. The terms "St. Louis area" and "St. Louis region" have generally referred to St. Louis City and St. Louis County. According to the 1990 U.S. census, however, the St. Louis Metropolitan Statistical Area consists of St. Louis City and eleven other counties, of which seven are in Missouri and five in Illinois (St. Louis City is counted as both city and county). Since an overwhelming majority of Chinese Americans reside in St. Louis City and St. Louis County of Missouri, the term "St. Louis region" in this study refers to St. Louis City and St. Louis County, Missouri, and all statistics are drawn accordingly.

4. Profile of General Demographic Characteristics: 2000 Data Set: Census 2000 Summary File 2 (SF 2) 100-Percent Data Geographic Area: St. Louis, MO-IL MSA Race or Ethnic Group: Chinese alone.

5. The Chinese in Metropolitan St. Louis include American-born Chinese and Chinese from mainland China, Taiwan, Hong Kong, Korea, Vietnam, and other Southeast Asian countries. Except for the census, there are no official statistics on the Chinese population in St. Louis, which has increased rapidly since 1990. The author has discussed the issue with leaders of various Chinese community organizations, and their estimate of the Chinese population in St. Louis ranges from 15,000 to 20,000.

6. Hsiang-shui Chen, *Chinatown No More: Taiwanese Immigrants in Contemporary New York* (Ithaca, N.Y.: Cornell University Press, 1992), 31; Yen-Fen Tseng, "Chinese Ethnic Economy: San Gabriel Valley, Los Angeles County," *Journal of Urban Affairs* 16, no. 2 (1994): 170; Jan Lin, *Reconstructing Chinatown: Ethnic Enclave, Global Change* (Minneapolis: University of Minnesota Press, 1998), 39; Peter S. Li and Yahong Li, "The Consumer Market of the Enclave Economy: A Study of Advertisements in a Chinese Daily Newspaper in Toronto," *Canadian Ethnic Studies* 31, no. 2 (1999): 43–60; Peter S. Li, "Self-Employment among Visible Minority Immigrants, White Immigrants, and

Native-Born Persons in Secondary and Tertiary Industries of Canada," *Canadian Journal of Regional Science* 20, nos. 1–2 (Spring–Summer 1997): 103–118; Peter S. Li, "Unneighborly Houses or Unwelcome Chinese: The Social Construction of Race in the Battle over 'Monster Homes' in Vancouver, Canada," *International Journal of Comparative Race and Ethnic Studies* 1, no. 1 (1994): 14–33; Peter S. Li, "Chinese Investment and Business in Canada: Ethnic Entrepreneurship Reconsidered," *Pacific Affairs* 66, no. 2 (Summer 1993): 219–243.

7. For studies of "urban ghettos," see Peter Kwong, *Chinatown, New York: Labor and Politics, 1930–1950* (New York: Monthly Review Press, 1979); Peter Kwong, *The New Chinatown* (New York: Hill and Wang, 1987). For studies of "ethnic enclave," see Min Zhou, *Chinatown: The Socioeconomic Potential of an Urban Enclave* (Philadelphia: Temple University Press, 1992). For studies of "suburban Chinatowns," see Timothy P. Fong, *The First Suburban Chinatown: The Making of Monterey Park, California* (Philadelphia: Temple University Press, 1994); Yen-Fen Tseng, "Suburban Ethnic Economy: Chinese Business Communities in Los Angeles" (Ph.D. diss., University of California, Los Angeles, 1994); Tseng, "Chinese Ethnic Economy." For studies of "ethnoburbs," see Wei Li, "Spatial Transformation of an Urban Ethnic Community from Chinatown to Chinese Ethnoburb in Los Angeles" (Ph.D. diss., University of Southern California, 1997).

8. Examples supporting such a pattern could be found in a number of works. See Oscar Handlin, *Adventure in Freedom: Three Hundred Years of Jewish Life in America* (New York: McGraw-Hill, 1954); Rowland T. Berthoff, *British Immigrants in Industrial America 1790–1950* (Cambridge, Mass.: Harvard University Press, 1953); R. A. Birchall, *The San Francisco Irish, 1848–1880* (Berkeley: University of California Press, 1980); Lawrence A. Cardoso, *Mexican Emigration to the United States, 1897–1931* (Tucson: University of Arizona Press, 1980); Dino Cinel, *From Italy to San Francisco: The Immigrant Experience* (Stanford, Calif.: Stanford University Press, 1982); Dennis Clark, *The Irish in Philadelphia: Ten Generations of Urban Experience* (Philadelphia: Temple University Press, 1974); Hasia R. Diner, *Erin's Daughters in America: Irish Immigrant Women in the Nineteenth Century* (Baltimore: John's Hopkins University Press, 1983).

9. See H. Arnold Barton, *A Folk Divided: Homeland Swede and Swedish Americans, 1840–1940* (Carbondale: Southern Illinois University Press, 1994); Chen, *Chinatown No More*; Irving Cutler, *The Jews of Chicago: From Shtetl to Suburb* (Urbana: University of Illinois Press, 1996); Eileen Tamura, *Americanization, Acculturation, and Ethnic Identity: The Nisei Generation in Hawaii* (Urbana: University of Illinois Press, 1994).

10. See Handlin, *Adventure in Freedom*.

11. See Kyeyoung Park, *The Korean American Dream: Immigrants and Small Business in New York City* (Ithaca, N.Y.: Cornell University Press, 1997).

12. See "100 Chinese Americans Will Be Speakers and Resources," *New York Times*, June 10, 1991.

13. Percentage computed according to *U.S. Census of Population: 1950*, Vol. 4, *Special Reports*, 3B-19.

14. Coolidge, *Chinese Immigration*, 402.

15. Rose Hum Lee, *The Growth and Decline of Chinese Communities in the Rocky Mountain Region* (New York: Arno Press, 1978), 147.

16. Rose Hum Lee, *The Chinese in the United States of America* (Hong Kong: Hong Kong University Press, 1960), 52.

17. Bernard P. Wong, *A Chinese American Community: Ethnicity and Survival Strategies* (Singapore: Chopmen, 1979), 18; Kay J. Anderson, *Vancouver's Chinatown: Racial Discourse in Canada, 1875–1980* (Montreal: McGill-Queen's University Press, 1991), 9.

18. David Lai, "Socio-economic Structures and the Viability of Chinatown," in *Residential and Neighborhood Studies in Victoria*, ed. C. Forward, 101–129, Western Geographical Series, No. 5 (Victoria: University of Victoria, 1973).

19. Lee, *Growth and Decline*, 34.

20. Victor G. Nee and Brett de Bary Nee, *Longtime Californ': A Documentary Study of an American Chinatown* (New York: Pantheon Books, 1972).

21. Thomas W. Chinn, *Bridging the Pacific: San Francisco Chinatown and Its People* (San Francisco: Chinese Historical Society of America, 1989).

22. Chalsa M. Loo, *Chinatown: Most Time, Hard Time* (New York: Praeger, 1991), 3.

23. Yong Chen, *Chinese San Francisco, 1850–1943: A Trans-Pacific Community* (Stanford, Calif.: Stanford University Press, 2000).

24. Nayan Shah, *Contagious Divides: Epidemics and Race in San Francisco's Chinatown* (Berkeley: University of California Press, 2001).

25. Wong, *Chinese American Community*.

26. Bernard P. Wong, *Chinatown: Economic Adaptation and Ethnic Identity of the Chinese* (New York: Holt, Rinehart and Winston, 1982), 107.

27. Bernard P. Wong, *Patronage, Brokerage, Entrepreneurship and the Chinese Community of New York* (New York: AMS Press, 1988).

28. Kwong, *Chinatown, New York*; Kwong, *New Chinatown*.

29. Kwong, *New Chinatown*, 5, 175.

30. Zhou, *Chinatown*, xvii.

31. Chen, *Chinatown No More*, ix.

32. Lin, *Reconstructing Chinatown*, xi, 12–17.

33. Renqiu Yu, *To Save China, to Save Ourselves: The Chinese Hand Laundry Alliance of New York* (Philadelphia: Temple University Press, 1992); Xiaolan Bao, *Holding Up More Than Half the Sky: Chinese Women Garment Workers in New York City, 1948–92* (Urbana: University of Illinois Press, 2001).

34. See, for example, Xinyang Wang, *Surviving the City: The Chinese Immigrant Experience in New York City, 1890–1970* (Lanham, Md.: Rowman and Littlefield, 2001).

35. Fong, *First Suburban Chinatown*.

36. John Horton, *The Politics of Diversity: Immigration, Resistance, and Change in Monterey Park, California* (Philadelphia: Temple University Press, 1995), 8.

37. Tseng, "Chinese Ethnic Economy."

38. Leland Saito, *Race and Politics: Asian Americans, Latinos, and Whites in a Los Angeles Suburb* (Chicago: University of Illinois Press, 1998).

39. Li, "Spatial Transformation."

40. Li, "Anatomy of a New Ethnic Settlement."

41. Tseng, "Chinese Ethnic Economy."

42. Lin, *Reconstructing Chinatown*, 107–120.

43. Theodore Dreiser, "The Chinese in St. Louis," *St. Louis Republic*, January 14, 1894.

44. "75 Years Ago—Wednesday, August 25, 1897," *St. Louis Globe-Democrat*, August 25, 1972; Chung Kok Li, interview by author, October 12, 1998, tape recording and transcript.

45. *U.S.A. v. Chu Dock Yuck*, Chinese Exclusion Cases Habeas Corpus Petitions, Case 3849, Box A-1, 849.

46. Claudia Phodes to Huping Ling, February 18, 2002, Huping Ling Collection, in author's possession.

47. *Gould's St. Louis Directory*, 1873–1889.

48. Many of the surnames mentioned here are probably not real Chinese surnames, as non-Chinese might refer to individual Chinese by the name of the store, or confuse

the Chinese given name with the surname. Kee, for instance, is the Cantonese pronunciation of "*ji*," meaning "a store" or "a brand."

49. Chung Kok Li, interview by author, October 12, 1998. The restriction was established by the Chinese laundry associations as early as the 1860s in San Francisco and Virginia City (the author thanks Sue Fawn Chung for providing this information).

50. *Gould's St. Louis Directory*, 1888.

51. *Gould's St. Louis Directory*, 1890–1910.

52. *Gould's St. Louis Directory*, 1912–1914.

53. *Gould's St. Louis Directory*, 1919–1929.

54. Ling, *Surviving on the Gold Mountain*, 64–70.

55. Dick Wood, "The Chinese Colony of St. Louis," *St. Louis Republic*, July 29, 1900 (Mag. Sec.), 2.

56. Annie Leong, interview by author, December 17, 1998.

57. Richard Ho, letter to Huping Ling, August 3, 2002, Huping Ling Collection.

58. Ling, *Surviving on the Gold Mountain*, 65–67.

59. Wood, "Chinese Colony of St. Louis."

60. "Housekeeping in St. Louis Chinatown," *St. Louis Republic*, August 14, 1910 (Mag. Sec.), 4.

61. Leong, interview.

62. *St. Louis Directory*, 1859.

63. *Kennedy's St. Louis Directory*, 1860; *Edward's St. Louis Directory*, 1864–1871; *Gould's St. Louis Directory*, 1872–1880.

64. *Missouri Republican*, December 31, 1869; *Kennedy's St. Louis Directory*, 1859–1863; *Edward's St. Louis Directory*, 1864–1871; *Gould's St. Louis Directory*, 1872–1879; 1860 census about Alla Lee; Blake, "There Ought to Be a Monument."

65. U.S. Census, 1940–1960.

66. James Neal Primm, *Lion of the Valley: St. Louis, Missouri* (Boulder, Colo.: Pruett, 1990), 468–469.

67. Earl C. Gottschalk, "Chinese Community Mourns Passing of Its Tradition," *St. Louis Post-Dispatch*, February 14, 1965.

68. *Census of Population: 1960*, Vol. 1, *Characteristics of the Population, Part 27, Missouri*, 153; *1970 Census of Population*, Vol. 1, *Characteristics of the Population, Part 27, Missouri*, 155–156; and *1980 Census of Population*, Vol. 1, *Characteristics of the Population, Chapter B. General Population Characteristics*, Part 27, Missouri, 14.

69. Wong, *Patronage*; Peter S. Li, "Chinese Investment and Business in Canada: Ethnic Entrepreneurship Reconsidered," *Pacific Affairs* 66, no. 2 (Summer 1993): 219–243; Linda Y. C. Lim, "Chinese Economic Activity in Southeast Asia: An Introductory Review," in *The Chinese in Southeast Asia*, vol. 1, *Ethnicity and Economic Activity*, ed. Linda Y. C. Lim and L. A. Peter Goaling (Singapore: Maruzen Asia, 1983).

70. Interviews with Chinese community leaders.

71. William Tao, interview by author, February 4, 1999; Walter Ko, interview by author, June 2, 2001.

72. St. Louis Chinese American News, *St. Louis Chinese American Yellow Pages*, 2003.

7

Chinese Week

Building Chinese American Community through Festivity in Metropolitan Phoenix

WEI ZENG AND WEI LI

This chapter documents the building of contemporary Chinese American identity and community in metropolitan Phoenix through Phoenix Chinese Week,[1] an annual celebration of the Chinese Lunar New Year. Due to its geographical proximity to California, and its role as one of the major settlement centers in Arizona, Phoenix has been a somewhat small-scale magnet for Chinese immigrants since the late nineteenth century. Chinese immigrants were involved in building railroads from California to Arizona in the 1870s, as well as in silver mining and grocery store and restaurant businesses. Despite this long settlement history, however, its traditional ethnic enclave—a downtown Chinatown—was wiped out several times. The last Chinatown, where the current US Airways Center resides, was demolished in the late nineteenth century though some physical remnants remained until the mid-twentieth century.[2] The fate of the last remnant of this historical Chinatown, the Sun Mercantile Building, built by the Chinese immigrant Tang Shing in 1929 and once the largest produce warehouse in Arizona, is at the center of the debate surrounding a major downtown development project at the end of 2005 that is widely publicized both in and beyond the state.[3]

The Chinese American population in metro Phoenix has continued to grow in terms of population and socioeconomic status as a result of generations of American-born Chinese and, more recently, increasingly heterogeneous Chinese immigrants. The number of Chinese immigrants has grown most since the 1965 Immigration Act, when changes to U.S. immigration policy resulted in a dramatic increase in the proportion and absolute number of non-European immigrants arriving in the United States. Chinese immigration has also burgeoned since the area developed a reputation as the "Silicon Desert" in the last two decades.[4] Metropolitan Phoenix continues to be the second-ranking metropolitan area in the nation in terms of overall population growth.[5] Concomitantly, a thriving ethnic economic sector has begun to draw a more heterogeneous Chinese immigrant

workforce. Historical and contemporary Chinese American community development has resulted in growing numbers of influential and important Chinese professional and community organizations. Many of the immigrants live in suburban
neighborhoods where native-born, non-Hispanic whites form the large majority
and minority groups a significant minority.[6] As of 2000, the Chinese American
population reached 15,156 in the Phoenix-Mesa Metropolitan Statistical Area
(which is the same as Maricopa County).[7]

Despite the rapid growth, however, the current Chinese population has
yet to reach enough critical mass to form an enclave, or "ethnoburb." None of
the known spatial models—invasion/succession, downtown versus uptown,[8] or
ethnoburb[9]—fits the current situation of the Chinese American community.
Rather, Chinese Americans in Phoenix are largely a community without geographical propinquity, that is, they maintain their culture and identity through
social networks and community events.[10] This community resembles a "cultural
community"[11] or "invisiburb,"[12] two newly developed concepts, and takes a "het-
erolocal" spatial form.[13] This chapter, therefore, will examine how the organizational efforts of the annual Chinese Week event serve to unite the contemporary
Chinese American community across class, nationality, and nativity boundaries
in order to re-create a Chinese American identity. We use Chinese Week and the
perspective of the organizers in particular to examine how Chinese American
ethnicity has been "defined and promoted, and how its meanings and practices
have been challenged and resisted."[14] As a result, this ethnic festival is examined as a venue for understanding Chinese American culture and identity formation through which the "cultural" or "invisible" Chinese American community
is constructed. The findings presented in this chapter are based primarily on in-
depth interviews with ten Chinese Week organizers by the first author in 2004,
our participation in Chinese Week events since 2002, and document analysis.
We argue that because of prior Chinese immigration and existing Chinese
American community structures, rapid growth in the high-tech industry, the
diverse Chinese populations and their businesses, and the rapid emergence of
multiethnic suburbs, what we found in this chapter may resonate with those
areas with similar characteristics of minority and immigrant community formation and mobilization.

Literature on Festivity and Community

"The increase in the ethnic diversity of North America is one of the most powerful demographic forces shaping U.S. and Canadian society."[15] Although Mexicans
represent the largest percentage of immigrants to the United States (29.5 percent), the second largest (4.9 percent) is Chinese—specifically immigrants from
Taiwan, Hong Kong, and the People's Republic of China.[16] In spite of the increasing number of Chinese in the United States, very little research has examined

either their leisure specifically[17] or that of Asians in North America in general.[18] Even more scant is the examination of the relationships between leisure activities and/or ethnic festivals and community formation and identity for the groups in question. This study on Chinese Week, therefore, also aims to fill this gap in existing academic research on ethnic festivals, identity, and community.

Chinese Americans are an ethnic group whose lifestyle is very different from other Americans as well as Chinese living in their homeland, but the literature does not contain studies specific to their leisure patterns. Both recently arriving Chinese immigrants and Chinese families who have been here for two or more generations strive to assimilate while retaining a sense of their roots. During the acculturation process, leisure activities provide a secure and supportive space for the expression and transmission of subcultural identity.[19] While past research on ethnicity in recreation has focused on park use and participation in recreation activities, few scholars have examined and interpreted participation in ethnic festivals, let alone the participation in celebrations by Chinese Americans.

A festival persists as a cultural form. A concentration of symbols, a festival displays ideational and material components of culture—language, religion, ceremony, myth, belief, values, folkways, mores, kinship, and worldview, as well as the worlds of art, music, tools, food, dress, and adornment.[20] In his study of San Francisco's Chinese New Year Festival, Yeh indicates that "exotic" and "foreign" cultural elements are emphasized to attract non-Chinese onlookers and to promote a commercial agenda.[21] For instance, women and children were encouraged to dress in Chinese-style clothes to provide more "oriental color" during the festival. In spite of the festival's economic motives and the resulting reinforcement of racial stereotypes, cultural forms and practices are in some ways revived and restored.[22] Yet at the time, Chinese New Year festival organizers often promoted a theme of compatibility between the East and West, which resulted in bands playing Western instruments in Chinese-style uniforms. Therefore, festivals observe cultural construction that includes cultural revivals/ restorations and cultural revisions/innovations. Nagel articulates that while cultural construction is a common response of communities threatened by the loss of cultural forms and practice, confronted with external pressures for assimilation, or engaged in competition with other ethnic groups for dominance or survival, construction of culture leads to revitalization of weakened ethnic boundaries, re-creation of ethnic identity, or reestablishment of ethnic group solidarity.[23]

Festivals are a phase of social concentration.[24] Cunha suggests that the reinforcement of the group solidarity, which is based on the similarity of the individuals, is a social function of festivals and other social gatherings.[25] Turner suggests "communitas" is engendered as collective participation in the liminality, a "sacred condition" that is "outside or on the peripheries of everyday life."

When communitas is achieved, it means an image of "the direct, immediate, and total confrontation of human identities which tends to make those experiencing it think of mankind as a homogeneous unstructured, and free community."[26] Turner's notion that "community is a felt reality" echoes in scholars' reflections on community as a "cultural construction."[27] Therefore, the community that festivals reinforce can be thought of as performed conjectures as well as bounded, essential entities. Literature suggests that festivals, particularly community and ethnic festivals, do inculcate community feeling, or putting it differently, the feeling of community solidarity.[28] Farber indicates festivals not only provide ideal entrees into a community's symbolic, economic, social, and political life for both members of the community and outsiders but also generate forces to respond to external influence and maintain community solidarity through, say, demonstration of community identity.[29]

In the past two decades, a growing number of scholars have come to recognize that group identities are not the spontaneous products of social conditions (structures) but are mediated through the replication of cultural experiences and practices. In this sense, festivals are among the most effective and universal mechanisms for inculcating fictive identities. Robert Orsi's work was the first study that examined ethnic identity formation through an ethnic festival.[30] Following Orsi, a series of studies on festivals focused on the role of festivals as a reflection of ethnicity and ethnic identity.[31] For instance, historian L. Kurshige interprets "the festival as a site of ethnic negotiation and appreciates it as both producer and product of ethnic definition."[32] Building on Kurshige's insights and strategies, Yeh uses the Chinese New Year Festival to examine how Chinese American ethnicity has been "defined and promoted, and how its meanings and practices have been challenged and resisted."[33]

Kaeppler's study demonstrated that festivals are the stage where "layering" of ethnic identity is produced; that is, ethnic boundaries, and thus identities, are constructed by both the individual and group as well as by outsiders, since festivals are cultural performances produced for the group themselves and various public audiences.[34] While Kaeppler examines the external forces existing in the festival shaping the formation of ethnic identity, Yeh looks closely into the tensions and conflicts within the ethnic group itself as the internal resistance that shapes and reshapes ethnic identity.[35] Her analysis of San Francisco's Chinese New Year Festival reveals the complex entanglement of ethnicity, class, gender, politics, and economics as they shape identity formation. She suggests heterogeneity as central to Chinese American community politics and starts from the intergenerational conflicts that are typical in areas with continuing waves of new immigrants. After providing the sociopolitical context of the festival, Yeh contrasts the picture of a happy, noisy, and affluent Chinatown that festival organizers, who are mostly Chinese entrepreneurs, try to present to the larger society and the "real" Chinatown behind the gilded celebratory scene with downplayed social problems including housing shortages, low pay, and neglected children. On the one hand, in addition to the economic motives, the festival organizers, Chinatown elite, sought to create through the festival an image of San Francisco's Chinese Americans as happy, loyal, assimilated, and a law-abiding model minority. On the other hand, "everyday resistance" employed by other community residents, particularly working-class youth, destabilized the Chinese New Year festivals.[36] Criticism of the Miss Chinatown U.S.A. beauty pageant, the production of an alternative celebration, and youth street violence symbolized the attempt of reformers and protesters to call attention to Chinatown's social issues and redefine the ethnic and gender identities imposed on the event by the festival organizers. Therefore, the multifaceted festival reflects the multidimensional ethnic identity. Yeh's study on San Francisco's Chinese New Year Festival has important implications for this study on Phoenix Chinese Week simply because the same ethnic group during a similar ethnic festival is studied. However, the special local contexts of the festival distinguish this study from past research.

In summary, past research has shown that festivals are cultural performances that reflect the dynamics of cultural construction. Festivals play an important role in unifying the community and engendering community solidarity. Last but not least, festivals are not only powerful mechanisms for claiming and expressing ethnic identity but also effective vehicles for re-creating and producing it, during which ethnic boundaries are maintained, negotiated, and invented.

Constructing Community through Festivity

Development of Chinese Week

The origins of Chinese Week arose from a discussion within the Phoenix Sister Cities Commission in 1991. At that time, the city of Phoenix had a sister city relationship with the city of Taipei for twelve years, and also with the city of Chengdu for five years. However, there was no organized Chinese festival celebrated in the Greater Phoenix area for a long time. To gain higher visibility for the Chinese community within the city of Phoenix outside its Chinese community, Phoenix Chinese Week was formed through the efforts of Clarence Teng from the commission, with the Phoenix Sister Cities Commission as cosponsor. With hard work from the members of local Chinese organizations, such as the Phoenix Chinese United Association, Phoenix Chinese Week was initiated in January 1991. A culture and cuisine festival held at Patriot Square Park, a major downtown public park, on the weekend was simple, with "basic entertainment," and quite a success. Gradually, the Phoenix Chinese Week Committee evolved into an independent nonprofit organization and started to collect funding and donations for this annual Chinese festival. The following years have seen Chinese Week expand from a small event with a few booths and entertainment

FIGURE 7.1 Chinese Week 2005 at Chinese Cultural Center; performance by Taipei Yoyo troupe.

at Patriot Square Park to an organized celebration with a three-day Cultural and Cuisine Festival attracting millions of people to the Phoenix Chinese Cultural Center since 1998.[37] Today, the spontaneous celebration has developed into a festival with programmed events, cohosted by the Phoenix Chinese Week Committee, the Phoenix Sister Cities Commission, and the city of Chengdu or Taipei (in alternate years), and sponsored by major corporations, small businesses, and community organizations alike. During the wide variety of festive and formal events, Chinese Week programs reflect the complexity of Chinese American culture. The persistent core elements include dance, music, martial arts, exhibits, fairs, and plays. Major events feature several genres of cultural performance, such as ritual, artistic, and dramatic performances; fairs; and carnivals. This diverse collection of cultural performances and symbols of Chinese Week not only portray multiple aspects of Chinese culture emphasizing a cultural heritage "of five thousand years" but also projects a self-image of Chinese Americans in Phoenix and a reconstructed Chinese American culture (see Figures 7.1 and 7.2). In addition to reproducing culture, Chinese Week serves an important collective end, that is, the construction of community. Through the construction of culture, Chinese Week initiates "the symbolic construction of community."[38] The following discusses how Chinese American community is constructed through Chinese Week with internal fundamentals and external forces.

FIGURE 7.2 "Chinese Culture Theatre" at Chinese Week 2005; Wei Zeng explains Chinese Zodiac to school children.

"Everybody Gets Together and Makes It Big!"

With the absence of a concentrated Chinese neighborhood in Phoenix, Chinese Week successfully involves a broad cross section of Chinese immigrants and native-born Chinese Americans in the process of working together as a community to present themselves to the larger society as a unified whole of distinct parts. During the process, fundamental bonds formed through common heritage, family, kinship, and friendship combine with reciprocity and coalition to form community networks, create community solidarity, and maintain community boundaries.

In the cultural construction of community, heritage and ethnic ancestry are important resources used by Chinese Week in the collective quest for meaning and community. Just as Tony Tang, president of Chinese Week 2003–2004, said, "We are from mainland China, Taiwan, Hong Kong, U.S. . . . ; yet we share one common thread—we love our great heritage and would love to share that with our American friends."[39] Tony Tang indicates that Chinese Week uses this "common thread," the self-esteem of being part of the same rich Chinese culture, to "unify the community." K. C. Tang (not related to Tony Tang) also reflects on the potential of cultural construction of Chinese community:

> Phoenix is the fifth largest city in the U.S. I understand that there are
> about 65,000 Chinese with a lot of new immigrants from Taiwan now.
> I looked back there were just 6,500 people [in the Chinese community].

But I hope more new immigrants come in and blend with us. That's why they come to the U.S. I see that Taiwanese congregate themselves; I believe Chengdu people do the same thing. I hope they can come and be part of the community. . . . Chinese Week is a place where they can get together and get to know how nice it is to know each other. So it is definitely a place where we can communicate and gather together.[40]

While K. C. Tang noted Chinese Week is able to offer a chance to "pull" Chinese from different places together, Lin Ling Lee, president of Chinese Week 2002–2003, identified another coalition that Chinese Week can make possible:

Chinese community differentiates old Chinese immigrants and new Chinese immigrants. Phoenix Chinese United Association represents the old immigrants. . . . I think it is our fate that brings us here together even though we come to the United States at different times. So we should not be separated into old and new immigrants; we are a big whole family. I think if you respect each other and offer services to each other, we can live together harmoniously. I heard a long time ago, there was a Chinatown, but it disappeared when downtown was rebuilt. After the absence of the old Chinatown, old immigrants held their activities in Phoenix area, like the Fourth of July celebration; while now new immigrants have their activities in Mesa or Chandler Center for the Arts. But people participate in each other's events. Like Chinese Week chooses China Doll restaurant as its meeting place which is located in the middle between the north and the south.[41]

The old Chinese immigrants Lin Ling mentioned actually refers to the later-generation America-born Chinese. What we see is Chinese Week's efforts to overcome the differences existing among the Chinese immigrating to the United States in different waves, its efforts to draw people together from various regional, social, ideological backgrounds, and yet a common cultural background.

In addition to fundamentals of ancestry and heritage, kinship, which is highly valued in Chinese culture, forms another force that "draws people, the community, back" to Chinese Week so that people will "be able to identify with each other."[42] For example, according to K. C. Tang and Paul Ong, Tang and Dong are actually the same Chinese surname, with different English spellings due to the differences in Chinese dialects. The Ong/Tang/Dong family is one of the "biggest clans" in Phoenix. The family and kinship system in Phoenix mobilizes people to participate in Chinese Week and therefore construct a "community." For instance, Paul Ong was encouraged to join the Chinese Week Committee by K. C. Tang and Lucy Yuen (chairperson of the Raffle Committee) in family gatherings such as funerals and banquets. Being actively involved in

Chinese Week now, Paul Ong hopes this kinship can also pull the younger generation back:

> Because the younger generation is so widespread, they do not know their relatives because we're all so spread out. And an event like Chinese Week could bring them all back together if they could attend one way or another. If they were to attend, they could gather together, renew friendships, and I could introduce them to other members of the family they did not even know existed![43]

What's more, Chinese Week also offers a chance to "see old friends."[44] As Lucy Yuen noted, Chinese American immigrants usually just see their relatives at family reunions, funerals, weddings, and birthday parties, while during Chinese Week, "it is something different. It's not just your relatives; you will see your friends and a lot of people in a festive gathering. You come across people you haven't seen for a long time." Chinese Week serves not simply as a site for friends gathering; the Chinese Week Committee keeps expanding through personal networking. For instance, during Chinese Week, Lucy met a woman who was interested in the photo exhibit at which Lucy was working. After talking about the Chinese and Chinatown in Phoenix for some time, that woman turned out to be Barbara Yim, whom Lucy had not seen since she was a little girl. Now Yim is the chair of the Chinese Week Photo Exhibit and the Chinese Week Scholarship Program.

In addition to these bonds and networks that occur during Chinese Week, community creation and maintenance are realized through reciprocity and coalition. Having membership that is associated with many ethnic organizations and providing support to one another, Chinese Week socializes and inculcates beliefs, values, and behaviors; establishes institutions, status, and authority relations; and symbolizes social cohesion or group membership.[45] As Lin Ling Lee observes:

> Because of the participation, we tend to attend more activities in Chinese community so as to expand our networking and improve the communication within the community and make the community better. The more you participate and involve in the community, the more organizations you know. The networking makes the reciprocal support and help possible and reinforces the community solidarity.[46]

Lin Ling notes that holding Chinese Week in the Chinese Cultural Center reflects the reciprocity of community. Like all the other organizers, she believes that while the "Chinese Cultural Center offers a matched background for Chinese Week" with the surrounding Chinese architecture, supermarket, stores, and restaurants, Chinese Week also attracts large numbers of potential customers each year to the businesses at the center. Similarly, the strong association between Chinese Week and local Chinese schools reflects the coalition of the Chinese community. Wen Chyi Chiu (daughter of Lin Ling and current Chinese Week president, who has been involved with Chinese Week since junior high school) comments on the interdependence of Chinese Week and local Chinese schools:

> We not only have the Chinese Culture Journey and School Outreach for our Chinese school, we do it also on behalf of Chinese Week. . . . Now we are representative of Chinese Week. . . . I can say that we actually unite Chinese Week and Chinese school together in some way. We borrow stuff from each other for the Chinese Week festival or for school outreach.[47]

As Alba suggests, ethnic social structures such as the Chinese Week festival and its organization harbor relationships where shared ethnicity becomes a salient element and where matters pertaining to ethnicity can be freely aired and discussed.[48] Therefore, while shared culture, family, kinship systems, and friendship emerged as the fundamental bonds that form community networks and create community solidarity, reciprocity and coalition mobilized by Chinese Week maintain the community.

However, community creation is not a simple process of accretion. For the young American-born Chinese, sporadic attendance at ethnic events constitutes the primary means by which ethnic identity is practiced. Yet lack of further involvement in the ethnic organizations or activities has led to repeated warnings by older Chinese that the group is doomed to extinction. As K. C. Tang noted, at an ethnic gathering, such as a banquet, "there are all senior citizens down there. The younger generations are so Americanized and they said they are always busy." Faced with a noticeable absence of young adults, older Chinese Americans hope to "encourage young kids to come out" as Chinese Week confronts the challenge "to attract more young people" who "join in the work end of it."[49] Therefore, the maintenance and development of Chinese community will be an ongoing task for Chinese Week.

Maintaining Chinese Culture

Chinese Week provides Chinese Americans with a stage for expressing their ethnic identity. Ethnic identity is most closely associated with the issue of boundaries. Chinese Week as the stage for community and identity reveals the negotiated nature of ethnic identity. The following sections focus on the cultural and political dimensions of ethnic identity and explore its dynamics as both a collective and personal identity.

"I just don't want to see Chinese culture fade away." Chinese Week provides Chinese Americans with a framework for reflecting upon their cultural and historical past. It gives meaning to an otherwise abstract assertion of ethnic

identity and breathes life into ethnicity as a social form.[50] Chinese Week allows
the Chinese to express their pride in being a part of Chinese culture and their
concerns of extinction of the culture. As Tony Tang remarks:

> Without any alternate motive, all Chinese Week members had one goal—
> to help to promote our great culture and tradition. We are from Mainland
> China, Taiwan, Hong Kong, U.S. . . . ; yet we share one common thread—
> we love our great heritage and would love to share that with our
> American friends.[51]

Tony came from Hong Kong. His comments underscore what emerged in
the interviews: a definite relationship between "being part of Chinese culture"
and involvement in Chinese Week. He noted, "The older you are, the more
attached to your own culture you will be, the more you think of your parents,
your family, and your culture." He believes that he is at the point that "I feel it is
so good to see that our culture be able to be showcased."[52]

Out of their love for Chinese culture, Chinese Week organizers are devoted
to the festival to "preserve and promote" that culture. Lin Ling Lee, from
Taiwan, expresses her appreciation of Chinese culture:

> In China everything around you is like that. You don't care about it, or get
> surprised by its glory; but in a foreign country, you will feel how valuable
> it is. It is very hard to get those ethnic costumes for the costume show in
> the event. Now you can wear them, in a foreign country! Some of them
> are really very beautiful.[53]

This echoes Lynn Pan: "Deep in their hearts they know that they love China best
when they live well away from the place."[54] As a corollary, Chang points out "the
overseas Chinese respect Chinese culture most when they are comfortably
removed from it."[55]

Anna Lee, from mainland China and past president of Chinese Week,
expresses her love of Chinese culture using artistic work:

> I was willing to do it. I was willing to spread out our Chinese culture. I want
> Americans to know that China has a lot of good things. Like my paintings
> for the Chinese Week Art Exhibition of this year, each of them belongs to
> a different style; I hope people can see the various styles of Chinese art.[56]

As Lin Ling noted, "Culture is the root; it represents our spirit." Chinese Week is
a reminder of the "root" and an occasion for the celebration of the "spirit."
Therefore, the commitment of constant involvement in the Chinese Week
Committee symbolizes a claim of ethnicity by itself.

The recent upward social and centrifugal geographic mobility of ethnics has
finally enabled Chinese Americans in Phoenix to enter the middle and upper

middle classes.[57] Dispersion and decentralization give other groups a chance to know Chinese people and accelerate the "Americanization" process of the Chinese. No matter whether it was to avoid racial conflict[58] or business competition,[59] or actually a result of the lack of interest in involvement in the Chinese community,[60] the Chinese in Phoenix spread out, and the Phoenix Chinatown disappeared. According to Paul Ong, who was born in mainland China and immigrated to the United States as an eighteen-month-old, "as the Chinatown went, so did our Chinese culture." He believes Chinese Week is "the closest thing that will keep the traditions and maintain and promote the culture." That is why he "enjoys working with it." Having lived in Phoenix for over fifty years, Paul regarded voluntary participation as a way to "give back to the community." Realizing the risk of the extinction of ethnic culture, he thinks "it is payback time."[61]

Similarly, their deep nostalgia for the past and their love for and pride in Chinese culture push Chinese Americans to perceive the duty to promote their culture:

> It is meaningful that we try to accomplish our responsibility to promote our culture. At the same time, I also participate in Asian Festival, representing Chinese culture which is part of Asian culture. We feel we have the duty to introduce what we know and experience with Chinese culture to the next generation and America society.[62]

Lin Ling and her entire family have been involved in Chinese Week for about thirteen years. Being the principal of a local Chinese school and chair of Chinese Week's Children's Pavilion, Lin Ling was deeply touched by the enthusiasm of the older American-born generation who may not be able to speak Chinese but devote a lot of energy, time, and money to the event to promote Chinese culture. She even fosters participation in Chinese Week in her Chinese school because she believes Chinese Week offers "a good opportunity to see, hear, and experience what Chinese culture is out of textbooks." She indicated that Chinese Week is the event that maintains and showcases the splendid Chinese culture.

Through the comparison with other events he has organized, Tony Tang also expressed the wish that Chinese culture be passed on to one generation after another in this new land:

> I have been the President of Kiwanis Festival for several years. . . . It is more community service-oriented. I feel nice to do good things, but I don't have the same strong feelings in those events as I do in Chinese Week. I have more personal interest in it: first, I would like MY culture to be recognized by the general public here; secondly, I am personally interested in it, because my kids live here. I hope they grow up with this culture imparted in their life and the rest of their life and keep this culture. I want to ensure this tradition is carried on.[63]

This sense of responsibility and desire to maintain culture is reflected in all interviews with Chinese Week organizers.

As Alba suggests, ethnic groups generally define their uniqueness in regard to other ethnic groups largely through the medium of culture.[64] In this case, Chinese Americans successfully maintain a distinctive sense of identity through Chinese Week as it presents some cultural elements seen as a positive heritage worth holding on to, even though ethnic culture need not represent an unchanging set of traditions. Our findings suggest that there is a strong emotional bond that ties Chinese Americans with Chinese Week, that is, the Chinese culture and heritage that they share. As Lee suggests, language, tradition, and festivals that immigrant groups participate in and celebrate, even though their contents may not be derived from the culture of origin, are nevertheless believed to be distinctively ethnic.[65] Chinese Week remains as a sign of ethnic identity when other traditions have faded.

Political dimension: Negotiating ethnic boundaries. In the process of creating cultural representations for the festival, another dimension of ethnicity is revealed. At one time, Chinese Week participants and organizers emphasized characteristics that differentiated the various Chinese immigrant groups from each other, emphasizing regional loyalties and identities.

The heterogeneity of Chinese Americans reflected by their national origins and political affiliations is revealed in Chinese Week. The conflicts between two competing governments (the People's Republic of China and the Republic of China—Taiwan) accentuated the Chinese community's inner political factions. Such tensions were often prominently reflected in Chinese Week. Faced with such tensions caused by homeland politics and international geopolitics, Chinese Week serves as a mechanism that removes people from the political arena, pulls them together, and transmits these differences into the production of the same ethnic festival to celebrate a common cultural tradition. At the same time, another tension resulting from different definitions of (regional) Chineseness and Americanness comes into play. We can see how these tensions become woven into Chinese Week and how ethnic boundaries are negotiated and the concept of ethnicity is redefined during the festival production process.

"By the time when the idea of celebrating Chinese New Year in Phoenix was brought out, Phoenix Sister Cities Commission was really with Taipei," Mai Young, one of the first organizers and past president, said about the origin of Chinese Week. She explained the embarrassing situation that was caused by the conflicts between foreign governments.

> We know each other and we were all friends in daily life. For a while, we invited both Taipei and Chengdu representatives to the Chinese Week banquet. You can see these two delegations walking towards each other, and when the two groups were about to meet, they turned around and headed in different directions.[66]

This case reflects the situated identities. Weinreich, Kelly, and Maja suggest that alternative states of identity might be engaged in by an individual cuing into different social contexts.[67] This explains the difference of behaviors of Taipei and Chengdu representatives in daily life and official settings. In the banquet, ideological and political identity is salient. Similarly, K. C. Tang, an American-born Chinese, also experienced the same kind of situation:

> The two sister cities, Taipei and Chengdu, used to co-host Chinese Week together with the Chinese Week Committee. We did that the first year, but we had a conflict there. I remember that when it was the mainland delegation's turn to speak, we had to grab the flag that Taipei people put up on trees and pull them down. It was embarrassing for me to climb up there and pull a flag down . . . so later we decided to alternate the two sister cities.

As a native-born person who is "looking at the Chinese community growing," K.C. notices that the differences and tensions caused by homeland politics exist in the Chinese American community in general. As he says, "Taiwanese congregate themselves . . . so do people from mainland."[68]

When it comes to social structures, the differences result in various voluntary organizations and associations with conspicuous ethnic labels yet differentiating the various Chinese groups from each other. Tony Tang's insight reflects this reality:

> We have different kinds of organizations. You can feel there is a line somewhere that most people don't want to step across between mainland China, Taiwan, Hong Kong, local ABC [American-born Chinese]. You can see that line at ASU [Arizona State University]: there is a Chinese Student Association for mainland China, there is one for Taiwan. Like the women's club here: if you are born in mainland China, Taiwan, or Hong Kong, you join in Oversea Chinese women organization, but if you are born in places other than China, you go to Desert Jade Woman's Club.[69]

Similarly, according to other organizers, the Chinese identify the Phoenix Chinese United Association as being primarily composed by later-generation native-born Chinese. Mai Young expresses her opinion from a personal stance:

> Some people from China and Taiwan don't get very well along with the Chinese United Association which is run by older generation. They just have different ideas, and even people from China and those from Taiwan are different. We can tell the difference, because we know both.[70]

These comments reveal the diversity of the Chinese population in Phoenix. Except for the regional and/or political distinctions, there is a distance between later-generation native-born Chinese and new immigrants. Differences in language, place of origin, and economic activity often further determine status and class in the Chinese American community and add another social distinction to the mix.

Tensions continue in discussions of what becoming and being American mean. For K. C. Tang, being American is a source of freedom from repression:

> I go to the meetings. They speak Mandarin that I don't understand. Well, we are in America, and we should learn to be Americans. We are not back in China or Taiwan. That's why we move to America. You won't learn if you stick to your own group all the time. There is a friction between China and Taiwan, but we are in America, it's different. We are here to get away from the suppression. They need to take advantage of it.[71]

Tensions and conflicts similar to those within the Phoenix Chinese population are seen in other cities as well. In his study of two Chinese associations in Philadelphia that are respectively composed of first generation and second generation Chinese, Lee points out that the rivalry between the two associations is not confined to the organizational level. It is derived from a more fundamental difference: "a contrasting definition of Chinese Americanness, a different set of assumptions, attitudes and behaviors, or a different 'culture.' "[72]

The tensions of being mainland Chinese or Taiwanese and being old/new immigrants and being Americans often prominently exhibit themselves in the Chinese Week festival. An ongoing question is: "Do distinctive regional identities that were not significant in the homeland have to be highlighted or recreated before the new Chinese American identity can emerge?" Chinese Week has been the stage where this question is presented and negotiated.

Chinese Week has been striving for an "apolitical" presentation of ethnic heritage and attempting to resolve the differences among Chinese originating from different regions. The above flag-pulling scenario K.C. described reflects the ways in which symbols are manipulated by Chinese Week as an ethnic collectivity to achieve the "apolitical" qualifier and promote the shared heritage and redefined concepts of ethnicity. Now Chinese Week "put up no flag but American flag or Arizona flag," said Margie Gin, a native-born Chinese. "After all, we are people from different places sharing the same Chinese heritage."[73] This is what Chinese Week demonstrates and expresses to the audience—their Chinese American identity.

Manifestation of ethnic identity. In addition to the "apolitical" cultural performance in the festival, the Chinese Week Committee as an ethnic organization tries to cut across the line generated from class and national origin differences. As Tony Yang indicates:

> Chinese Week offers an excuse to pull us together . . . Chinese Week doesn't have that [line], we blend them all together. It is among very few

organizations which successfully do that. I think one of the reasons that help is that everyone likes Chinese New Year, no matter where you come from and what backgrounds you have, it makes no different. This is one organization that crosses the borders now.[74]

Producing an ethnic festival that "everyone likes" mobilizes people and local Chinese organizations and transmits the differences into the festival production. But the ethnic festival is not a mere moment of fun and celebration. As Lin Ling Lee notes, what draws local organizations together is the common wish to promote Chinese culture:

> The goal and policy of our Chinese school is to provide the next generation a chance to learn Chinese and know Chinese culture, it resembles the goal of Chinese Week. So we think it will be really nice if we can expand our student population to the general public instead of limiting to those students coming to our school. Since our goal and interest are the same with those of Chinese Week, Chinese school started participating in this event actively.[75]

Lin Ling shared how local Chinese schools gradually become involved in Chinese Week and its organization. Similarly, other local ethnic organizations such as the Phoenix Chinese United Association, Desert Jade Women's Club, and Arizona State University Chinese Student Association are frequently associated and have overlapping membership with Chinese Week. They work together in groups that cut across regional, class, and ideological lines. As Lin Ling says, "Chinese Week Committee is like a big family."[76] Not only is it a big family that is associated with other local organizations and in some way functions to organize the Chinese community's social network, it also mobilizes individuals with the common interest to produce the festival.

In absence of a Chinatown in a multicultural metropolis, Chinese identity is maintained in the Chinese Week Committee, where people who identify with a group can come together, inter alia, to socialize with fellow ethnics, to discuss matters of common concern, and to introduce the next generation to an ethnic social circle and to ethnic ways. K. C. Tang believes that "Chinese Week is a place where they can get together and get to know how nice it is to know each other. So it is definitely a place where we can communicate and gather together."[77] Similarly, Tony Tang states that his favorite part of the committee is to be able to work with people toward a common interest, despite differing national origins:

> A lot of things mean to an end. Chinese Week is all year around process. By doing Chinese Week, you get to know people, people involved in the process, you respect how dedicated people are, like Johnny and Mai. I have difficult time to get these people not to work than get them to work. So I think that is what I enjoy: working with people side by side, dedicated people having a very un-selfish motive to put our culture in front of public.[78]

Tony is proud to share that the Chinese Week Committee has a very diversified membership. For instance, as far as place of origin is concerned, in addition to the U.S.-born, it has members who emigrated from mainland China, Taiwan, Hong Kong, the Philippines, and the United Kingdom at different periods of time.

As Nagel suggests, cultural construction is especially important for groups that are composed of subgroups with histories of conflict and animosity.[79] Faced with tensions and conflicts within the group, Chinese Week and its committee forge their own culture and redefine ethnic boundaries through the production of the festival and construction of culture. During the ethnic boundaries negotiation process, ethnicity is maintained, modified, and invented. When Chinese culture is brought "to the forefront" vis-à-vis the general public, Chinese Week has shown the potential to continue to successfully involve a broad cross section of Chinese Americans in the process of working together as a community to present themselves to the larger society as a unified whole of distinct parts.

The presence or absence of a Chinese neighborhood in which a person grows up also influences the identity formation process. Paul Ong believes that absence of a Chinatown with explicitly ethnic features is partially responsible for his ignorance of his own ethnic culture:

> In Chinese Week, I feel proud to be able to explain to them what I do know about my own tradition. In my own mind I ask myself, "do I really know that much?" To be truthful, I really don't know that much. Growing up here in Phoenix . . . without a Chinatown which is a central location where we can all get together, I don't know a whole lot about my own heritage where I came from.[80]

Paul gets excited when recalling the old Phoenix Chinatown where the US Airways Center is now located:

> It is neat to remember what the Chinatown used to be and say, "Yes! My dad's store was right there! That was used to be so and so's restaurant or grocery store. . . ." Actually we still own and rent out the old house that is four blocks away from the old Chinatown. It's still there. When I go down to check those house, just driving down that street, I can just picture the old Chinatown and picture where my dad's store was, picture how old men sitting down having nothing else to do just drinking tea. That's how I remember the old Chinatown is.[81]

Although in Lucy Yuen's memory the old Phoenix Chinatown was "a series of little shops that were built around the square there selling Chinese stuff," it housed the small businesses that catered to special ethnic needs and served as sites for ethnic festivals.[82] As Paul Ong remembers, "during Chinese New Year, we used to have traditional lion dances marching down the streets of the

Phoenix Chinatown, with firecrackers." As time went on, "because the downtown Phoenix business area was growing, most of the buildings were torn down to make room for parking lot." Paul explains why he thinks there is no longer a Chinatown:

> The younger generation is not interested or don't want to get involved. . . . Traditionally, they are not really knowledgeable about Chinese culture, how Chinatown used to be in Phoenix, or how Chinatown in Los Angles or San Francisco is like. Our fathers were in business; today's generation isn't any more because of the long hours. They run off to work for somebody else; they have very nice eight-to-five jobs, clean professions. I think that's a lot to do with why we don't have a Chinatown as it was fifty years ago.[83]

Recent upward social and centrifugal geographic mobility of the later generation has finally enabled them to enter the middle and upper middle classes. Yet a lack of interest and involvement in ethnic culture and traditional family business also resulted in the extinction of the Phoenix Chinatown. Having his childhood memory in the old Chinatown, Paul laments, "Once a lot of them have been lost, and it's very difficult to get back":

> As the Chinatown went, so did our Chinese culture. Phoenix Chinese population is spread out. The only chances we can get together are banquet, funeral, birthday and wedding. So the only time we get to see each other than, say, Chinese Week seldom we can get back together. So basically Phoenix Chinese just spread out and don't get together as an ethnic groups any more.

He thinks there will never be a Chinatown again:

> The closest thing we'll have is the Chinese Cultural Center here and the biggest event, theoretically, the Chinese Week celebration during New Years. Other than that, the family associations, like Ong Family Association and Wang Family Association, get together every year. But they are just limited to the family, although members out of the family are invited. But I don't think we will get together as a whole Chinatown again to visit and say we have Chinese herb shops, Chinese merchants or all kinds. So I don't think we will have an area designated as Chinatown again in Phoenix, not in my lifetime.[84]

In the meantime, other U.S.-born organizers go some way toward recognizing the bright side of living out of Chinatown and "being spread-out." Lucy Yuen believes that growing up in a Mexican neighborhood gave her a chance to be

exposed to and learn to appreciate other ethnic cultures. Similarly, K. C. Tang
believes that the absence of Chinatown is a good thing for communication:

> But we all moved out in community. It's good for us. There is hardly prej-
> udice for us. We moved to Glendale. We went to schools with Mexican,
> Russian, and Japanese. We got along well. I don't think we have the prej-
> udice like those in San Francisco or New York. I think it's good to spread
> out in Phoenix. We have no Chinatown, and we have business all over
> Phoenix so that we are able to communicate with Caucasian and Mexican
> people. They got to know us.[85]

Lucy's and K.C.'s perspectives reflect that ethnic social and territorial boundaries sometimes have to be broken down and/or more permeable in order to
foster interethnic understanding and interactions.

Although residence in areas of ethnic concentration is independent of ethnic identity, the ethnic neighborhood as a physical setting and ethnic social
structure enhances some ethnic traits due to its capacity to concentrate the
institutions and cultures of an ethnic group, thereby keeping alive the sentiments and loyalties associated with ethnicity in adult residents and socializing
a new generation to ethnic ways.[86] As indicated by Chinese Week organizers, the
absence of a Chinatown in Phoenix represents a loss of embodiment of
ethnicity that contributes to the assimilation process of local Chinese American
immigrants.

In summary, ethnicity loses the foundation for an elaboration of common
expressions of ethnicity when family and ethnic neighborhoods no longer function as perpetuators of ethnicity. In contrast to the self-defined Chinese ethnicity, U.S.-born Chinese members in Chinese Week are experiencing the
inevitable and unidirectional "Americanization" process, where "symbolic ethnicity" persists in the face of apparent assimilation, and sometimes external
ascription is no longer consistent with internal identification. Therefore, in the
Chinese Week Committee, the U.S.-born Chinese or those who came to the
United States in their early childhood claim that "I am Chinese" while simultaneously searching for and inventing their own ideas of what being Chinese
means while also being American.

Conclusion

On Sunday afternoon when Chinese Week was about over, the crowds resumed
their visiting, playing, and tasting until the booths were taken down and the
streets reopened. The Chinese Cultural Center returned to its everyday routine.
Chinese Week ends, but the sense and reality of the Phoenix Chinese community persist. Chinese Week effectively unifies diverse Chinese American groups

and provides them with an arena for creating a synthetic Chinese American identity.

Chinese Week stages a cultural performance of identity that is strengthened, altered, shaped, and reshaped among diverse groups of immigrants and allows them to represent themselves to the larger society. Chinese Week reveals the multidimensional and negotiated nature of ethnic identity, which is cultural and political, collective and individual. On the one hand, Chinese Week provides a purpose and an arena for diverse groups to interact with each other, to reflect on their experiences, to celebrate the same Chinese New Year, and to represent themselves in a public performance as they would not otherwise have done. Vis-à-vis a larger audience, Chinese Week encourages immigrants from different places and backgrounds to work together in groups that cut across regional, class, and ideological "borders."[87] On the other hand, Chinese Week provides Chinese Americans as individuals with a framework for reflecting upon their ethnic identity.

The process of the formation of general ethnic renewal that Nagel explores provides a description of how personal identity and collective identity are created at Chinese Week.[88] However, the case of Chinese Americans is a bit more complicated. In the formation of personal identity as well as collective identity, tensions and conflicts caused by definition of "Chineseness" (including different regional Chineseness) and "Americanness" arise, and ethnic boundaries are negotiated, modified, and redefined. Hence, using Nagel's notion of "ethnic renewal," a new ethnic identity is defined. It is a Chinese American identity.

In her theoretical explorations based on a Chinese American novel, *Bone*, Chin proposes that a "dual personality" in which "Chinese" elements battle against "American" elements can be rejected.[89] Instead of being a stereotypical "model minority" who can overcome all obstacles or achieve the ultimate goal of becoming an American according to the assimilationist paradigm, Chin argues that the end goal in *Bone* is to become a certain kind of acceptable Chinese American.[90] Extending her argument, the festival can provide a stage on which Chinese Americans can perform, produce, and reinvent ways of being Chinese in America. In other words, Chinese Americans can show their self-image and tell their own stories at ethnic festivals in which characters are not torn between Chinese and American. For instance, Yeh notices the "model minority" stereotypes and "authentic" Chinese culture that festival organizers sought to create at the San Francisco Chinatown New Year Festival.[91] Yeh further indicates that, conforming to middle-class American expectations and values to promote tourism, the festival leaders' monolithic inclusion of "model minority" stereotypes and the neglect of social problems of San Francisco Chinatown finally resulted in resistance from the Chinese Americans themselves and hate crimes.[92] The San Francisco Chinese New Year Festival sends out a warning with extreme cases to other ethnic festivals, including Phoenix Chinese Week.

Therefore, Chin's theoretical notion of "being Chinese in America" and Yeh's empirical research of the San Francisco Chinese New Year Festival, along with our study of Phoenix Chinese Week itself, can provide some ideological implications for Phoenix Chinese Week organizers.[93]

As time moves on, another year of preparation for Chinese Week has drawn to an end. While showcasing their understandings of a culture "five thousand years old" to the public, Chinese Americans have redefined and continue to redefine their own identities while uniting and transforming their community through festivity.

NOTES

We dedicate this chapter to the late Paul Ong and Johnny Young, two devoted Chinese Week organizers with whom we worked closely and whom we interviewed. Their legacy will continue to enrich all our lives, and they are truly missed. The research project is partially funded by the Initiative Grant, Office of Vice Provost for Research; and Dean's Incentive Grant, College of Public Programs, Arizona State University (MRR N029).

1. Hereafter, "Phoenix Chinese Week" and "Chinese Week" will be used interchangeably.

2. S. Bush, *Arizona's Gold Mountain: Oral Histories of Chinese Americans in Phoenix* (Tempe: Arizona State University, 2000); M. Keane, A. E. Rogge, and B. Luckingham, *The Chinese in Arizona 1870–1950* (Phoenix: Arizona State Historic Preservation Office, 1992); Bradford Luckingham, *Minorities in Phoenix: A Profile of Mexican American, Chinese American, and African American Communities, 1860–1992* (Tucson: University of Arizona Press, 1994).

3. The debate around this building and the overall issue of downtown renovation at the expense of ethnic minorities' historical legacies and physical landscapes is beyond the scope of this chapter. Interested parties may read newspaper reports, such as "Builder Remarks Sting Asian Community," *Arizona Republic*, December 23, 2005; "Pressure Is Building on Phoenix Warehouse," *Los Angeles Times*, November 30, 2005, http://www.latimes.com/news/nationworld/nation/la-naphoenix30nov30,0,4115301.story?coll=la-home-nation; "Chinatown Phoenix: Saving the SunMerc Building," *Asia Week*, November 18, 2005, http://news.asianweek.com/news/view_article.html?article_id=639cd2d25357b2c6c4e1b282cfc4d5db&this_category_id=172; "Remnant of Phoenix's Chinatown to Be Incorporated in Development," *Asian-American Village Daily News*, October 31, 2005, http://www.imdiversity.com/Villages/Asian/Daily_News_Oct31.asp; "Sun Mercantile Building Is Part of Phoenix's Asian Heritage," *Arizona Republic*, October 28, 2005, http://www.azcentral.com/arizonarepublic/centralphoenix/articles/1028exwong1028.html; "Hotel Extension Would Set Bad Precedent for Historic Preservation," *Arizona Republic*, October 27, 2005, http://www.azcentral.com/arizonarepublic/phoenixopinions/articles/1105weiss04.html; "High-rise Plan Stirs Fear of Losing History," *Arizona Republic*, October 24, 2005, http://www.azcentral.com/sports/suns/articles/1024sarver24.html; "Surveying History after It's Demolished," *Arizona Republic*, October 15, 2005, http://www.azcentral.com/arizonarepublic/opinions/articles/1015quickhit-phoenix.html.

4. Tom R. Rex and Katrian S. Walls, *Employment in Metropolitan Phoenix* (Tempe, Az.: Morrison Institute of Public Policy, 2000).

5. Audrey Singer, *The Rise of New Immigrant Gateways* (Washington, D.C.: Brookings Institute, 2004).

6. Wei Li and Emily Skop, "Enclaves, Ethnoburbs, and New Patterns of Settlement among Asian Immigrants," in *Contemporary Asian America: A Multi-Disciplinary Reader*, 2nd ed., ed. Min Zhou and John Gatewood, 222–236 (New York: New York University Press, 2007); Emily Skop and Wei Li, "Immigrants in America's Suburbs: New Patterns of Settlement," *Geographic Review* (forthcoming).

7. This number is based on one-race data. The total number of Chinese Americans, including those who are multiracial Chinese, was 18,976 in 2000. Data source: 2000 U.S. census http://factfinder.census.gov/servlet/DTTable?_bm=y&-context=dt&-reg= DEC_2000_SF2_U_PCT001:001|016|035&-ds_name=DEC_2000_SF2_U&-CONTEXT= dt&-mt_name=DEC_2000_SF2_U_PCT001&-tree_id=402&-all_geo_types= N&-geo_id=05000US04013&-search_results=01000US&-format=&-_lang=en, accessed December 29, 2005.

8. P. Kwong, *The New Chinatown*, rev. ed. (New York: Hill and Wang, 1996).

9. Wei Li, "Anatomy of a New Ethnic Settlement: The Chinese *Ethnoburb* in Los Angeles," *Urban Studies* 35, no. 3 (1998): 479–501.

10. Kathleen Wong (Lau), "The Asian American Community in the Southwest: Creating 'Place' in the Absence of Ethnic 'Space,'" in *Asian Pacific Americans and the U.S. Southwest*, ed. T. K. Nakayama and C. F. Yoshioka, 79–90 (Tempe: Arizona State University, 1997).

11. Huping Ling, *Chinese St. Louis: From Enclave to Cultural Community* (Philadelphia: Temple University Press, 2005).

12. Emily Skop and Wei Li, "From the Ghetto to the Invisiburb: Shifting Patterns of Immigrant Settlement in Contemporary America," in *Multi-Cultural Geographies: Persistence and Change in U.S. Racial/Ethnic Geography*, ed. John W. Frazier and Florence L. Margai, 113–124 (Binghamton, N.Y.: Global Academic, 2003).

13. Wilbur Zelinsky and Barrett A. Lee, "Heterolocalism: An Alternative Model of the Sociospatial Behavior of Immigrant Ethnic Communities," *International Journal of Population. Geography* 4 (1998): 1–18; Wilbur Zelinsky, *The Enigma of Ethnicity: Another American Dilemma* (Iowa City: University of Iowa Press, 2001).

14. L. Kurashige, "Made in Little Tokyo: Politics of Ethnic Identity and Festival in Southern California, 1934–1994" (Ph.D. diss., University of Wisconsin–Madison, 1994), 12.

15. J. H. Gramann and Maria T. Allison, "Ethnicity, Race, and Leisure," in *Leisure Studies: Prospects for the Twenty-first Century*, ed. E. Jackson and T. Burton, 283–297 (State College, Pa.: Venture, 1999).

16. U.S. Bureau of the Census, "The Foreign-Born Population: 2000," in *Census 2000 Brief* (Washington, D.C.: Government Printing Office, 2003).

17. See, for example, M. T. Allison and C. W. Geiger, "Nature of Leisure Activities among the Chinese-American Elderly," *Leisure Studies* 15 (1993): 309–319; P. Yu and D. L. Berryman, "The Relationship among Self-esteem, Acculturation, and Recreation Participation of Recently Arrived Chinese Immigrant Adolescents," *Journal of Leisure Research* 28 (1996): 251–273.

18. See, for example, M. F. Floyd, "Race, Ethnicity and Use of the National Park System," *Social Science Research Review* 1 (1999): 1–24; Gramann and Allison, "Ethnicity, Race, and Leisure."

19. S. L. Shaull and J. H. Gramann, "The Effect of Cultural Assimilation on the Importance of Family-Related and Nature-Related Recreation among Hispanic Americans," *Journal of Leisure Research* 30 (1998): 47–63.

20. J. Nagel, *American Indian Ethnic Renewal: Red Power and the Resurgence of Identity and Culture* (New York: Oxford University Press, 1996).

21. C. L. Yeh, "Contesting Identities: Youth Rebellion in San Francisco's Chinese New Year Festivals, 1953–1969," in *The Chinese in America: A History from Gold Mountain to the New Millennium*, ed. Susie Lan Cassel, 329–350 (Walnut Creek, Calif.: AltaMira Press, 2001).

22. Nagel, *American Indian Ethnic Renewal*.

23. Ibid.

24. Emile Durkheim, *The Elementary Forms of the Religious Life* (New York: Free Press, 1915).

25. M. W. Cunha, "Festivals and the Social Rhythm Considered in the Light of Functionalist Theories" (master's thesis, University of Chicago, 1943).

26. V. Turner, *Dramas, Fields, and Metaphor* (Ithaca, N.Y.: Cornell University Press, 1974), 169.

27. A. P. Cohen, *The Symbolic Construction of Community* (New York: Tavistock, 1985); E. Hobsbawm, "Introduction: Inventing Traditions," in *The Invention of Tradition*, ed. E. Hobsbawm and T. Ranger, 1–14 (Cambridge: Cambridge University Press, 1983); D. Noyes, "Group," *Journal of American Folklore* 108 (1995): 449–478.

28. M. Ashkenazi, *Matsuri: Festivals of a Japanese Town* (Honolulu: University of Hawaii Press, 1993); O. Cadaval, *Creating a Latino Identity in the Nation's Capital: The Latino Festival* (New York: Garland, 1998); C. Farber, "High, Healthy and Happy: Ontario Mythology on Parade," in *The Celebration of Society: Perspectives on Contemporary Cultural Performances*, ed. F. Manning, 33–50 (Bowling Green, Ohio: Bowling Green University Popular Press, 1983); R. Grimes, *Symbol and Conquest: Public Ritual and Drama in Santa Fe, New Mexico* (Ithaca, N.Y.: Cornell University Press, 1976); R. H. Lavenda, "Family and Corporation: Two Styles of Celebration in Central Minnesota," in Manning, *Celebration of Society*, 51–64; M. Singer, "On the Symbolic and Historic Structure of an American Identity," *Ethos* 5 (1977): 431–454; W. L. Warner, *The Living and the Dead: A Study of the Symbolic Life of the Americans* (New Haven, Conn.: Yale University Press, 1959).

29. Farber, "High, Healthy and Happy."

30. Robert A. Orsi, *The Madonna of 115th Street: Faith and Community in Italian Harlem, 1880–1950* (New Haven, Conn.: Yale University Press, 1985).

31. Cadaval, *Creating a Latino Identity*; A. Kaeppler, "Pacific Festivals and Ethnic Identity," in *Time Out of Time: Essays on the Festival*, ed. A. Falassi, 162–170 (Albuquerque: University of New Mexico Press, 1987); Kurashige, "Made in Little Tokyo;" L. Kurashige, *Japanese American Celebration and Conflict: A History of Ethnic Identity and Festival, 1934–1990* (Berkeley: University of California Press, 2002); R. Swiderski, *Voices: An Anthropologist's Dialogue with an Italian-American Festival* (Bowling Green, Ohio: Bowling Green State University Popular Press, 1987); Yeh, "Contesting Identities."

32. Kurashige, "Made in Little Tokyo," v.

33. Yeh, "Contesting Identities;" Kurashige, "Made in Little Tokyo," 12.

34. Kaeppler, "Pacific Festivals;" S. McBeth, "Layered Identity Systems in Western Oklahoma Indian Communities" (paper presented at the annual meeting of the American Anthropological Association, 1989).

35. Yeh, "Contesting Identities."

36. J. C. Scott, *Weapons of the Weak: Everyday Forms of Peasant Resistance* (New Haven, Conn.: Yale University Press, 1985).

37. The name "COFCO Chinese Cultural Center" is derived from the China National Cereals, Oils and Foodstuff Import and Export Corporation, the company that founded the center. A business center built in 1997 in southeastern metropolitan Phoenix, the Chinese Cultural Center contains a Chinese shopping center, executive suites, and retail and other specialty stores, which are surrounded by elaborate Chinese architectural flourishes. A traditional two-acre Chinese garden envelops the center in classic

Jiangsu-Zhejiang provincial style, with attractions such as pavilions and a pond replete with water lilies and fish. It is a small commercialized "Chinatown" in the Greater Phoenix area.

38. Cohen, *Symbolic Construction of Community.*
39. Tony Tang, interview by Wei Zeng, January 31, 2004, Phoenix.
40. K. C. Tang, interview by Wei Zeng, March 1, 2004, Phoenix.
41. Lin Ling Lee, interview by Wei Zeng, March 3, 2004, Phoenix.
42. Paul Ong, interview by Wei Zeng, February 26, 2004, Phoenix.
43. Ibid.
44. Lucy Yuen, interview by Wei Zeng, March 3, 2004, Phoenix.
45. Hobsbawm, "Introduction."
46. Lin Ling Lee, interview.
47. Wen Chyi Chiu, interview by Wei Zeng, March 3, 2004, Phoenix.
48. R. D. Alba, *Ethnic Identity: The Transformation of White America* (New Haven, Conn.: Yale University Press, 1990).
49. Yuen, interview.
50. Alba, *Ethnic Identity.*
51. Tony Tang, interview.
52. Ibid.
53. Lin Ling Lee, interview.
54. Lynn Pan, *Sons of the Yellow Emperor: A History of the Chinese Diaspora* (New York: Kodansha Globe, 1994), 379.
55. G. H. Chang, "Writing the History of Chinese Immigrants to America," *South Atlantic Quarterly* 98 (1999): 135–142.
56. Anna Lee, interview by Wei Zeng, February 25, 2004, Phoenix.
57. Luckingham, *Minorities in Phoenix.*
58. R. Nagasawa, *The Elderly Chinese: A Forgotten Minority* (Tempe: Arizona State University, 1980).
59. Yuen, interview.
60. Ong, interview.
61. Ibid.
62. Lin Ling Lee, interview.
63. Tony Tang, interview.
64. Alba, *Ethnic Identity.*
65. J. H. Lee, *Dynamics of Ethnic Identity: Three Asian American Communities in Philadelphia* (New York: Garland, 1998).
66. Mai Young, interview by Wei Zeng, January 18, 2004, Phoenix.
67. P. Weinreich, A. J. D. Kelly, and C. Maja, "Black Youth in South Africa: Situated Identities and Patterns of Ethnic Identification," in *Environmental Social Psychology*, ed. D. Canter, C. Jesuino, L. Soczka, and G. Stephenson, 231–245 (Dordrecht: Kluwer Academic, 1988).
68. K. C. Tang, interview.
69. Tony Tang, interview.
70. Young, interview.
71. K. C. Tang, interview.
72. Lee, *Dynamics of Ethnic Identity*, 141.
73. Margie Gin, interview by Wei Zeng, February 23, 2004, Phoenix.
74. Tony Tang, interview.
75. Lin Ling Lee, interview.

76. Ibid.

77. K. C. Tang, interview.

78. Tony Tang, interview.

79. Nagel, *American Indian Ethnic Renewal.*

80. Ong, interview.

81. Ibid.

82. Yuen, interview.

83. Ong, interview.

84. Ibid.

85. K. C. Tang, interview.

86. Alba, *Ethnic Identity*; Raymond Breton, "Institutional Completeness of Ethnic Communities and the Personal Relations of Immigrants," *American Journal of Sociology* 70 (1964): 193–205.

87. Tony Tang, interview.

88. Nagel, *American Indian Ethnic Renewal.*

89. V. F. Chin, "Finding the Right Gesture: Becoming Chinese American in Fae Myenne Ng's *Bone*," in Cassel, *Chinese in America*, 365–377.

90. Ibid.

91. Yeh, "Contesting Identities."

92. Ibid., 341.

93. Chin, "Finding the Right Gesture;" Yeh, "Contesting Identities."

8

Virtual Community and the Cultural Imaginary of Chinese Americans

YUAN SHU

With the advancement of information technology and the increase of users across different strata in American culture and society, the Internet has become increasingly important in our understanding and articulation of the changing senses of identity and community. According to the seventh-year study of the Internet released by the University of Southern California (USC) Annenberg School Center for the Digital Future in January 2008, "the Digital Future Project found that membership in online communities has more than doubled in only three years."[1] As the majority of Americans have gone online by 2008, this study further reports that the Internet has ranked above all other media as the most important source of information among experienced users and that three-quarters of online community members use the Internet to participate in community related to social causes. Indeed, in noting the expansion of the Internet across North America and around the world, the United States Internet Council, in its final edition of "The State of the Internet Report" announced that the online population had crossed the half a billion milestone globally and that online demographics have finally begun to reflect offline realities.[2] What is most interesting about this report, however, is its declaration that English speakers have now for the first time lost their dominance in the online world, and represent approximately 45 percent of the total online population. Though the United States, the European Union, and Japan still lead the Internet in terms of technology and language content today, the council further observes, "several other nations such as China, India, and South Korea [have begun] to play larger roles."[3] The latest development of the Internet and the emergence of the three Asian nations as new major players in the information technology industry have important political and cultural implications. To begin with, as the Internet continues to facilitate the free flow of information across regional and national boundaries, these three Asian national governments have promoted the technology as a means to integrate their national economies into the global one and bridge the gap between their countries and the more advanced ones such as the United States, even though it means that they have to wrestle with issues of authority, jurisdiction, and law enforcement in their traditionally defined nation-states. As a result of their efforts, the Internet and their native-language contents on the Internet have now flourished in these nation-states.[4] Moreover, with the Internet continuing to grow at a phenomenal pace, Internet architecture has now expanded to accommodate new multilingual domain names as well as to develop new multicultural Top-Level Domains. What all these changes mean culturally and technologically is that the Internet has finally experienced transformation from an initial English-language-oriented and U.S.-centered environment to the present multipolar, multilingual, and multicultural one, the meaning of which remains to be determined and interpreted by scholars of technology and cultural studies.

At this moment of change that has redefined the function and content of the Internet, how should we reconsider the generalization and speculation made on the Internet and virtual communities that have usually privileged U.S. Internet users as well as have been based primarily on English-language content? How should we assess the role that multilingual content on the Internet has played in prompting new social interactions and cultivating new cultural spaces? In this essay, I examine specifically the function that the Internet and Web-based Chinese-language networks have performed in informing and reshaping Chinese professionals and their transnational communities in the U.S. context. By the phrase "Chinese professionals," I refer specifically to the growing number of professionals originally from mainland China who either come to study and do research in the United States as students or scholars but wind up working in U.S. industries and academic institutions and traveling back and forth between North America and East and Southeast Asia, or are directly recruited by U.S. transnational corporations from mainland China because of their background in the information technology industry and their potential capability to open up the supposedly huge Chinese markets for these corporations and businesses. I use the term "transnational communities" to call attention to the emergence of Chinese professionals as a group in the United States whose legal statuses as naturalized citizens, permanent residents, and H-1B workers, and whose professional interests in both East Asia and North America, have frequently prevented them from fully participating in American public life. Though these professionals cannot articulate their interests and concerns within the parameters of the traditional Asian American identity politics based on the civil rights movements of the 1960s, they have nevertheless been perceived by the general American public as foreigners and Asian Americans interchangeably, or both, and have to travel back and forth between East Asia and North America. On the one hand, unlike the traditional working-class immigrants from southern China in the early twentieth century, whose life and work revolved around the geopolitical space of Chinatown in the United States, these Chinese professionals usually hold advanced academic degrees in hard science and technology, speak functional English, and travel extensively worldwide for professional and business reasons. On the other hand, like the early traditional immigrants in Chinatown in many ways—even though the ethnic enclave itself has recently undergone significant changes and directly attracted transnational capital from Hong Kong, Taiwan, and mainland China[5]—these Chinese professionals remain politically invisible and culturally irrelevant in the dominant American culture and society. The only moment that they make national headlines is when the few Chinese prodemocracy activists testify in congressional hearings as victims of Communist China and side, ironically, with the most conservative right-wing politicians in the United States. Recently, they have garnered more attention from the media because they have been singled out by the same batch of right-wing politicians as potential Chinese Communist spies who may someday steal high-tech secrets from U.S. military industries and research institutions and create a potential problem for U.S. national security. In foregrounding such political liability and cultural indifference that these Chinese professionals have been subjected to in American culture and society, I argue that the Internet and the Web-based Chinese-language networks have not only served as a medium of communication for the transnational professionals to negotiate their political power and cultural spaces in the United States, but they have also cultivated and performed a sense of "Chineseness," a cultural imaginary that allows these professionals to achieve what cultural anthropologist Aihwa Ong, in her work *Flexible Citizenship*,[6] describes as "flexibility" across national boundaries and "visibility" within a global context.

The Emergence of Virtual Communities:
Information Technology and Chinese-Language Networks

In the report "Chinese Language Internet Users," released in January 2001, Global Reach, a U.S.-based marketing communications consultancy, noted that the highest concentration of Chinese speakers outside of China was in the United States.[7] While there were only 1.3 million Chinese speakers living in the United States in 1990, the report noted that the number had reached 2.2 million in 2000, with a majority not only owning personal computers but also having Internet access. Indeed, as stated in a similar survey that was conducted by NUA Internet Surveys in February 2001, "almost all Chinese-Americans in the U.S. and [Chinese Canadians in] Canada own a PC and about 60 percent have Internet access." Among these Chinese Americans and Chinese Canadians, the survey concluded that most of them "regularly visit Chinese-language sites—73 percent in the U.S. and 63 percent in Canada."[8]

Though these sources never explain explicitly their research methodology or their definition of "Chinese Americans," their statistics do provide us with a snapshot of Chinese-language Internet users in the United States, which is to say that there are a large number of Chinese speakers in the United States who are comfortable with information technology as well as interested in Chinese-language content. Who are these Chinese-language Internet users, and why do they read Chinese-language content if they are working and living in the United States? Simply put, what kind of information and services do these Chinese speakers usually expect to get from Chinese-language Web sites? As the other side of the same coin, who are these providers of Chinese-language services in the United States? What are their objectives in providing such services? Which Chinese speaker groups do they target?

In responding to these questions, I examine closely two of the most frequently visited Chinese-language Web sites among Chinese professionals in the United States in two different periods: Chinese News Digest (CND) and Chinese Media Net (*duowei*).[9] While the former network represents an early effort of Chinese students and scholars in the United States who took advantage of information technology and provided Chinese-language services to their communities in the early 1990s, the latter indicates the changing nature of such services, which have become more commercial and business oriented in the wake of the booming economy in China since the late 1990s. I concentrate on the roles that these two Web-based Chinese-language networks have played in informing and reshaping Chinese professionals and their transnational communities in the United States at different historic junctures.

According to the essay "The Making of 'China News Digest,'"[10] collaboratively written by the network's staffers and published in a special issue celebrating the tenth anniversary of the network, CND was first established by a group of Chinese students and scholars in the United States and Canada as a nonprofit organization on March 6, 1989, in direct response to the political crisis intensifying in China at the time, which would lead to the Tiananmen Square massacre on June 4. It started as an English-language service that aimed to search for news items related to China on what has been known as Usenet and to deliver them to Chinese students and scholars on campuses across the United States and Canada. In its first month of service, the network had 400 direct subscribers, most of them based in Canada. In September 1989, the network not only formally adopted its current name, but it also boasted 4,000 direct subscribers from the United States and Canada, two Listserv accounts based at Arizona State University and at Kent State University in Ohio, and a mailing list maintained at the University of Toronto. From the outset, CND successfully overcame the geographical barriers and incorporated the resources from different college campuses in North America.

Such a rapid growth of the network and collaboration among Chinese students and scholars on both sides of the U.S.-Canadian border reflected their urge to keep themselves informed about the political situation in China as well as the need to communicate among the estimated 80,000 students and scholars studying and living across the United States and several thousand in Canada during that period.[11] As they were shocked by the atrocities committed by the Chinese military machine, which had always claimed to be the people's liberation army, these students and scholars were very concerned about the political uncertainty in China and the safety of the demonstrators. The most urgent question that they confronted at the moment, however, was whether they should take advantage of the political situation in China to seek political asylum collectively in the United States and Canada. Since such a question would trigger political tension and create psychological confusion, in December 1989 CND started offering individual-based as well as community-related services, which included "Introduction to Organizations," "Questions and Answers," and "Books and Journals Review." While the former two functioned as advising, counseling, and referral services, the latter enabled these students and scholars to maintain their connection with China and Chinese culture psychologically.

In facilitating debates on issues such as Chinese nationalism, survival strategies in American culture and society, and the intellectual responsibility of their generations, CND helped the students and scholars to make the psychological transition from identifying themselves with mainland China to considering the alternative of working and staying in the United States or Canada. Moreover, CND also technologically made it possible for the headquarters of the Independent Federation of Chinese Students and Scholars (IFCSS), based in Washington, D.C., to organize and mobilize its local chapters and constituencies on college campuses across the United States. As an organization initially meant to replace the official student associations endorsed by the Chinese embassy in the United States, the IFCSS launched a massive lobbying campaign coordinated by the CND network on both the national and local levels, and successfully pressured the George H. W. Bush administration (1988–1992) to issue an executive order in April 1990 that would allow Chinese nationals to work and stay in the United States temporarily regardless of their legal status. Before the executive order expired in March 1993, CND stepped up its effort to orchestrate a second massive lobbying campaign and helped to convince Congress to pass the Chinese Student Protection Act, which would allow 52,425 Chinese students and scholars and their immediate families to adjust their legal status and apply for permanent residency in the United States.[12]

As Chinese students and scholars recognized the importance of information technology in developing their political awareness and consolidating their sense of community, they equally realized that the English language had greatly limited their communication abilities and failed to convey their sensibilities. On April 5, 1991, CND launched its groundbreaking project—the first online Chinese-language journal, Hua Xia Wen Zhai (*China Digest*)—and started Chinese-language services on Usenet. The Chinese journal primarily featured political critiques of Chinese and American historical events and social issues, such as the Chinese Exclusion Act and its impact upon early Chinese Americans and their communities, McCarthyism and the wave of Chinese students and scholars returning to China in the mid-1950s, and the political power struggle in the current Chinese Communist government and its implications for the future of China. Moreover, the journal also created a section of personal narratives that would enable these students and scholars to articulate their individual sense of cultural dislocation and their nostalgic feelings for the distant homeland.

As the early volunteers landed professional jobs both inside and outside the academe, and new students and scholars continued to come and study in the United States, CND made an important structural change and moved its entire operation to the World Wide Web on June 4, 1994. The new content of CND includes the categories of publications, communities, services, and InfoBase. While it continues to provide daily bilingual news service and publish the weekly Chinese-language journal, CND has also expanded its services to include "Matchmaking Cupid (*yuanyangqiubite*)," "Job Openings (*gongzuojihui*)," "Alumni Associations (*tongxuexiaoyouhui*)," and "Chinese Students and Scholars Associations (*xiaoyuanlianyihui*)" on major college campuses in the United States and around the world.[13] InfoBase, serving as a virtual museum and library, features subjects such as "The Cultural Revolution," "China in 1989," "Chinese Scenery," "Chinese Classic Literature," and "Nanjing Massacre." While "The Cultural Revolution" and "China in 1989" reflect the political interests of the students and scholars as the generations that have been directly affected by these two major events in contemporary Chinese history and culture, "Chinese Scenery" and "Chinese Classic Literature" target a broader audience who have not necessarily visited China but have been interested in China and Chinese culture in a more abstract sense.

In incorporating matchmaking and alumni associations into their services in 1994, the network showed its awareness of the transition that these former students and scholars had experienced legally and professionally as permanent residents and professionals in the United States. While they were building their professional lives and finding their own niches in American culture and society, their interest in Chinese politics and society had declined, but their needs for having their own lives, raising families, and building local communities had surfaced as priorities. Such needs were followed by an increasing concern over the problem of racism in American culture and society and the question of protecting their own civil rights as naturalized citizens and permanent residents. Articulations of these concerns and anxieties, however, were usually not direct inquiries into the fairness of the American political system per se or a matter of familiarizing themselves with the tradition of the civil rights movement in the United States, but rather were personal narratives reflective of their own awkward situations and measuring the impact of these situations upon themselves and their children. In other words, the glass ceiling in the workplace and unfair treatment in their daily lives were often billed as the price they would have to pay as nonnative speakers of English working and living in their country of adoption and the sacrifice they would have to make for the well-being of their children. As a result, discussion on racism and civil rights usually wound up with some wishful thinking that their children would not have to follow their own paths to work and live as computer programmers in the United States but could choose more lucrative professions such as physicians, attorneys, and business executives. Moreover, since most professionals were more interested in telling their stories of triumph in American culture and society rather than sharing their stories of bitterness, which would be construed as their personal failures or professional incompetence, victims of institutional racism and individual prejudices usually preferred to retain a low profile in both their online and offline communities, quitting their jobs if they could afford to or simply leaving the United States for China or a third country if they had to.

Since 1995, there have been some significant changes concerning Chinese professionals and their communities in the United States. While many Chinese students and scholars continue to follow their predecessors in their preference to work and live in the United States, there have also emerged new groups of Chinese professionals, H-1B workers, who have been recruited directly from mainland China by U.S. transnational corporations. Though Japan studies specialist Masao Miyoshi identifies transnational professionals entirely with their respective transnational corporations in terms of economic interests as well as language abilities,[14] language and ethnicity still play an important role in shaping these professionals with regard to their personal interests and sensibilities, at least in the case of Chinese transnational professionals who have emerged as a group since 1995. Young and outspoken, these Chinese professionals are not only more proficient in the English language and skilled in information technology compared with those who came to Western countries before 1989, but they are also more confident about their own marketability globally and the future of a prosperous China. As a result, they retain their contacts as well as keep up with the latest economic and cultural developments in China. Furthermore, since their professional interests are not necessarily confined to China or the United States, they also look for opportunities in other countries and regions, which may vary from Singapore to Australia, from Hong Kong to Japan, and from Switzerland to South Africa. To attract these young professionals and other Chinese speakers in North America and around the world, Web-based Chinese-language networks have sprung up in North America since the late 1990s; among them was Chinese Media Net (CMN), a multimedia network that began operations in January 1999.

As noted in its mission statement, CMN aims to be an equivalent of CNN for ethnic Chinese in North America and around the world, and thus tries to offer services on various technical, linguistic, and cultural levels. First, it tends to be multimedia; it includes a Chinese news net, an English news net, a radio news net, a TV news net, a weekly magazine net, a picture news net, and a global newspaper net. Second, it tries to be comprehensive technically; the Chinese news net alone contains twenty-one news categories, which include important current events, global trends, North American news, Taiwan news, overseas Chinese news, business news, and so forth. It not only has its own news agency and journalists to report on current events in North America and China, but it has also developed partnerships with Reuters, New China News Agency and China News Agency based in Beijing, and Central News Agency based in Taiwan. The news net offers its services twenty-four hours a day, seven days a week, updating news entries and commentaries every few minutes. Third, it is entertaining when it carries martial arts fiction and some controversial books in Chinese, which readers may have difficulty in locating locally in their countries of adoption and regions of sojourn. Above all, the network, making good use of the interactive feature of information technology, has created six major discussion forums: everybody's forum, everybody's thoughts and comments, reader's forum, net users' report, ball game fans' forum, and documentation of the corrupt officials in mainland China. The last forum not only enables users in China to expose corruption and injustice on the mainland, but it also aims to cultivate a sense of connection among ethnic Chinese around the world, who hope to see an economically strong as well as politically healthy China.

Founded by a group of Chinese journalists and computer professionals based in the United States and Canada, CMN has become important in several ways. Equipped with the advanced technologies and operated by U.S.- and Canadianeducated professionals, the network aims to compete with the traditional Chinese-language media such as newspapers and television based in North America and East Asia, and even to emulate major English-language networks in range and scope in the United States. Moreover, the network targets Chineselanguage speakers across regional and national boundaries and endeavors to foster a sense of community based on language, culture, and ethnicity, even though the discussion columns often reveal the fact that their users are primarily Chinese professionals based in North America, western Europe, and mainland China. Occasionally, those who work and stay in Japan, Israel, or South Africa may join the forums by airing their opinions on current world events and pointing out their relevance to ethnic Chinese around the world. Finally, as information technology makes interactivity a reality, the network attempts to bridge political, linguistic, and cultural gaps among Chinese speakers around the world, particularly the gap between those in the United States and those in China. Ironically, however, the discussion columns often turn out to be a virtual battleground for mainland Chinese students studying in the United States who promote reunification with Taiwan and their Taiwanese counterparts who articulate their own desires and anxieties for an independent Taiwan.

Because of its technological capacity and information resources, CMN reports on the changing culture and society in mainland China, keeps track of the ups and downs of U.S.-China relations and major political and cultural events in the United States, and focuses on political freedom in Hong Kong and the military tension between mainland China and Taiwan. The column "News in Focus," which features major current events and facilitates follow-up discussions, reflects concerns and anxieties shared by Chinese professionals in the United States, and in that regard fosters a sense of community that has been conditioned by language and ethnicity. In fact, incidents such as the bombing of the Chinese embassy in Yugoslavia in May 1999, the Wen Ho Lee case starting in early 1999, and the collision between the U.S. spy plane and the Chinese jet fighter in April 2001 have all generated heated discussion about and speculation upon a potential confrontation between the United States and China and the future of Chinese professionals and Chinese Americans in the United States. There have not only been angry comments on U.S. imperialism and racism but also suggestions on how Chinese professionals should help American politicians abandon their Cold War mentality and educate the uninformed American public about a changing China. For instance, when the Chinese embassy was bombed in May 1999, many network users, students and professionals alike, actually organized protests in front of their local courthouses in the United States and around the world and condemned what they had considered as the deliberate bashing and provocation of China.[15]

From the emergence of CND to the popularization of CMN, we can see some changing features concerning Chinese-language networks based in North America. First, as the pioneering Chinese-language online network in the United States, CND from the outset had clear political objectives as well as specific readers and communities in mind, that is, the Chinese students and scholars studying and working in the United States and Canada. CMN, on the other hand, has to define and attract its net users by offering extensive coverage of current events and creating follow-up discussion forums for them to air their positions and opinions. Precisely because of this difference in assessing and targeting net users, CND tends to be more critical of the Chinese Communist regime but less willing to challenge U.S. institutional racism and cultural imperialism, whereas CMN carries a wide range of essays that not only question U.S. domestic and foreign policies but also explore the possibility of reforming the political system in China. In this light, CND has been more reflective of a U.S.-centered environment in which the early Chinese students and scholars, as the generations of the Cultural Revolution (from 1966 to 1976) and of the Tiananmen Square incident in 1989, celebrate their presence in the United

States and consider themselves victims of the Chinese Communist regime. CMN, by contrast, has centered on the recent booming economy in China and catered to the needs of a new generation of Chinese professionals who are outspoken and confident about the future of China as well as eager to see a new China emerging from its historical humiliation imposed by Western powers and Japan since the First Opium War in 1840, and a new China being acknowledged and respected economically and politically by the United States, western Europe, and the whole world.

Transnational Connection: Nationalism, Cultural Imaginary, and Flexible Citizenship

If the aforementioned two Chinese-language networks demonstrate different attitudes toward China, how do we understand their respective transnational communities in relation to the Chinese nation-state? Should we consider these transnational communities as being imagined outside the Chinese nation-state by virtue of language, ethnicity, and information technology? Rather than simply evoking Anderson's critique of nationalism as imagined communities, I argue that information technology and Chinese-language networks have reinforced transnational communities by performing "Chineseness" in the sense described by Aihwa Ong in *Flexible Citizenship*, as a cultural imaginary that would enable ethnic Chinese professionals to negotiate with national governments as well as maintain their flexibility within the global context. This "Chineseness," argues Ong, serves as an open signifier that acquires its dynamic meanings "in dialectical relation to the practices, beliefs, and structures encountered in the spaces of flows across nations and markets."[16] In employing the term "Chineseness," I do not want to explore the sense of relativity implied by Ong's critique, but instead seek to investigate the changing meanings of the term that have corresponded to the rise and fall of the Chinese nation-state.

When Anderson introduces the notion of nationalism as an "imagined community" based on his own observation of the formation of the Indonesian nation-state in Southeast Asia, he highlights the function of print technology as an effective medium in disseminating the native language and consolidating the national consciousness, but downplays the significance of the national consciousness in organizing and mobilizing the native people in their political and military struggle against colonial rule.[17] It is precisely at this point that Partha Chatterjee intervenes in the Western critique of nationalism and introduces the concept of the inner domain of a national culture as an important component of national consciousness.[18] Though important in its opposition to Western trivialization of nationalism in the course of the de-colonization movement, the concept of the inner domain itself is grounded in some essentialist understanding of native culture, and in that sense fails to recognize the changing dynamics of native culture in response to and in interaction with colonial rule and different dimensions of modernity. As we have moved into the information age, not only have the boundaries of the nation-state been questioned, the concept of national consciousness itself has also become suspect. To integrate information technology into his reconstruction of nationalism, Manuel Castells redefines the term as being "more oriented toward the defense of an already institutionalized culture than toward the construction or defense of a state."[19]

Though it is important to discuss the distinction between culture and state, Castells has nevertheless been tempted to salvage the notion of nationalism from its wreckage. In critiquing what she dubs as flexible citizenship, Ong introduces the term "Chineseness" as an alternative notion to nationalism and highlights its dynamic dimension that would encompass the plurality of ethnic Chinese identities across national boundaries and incorporate the diverse factors of gender, class, and sexuality in informing and reshaping ethnic Chinese identities and communities. As Ong convincingly argues in her work from *Flexible Citizenship* to *Ungrounded Empires*,[20] ethnic Chinese in Southeast Asia have never identified themselves with any Chinese nation-state in the first place, but they have always wanted to articulate their own sense of cultural difference and economic accomplishment in terms of abstract Chinese notions such as Confucianism. As Ong spells out this "Chineseness," the term winds up being something between ethnicity and cultural beliefs that have constantly been reconstructed by global capitalism and national government. In my own use of the term, I do not want to rule out the Chinese nation-state as an irrelevant element in constituting this "Chineseness," but on the contrary, I examine the ways in which the term has been deployed by Chinese professionals in juxtaposition to the Chinese nation-state at different historical junctures and interrogate what this deployment means to the transnational communities in the United States.

When CND started its service in 1989, "*huaren*" (ethnic Chinese), "*zhonghuawenhua*" (Chinese culture), and "*huaxia*" (China proper) were terms conveniently employed by Chinese students and scholars to replace the terms related to the People's Republic of China and to exonerate themselves from any negative association with the Communist regime in American culture and society. The uses of these terms were also meant to appeal to overseas Chinese and Chinese American communities in the wake of the political crisis of 1989 so that the students and scholars would get more support from these established communities when they tried to cut off their own ties with the Chinese nation-state. These terms were most effectively used in the political mobilization of the Chinese students and scholars concerning the protection bill in 1992, when the leaders of the IFCSS tried to convince their communities that they were collective victims as citizens of the People's Republic of China. Only by acquiring permanent residency in the United States and becoming ethnic Chinese in the pure cultural sense of the term could they cherish their dreams of "life, liberty, and the pursuit of happiness." The point of their argument, however, did not lie so much in the protection of the Chinese students and scholars as in its gesture to dissociate themselves from the Chinese nation-state and reinvent themselves as freedom fighters and competent professionals in the U.S. and global contexts.

Meanwhile, the IFCSS also explored the cultural dimension of "Chineseness" that had been manifested in values such as education and meritocracy. In their lobbying activities, the IFCSS task force emphasized the uniqueness of Chinese students and scholars in terms of their education levels and potential contribution to the advancement of science and technology in the United States, a strategy that would easily evoke the "model minority" myth surrounding Asian Americans and would likely gain support from both parties in Congress. The subtext was that, as Chinese professionals, they would not create any welfare problem for the U.S. government, and that the United States would have nothing to lose in granting them permanent residency, a point that would appeal particularly to Republicans. Journalist Susan Lawrence drove the point home by comparing these students and scholars with the refugees from Haiti, whose status and future were pending and gloomy at that time:

> As an immigrant group, the students are unusually appealing. The vast majority either hold Ph.D.'s or are studying for them now. Many are skilled scientists—biologists, physicists and engineers. The Haitian refugees may face greater physical danger in their homeland. But, as Cheryl Little, a Miami lawyer who represents the Haitians, notes ruefully, "the perception is that they are poor, they are uneducated, they are black, they are 'undesirables.' "[21]

To ensure the passage of the protection bill, the IFCSS played the political and cultural meanings of "Chineseness" right into the anti-Communist sentiment prevalent in Congress at the moment. During the congressional hearings, one question that had frequently been debated was what would happen to the United States if Communist China got all the estimated 80,000 students and scholars, the majority of whom were holding or studying for Ph.D.'s in science and technology. This fear was not entirely groundless considering the fact that when McCarthyism drove back to Communist China some 200 Chinese students and scholars with Ph.D.'s in the hard sciences in the mid-1950s, China embraced these returnees, as they provided a unique opportunity for the new country to lay down the foundation for higher education and scientific research as well as to build up its nuclear arsenals in the following decades. Included in this list were distinguished scientists such as Qian Xuesen, "the father of Chinese rockets," and Deng Jiaxian, "the father of Chinese atomic bombs."[22] In light of this history, the legislators perceived the passage of the bill as being crucial to U.S. national security and U.S. global hegemony. At the moment when the IFCSS leaders celebrated the passage of the bill as a victory and an example of the most successful involvement of Chinese students and scholars in the U.S. legal and political system, little did they realize that there had been elements of racism and cultural imperialism vested in the anti-Communist rhetoric in Congress, which would take its toll on the very same Chinese professionals years later.

Though there was no major voice on CND opposing the tactics of the IFCSS, not every Chinese student and scholar bought the IFCSS's argument or took advantage of the legislation to stay in the United States. According to the initial projections of most reports,[23] there would be 80,000 students and scholars and their immediate families eligible for permanent residency in the United States, but the data collected and released by the U.S. Immigration and Naturalization Services (INS) suggested that there were only 26,915 applicants in 1993 and 21,297 applicants in 1994 for permanent residency under the Chinese Student Protection Act, which was effective from April 1993 to April 1994.[24] The total number of applicants was 48,212 during that yearlong period, a figure that fell far below the projection of 80,000.[25] While there could be different explanations for this discrepancy, such as that some students and scholars had already applied for permanent residency under other immigration categories, it did suggest that many students and scholars actually had given up their opportunities to become permanent residents in the United States and left for mainland China and other countries for different reasons. One Ph.D. candidate in material science at Purdue University in Indiana, after his grant proposal on submarine material was rejected allegedly on the basis of his Chinese citizenship, stated explicitly on CND in 1993 that he would never be trusted by the U.S. government as a scientist even though he might become a permanent resident or a naturalized citizen in the future. He concluded that he would rather go back to China than live in a racist country and work as a second-class citizen for the rest of his life. True to his words, he went back to China and started his own high-tech firm in Beijing in 1995, as reported in the official newspaper of the Chinese government, the *People's Daily*.[26] Moreover, even for those who had become permanent residents and obtained academic positions, many of them left for China or a third country several years later. In early 1996, ten senior research scientists at Indiana University Medical School in Indianapolis decided to leave their academic positions and started their new careers as a team at a university in Guangzhou, Guangdong Province, China.[27]

When CMN began operations as a Web-based Chinese-language network in January 1999, the profile of Chinese-language speakers in the United States was quite different from that for CND a decade earlier. Not only has an entire new generation of Chinese professionals in North America and East and Southeast Asia emerged, the meaning of "Chineseness" itself has also undergone some dramatic changes. As the economy continues to boom in China, the term "Chineseness" has expanded in an economic sense to include the regions of the mainland, Hong Kong, and Taiwan, and resisted political identification with any

specific regime even though the governments in all three regions have com-
peted to influence this economic integration according to their own political
ideologies and economic models. Because of this economic expansion and prosperity, a new sense of optimism and confidence has widely spread among
Chinese professionals. Ironically, this optimism and confidence could easily
turn into vulgar nationalism and virtual patriotism, as evidenced in the reactions toward the bombing of the Chinese embassy in Yugoslavia in May 1999,
when this new economic dimension of "Chineseness" was not honored or
understood by Western powers and Japan. As the United States and China are
becoming increasingly confrontational, this new meaning of "Chineseness" has
finally become a self-reflexive moment for Chinese professionals in North
America to reconsider their own positions and their transnational communities
in terms of the fluctuating U.S.-China relations.

When the news broke on CMN that the U.S.-led North Atlantic Treaty
Organization (NATO) bombed the Chinese embassy in Yugoslavia and killed
three Chinese journalists in May 1999, the network immediately exploded as an
important source of information and a forum for discussion for Chinese professionals as well as Chinese students and scholars in the United States, China, and
around the world. Though some net users doubted that NATO had any real
motivation in doing it deliberately, the majority of the users believed that the
Western powers had always intended to bash an emerging powerful China and
expressed their outrage that China had been humiliated at its strongest
moment since the First Opium War in 1840. As these students and professionals
called for investigation and retaliation, their sense of optimism and confidence
based on the Chinese economy suddenly turned into vulgar nationalism and
virtual patriotism. While some student hackers based in China broke into U.S.
government Web sites to post a red flag or a message reading "I'm proud of
being Chinese," and others protested in front of the U.S. embassy in Beijing
shouting slogans and throwing eggs at the U.S. property, Chinese students and
professionals in the United States also joined the chorus of protests. On May 11,
1999, sponsored by organizations such as the Chinese Students and Scholars
Society at Ohio State University and the Midwest Chinese Science and Culture
Association, over 100 Chinese students and scholars and professionals demonstrated in front of the courthouse in Columbus, Ohio, holding a banner with the
words "Peace! Truth! Justice!" and carrying signs that read "Shame On NATO!"
"Stop Killing the Innocent," "Violence Breeds Violence!" "NATO Is the Mistake!"[28]

Before the impact of the bombing was over, the collision between the
Chinese jet fighter and the U.S. spy plane took place in April 2001. Chinese professionals in the United States began realizing that there could be a real war
between China and the United States and that they, as Chinese professionals
and Chinese Americans, would be particularly vulnerable of being caught in the
middle. In the discussion forum on CMN in the following weeks, there were

heated discussions on the strategies and positions that Chinese professionals should hold in the wake of the crisis. All the participants showed their concerns about the awkwardness that would result if they were caught in a scenario of war between the United States and China. In the second week of the incident, one person predicted pessimistically that the U.S. government would not hesitate to put everybody of Chinese descent into some kind of internment camp, as they had done to Japanese Americans during the Second World War. Another person countered the prediction by arguing that the U.S. government would not make the same mistake twice to violate the U.S. Constitution. As naturalized citizens, the person argued further, Chinese professionals should fight for their civil rights as protected and guaranteed by the First Amendment and should have a strong case if anything like that would happen. However, the same person expressed more concern over "patriotism" of individual U.S. citizens who might take things into their own hands, breaking the windows of his house or abusing his children verbally and physically at public schools. A third person suggested that as Chinese professionals and immigrants, they should probably do more to promote understanding between the Chinese and Americans. A good relationship between the United States and China, she argued, would not only benefit people in both countries but would also become crucial to Chinese professionals working and living in the United States like herself. She concluded by suggesting that people of Chinese descent at the moment should be united in their fight against all sorts of warmonger "hawks" in the U.S. government, the Chinese government, and the Taiwanese government.

Discussions like this highlight three things. First, the transnational communities are consolidated at the moment of a crisis when the professionals believe that their own interests and welfare are at stake. Second, these professionals have always been interested in both U.S. domestic politics and U.S. foreign policy, particularly those policies that would have a direct impact upon Chinese immigrants and transnational professionals. Finally, these professionals usually consider the situations of Chinese Americans in light of U.S.-China relations.

The Changing Cultural Imagination: Transnational Professionals and Asian American Identity Politics

In their essay "Changing of the Guard? The Emerging Immigrant Majority in Asian American Politics," Paul Ong and David Lee examine the transition of the Asian American population from a U.S.-born majority to an immigrant majority and speculate upon one of the major consequences of this transition as a potential threat to progressive activism, "which has been an important force within Asian American communities." In defining "progressive activism" as the leadership of the "Asian American Movement" between 1965 and 1980, as well as the new group of social service providers and civil rights advocates who "share a liberal or progressive agenda centered on social justice, economic equality, and ethnic/ racial pride," the authors ground their perception on two basic assumptions about immigrants.[29] One is that Asian immigrants are more Republican in their political orientation and may not care much about working-class and social justice, an issue that the two authors address at length in their essay. The other assumption is that immigrants are more interested in the politics of their home country than in the politics of their country of adoption.

Though there indeed has been a tradition of engaging in their home-country politics among immigrants since the late nineteenth century, as discussed in Gordon Chang's essay, "Asian Americans and Politics,"[30] Ong and Lee have failed to address several important questions. First, are progressive activism and immigrant interest always in conflict or in opposition? Is there any common ground that U.S.-born activists and immigrants share? Second, why are immigrants still interested in their home-country politics if they are working and living in a new country? To what extent is their home-country politics relevant to their experience in their country of adoption? Finally, how should U.S.-born Asian Americans educate immigrants about Asian American history, culture, and politics? What can Asian immigrants teach U.S.-born Asian Americans about the specific history, culture, and language of a given Asian nation?

In reconsidering incidents such as the collision of the U.S. spy plane and the Chinese jet fighter and the Wen Ho Lee case, I suggest that U.S.-born and Asia-born Asian Americans do share many common interests. In "Lee Case Smashes Students' Dreams," published in the *Boston Herald* on September 23, 2000, Charles Bu, a tenured faculty member in mathematics at Wellesley College who had benefited from the Chinese Student Protection Act, discussed the frustration and sentiments that the Wen Ho Lee case had produced among Chinese professionals in the United States.[31] Most of them, Bu argued, believed that they could be the next victims of a U.S. politics that had needed to demonize China as its next major evil empire in lieu of the former Soviet Union. Condemning this right-wing politics as a revival of 190s McCarthyism, Bu warned that this Cold War reasoning could drive many Chinese professionals in high-tech sectors back to China and in that sense would self-fulfill the so-called disloyalty of Chinese Americans. Bu concluded his essay by suggesting that he would never let his own son study any field related to nuclear technology or the defense industry in the future and would call on all his Asian and Asian American students on campus not to work for U.S. national laboratories on weaponry research.

Like Bu, many Chinese professionals do identify with Wen Ho Lee and have answered the call from various Asian American organizations to boycott the three major U.S. national laboratories on weaponry research. As reported on CMN in early 2000, the famous Chinese dissident Fang Lizhi (who sought political asylum in the U.S. embassy in Beijing during the political crisis of 1989 and left China under the auspices of the U.S. government, and is currently teaching physics at the University of Arizona in Tucson) wrote an open letter to the U.S. Department of Energy, condemning its racial profiling in the Wen Ho Lee case and demanding justice for the Taiwan-born scientist. When his political disciple, Wang Dan, a well-known student leader at Tiananmen Square in 1989, was released from a Chinese prison and came to study history at Harvard University in the mid-1990s, Fang was reported to have told Wang not to make too many public appearances or talk about democracy until he had a solid understanding of U.S. politics, history, and culture. Fang's advice was not only meant to protect Wang from political vulnerability, but it also reflected his own concerns and experience with the political system and cultural practices in the United States as a prominent Chinese dissident as well as an immigrant scientist. The Wen Ho Lee case was certainly a wake-up call for the former Chinese students and scholars and the more recent Chinese professionals, and it should probably serve to bridge the gap between what Ong and Lee call "progressive activism" and immigrant concerns, if there were any gap in the first place.

In her critique of Asian American identities and politics, Aihwa Ong argues that the strategy of Asian Americans in distancing themselves from transnational communities "discloses an ongoing political vulnerability that merely reifies the ethnic-racial divide between Asian Americans and white Americans." Such a strategy, Ong further suggests, ignores "the objective reality that a majority of Asian Americans are now linked to transnational family networks." The real problem, Ong concludes, is that Asian Americans have bought into an American ideology that "limits the moral claims to social legitimacy of nonwhites."[32] As a cultural anthropologist whose expertise is focused primarily on ethnic Chinese identities in East and Southeast Asia, Ong's critique might not be an accurate description of Asian American reality, but it certainly points out some pitfalls in Asian American identity politics as well as the urgency to theorize and integrate the transnational professionals and their communities into Asian American identity politics.

As a matter of a fact, since 1995, when Sau-ling Wong, in her seminal essay "Denationalization Reconsidered: Asian American Cultural Criticism at a Theoretical Crossroads," proposed a paradigm shift in Asian American studies from the domestic perspective to the transnational one to empower the field, new scholarship on transnational aspects of Asian American identities and communities has flourished.[33] Now it is time not just for Chinese professionals to reimagine their communities and negotiate their own political and cultural spaces by applying information technology and Chinese-language networks, but it is also a critical moment for U.S.-born Asian Americans to reimagine their own broadly defined community by helping and working together with these professionals and their transnational communities. U.S.-born Asian Americans can teach these transnational professionals about Asian American history, culture, and politics, and at the same time learn from the latter about the history, culture, and politics of a specific Asian country or countries, and their transnational perspectives on issues such as how U.S.-China relations would inform and shape Asian American identities and communities. If U.S.-born Asian Americans do not take the initiative to reach out to these new professionals and transnational communities, then who will?

NOTES

This is an expanded version of "Reimagining the Community: Information Technology and Web-Based Chinese Language Networks in North America," in *AsianAmerica.Net: Ethnicity, Nationalism, and Cyberspace*, ed. Rachel Lee and Sau-ling Cynthia Wong (New York: Routledge, 2003), 139–157. Used by permission of Routledge/Taylor & Francis Group, LLC.

1. Initially housed at UCLA, the Center for the Digital Future has moved to the Annenberg School at the University of Southern California and conducted its seventh year of study of the Internet since 2001. For more information, see the report online at http://digitalcenter.org.

2. United States Internet Council, "State of the Internet 2001 Edition." For some reason, the agency did annual reports on the state of the Internet for only three years, from 1999 to 2001. No update is available. For more information, see their Web site at http://www.usintenetcouncil.

3. Ibid.

4. For the past few years, the Chinese government has tried to crack down on Internet bars and install filters to prevent Chinese Internet users from gaining access to some politically sensitive Web sites based in the United States. However, most students and professionals in China can still access these Web sites by different means. In July 2002, hackers in the United States gathered in New York City and made a manifesto to fight the Chinese government's control of the Internet by all means necessary. This means that they are going to provide free software to Chinese Internet users to circumvent the filters and deactivate the surveillance software. See http://www.duoweinews.com.

5. In *Reconstructing Chinatown: Ethnic Enclave, Global Change*, Jan Lin argues that the stereotypical representation of Chinatown simply as a filthy and exotic ethnic enclave in American popular culture is far from accurate. There are not only discrepancies among businesses and residents in Chinatown these days but also transnational capital involved in Chinatown renovation and development. See Jan Lin, *Reconstructing Chinatown: Ethnic Enclave, Global Change* (Minneapolis: University of Minnesota Press, 1998), 1–22.

6. Aihwa Ong, *Flexible Citizenship: The Cultural Logics of Transnationality* (Durham, N.C.: Duke University Press, 1999).

7. "Chinese Language Internet Users," Global Reach Web site at http://www.glreach.com/, accessed February 26, 2001.

8. "CyberAtlas: Chinese-American Lead the Way Online," http://www.nua.ie/surveys/, accessed February 26, 2001.

9. See Chinese Media Net (*duowei*) Web site at http://www.chinesemedianet.com/AboutUs.html; Chinese News Digest Web site at http://www.cnd.org/.

10. Bo Xiong and Gang Yu, "The Making of 'China News Digest,'" http://www.cnd.org/CND-Tech/, accessed February 28, 2001.

11. See Jordana Hart and Cheong Chow, "Joy, Envy at Green Cards for Chinese," *Boston Globe*, June 27, 1993. See also L. A. Chung, "Refuge Program in Response to Tiananmen," *San Francisco Chronicle*, July 2, 1993.

12. The Chinese Student Protection Act was effective from April 1993 to April 1994. Based on the data from the INS, there were 26,915 applicants in 1993 and 21,297 applicants in 1994 for the adjustment of their legal status. There were 4,213 applicants in 1995. My understanding is that the applicants in 1995 were mostly spouses and family members of these Chinese students and scholars. For more information, visit the INS Web site at http://www.ins.usdoj.gov/graphics/aboutins/annual/fy95/125.htm.

13. Both the Chinese and English terms used here are the original ones on the Web site. They are not exact translations.

14. Masao Miyoshi, "A Borderless World? From Colonialism to Transnationalism and the Decline of the Nation-State," *Critical Inquiry* 19 (Summer 1993): 726–751.

15. See "Chinese Group Protests NATO Bombing," *Columbus Dispatch*, May 11, 1999. According to the reports on CNN on May 12, 1999, there were major protests organized by Chinese students and scholars in Great Britain, Germany, France, Australia, Japan, South Africa, and other countries around the world.

16. Ong, *Flexible Citizenship*, 24.

17. Benedict Anderson, *Imagined Communities: Reflections on the Origin and Spread of Nationalism*, rev. ed. (New York: Verso, 1991), 46.

18. Partha Chatterjee, *The Nation and Its Fragments: Colonial and Postcolonial Histories* (Princeton, N.J.: Princeton University Press, 1993), 9.

19. Manuel Castells, *The Rise of the Network Society*, Vol. 1 of *The Information Age: Economy, Society and Culture Series* (Cambridge, Mass.: Blackwell, 1996), 31.

20. Aihwa Ong and Donald Nonini, eds., *Ungrounded Empires: The Cultural Politics of Modern Chinese Transnationalism* (New York: Routledge, 1997).

21. Susan Lawrence, "Chinese Students Hit the Jackpot," *U.S. News and World Report*, 115, no. 11 (1993), 38.

22. See Iris Chang, *Thread of the Silkworm* (New York: Basic Books, 1995).

23. See Hart and Chow, "Joy," 1.

24. See INS Web site at http://www.ins.usdoj.gov/graphics/aboutins/annual/fy95/125.htm.

25. See Hart and Chow, "Joy," 1.

26. The official Chinese Communist flagship newspaper, *People's Daily* (overseas edition), gave extraordinary coverage of the Chinese students and scholars who had returned to China during 1990 to 1995. It was understood as a strategy and gesture to lure these students and scholars in hard sciences and technology back to China. See *People's Daily*, April 20, 1995.

27. I first heard this story from a friend who had been working at Indiana University Medical School in Indianapolis. The story was reported in the Chinese-language journal *Shenzhouxueren* 2 (April 1996): 5.

28. See "Chinese Group Protests NATO Bombing."

29. Paul Ong and David Lee, "Changing of the Guard? The Emerging Immigrant Majority in Asian American Politics," in *Asian Americans and Politics: Perspectives, Experiences, Prospects*, ed. Gordon H. Chang, 153–172 (Stanford, Calif.: Stanford University Press, 2001).

30. Gordon H. Chang, "Asian Americans and Politics: Some Perspectives from History," in Chang, *Asian Americans and Politics*, 13–38.

31. Charles Bu, "Lee Case Smashes Students' Dreams," *Boston Herald*, September 23, 2000.

32. Ong, *Flexible Citizenship*, 180.

33. Sau-ling C. Wong, "Denationalization Reconsidered: Asian American Cultural Criticism at a Theoretical Crossroads," *Amerasia Journal* 21, nos. 1–2 (1995): 1–27.

9

Ethnic Solidarity in a Divided Community

A Study on Bridging Organizations in Koreatown

ANGIE Y. CHUNG

Although theorists have come to recognize the continuing significance of ethnic political solidarity for black and Latino groups, there have been few studies that have analyzed how post-1965 Asian immigrant communities are able to sustain ethnic political solidarity amid increasing generational cleavages, class polarization, and residential sprawl. This inattention to the social dynamics of Asian American politics may partly be attributed to both the relative recent emergence of most post-1965 Asian American communities and the political inactivity of those Asian Americans who preceded them because of historical disenfranchisement and discrimination, cultural and linguistic barriers, electoral divisions, and negative experiences with politics in the ancestral homeland.[1] However, the potential impact of Asian American political activity and influence has become particularly clear in recent decades with the slow but inevitable emergence of Asian American politicians, the growing importance of Asian and Asian American financial contributions to politicians, and the proliferation of Asian American community-based organizations and activities across the nation.

At the same time, new patterns of residential settlement among select post-1965 immigrants have raised questions about the overall capacity of ethnic communities to cultivate ethnic political solidarity in the current era. In particular, the possibility of maintaining ethnic political solidarity without residential concentration has become particularly poignant, considering the rapid pace at which Korean, Chinese, Japanese, and other Asian American groups have achieved socioeconomic mobility and spread out into diverse residential settings. While there is growing literature on the role of mainstream politics in shaping the development and political integration of immigrant organizations into the host society, relatively few works have looked at political organizations, relationships, and inequality *within* ethnic opportunity structures. In this light, ethnic community-based organizations may better help us to understand what happens with generational transitions in political leadership. Ethnic organizations led by American-raised/American-born ethnic constituencies, or the so-called 1.5/second generation, provide a compelling case with which to study the dynamics of ethnic political solidarity for two reasons: because of their intermediary role between the immigrant community and mainstream society; and because such organizations provide one of the few institutional spaces where younger generations can find a developed sense of ethnic political identity, a vehicle to act upon their political beliefs, and a means to network with the ethnic community despite residential dispersal.

The general objective of my research is to examine the different strategies that ethnic organizations among the native-born Korean American generation use to create a sense of ethnic political solidarity among their constituents despite the community's increasing residential dispersion, class disparities, and ideological differences. To this end, I discuss how traditional assimilationist theories have conceptualized ethnic solidarity in a way that underestimates the ability of nonprofit organizations to accommodate the shifting demographics of new ethnic communities through institutional consolidation and diversification. The next section describes how the introduction of mainstream support changed Korean American political structures such that the fate of 1.5/second generation ethnic organizations became intertwined with immigrant power-holders despite increasing tensions and resource competition. However, intergenerational dependency means that bridging organizations must also negotiate their political agenda within traditional ethnic hierarchies—a process that lays the basis for diverse organizational frameworks of ethnic political solidarity. In this light, the third section takes a closer look at how two specific Korean American organizations in the upper and lower tiers of ethnic power structures have come up with distinct political frameworks for organizing and mobilizing 1.5 and second generation subgroups based on differential relations with immigrant power-holders. The final section discusses the implications of this organizational specialization and diversity on ethnic political solidarity among the 1.5/second generation leadership.

The Institutional Bases of Ethnic Political Solidarity

For the most part, traditional assimilation theory has been the dominant paradigm to explain the long-term incorporation of immigrants in the United States, but the direct link between assimilation and ethnic political involvement has yet to be clearly articulated. First, traditional approaches provides little framework for understanding the formation and persistence of ethnic political solidarity throughout the processes of assimilation. These paradigms conceptualize immigrant adaptation as a unidirectional, straight-line process, where immigrants begin on the peripheries of the ethnic enclave economy but eventually achieve full cultural and socioeconomic integration into mainstream social structures over generations.[2] From this perspective, ethnic political solidarity is feasible only when there are low levels of class and generational differences among coethnics, and interests are reinforced by residential proximity and day-to-day interactions within the confines of the immigrant enclave.[3] It is presumed that as future descendants of immigrants start to achieve upward mobility and intermix with other racial groups, the structural foundations of ethnic political structures will dissolve and give way to more "useful" ties with mainstream institutions and greater involvement in electoral politics.

Furthermore, the disintegration of homeland-based cultural and normative systems and acculturation into the mainstream assist in undermining the ideological basis for ethnic political solidarity. As discussed in Abelmann and Lie's study of the Korean American community, there is an underlying assumption that without any structural basis to uphold ethnic solidarity, different generations of political leadership will be increasingly fractured along ideological, class, and generational cleavages until ethnic solidarity becomes a thing of the past.[4] This approach, however, proves problematic for understanding the evolution of ethnic politics, because it is based on an individual socioeconomic mobility–driven model such that there is seemingly no structural basis for political solidarity or returning to the ethnic community upon assimilation.

Other scholars such as Breton, Zhou, and Portes have suggested the possibility that ethnic networks and institutions can providing a stepping stone for both the socioeconomic mobility and political advancement of new ethnic communities.[5] That is, the information, resources, and assistance derived from strong networks of ethnic-based support may actually help new ethnic groups to overcome the disadvantages associated with adaptation to a foreign culture, marginal social status, and spatial isolation within low-income urban communities and, in some cases, provide them with a competitive edge over their coethnic and non-coethnic counterparts. Institutional development can be the key to understanding how some Asian American groups can overcome some of the difficulties they face in seeking political representation and empowerment in mainstream society. Rooted in these strong networks of support, ethnic political solidarity reflects the continuing importance of ethnic-based infrastructures in representing immigrants and their children to the outside world and helping younger generations of leadership to transition into mainstream American politics. The question remains: how do ethnic communities cultivate networks and institutions considering the residential dispersal of populations like Korean Americans in Los Angeles, the increasing cultural tensions between immigrants and the American-born generation, and political inequality and uneven resource distribution even *within* ethnic opportunity structures?

I argue that despite the suburbanization of the ethnic community, Korean American organizations are able to cultivate ethnic political solidarity through the centralized resources and institutional infrastructures of the old enclave. The status of Koreatown as the institutional powerhouse of a spatially dispersed community provides ethnic organizations with the general resource base and infrastructure within which to pursue their political goals.[6] Because the immigrant elite control enclave resources, the next generation of leadership has not simply detached from the immigrant leadership, as one might expect according to assimilation theory, but has rather worked to negotiate their political agenda within traditional ethnic hierarchies.

However, conflicts with the immigrant leadership and the availability of mainstream resources also mean that "bridging" organizations like the Korean Immigrant Workers Advocates (KIWA) and the Korean Youth and Community Center (KYCC) must leverage mainstream networks to negotiate their position within ethnic power structures. In other words, these organizations have used their mainstream resources to engage with, not detach from, ethnic power structures. More specifically, depending on how 1.5/second generation ethnic organizations negotiate their political agendas within traditional immigrant hierarchies, they will construct different organizational frameworks of ethnic political solidarity that attract specific substrata of Korean Americans. Hence, support from outside constituencies has not diminished the salience of ethnicity in these community-based organizations so much as given them the tools to promote new and diverse frameworks of "Korean Americanness" that appeal to specific subgroups within the Korean American population. Both cases challenge the traditional assumption that assimilation undermines ethnicity as a meaningful framework for political solidarity among the American-born generation, but rather it pushes them to reconstruct ethnic political identity in more diverse ways.

Data and Methods

This research examines 1.5/second generation–led community-based organizations within the ethnic enclave community. The classification of organizations as 1.5/second generation versus first generation is determined by the generational status of the executive director and the dominant majority of full-time staff members.[7] The data for the study was collected over a five-year period, from 1997 to 2001. The first part of the research project focuses on the broader organizational structures of the Korean American community through interviews with community leaders and participatory observation of various organizational events and meetings. Based on this research, I identified two organizations as being progressive 1.5/second generation organizations situated in different tiers within ethnic organizational structures: Upper tier—the first organization, the KYCC, is a nonprofit social service agency that was originally established in 1975 to service economically disadvantaged youth and their families but has expanded its programs to encompass a variety of other health, advocacy, community, business, housing, and employment-related services; Lower tier—founded in March 1992, the KIWA has worked to organize, empower, and advocate for workers in the Koreatown community through legal assistance, protest demonstrations, educational seminars, and other political activities.[8]

The interview sample includes a total of eighty interviewees: sixty respondents who are affiliated with the KYCC and the KIWA and the remaining twenty who are representatives of various first and second generation Korean American organizations, church leaders, academics, youth, and business owners, all of whom were intimate with the organizations and political history of Koreatown. The majority of interviews were personally administered and audiotaped using open-ended, semistructured questionnaires. Based on an inductive reading of the field notes and interview transcripts, I analyzed and compared resource distribution and political influence within ethnic community structures, relations with the ethnic elite, public and private interactions among different organizational staff and leadership, the content of interorganizational alliances and networks, the perceived benefits and difficulties of community work, the dynamics of ethnic identity and political beliefs among organizational affiliates, and the organization's strategic approaches to various community issues.

The research data also includes both nonintrusive and participant observations in the organizational and sociopolitical spaces of Koreatown. In an effort to immerse myself in the setting, I devoted fifteen to twenty hours of volunteer work per week at two of the organizations for more than a year. In addition to volunteer work, I participated in the various meetings and events sponsored by each organization, including protest demonstrations, staff/youth/worker meetings, annual fund-raisers, interorganizational meetings, social events, canvassing, and conferences. My data is also informed by my own active participation and nonintrusive field observations in the Koreatown community—activities that included attending language classes and political study groups, teaching at a tutoring school, and attending church, among other things. The above data was supplemented with archival material, such as mainstream media (for example, *Los Angeles Times*), local ethnic media (for example, *La Opinion*, *Korea Times*, *Korean Central Daily*, and *KoreAm Journal*), documentaries (for example, *Sa-i-gu*), and organizational media (for example, newsletters and informational pamphlets).

The Demographic Context of Koreatown Politics

The dynamics of ethnic solidarity within the Korean American community is formatively shaped by the demographic characteristics of the ethnic population, which has weakened the overall political empowerment of the broader community. The setting of the study is the urban ethnic enclave of Koreatown—a roughly sixteen-square-mile region west of downtown Los Angeles. Although most well

known for its abundance of Korean-owned businesses, Koreatown is more anal-
ogous to a multiracial community, with Koreans comprising only 20.4 percent of
the residential population and Latinos more than half (52.4 percent) of its residents. Korean residents in Koreatown are mostly poor and elderly, with the
remainder of the community having moved to suburban neighborhoods of Los
Angeles and Orange counties, including Fullerton, Garden Grove, and Glendale.

So what does this mean for the political development of institutionally centered communities like Koreatown Los Angeles? One thing to note is that the pace
at which ethnic groups socioeconomically assimilate does not necessarily parallel
the pace at which they achieve political and social recognition from their white
American peers and discard ethnic ties and identities. In the case of Korean
Americans, the extent to which many Korean immigrants and their children have
assimilated into mainstream economic structures may have lessened some of the
socioeconomic hardships of the upwardly mobile but have not necessarily fulfilled
all of their social and political needs. Events like the 1992 Los Angeles riots
impressed upon the community the need to build their base of political empowerment, even as their ability to mobilize votes has become increasingly diluted by
residential out-migration. Socioeconomic mobility has allowed Korean Americans
to move into more affluent parts of metropolitan Los Angeles, but the demographic distribution of the ethnic community has also been the Achilles' heel of
Koreatown's political development. The situation has been compounded by the
relatively small demographic size of the Korean American population and the sec-
tionalization of Koreatown into four electoral districts.

Despite residential dispersion, Koreatown is most distinctive from other
enclaves by its abundance of ethnic organizations, services, and resources
that cater to the needs of different interest groups within the community.
Furthermore, Koreatown has witnessed continuing entrepreneurial expansion
as a result of the influx of transnational capital and recent local public-private
redevelopment partnerships in the downtown Los Angeles area, among other
things. Almost all of the major politically active organizations of the ethnic community are located in the enclave of Koreatown. An informal count of the
2000–2001 Korean business directory (*Korean Central Daily* version) and the
1998–1999 Asian and Pacific Islander Community directory (UCLA Asian
American Studies Center) shows that there are at least fifty major Korean community–based organizations located within the general Koreatown zip code
area servicing the cultural, social, economic, and political needs of Korean
Americans. This number does not even include religious organizations or the
multitude of smaller friendship, recreational, hobby, and service groups listed
in the directory.

Institutional concentration in the immigrant enclave plays an even more
vital role for sprawling ethnic populations. Although their electoral impact has
been severely handicapped by their small numbers, residential dispersion, and

electoral fragmentation, Korean Americans have maintained some semblance of political solidarity by consolidating their organizational infrastructures within the old Koreatown enclave. Unlike businesses and institutions like the Church, which can establish themselves far away from the enclave, political organizations rely more heavily on a fixed and concentrated ethnic membership and the combined support of surrounding ethnic institutions. For instance, community-based organizations must have active members from the local neighborhood in order to solicit government contracts, solidify their political representation within council districts, or garner supporters for their protest demonstrations.

By building on adequate resources and entrepreneurial development, institutional concentration can provide a strong political foundation for communities whose voting power is significantly diminished by small population size and residential diffusion. Spatial clustering enables such organizations to coordinate their services, combine resources, and instantly band together in response to urgent events. Of course, internal ethnic solidarity does not fully compensate for the disadvantaged status of Korean Americans in mainstream politics, but maintaining the integrity of such institutions gives them the political cohesiveness necessary to consolidate their ethnic resources and networks, to enhance their political visibility, and to cultivate alliances with non-Korean residents.

Making Bridges in Postriot Koreatown

For the most part, Korean communities in America did not emerge to any significant extent until the provisions of the Hart-Cellars Immigration Act opened the doors to massive immigration from Asia and Latin America during the late 1960s and 1970s. The picture of Koreatown politics in Los Angeles during this early period of immigration was one similar to past Asian immigrant enclaves in that it was characterized by preoccupation with homeland affairs and extreme cultural and political detachment from mainstream society.[9] My research indicates that power-holders in the Korean American community re-created new lines of stratification in the United States based on the conservative ideologies and material privileges of the male-dominated Seoul elite. Their position was reaffirmed not only by their wealth and status vis-à-vis the poverty of rural Koreans but also by pro-U.S. principles of democracy directed against the Communist threat of North Korea. In the early years of Koreatown's formation, the three branches of what I call the "ethnic elite"—namely, church leaders, entrepreneurs, and select immigrant institutions (for example, Korean Federation)—were able to dominate enclave politics as a result of the demographic composition of the immigrant-dominated population and also because of the elite's control over the resource-rich social networks of the Korean American community. In situations where their positions were threatened, the ethnic elite took advantage of their extensive networks and resources to stifle opposition and reassert their authority over local community affairs. The authority of this primarily elderly male consortium was backed by the intervention of the Seoul government through institutions like the Consulate General and the Korean language media.[10]

A series of events throughout the 1980s and 1990s dramatically altered the political landscapes of the Korean American community by weakening the influence of the ethnic elite and redistributing power among different generations of leadership. These events included the Kwangju Rebellions in Korea when demonstrations by prodemocratic student leaders were brutally repressed by the Seoul government in 1980, as well as tensions between Korean immigrant entrepreneurs and black activists throughout the 1980s and 1990s.[11] Although these internal crises set the backdrop for future events, the most critical turning point in Korean American history began on April 29, 1992, when more than 2,000 Korean-owned businesses throughout South Central, Koreatown, and Pico-Union were looted, burned, and destroyed at the hands of rioters, who were left unchecked by law enforcement agencies for several days.[12] Sparked by the acquittal of police officers accused of beating up a black motorist, the 1992 Los Angeles civil unrest represented the culmination of a long history of poverty, police abuse, discrimination, and tensions between Koreans and blacks in Los Angeles. In the absence of police protection, Korean business owners were forced to defend their stores and find alternative means of support through ethnic community-based institutions like Radio Korea. Yet despite this show of solidarity, they suffered the greatest property loss among all ethnic groups.

The 1992 riots had a notable effect on ethnic politics by directing mainstream attention toward leaders within the community best able to articulate the concerns of the Korean American community—namely, English-speaking 1.5 and second generation Korean Americans. During the rebuilding processes, this new wave of ethnic leadership became the intermediary between the immigrant population and mainstream institutions, because of their English-language skills, greater knowledge of American politics and culture, and general exposure to American society. As a result of greater sensitivity to the plight of racial minority groups, these leaders were also better able and more willing to participate in coalition-building efforts with other Asian American and minority communities through organizations like the Asian Pacific Americans for a New Los Angeles (APANLA), the Black-Korean Alliance (BKA), and the Multi-Cultural Collaborative (MCC).

One of the consequences of the newly found attention in the post–civil unrest era was the establishment and strengthening of organizational networks outside the ethnic community. Thus, I find that the 1992 civil unrest was critical in opening the doors to outside resources and networks, which had two main effects on the internal structures of 1.5/second generation ethnic organizations. First, it allowed more established organizations like KYCC to extend and diversify their services to the surrounding area, thus increasing their influence both within and outside the Korean American community. According to several sources, KYCC was able to use the governmental connections it had cultivated through social service contracts to receive many of the postriot recovery funds that were channeled into the Korean American community as a result of the devastation inflicted on Korean immigrant merchants. Within a matter of years, KYCC went from being a small, drop-in community center to an agency working with a $3 million budget that was well recognized in both the ethnic community and the outside world.

Second, events since the 1992 riots helped smaller, lower-tier Korean American organizations like KIWA, which had until then suffered from lack of ethnic elite support, to begin to build a progressive base within the community and mobilize disempowered Koreans. A distinguishing feature of ethnic politics has been the increasing presence of women and immigrant workers in both leadership and staff positions—a significant departure from the male-dominated political culture of the past. Through its incorporation of Korean and Latino immigrant workers and progressive Asian Americans, KIWA epitomizes the ideal to not only include marginalized segments of the Korean American population but to represent and actively advocate for their often-neglected interests— even if this means challenging the immigrant elite of the community. As a result, KIWA could not have expanded and emerged politically to the extent that it did without the support it received from outside organizations.

In the end, mainstream networks allowed ethnic organizations to diversify and be better positioned within ethnic power structures. On one hand, this newly emerging leadership brought with it diverse Americanized ideologies about the Korean American experience that oftentimes clashed with those of the traditional ethnic elite. As one editorial by a first generation Korean reporter bitterly comments, "The fact that English-speaking Korean Americans use terms other than riot to refer to the economic holocaust indicates how removed they are from the community and how unqualified they are to deal with this most pressing Korean American issue."[13] In addition, the political emergence of 1.5/second generation ethnic organizations played a huge role in aggravating interorganizational competition between first and 1.5/second generation leadership. In one *Los Angeles Times* article, a prominent immigrant leader in the Koreatown community remarked on the unwillingness of the younger generation to "share [their] resources with small community-based groups that lack the administrative savvy and connections to compete for funding" because they have been "viewed by mainstream politicians and institutions as the representative of the Korean American community."[14]

At the same time, these events also provided the new leadership with the opportunity to engage actively in the ethnic political structures of the community— albeit in different ways. The perceived plight of Koreans in America and their

isolation from mainstream society renewed a strong sense of ethnic consciousness among younger Korean Americans. This political consciousness set the
context for the integration of 1.5/second generation organizations into existing
power structures. For KYCC, its access to valuable information, resources, and
networks with mainstream institutions made it an invaluable partner for immigrant elite leadership, who also sought some of the same goals despite divergent, generation-based approaches and outlooks. For KIWA, its gradual
entrenchment within the political structures of the ethnic community was
much more strategic and initially surreptitious, because its progressive politics
and goal to empower Koreatown workers clashed with those of the ethnic elite.
As one of the cofounders described to me, the organization began with "non-
threatening" service work and progressed to mainstream political issues, until
the group's leaders thought they had enough widespread support to finally
tackle labor issues within the Korean American community. In either case, both
organizations recognized the need to deal with the pervasive influence of the
immigrant elite and developed their strategies accordingly.

My research indicates that the ethnic elite continues to play a vital role in
the development of new ethnic organizations. Despite ideological tensions and
competition between the two generations, there is a general consensus among
most organizational representatives that the fate of the first generation is still
intertwined with that of the 1.5 and second generations, as shown in this quote
by a second generation activist:

> I remember way back when welfare reform was going on, we had a task
> force in the Korean community. We had first generation and 1.5/second
> generation involved with this. And basically what happened was that the
> first generation said that we don't know what we need to do. So it was the
> second generation that came up with the strategy, okay? There was five of
> us that came up with a strategy. You know what happens? The senior cit-
> izens, they went out and got all these petitions signed and they came
> back with almost like three thousand letters, you know. So I was very sur-
> prised. To me, it blew my mind away . . . that the younger generation we
> came with the plan and the first generation, they implemented it.

According to the interviewee, it is the first generation's networks within the
immigrant-dominated population and the 1.5/second generation's stronger
linkages with networks outside the ethnic community that provide a compelling basis for ethnic solidarity.

Although more advantaged than the first generation organizations in terms
of political expertise, English proficiency, citizenship rights, and access to mainstream resources, 1.5/second generation Korean American organizations are still
constrained by their relations with first generation power-holders who are better equipped to mobilize financial capital, ethnic-based networks of support,

and other community resources within the immigrant-dominated population. For some organizations, mainstream institutions may offer more in the form of financial resources, particularly in the post–civil unrest era. Nevertheless, ethnic-based networks contribute to organizational development by conferring upon organizations other valuable forms of support, including political legitimacy and community backing, immigrant clientele upon which their programs depend, and financial resources that are not subject to strict federal or institutional regulations.

With a large population of native-born Korean Americans in outlying areas, the majority of clientele in Koreatown comes from the immigrant-dominated population. As one counselor notes, "When the mainstream government thinks about community, they mostly think about geographic community, not necessarily the ethnic community." Because the more disadvantaged segments of the Korean American population are foreign-born, organizations like KYCC and KIWA would be unable to justify their social service contracts or even their political mission without some support from the first generation. In addition, several interviewees have remarked on the severe restrictions imposed by government contracts, which cause them to seek other sources of support within the Korean immigrant community. As one social service worker notes, "I think a lot of times the way the program's designed is not culturally sensitive to the Korean American community. Some of the things that [funders] want us to do with our clients is very difficult—you know like financial screening. Koreans hate that."

Certainly, the 1992 Los Angeles civil unrest did much to heighten tensions among the various political leaders, but it also reaffirmed a stronger sense of emotional connectedness among the second generation for the plight of Korean immigrants. The influx of outside resources facilitated alliances and collaborative projects among the various ethnic organizations. In the post-riot era, younger generations of leadership could no longer be ignored or relegated to menial duties within existing immigrant organizations because of their influential position outside the community, such that both sides were forced to collaborate with one another. As a testament to this higher level of intergenerational cooperation, 1.5/second generation–led organizations have engaged in numerous joint projects with the immigrant elite.

One example of this is the intergenerational alliance that spontaneously developed after the suicide of M. S. Lee, a Korean immigrant who had allegedly been harassed and discriminated against by his coworkers and employers at a Japanese corporation. A conglomerate of immigrant and native-born leaders worked together to publicize the tragedy in ethnic and mainstream newspapers and organized protests outside the company. Despite the integral role of more formal alliances, immigrant and second generation leadership have been better known for collaborating with each other on a more informal level, because such flexible relationships are easier to sustain in light of cultural differences.

Sometimes, first or 1.5 generation board members of the organization are critical in mediating between traditional and newly emerging organizations. In contrast, other efforts by native-born leadership to address urgent immigrant-related issues without widespread support from the immigrant community, such as the BKA in the 1980s, ultimately failed to produce any substantive outcomes. The lack of traditional Korean immigrant representation was cited as one of the reasons for BKA's ultimate demise.[15]

Frameworks of Ethnic Political Solidarity

The Case of KYCC

This section takes a closer look at two progressive 1.5/second generation ethnic organizations situated in different circuits of ethnic power structures. The first organization, KYCC, may be considered one of the upper tier organizations that is able to work in relative accommodation with the immigrant elite because of KYCC's orientation around middle-class ethnic goals and its partial dependency on elite resources. The organization gets the information, funding, and political influence it needs to achieve its ambitious political agenda through established, resource-rich institutions within the ethnic community and mainstream society. Based on organizational records, interviews, and general observation of KYCC events, I compiled the following categories of individuals and institutions as being the primary donors or supporters of the organization. The organization's main bases of support come from the elite sectors of the ethnic community, such as businesses and churches and established mainstream institutions and corporations. These include:

1. Governmental agencies and politicians on the city, county, state, and federal levels
2. Private foundations
3. Large mainstream corporations (for example, Southern California Edison)
4. Large Korean corporations (for example, Korea Times, Korean Air, Korean Television Enterprise, Hanmi Bank)
5. Established first generation immigrant organizations (for example, Korean Consulate General, Korean Chamber of Commerce, Korean Federation)
6. Small businesses
7. Churches and religious organizations
8. Other Korean community-based organizations (for example, Korean Health Education, Information, and Research Center [KHEIR], Korean Garment Wholesalers Association)
9. Non-Korean ethnic organizations, coalitions, and social service agencies (for example, Little Tokyo Service Center, El Centro de Pueblo, Salvation Army)
10. Individual sponsors, especially young professionals such as CPAs and lawyers

Many of these supporters are well positioned to offer KYCC considerable financial support in the form of program endowments or donations during the organization's annual fund-raising dinners.

Other than financial support, KYCC has been shown to depend on the
ethnic elite to maintain political legitimacy within the ethnic community.
Although a few interviewees complained about the organization's preoccupation with its image over the needs of its clientele, others contend that KYCC's
reputation and backdoor networking allow the organization to draw in and
effectively serve clients in the first place. As one third generation Korean
American board member comments, "I think the board feels that it's important to maintain those ties, because when you look around at the community,
we still are an immigrant community. We are recognizing much more the need
to deal with the community or deal with families as much as the individual
youth." Political stature is a key factor in the organization's ability to bring in
clients, provide the resources to serve the clients, and gain the kind of recognition within the ethnic community needed to justify funding from outside
mainstream agencies. KYCC has collaborated with the immigrant elite on various levels, from individual consultation exchanges to interorganizational collaborative projects.

The organizational leadership perceives the success of the community as
depending on the ability to both unite on an ethnic level and integrate into
mainstream society through traditional routes of acculturation and upward
mobility. One second generation board member describes the political mission
of KYCC:

> Many Korean Americans [in KYCC] generally promote the idea of trying
> to integrate this agency into the fabric of the city. Integrate not in the
> sense of you know becoming a Red Cross or United Way, [or] a YMCA that
> is wholly homogenized. The second and third generation still see the very
> significant importance of keeping a Korean orientation. But as part of
> that Korean orientation, the role of making sure that the Korean
> [American] community is a part of the LA community. And that's both
> about putting KYCC out into the community as well as bringing members
> of the community into KYCC.

The organization's political mission reflects values that are in some ways com-
patible with those of the immigrant elite (for example, entrepreneurs). Among
other things, its programs and services are aimed at promoting education and
career mobility, the healthy functioning of the traditional family unit, the
growth of elite political leadership, and greater ties with the ethnic community.

Within this context, staff members generally perceive the role of the organization as helping underprivileged Korean American youth and their families
to develop the knowledge and skills to succeed on an individual level while also

empowering and uniting the ethnic community on a collective level. A second generation male youth coordinator explains:

> I was raised in the suburbs, Cerritos, and it's kind of well known for a lot of Asians there. It's a very affluent suburb. Kids tend to be pressured more to do well in school, because kids around them, the peers and their environment, they're focused a lot on education so college is not an option. It's another step for kids in the suburbs, and they are very career-driven and have a lot of other activities like involving themselves in church or other organizations. In Koreatown, the resources are very limited, and the environment itself is not geared towards academic issues. Just remembering how it was in middle school and how I was studying all the time versus these kids are missing a lot of things in their lives and I feel really bad for them. So it motivates me to do more for them.

This collective consciousness also pervades the accounts of KYCC's clientele. For instance, one ex-gang member, who told me that he did not have high aspirations before coming to KYCC, excitedly relayed to me his plans to start up a juice bar business—an idea he got from his supervisor. He would use part of the profits to employ other ex-gang members like himself. Thus, he could start up a successful business while also contributing to the betterment of the community.

Most employees I interviewed told me that they had come to KYCC because they needed a job, a different type of work experience, a chance to hone their knowledge and skills with a nonprofit organization, or the chance to learn from more experienced mentors. KYCC's membership is primarily composed of 1.5 and second generation college-educated Korean Americans mainly but not exclusively in their twenties and thirties, most of whom live in outlying suburban areas of the county (see Table 9.1). My interview with KYCC affiliates indicates that the majority of the line staff are either in the beginning of their career trajectories or have had some experience working with service-oriented orga-nizations in the past. Many are also involved with churches, which reaffirms their roots with the ethnic elite and their ideologies about ethnic solidarity, social service, and humanitarianism. Ultimately, they hope either to continue working with social service agencies or the general nonprofit sector or to pursue middle-class professional careers in medicine, law, government, or education, among other things.

The organization's hierarchical, bureaucratic structure helps to create a professional environment within which to foster elite leadership skills, networks, and resources for upwardly mobile members. KYCC is able to provide these types of opportunities only because it has the financial resources and support networks to build a large, bureaucratic organization with the capacity to train, develop, and promote individual staff members. Furthermore, because of its interconnectedness with elite leadership in the Korean American community and mainstream society, KYCC can help members to develop and promote their

TABLE 9.1
Profile of Past and Present Korean Members at KIWA and KYCC, 2000

	KYCC		KIWA	
	No.	%	No.	%
Gender				
Male	14	46.7	5	35.7
Female	16	53.3	9	64.3
Age				
Under 22	5	16.7	0	0.0
22–29	10	33.3	7	50.0
30–39	8	26.7	5	35.7
40+	6	20.0	2	14.3
Not available	1	3.3	0	0.0
Generation				
1st generation	7	23.3	4	28.6
1.5 generation	7	23.3	5	35.7
2nd generation	15	50.0	5	35.7
Not available	1	3.3	0	0.0
Education				
No/some high school	2	6.7	1	7.1
High school grad	4	13.3	3	21.4
B.A. degree	15	50.0	6	42.9
M.A. degree	3	10.0	0	0.0
Post-grad degree	3	10.0	2	14.3
Not available	3	10.0	2	14.3
City of residence				
In/near Koreatown[a]	9	30.0	5	35.7
Outside Koreatown	20	66.7	9	64.3
Not available	1	3.3	0	0.0

(Continued)

TABLE 9.1

Profile of Past and Present Korean Members at KIWA and KYCC, 2000
(Continued)

	KYCC		KIWA	
	No.	*%*	*No.*	*%*
Language				
Mostly English	13	43.3	3	21.4
Mostly Korean	3	10.0	4	28.6
Korean-English	12	40.0	2	14.3
Korean-Spanish	0	0.0	1	7.1
Korean-English-Spanish	2	6.7	4	28.6
TOTAL	30	100.0	14	100.0

[a] Indicates those who reported living in an area within a mile radius of Koreatown.

career aspirations by exposing them to new experiences and critical social networks for future occupational mobility. As an example of this, one female staff member with experience working in political offices informs me that Korean Americans interested in going into mainstream politics oftentimes start out by working in ethnic nonprofits like this, because it provides them with critical networks and legitimacy within the ethnic community.

The Case of KIWA

Although organizations like KYCC are integral in building the resource base of the ethnic community, community-based organizations like KIWA can be credited for broadening the meaning of "ethnic solidarity" to include the diverse ethnic-centered experiences of second generation Korean Americans. In the process, they have expanded the political terrain in a way that enables the ethnic community to move beyond the narrow political goals of traditional immigrant elite leaders. Although they attract a strong Korean immigrant worker clientele, KIWA's progressive mission and strong stance against exploitative labor practices of Korean business owners have raised major opposition from the Korean business elite and hence tensions with other members of the traditional ethnic elite. The organization has worked with immigrant power-holders on an issue-to-issue basis, but they have been most well known for their boycotts of Korean-owned businesses and for militant protests against injustices within the Korean American community and have thus relied on a stronger base of support outside the ethnic community. KIWA's main networks of support include:

1. Labor unions
2. Other labor organizations (for example, Sweatshop Watch, ACORN)
3. Private progressive foundations (for example, Liberty Hill Foundation)
4. Small, progressive Korean organizations (for example, National Korean American Service and Education Consortium [NAKASEC])
5. Non-Korean Asian American organizations (for example, Thai Community Development Center, Filipino Workers Center)
6. Latino organizations (for example, Coalition for Humane Immigrant Rights of Los Angeles [CHIRLA])
7. South Korean progressive student and labor groups (for example, Korean Federation of Trade Unions)
8. Other outside liberal organizations
9. Individual supporters, especially workers

KIWA's main networks include other similar organizations outside the ethnic elite circle as well as many organizations outside the ethnic community itself. Interestingly, their non-coethnic bases of support include a diversity of constituencies, including labor unions, Asian American and Latino organizations, and South Korean leftist groups.

KIWA challenges the ideology of meritocracy, capitalist wealth, and "family values" that underlies the entrepreneurial success of Korean immigrants in the United States and instead argues that to succeed, the community must rely on broader visions than the middle-class aspirations of individual achievement and hard work. A 1.5 generation male staff member argues:

> A lot of people still think immigration to U.S. is opportunity to prosper in terms of economically and lot of their excuse is to provide education to their children. So they're still really, really working hard . . . and trying to improve their economic conditions. I think KIWA is saying that it's true that community's working hard to improve their lives and community as a whole. But if all these different issues, such as workers' issue, and other political issue is not addressed, the Korean community's not developing with balance.

The activities of the traditional ethnic elite are seen as supporting American hierarchies of race/ethnicity, class, and gender by aspiring to work within the system and promoting hierarchical ideologies (for example, entrepreneurial values about family and upward mobility that perpetuate the model minority myth).

Considering the organization's position of marginality within local power structures and their lack of financial resources, how is KIWA able to fulfill its political agenda of empowering workers against business owners who have on their side blacklisting tactics, organizational support, and financial resources? One of the downsides of KIWA's ethnic network structure is that it is mainly based on other lower-tier organizations whose financial base is already spread thin. Furthermore, few of these organizations wield enough political influence within the ethnic community to sway public opinion in their favor on numerous political issues. As a second generation staff member complained, "[People] have this view that KIWA only survives to be like in opposition. You know, they see us as the rioters and the picketers . . . not a friend to the Korean immigrant." Although they acknowledge the benefits of making their own rules and regulations (as opposed to following those of funding agencies), others have remarked on the challenges KIWA faces in trying to work with the limited funding it is able to tap.

Nevertheless, such support networks still provide a crucial source of support in the form of manpower, organizing experience, and outside publicity. As one interviewee related to me, being a relatively new organization in a largely conservative community, KIWA tends to find role models with longer histories of organizing experience from outside the Korean American community. For instance, the executive director has been known to visit other organizations with limited resources to gain insights on how to fight more powerful groups. As the case of KIWA shows, direct action is a critical tool for organizations situated on the peripheries of ethnic power structures, because it achieves several goals: it publicizes injustices to organizations outside the Korean community, bringing external pressure through negative publicity; it allows them to do this with minimal time and financial costs; and it helps immigrant workers to gain both leadership skills and greater political knowledge in the American system.

Staff and volunteers are less career oriented in their motivations and more drawn to the organization by its broader vision of social justice, coalition building, and progressive politics within the Korean American community. I have found that members are drawn to ethnic community work because of ideological linkages they make between KIWA's framework of social justice and their personal ethnic-centered experiences as Korean Americans. KIWA mostly attracts liberal, college-educated Korean Americans in their twenties and thirties. The political consciousnesses of most staff members were shaped by earlier formative life experiences and political involvement with other progressive organizations and social movements in the United States and Korea, including labor organizations, Korean American organizations, progressive movements in Korea, and other Asian American/racial minority organizations. Some were raised in predominantly white suburbs and became involved with Korean/Korean American, Asian American, or other race-based organizations in order to find a sense of connectedness with their ethnic community. Very few are associated with churches, much less Korean churches. Only a few of them hope to pursue upper white-collar professional careers, and even those who do are committed to careers that help the community (for example, public interest law). Instead, the majority of them have expressed the desire to continue struggling for the larger goal of social justice through less profitable but community-oriented jobs like teaching and participation in liberal organizations like KIWA and in the non-profit sector.

But because the Korean American community is predominantly immigrant as well as conservative, current members initially sought sanctuary in other racial and ethnic communities. The dominance of traditional ethnic elite interests in the new immigrant community shapes politics in such a way that more progressive Korean Americans—from students to workers to leftist and coalitional activists—have had a difficult time finding an established channel through which to voice their concerns to both the ethnic community and mainstream society. A second generation female activist explains it in this way:

> I don't really feel connected to the Korean American community, but I feel like it is diverse and that diversity isn't often represented but then I'm still part of the Korean American community. But sometimes I feel like there's no one that I can relate to in the Korean American community as opposed to the Filipino community or Japanese or Chinese. It's just different, because Korean Americans are still very traditional and more conservative and stuff, even in areas like homosexuality and religion. I guess in other communities, it seems like they're a little bit more accepting, because they've been here longer. I kind of see Korean Americans going in that direction. But I still feel like I'm a Korean American and I need to work toward my immediate community.

The passage underscores the centrality of the respondent's ethnic identity in her sense of political consciousness but suggests how this comes into conflict with the conservative nature of ethnic power structures. In this way, KIWA offered an ideological passageway and training ground for progressive Korean Americans to take part in larger organizations and movements for social justice as well as developing the organizing skills to help workers to empower themselves.

The Multiple Bases of Ethnic Solidarity

The case of Koreatown politics demonstrates how ethnic organizational structures can create new ways of adapting to the internal fragmentation of post-1965 immigrant communities when there are both compelling reasons and substantial resources to mobilize around shared ethnic-based interests. The status of Koreatown as the institutional powerhouse of a spatially dispersed community has provided ethnic organizations with the general resource base and infrastructure within which to pursue their political goals. In this sense, the rise of vibrant ethnic enclave economies in an era of globalization has created new incentives for political actors to engage with one another despite increasing dissonance over the terms of this partnership.

Based on these findings, I have challenged traditional approaches that interpret residential dispersion, class polarization, and generational differences as signaling the disintegration of ethnicity as a meaningful basis for collective action in community politics. Clearly, complementary resources link the fate of 1.5/second generation organizations to the traditional power structures of the ethnic community, but organizational approaches to ethnic solidarity are based not simply on ties to the ethnic community but also on how organizations relate to those who control the community's resources.

At the same time, ethnic organizations have stratified themselves along two interactive but divergent circuits of power. One is based on a middle-class approach to ethnic political solidarity that works in accommodation with the immigrant elite and is somewhat closer to traditional notions of ethnicity and middle-class ethnic success. The other is based on a broader notion of ethnic political solidarity that encompasses the wide range of ethnic identities that 1.5/second generation embrace as Asian Americans, women of color, children of immigrants, and so forth, and relies on alliances with outside interest groups.

These organizational frameworks focus on the salience of ethnicity as a central feature of the American experience, yet how they conceptualize the ethnic community and where this fits within the broader schemata of ethnic politics vary depending on the way they navigate immigrant power structures. Indeed, these diverse strategies ultimately lead to the diversification and specialization of ethnic political structures, not its disintegration, which enables organizational leadership to better connect with an increasingly heterogeneous ethnic population and thus to enhance a sense of community and political unity across multiple lines of stratification. The greater the resources, the greater the capacity of ethnic organizational structures to cater to an internally diverse population, including marginalized segments of the community as well as non-coethnic constituencies (for example, Latinos). In the process, bridging organizations have completely rearticulated the sociopolitical meanings of "ethnic solidarity," which are no longer based on spatially bound, monolithic conceptualizations of ethnic community but rather on specialized political agendas that arise from navigating the rapidly diversifying context of Koreatown and the Korean American community.

NOTES

Portions of this chapter were taken from Angie Y. Chung, *Legacies of Struggle: Conflict and Cooperation in Korean American Politics*, © 2007 by the Board of Trustees of the Leland Stanford Jr. University. Special thanks to KIWA and KYCC for their assistance with the research. I would like to acknowledge Edward J. W. Park, Min Zhou, Walter R. Allen, John

Horton, and John Logan for their helpful comments on different versions of this essay. The research was assisted by a fellowship from the International Migration Program of the Social Science Research Council (with funds provided by the Andrew W. Mellon Foundation), resources from the Center for Comparative Immigration Studies, and a grant from the Institute of American Cultures and UCLA Asian American Studies Center. Please direct all correspondence to: Angie Y. Chung, Department of Sociology, University at Albany, 1400 Washington Avenue, Albany, NY 12222 (e-mail: aychung@albany.edu).

1. Pei-Te Lien, *The Making of Asian America through Political Participation* (Philadelphia: Temple University Press, 2001); Don Nakanishi, "The Next Swing Vote? Asian Pacific Americans and California Politics," in *Racial and Ethnic Politics in California*, ed. Bryan O. Jackson and Michael B. Preston, 25–54 (Berkeley, Calif.: Institute for Governmental Studies, 1990); L. Ling-chi Wang, "Exclusion and Fragmentation in Ethnic Politics: Chinese Americans in Urban Politics," in *The Politics of Minority Coalitions: Race, Ethnicity, and Shared Uncertainties*, ed. Wilbur C. Rich, 129–142 (Westport, Conn.: Praeger, 1996).

2. Ernest W. Burgess, "The Growth of the City: An Introduction to a Research Project," in *The City*, ed. Robert E. Park et al., 47–62 (Chicago: University of Chicago Press, 1925); Milton Gordon, *Assimilation in American Life: The Role of Race, Religion, and National Origins* (New York: Oxford University Press, 1964); David Ward, *Poverty, Ethnicity, and the American City, 1840–1925: Changing Conceptions of the Slum and Ghetto* (Cambridge: Cambridge University Press, 1989).

3. Mark Edward Pfeifer, " 'Community,' Adaptation and the Vietnamese in Toronto" (Ph.D. diss., University of Toronto, 1999).

4. Nancy Abelmann and John Lie, *Blue Dreams: Korean Americans and the Los Angeles Riots* (Cambridge, Mass.: Harvard University Press, 1995).

5. Raymond Breton, "Institutional Completeness of Ethnic Communities and the Personal Relations of Immigrants," *American Journal of Sociology* 70, no. 2 (1964): 193–205; Min Zhou, *Chinatown: The Socioeconomic Potential of an Urban Enclave* (Philadelphia: Temple University Press, 1992); Alejandro Portes and Alex Stepick, *City on the Edge: The Transformation of Miami* (Berkeley: University of California Press, 1993).

6. Angie Y. Chung, *Legacies of Struggle: Conflict and Cooperation in Korean American Politics* (Stanford, Calif.: Stanford University Press, 2007).

7. Generational status itself is based on levels of socialization within the educational systems of the United States. Thus the "first generation" includes all those who were born in Korea and arrived after the age of eighteen (post–high school stage); "1.5 generation" are those who immigrated between the ages of six and eighteen (elementary school and high school stages); and "second generation" are those who were either born in the United States or had arrived before primary school age.

8. Chung, *Legacies of Struggle*.

9. Edward Tea Chang, "The Post–Los Angeles Riot Korean American Community: Challenges and Prospects," *Korean and Korean American Studies Bulletin* 10, nos. 1–2 (1999): 6–26.

10. Ibid.; Edward Tea Chang, "Korean Community Politics in Los Angeles: The Impact of the Kwangju Uprising," *Amerasia Journal* 14, no. 1 (1988): 51–67; Ilsoo Kim, *New Urban Immigrants: The Korean Community in New York* (Princeton, N.J.: Princeton University Press, 1981).

11. Chang, "Korean Community Politics in Los Angeles;" Edward J. W. Park, "Competing Visions: Political Formation of Korean Americans in Los Angeles, 1992–1997," *Amerasia Journal* 24, no. 1 (1998): 41–57.

12. Paul Ong and Suzanne Hee, *Losses in the Los Angeles Civil Unrest* (Los Angeles: UCLA Center for Pacific Rim Studies, 1993).

13. "Sa-ee-gu (April 29) Was a Riot, not 'Civil Unrest,'" *Korea Times*, March 26–April 29, 1997.

14. "A Cause for Korean American Celebration—and Controversy," *Los Angeles Times*, May 13, 1994.

15. Edward Tea Chang and Jeannette Diaz-Veizades, *Ethnic Peace in the American City: Building Community in Los Angeles and Beyond* (New York: New York University Press, 1999).

PART FOUR

Asian Communities
in Canada

10

The Social Construction of
Chinese in Canada

PETER S. LI

Two main perspectives have been used to understand the development of Chinese communities overseas. The first stresses the historical origin of emigration, focusing on the influence of ancestral roots and homeland ties on Chinese community formation. According to this view, the Chinese overseas share a common history of emigration and displacement, a collective memory of the ancestral home, and a sense of estrangement that arises from being uprooted in the home country and marginalized in the country of adoption.[1] In short, the experiences of emigration and estrangement provide the common grounds for strengthening the cultural identity within a diaspora, and for nurturing an often exaggerated image of the distant ancestral home based on its reconstructed historical and cultural richness. Chinese communities overseas have been able to maintain a strong ethnic identity and cultural resilience because of the strength of the Chinese kinship system, affinity to homeland and ancestral roots, and commonality in language, tradition, and place of origin.[2]

The second perspective focuses on changes of diaspora communities as a result of increased migration and transnational flow under globalization. The term "new diasporas" has been used to describe the reconfiguration of global diasporas in the second half of the twentieth century that has been produced by complex migration processes and to stress the multiple memberships of migrants in different societies and their multiple allegiances.[3] This perspective highlights the importance of migration shifts in shaping ethnic diaspora configurations and identity formation. If "place" provides the stability and continuity for cultural identity in classical diasporas, then movements between places give rise to flexibility and identity shifts in new diasporas. In the case of Chinese overseas, Ong and Nonini have argued that economic globalization has de-territorialized the Chinese diaspora communities, making them flexible and highly mobile, and that the shifting experiences of the diaspora Chinese require them to rework the conditions of flexibility.[4] The view of flexible identity and multiple allegiances as characteristics of contemporary Chinese overseas stands in sharp contrast to the conventional wisdom of seeing the Chinese diaspora as

transplanted communities with enduring Chinese cultural values and organizations, such as the persistence of Chinese commercialism, extended familism,
and homeland affinity.[5]

Despite the fundamental differences between the two views, they both in
fact dwell on opposite aspects of identity formation, stressing either the
resilience of traditional homeland culture or the fluidity of postmodern
transnational relations. Both perspectives tend to interpret Chinese communities overseas as defined by cultural identity, in the first instance influenced by
the persistence of homeland traditions and affinity, and in the second instance
by the adoption of fluid identity and multiple allegiances.

Notwithstanding the merits of studying Chinese communities overseas in
terms of identity formation, this chapter focuses on the social construction of
Chinese as a racial minority in a majority setting, using the case of Canada. The
attention here is on explaining the historical and contemporary processes by
which the notion of Chinese has been given social significance. Rather than
treating the Chinese either as a transplanted cultural entity shaped by homeland traditions and forces or as an amorphous transnational collectivity sustained by transnational connections and pragmatic considerations, the
approach here is to explain how the Chinese came to be a racial minority in
Canada. In order for the Chinese to be understood as a racial minority in the cultural framework of majority Canadians, there must have been a process of
racialization by which selected cultural and physical features of the group,
whether real or presumed, have been paired with social characteristics to
become markers of the racial minority.[6] Over time, the social characteristics
and cultural meanings imputed to a racial minority become ingrained in the
hearts and minds of people as though they are primordial features and not
products of social relations between the majority and the minority. Hence,
understanding the Chinese community in Canada requires deconstructing the
notion of Chinese to see how the concept was given social content and meanings in the first place and how it has changed over time.

The Making of the Chinese Minority in Canada

Chinese immigration to Canada began in 1859, after gold was discovered in the
Fraser Valley of British Columbia.[7] Initially, the Chinese came as gold miners from
California. Shortly after, the Chinese came directly from China to Canada, mainly
as laborers, in response to labor shortages in railway construction and in other
labor-intensive industries of the bourgeoning West. At the height of railway construction in 1881 and 1882, over 11,000 Chinese came by ship to Victoria from
China directly.[8] The Chinese quickly became the target of racial discrimination in
the late nineteenth and early twentieth centuries. Many laws were passed to
restrict Chinese immigration and to curtail the rights of those already in Canada.

Between their initial arrival in 1859 and the passage of the 1923 Chinese Immigration Act, the Chinese in Canada were frequent targets of discrimination and were subjected to many legislative controls. For example, as soon as the Canadian Pacific Railway was completed, the federal government imposed a head tax of $50 on virtually every Chinese person entering the country. The head tax was raised to $100 in 1900 and then to $500 in 1903.[9] Between 1886 and 1924, 86,000 Chinese entering Canada paid a total of $23 million in head taxes. In addition, British Columbia passed numerous laws against the Chinese between 1875 and 1923, disallowing them to acquire Crown lands, preventing them from working in underground mines, excluding them from admission to the provincially established home for the aged and infirm, prohibiting them from being hired on public works, and disqualifying them from voting.

The 1923 Chinese Immigration Act required every Chinese person in Canada, regardless of citizenship, to register with the federal government within twelve months and to obtain a registration certificate, with a heavy penalty for failing to do so.[10] Furthermore, every Chinese person in Canada who intended to leave Canada temporarily had to file an official notice of departure and register with the government. Chinese leaving Canada for more than twenty-four months would forfeit the right to return even with the registration.

The 1923 act also prohibited further Chinese immigration to Canada. As a result, many Chinese in Canada, mostly men, endured long periods of permanent separation from their family in China. Before 1923, financial hardship and social animosity discouraged the Chinese from bringing their family to Canada when it was legally possible to do so. The 1923 act dashed any hope of the Chinese immigrants to bring their family, as virtually no Chinese were allowed to come to Canada between 1923 and 1947.[11]

The exclusionary policies and discriminatory legislation against the Chinese effectively reduced them to second-class citizens. They were denied many basic rights, including the right to pursue a living in many occupations, the right to vote, and the right to travel freely in and out of Canada. The Chinese were frequent targets of political demagogy and social hostility. The unequal treatment of the Chinese further contributed to their marginal social status in Canadian society. The restriction on citizenship rights and their legal exclusion from higher-paying jobs forced the Chinese to seek refuge in service industries, notably the laundry and restaurant businesses. By 1931, about 40 percent of the Chinese in Canada were servants, cooks, waiters, or laundry workers. The restaurant business was a survival haven for many Chinese before the Second World War, and it remained an important sector of employment and self-employment for the Chinese after the war, even when opportunities in professional and technical occupations became available to them.

Another consequence of institutional racism was to retard the development of the Chinese Canadian family. The Chinese Canadian community remained a predominantly male society until decades after the Second World War. In 1911, among the 27,831 Chinese in Canada, the sex ratio was 2,800 men to 100 women; in 1931 the sex ratio was 1,240 men to 100 women among the 46,519 Chinese.[12] Throughout all the census years before 1946, the imbalance in the sex ratio among the Chinese population was the most severe among all ethnic groups in Canada. In the absence of Chinese women, many Chinese men in Canada maintained a "married bachelor" life—living as a bachelor in Canada separated from their wives and children in China. Those who had the means would periodically travel to China for a sojourn with their families. The absence of Chinese women and family in Canada also meant that the delay of a second generation in Canada. Many wives of Chinese Canadian men endured severe emotional and financial hardships in China, raising the children on their own. Throughout this period, the Chinese in Canada organized many voluntary associations as a means to answer community needs. These associations provided important functions, such as organizing social services, mediating internal disputes, sending remittances to China, and dealing with external pressures of discrimination and segregation.

Historical Social Construction of the Chinese

Historically, the immigration discourse in Canada has racialized its territorial and social boundaries by upholding the value of European immigrants, notably those from Britain, northern Europe, and the United States, and discounting the contributions of nonwhite immigrants, particularly those from Asia.[13] In other words, Canada's territorial security and social boundaries were expressed in clear racial terms, with an unequivocal understanding that the value of non-European races to Canada was questionable even though their contribution to some developing industries was essential. This discursive framework has been influenced by Canada's long-standing racial ideology, which saw Oriental immigrants as racially, morally, and culturally inferior to the Occidental tradition of Canada.[14] Hence, the historical restriction and exclusion of Asian immigrants, in particular the Chinese, were equated with safeguarding Canada's borders and its European traditions from what was seen as the "yellow peril."

There is no doubt that the various federal and provincial laws passed against the Chinese between 1885 and 1923 had the adverse effect of reducing the social image and market worth of the Chinese, as they were branded by legislation as an undesirable racial minority that, unless harnessed by law, would be harmful to Canadian society. But even around the time the Canadian Pacific Railway was completed, the Chinese had been painted as a race that was unworthy of Canada, despite the usefulness of Chinese labor to the various bourgeoning industries of British Columbia. A royal commission headed by John Gray produced a report in 1885 that contained substantial damning testimonies against the Chinese regarding their alleged moral character and social habits.

Commissioner Gray summarized the allegations under six headings: (1) Chinese laborers displaced white workers and retarded the settlement; (2) the Chinese dominated domestic service and endangered the country with immorality; (3) the Chinese were known for their uncleanliness and filthy habits and for bringing diseases; (4) the Chinese engaged in opium smoking, prostitution, slavery, and immorality; (5) the Chinese maintained secret organizations, evaded taxes, and became public burdens; and (6) the Chinese did not identify with Canada and withdrew their economic gains from Canada.[15]

Although many of the allegations—such as those regarding Chinese criminality, tax evasion, and lacking economic contributions—were found to be exaggerations that were not supported by the evidence, there was substantial convergence in testimonies against their moral character and their undesirability for Canada.[16] These testimonies reflected how the Chinese race was constructed in the cultural framework of European Canadians, despite the economic values the Chinese brought to many industries.

The idea that the Chinese belonged to an inferior race that could never mix properly with the European race was a central aspect in the social construction of the Chinese. For example, a Mr. Thompson, a member of the Parliament from Cariboo, British Columbia, described the Chinese:

> They are a separate race from the whites. They do not amalgamate with the whites, nor do they adopt our customs. They live among themselves. They have their own religion and also they have secret societies. . . . They contribute very little to the wealth of the country, and, to a certain extent, they impoverish it by competing with white men.[17]

A Dr. McInnis, another member of Parliament, was more blatant in giving his view about the "inferior Chinese race":

> I consider them a low class—certainly much lower than any white class of people I have ever come in contact with. . . . They have certainly a very demoralizing effect upon the white people of British Columbia, or any other country in which they have gained a permanent foothold.[18]

Several alleged features of the Chinese race or the Chinese culture were depicted, and these testimonies implied that the Chinese could not be assimilated with the European race because of the fundamental nature of the "inferior race." One of these features had to do with the untrustworthiness of the Chinese. A Mr. Thompson testified:

> Yes; they will steal any thing they can lay their hands on if they get a favourable opportunity for doing so. Of course, there are white men who will steal too, but the Chinamen can never be trusted to work by himself in any place where there is coarse gold that can be picked up.[19]

Not all testimonies were on the undesirability of the Chinese social habits and moral character. Several witnesses spoke about the Chinese workers as being industrious, frugal, and diligent, making them particularly suitable for harsh labor, and about the Chinese businesspeople as being trustworthy in business transactions. But few had anything positive to say about the moral character of the Chinese as a racial group.[20]

At times, conflicting evidence about the Chinese character was given even by the same witness. A Mr. Bernard, another member of Parliament from British Columbia, described the Chinese as both "smart" or "cunning" but "low in intelligence." He warned that the Chinese were "too smart" for the Europeans and that they would beat them "everywhere they got a foothold," but at the same time, the Chinese worker is "a grade lower" than "the ordinary white labourer of this country."[21] A Mr. Cornwall, a senator from British Columbia, also testified that the Chinese were useful because they provided low-cost labor, but they should never be given the right to vote because of what he called their "ignorance of our institutions and language."[22]

By the beginning of the twentieth century, the Chinese as a minority assumed an unmistakable image of being suitable only to harsh labor but also being inferior to Europeans racially due to their questionable character and incompatible nature. In addition to the stereotypic construction of the Chinese race in general, there were special ideological contents attributed to Chinese women and to the Chinese quarter dubbed Chinatown.

Historically, the number of Chinese women relative to Chinese men was always small, as the financial cost of the head tax and the hostile social atmosphere prevented many Chinese men from bringing their family to Canada even in the period prior to the total exclusion of Chinese.[23] The 1911 Census of Canada indicated that there were only 961 Chinese women among 26,813 Chinese men; by 1921 there were 2,424 Chinese women and 37,163 Chinese men.[24] With the exception of the small Chinese merchant class who could afford to bring their wives and families with them to Canada before 1923, the vast majority of the working class Chinese were deprived of married life in Canada.

Another category of Chinese women that often caused public scrutiny in the nineteenth century was Chinese prostitutes. There is little direct evidence on the conditions facing Chinese prostitutes in Canada. In 1885, the Royal Commission on Chinese Immigration indicated that British Columbia had 154 Chinese women, of whom 70 were prostitutes, among 10,550 Chinese.[25] There were also a small number of Chinese women who were concubines and maids purchased in China and brought over to Canada, most likely by merchants.[26]

Despite the conspicuous absence of Chinese women in Canada in the nineteenth century, they shared a poor social image in the minds of white Canadians. The few Chinese women in Canada were widely believed by the Canadian public to be mostly slave girls, concubines, or prostitutes, and considered to be more injurious to the community than "white abandoned women."[27] The image of Chinese women as syphilis-infested prostitutes luring young white men was also popularized by some newspapers.[28] Some Canadian legislators in the late nineteenth and early twentieth century were convinced of the need to exclude Chinese women from Canada in order to limit the growth of the Chinese population.[29]

The Chinese urban living quarters, commonly known as "Chinatown," also assumed an inferior racial content. The term "Chinatown" was developed in the nineteenth century as a European concept to represent an undesirable neighborhood filled with unsanitary conditions and vices and populated by an inferior race.[30] Accordingly, the concoction of such a concept reflected the cultural hegemony of European settlers in being able to abstract from the unequal conditions facing the Chinese into a racial ideology about the Chinese race and their moral threat to Canadian society. The term "Chinatown" was widely used in the nineteenth century in the media and public discourse, often with a negative and exotic connotation. Over time, the stereotypic symbols and racial mystics associated with "Chinatown" were entrenched in the ideology of white Canadians, and both Europeans with the power to coin the ideological meanings of Chinatown, and the Chinese to whom those meanings were applied, came to accept the label as legitimate.

Changing Conditions for the Chinese Minority after World War II

It was after World War II that the legally sanctioned exclusion and discrimination against the Chinese were removed. Further changes to the immigration regulations in the 1960s removed the remaining barriers of immigration for Chinese. However, it was not until 1967 when Canada adopted a universal point system of assessing potential immigrants that the Chinese were admitted under the same criteria as others. The Chinese population increased substantially after 1967. In 1971, the Chinese Canadian population was 124,600; by 1981, it had expanded to 285,800, and it further increased to 412,800 in 1986 and to 922,000 in 1996. About two-thirds of Chinese Canadians now live in Vancouver and Toronto. Slightly over one-quarter of Chinese Canadians were born in Canada; most foreign-born Chinese came to Canada after 1967.[31]

The new wave of Chinese immigrants who came after 1967 contributed to the growth of a new generation of Chinese Canadians. They tended to be better educated, more cosmopolitan, and upwardly mobile. The arrival of these immigrants and the growth of native-born Chinese Canadians helped to produce an emergent new Chinese middle class. They began to take up professional, technical, and managerial jobs, which historically were denied to the Chinese. Further changes in the immigration policy in the mid-1980s in favor of business immigrants and the prospective return of Hong Kong to China in 1997 triggered another wave of Chinese immigrants to Canada. Many of the new immigrants brought substantial wealth and human capital to Canada; they came from Hong Kong, but also Taiwan and other parts of Asia that had experienced rapid economic growth in the 1970s and 1980s. By the late 1980s, there were many indicators that a new affluent class of Chinese Canadians had emerged, and their spending power and investment capacity stimulated the expansion of a new "ethnic" consumer market.[32] In turn, urban Canada went through many changes: middle-class Chinese Canadians moved to traditional white neighborhoods, Chinese businesses flourished in suburban malls, and Canadian corporations and investment houses went after the fast-growing lucrative consumer market created by the new wealth of Chinese immigrants and the social mobility of middle-class Chinese Canadians. Changes in economic and political conditions in Hong Kong and China in the 1980s and amendments to Canada's immigration policies in the 1990s to emphasize the immigration of economic-class immigrants further encouraged immigration from Hong Kong and later mainland China. As a result, the population of those of Chinese origin continued to grow, reaching 1,094,700, or about 3.7 percent of Canada's population, in 2001.[33]

One of the conspicuous changes in the Chinese community has been the growth of the new Chinese middle class.[34] Counting those in managerial, professional, supervisory, and administrative occupations as belonging to the middle class, about 18 percent of the Chinese in Canada's labor force were estimated to belong to the middle class in 1971, 23 percent in 1981, and 28 percent in 1991.[35] By 2001, Chinese in managerial and professional positions accounted for 33 percent of those in Canada's workforce. But if those in semiprofessional, supervisory, and administrative and senior clerical positions are included, then as many as 48 percent of the Chinese in the Canadian labor force in 2001 can be classified as middle class.

Transnational migration has been the main factor that accounts for the growth of the workforce and, along with it, the middle class, among the Chinese in Canada. For example, in 2001, 84 percent of the Chinese middle class, as well as the Chinese in the Canadian labor market, were born outside of Canada. In other words, without transnational migration, the Chinese middle class in Canada would have been reduced from 272,000 to slightly over 44,000 persons.[36]

Among the foreign-born Chinese middle class, about 70 percent immigrated to Canada between 1981 and 2001. The importance of transnational migration in the making of the Chinese middle-class population between 1991 and 2001 is particularly clear. It accounts for 44 percent of the total foreign-born Chinese middle class, and 47 percent of those in professional and semiprofessional jobs.

The region from which the foreign-born Chinese middle class originated has shifted over time. In the 1970s and 1980s, about 42 percent came from Hong Kong. However, in the 1990s mainland China accounted for about 51 percent of the foreign-born Chinese middle class, and Hong Kong accounted for 27 percent in this period. These changes reflect the changing economic and political conditions in mainland China and Hong Kong and their impact on transnational migration.

Immigration from Hong Kong to Canada rose from the late 1980s to the early 1990s, culminating in record numbers in the mid-1990s prior to Hong Kong's return to China in 1997. After 1995, immigration from Hong Kong declined, falling from a peak of over 40,000 a year in the mid-1990s to 2,000 to 3,000 in 2000. In contrast, immigration from mainland China has risen slowly and steadily since the early 1990s; by the early 2000s immigrants from mainland China accounted for the largest number of new immigrants to Canada from a single country.[37]

On the surface, it would appear that changing political uncertainty related to Hong Kong's return to China affected the rise and fall of Hong Kong immigration to Canada. In reality, the Tiananmen Square incident of 1989 and its aftermath probably had a greater effect to encourage Hong Kong emigration in the early 1990s than Hong Kong's imminent return to China. At the same time, Hong Kong's economic prosperity and growth in the early 1990s also facilitated capital accumulation and provided the middle class with the financial means to immigrate. The surge in the level of immigration from Hong Kong was mainly driven by the growth of business immigrants from Hong Kong in the late 1980s and early 1990s. However, emigration levels from Hong Kong and arrivals in Canada fell dramatically after 1995, when Hong Kong's economy was beginning to slow down. The Asian financial crisis of 1997 further devastated Hong Kong's economy, which entered a period of negative growth, deflation, rising unemployment, and falling real estate prices. The economic downturn affected the wealth and assets of the property-owning middle class.

On the other hand, China maintained steady economic growth, especially in urban centers, despite the Asian financial crisis. The expansion of the market economy and the growth in foreign investment enriched many urban centers in China and created the urban prosperity driven by middle-class affluence and consumption. As the stock of well-educated middle class increased, and as Canada placed more emphasis on admitting economic-class immigrants with human capital, a growing number of immigrants from China, mainly the economic class, have been admitted into Canada since the mid-1990s.[38]

Social Construction of the Chinese in Canadian Society

It took the Chinese almost ninety years after their initial immigration to Canada in 1859 before they were given the franchise and other civil rights that other Canadians had long taken for granted. Throughout the 1950s and 1960s, despite the removal of legalized discrimination against them, the Chinese did not gain full social acceptance in Canadian society. Stereotypes of the Chinese race and Chinatowns have been deeply ingrained in the Canadian popular culture. The

Chinese, irrespective of their nationality or political allegiance, are often equated with a foreign race with incompatible values and customs, and Chinatown retains an Oriental mystique and remains a novelty in urban Canada. Canada's guarded postwar immigration policy toward the Chinese was in part influenced by the historical stereotype and in part by Sinophobia during the Cold War of the 1950s.

The need to safeguard Canada's border from racially undesirable immigrants was reaffirmed by the then prime minister Mackenzie King in 1947, in his famous statement to reject what he called "large-scale immigration from the Orient" because of its potential harmful effects on Canada, at a time when Canada was planning to expand immigration. Throughout the 1950s, Canada restricted Chinese immigration on the grounds that it could become what J. W. Pickersgill, minister of citizenship and immigration from 1954 to 1957, called "an avenue for the back door infiltration of communist agents."[39] Indeed, during the Cold War, Canada's concerns about national and border security were guided by its anti-Communist stance, which interpreted Communist regimes as a threat to Canada and Western democracy. Since Chinese immigrants originated from China, a Communist state, they were seen as posing a potential security threat to Canada.[40] No doubt the historical image of the Chinese as morally questionable, culturally inferior, and socially unassimilable could only contribute to the stereotype of their being untrustworthy.

Even today, despite the financial and occupational achievement of Chinese Canadians, segments of Canadian society have shown reluctance to accept them as full-fledged Canadians, and have branded them as belonging to a foreign race whose increased presence and implied cultural differences have allegedly upset the complacency and security of traditional Canada. However, due to the changing class structure of the Chinese community and Canada's adoption of the Charter of Rights and multiculturalism policy,[41] there have been corresponding changes in how the Chinese have been represented in the cultural framework of Canada. Such a representation tends to be multifaceted, racially subtle, and situationally specific. Consequently, depending on specific circumstances, the public's articulation of what the Chinese minority means in contemporary Canadian society shifts in content and representation within the constraints of Canada's widely accepted values of equality and nondiscrimination.

Social Construction of Chinese Malls in White Suburban Neighborhoods

With the growth of the Chinese Canadian population throughout the 1980s and the arrival of more affluent Chinese immigrants, there has been a tendency for middle-class Chinese to move into desirable residential neighborhoods that were traditionally favored by white middle-class Canadians. As well, the expansion of the Chinese middle-class consumer market has prompted the proliferation of Chinese business concentrations in different parts of major cities in

Canada. These developments have caused some tension, as some residents oppose the coming of Chinese neighbors and Chinese-owned businesses as encroachments to what they perceive as traditional European neighborhoods.

In 1984, the Chinese Canadian community in Scarborough, Ontario, was the target of a public debate. Earlier, many Chinese residents and businesses had moved to Scarborough as rising land prices in Toronto made suburban living more attractive. The apparent increase in the Chinese population caused considerable public concern. In particular, many local residents were unhappy about the development of Dragon Centre in the Agincourt area in Scarborough, which housed Chinese restaurants, grocery stores, and shops, and attracted many Chinese patrons on weekends. A meeting to discuss the alleged traffic and parking problems caused by the Chinese drew 500 people, and afterward one participant frankly admitted that there was an anti-Chinese sentiment at the meeting.[42] The public reactions toward the Dragon Centre and the underlying racial tension prompted the mayor to appoint a task force on multicultural and race relations in Scarborough. Four years later, Alderman Doug Mahood conceded that many of the traffic problems were the result of "poor planning by city staff," but "a lot of the wrath was taken out on the Chinese."[43]

An element of public concern seems to be related to the fact that the so-called Asian malls like Dragon Centre were able to prosper with ethnic businesses that catered to the growing Chinese middle-class consumer market, while surrounding traditional retail businesses were struggling to survive due to the growth of large-scale suburban shopping malls. As a shopkeeper in the Agincourt area described it in 1988, "Many of the original merchants have left because their business dropped off—the Anglo community just doesn't shop here as before."[44] It would appear that hostilities toward Chinese businesses was partly because they were prosperous in suburban shopping areas where other small businesses were unable to survive, while the animosity toward the Chinese was premised upon the stereotype of Chinese as foreigners who were seen as encroaching in large numbers upon the affluent suburbs unaccustomed to racial diversity.

In 1995, another controversy surfaced concerning the growing number of Chinese residents and the expansion of Chinese businesses in Markham, a suburb north of Toronto. In June 1995, Carole Bell, the deputy mayor of Markham and regional councilor of York Region, warned in a regional council retreat that the growing concentration of ethnic groups was causing conflict and prompting some residents to move out of Markham. She said that citizens demanded that councilors pass laws prohibiting what she called "signage in a language we can't read," and cited as an example many new developments in Unionville that were exclusively marketed to the Chinese community.[45] Bell suggested that the growing concentration of Chinese Canadians in Markham and the development of malls with Chinese signs were driving longtime residents to leave.[46] Despite strong protests from the Chinese Canadian community and the written condemnation of her statement by twelve mayors from across Greater Toronto, Bell refused to apologize and reiterated her position as reflecting the true perception in the community.[47] One Markham resident was reported to have said that she was tired of driving through town and seeing signs only in Chinese, and that she was glad Bell didn't apologize.[48] Eventually, the municipality council of Markham appointed an advisory committee to address the public concerns, with seven of the fourteen members being from the Chinese Canadian community. In addition, the councilors adopted a statement that said, "We welcome all races, nationalities and cultures to live and work together and we value everyone's contribution."[49]

The Markham incident illustrates that segments of the Canadian public were unprepared to accept the Chinese as middle-class Canadians with the same mobility rights as other Canadians. Throughout the incident, superficial racial and linguistic differences of the Chinese were used as prima facie evidence of the foreign nature and foreign appearance of a group deemed disrupting the harmony of the white neighborhoods of Canada. In short, the Chinese minority was constructed as a foreign race with different linguistic and racial characteristics that were threatening the complacency of white middle-class communities. In 1991, the Chinese Canadian population made up about 14 percent of the population of Markham,[50] which was considered by some as too large and too concentrated, thus warranting a restriction on its future growth and development.

Racialization of "Monster Houses" in Vancouver

Toward the end of the 1980s and in the early 1990s, there were heated debates in Vancouver concerning changes in the urban landscape of white middle-class neighborhoods, as mansion-style homes were being built in record numbers in response to demands that were created in part by increased Chinese immigration. In the course of the debate, the terms "monster houses" and "unneighborly houses" were used in the media and public discourse to refer to what some people considered to be bulky houses that overshadowed surrounding homes in desirable neighborhoods. Over time, however, the term "monster houses" acquired a subtle but clearly understood meaning to refer to big houses that were deemed architecturally unpleasant and environmentally destructive, and were believed to be built by greedy developers to suit the poor tastes of wealthy Chinese immigrants, mainly from Hong Kong.[51] The case of "monster houses" in Vancouver illustrates how a negative racial connotation about the Chinese is socially constructed in the contemporary context, and how the Chinese are being stigmatized as wealthy foreigners who have little regard for the aesthetic values and traditional lifestyle of Canadians.

The controversy of "monster houses" began during the mid-1980s when housing prices in Vancouver started to rise precipitously and builders were constructing larger new houses in prestigious neighborhoods to maximize the land value. The mid-1980s also witnessed increased immigration from Hong Kong,

especially the migration of business immigrants, many with substantial investment capital. As immigrants from Hong Kong and also Taiwan bought mansion-
style homes in affluent neighborhoods of Vancouver West, such as Shaughnessy,
Kerrisdale, and Oakridge, there were hostilities toward the opulence of the
Chinese and the glamour of their large homes. The construction of these mansion-style houses, or so-called monster houses, on the west side of Vancouver
prompted many protests by residents to officials and councillors throughout the
late 1980s and early 1990s. Many heated public meetings were held, and in
response to public pressure, the city council of Vancouver made substantial
changes to the zoning laws between 1986 and 1989 aimed at restricting the height
and size of houses relative to the size of the lot.[52] As they increased their presence
and influence on the West Coast, the Chinese also became the new target of racial
antagonism, and were continuously blamed for destroying the traditional neighborhoods of Vancouver and for transforming Vancouver into another Hong Kong.
The media also reported anti-Chinese signs appearing in affluent neighborhoods
of Vancouver, and T-shirts with imprints unfriendly to Chinese immigrants.[53] Two
Angus Reid surveys conducted in 1989 showed that about 60 percent of the
respondents in British Columbia agreed with the statement that "immigrants are
driving housing prices up," whereas nationally, only about 30 percent agreed with
the statement.[54] However, in the same year a report published by the Laurier
Institute showed that the major factors contributing to the housing demand in
Vancouver had to do with many demographic factors, including natural population increase, net migration, and changing household structures.[55]

By the end of the 1980s, there was a general perception that the overheated
real estate market in Vancouver was largely caused by wealthy Hong Kong immigrants and offshore Asian investors buying into the housing market, and that
the problem of "monster houses" was aggravated by the wealth of Chinese
immigrants and their cultural tastes, which supported the demand for the
bulky, "unneighborly" houses. As several commentators pointed out, the hostility toward the Chinese had to do with the simple fact that they were able to
move into established white middle-class neighborhoods and buy big houses
that were beyond the reach of average white Canadians.[56]

The perception of Hong Kong immigrants driving up real estate prices and
causing radical changes to traditional neighborhoods was reinforced in many
newspaper reports. For example, in a front-page article entitled "Hong Kong
Connection: How Asian Money Fuels Housing Market," a reporter stated that
Asian investors were driving up housing prices and that Hong Kong buyers were
concentrating in west-side neighborhoods; she further lamented how bilingual
English and Chinese signs were changing the streets of Kerrisdale, a neighborhood she described as "once a WASP bastion."[57]

In letters of complaint to the city hall about "monster houses," many residents blatantly blamed Chinese immigrants—including their social behavior and

foreign cultural tastes—for a wide range of issues, sometimes unrelated to hous-
ing.[58] Complaints about "monster houses" sometimes had to do with average
Canadians not being able to afford them, and sometimes were generalized into
"Vancouver's problem" believed to be caused by non-European immigrants.[59]

The opposition to "monster houses" was sometimes directed toward the
design of the new homes, and other times toward the Chinese owners and their
alleged differences in lifestyle and aesthetic taste. Over time, a negative connotation of the Chinese was constructed, and recent Chinese immigrants and their
alleged preference for "monster houses" came to symbolize unwelcome outsiders and foreign values deemed contrary to the nostalgic Canadian lifestyle.

Some white Canadians, through their protest actions and neighborhood
associations against the building of "ugly large homes," almost equated their
actions to a crusade to save Vancouver from being overurbanized. In the process,
Chinese immigrants became scapegoats for many of Vancouver's problems. The
protest movement also helped to racialize the Chinese immigrants, in the sense
that their habits, preferences, and spending styles took on a racial meaning that
demarcated the difference between white Canadians and Chinese immigrants.

By the mid-1990s, the issue of "monster houses" began to subside, in part
because Vancouver passed numerous laws to control the building of new houses,
and in part because of a slowing down of housing construction as real estate
prices fell. However, there were also indications that racial tensions in Vancouver
remained high in the mid-1990s as some white Canadians moved out of central
Vancouver to settle in neighborhoods that were more racially homogeneous.[60]
The case of "monster houses" reveals the negative images constructed of the
Chinese as they ventured into affluent white neighborhoods. It also shows how
the notion of the Chinese as a foreign race with incompatible values and tastes
has been appealing to many white Canadians in providing them with a convenient and simple explanation of many complex urban problems around them.

Other Themes in the Social Construction of Chinese

Specific adverse sentiments against the Chinese seemed to have emerged under
special circumstances, especially when some segments of the Canadian public
perceive the nation's security or their well-being as being threatened. Two
examples further illustrate how the public, the media, and some politicians
were quick to attribute negative connotations to the Chinese when the country
was swept by a moral or health panic.

In the summer of 1999, four ships carrying a total of 599 Chinese migrants
from the Fujian Province of China ended up on the west coast of Canada. The
arrival of these unexpected Chinese migrants caused sensational responses
from the public and the media. Major newspapers in Canada published many
articles on the episodes, using conspicuous headlines and articles to highlight
illegal migrants from China and the lax refugee system of Canada.[61] By the time

the third ship arrived in August 1999, the issues of Chinese "illegal" migrants, the arduous journey across the sea, and smugglers taking advantage of Canada's generous refugee system had become common topics in the media. A reporter from the *Globe and Mail* described the arrival of the third ship as "an increasingly familiar scenario in human struggling."[62] There was a clear angry response from the Canadian public. The *Globe and Mail* described what it called the "backlash": "The arrival of the two ships has sparked an angry backlash against the illegal migrants and debate over Canada's refugee laws. . . . The second ship was met by protests in Port Hardy. A Victoria newspaper ran a front-page headline saying 'Go home,' along with a poll in which 97 per cent of respondents favoured deporting the group."[63]

A public opinion poll commissioned by the *Globe and Mail* and CTV, a major television station, in August 1999 found that about half of the respondents in Canada, and 56 percent in British Columbia in particular, favored immediately deporting the Chinese migrants to China.[64] A Canadian official said that human cargo smugglers were flouting the law and that their boatloads of people were stirring up an anti-immigration backlash in Canada.[65]

The 599 Chinese who landed illegally on the West Coast in 1999 were seen as a threat to Canada's security because the migrants were viewed as pauperized and bogus migrants encouraged by greedy smugglers to take advantage of Canada's refugee system. The Canadian public reacted with panic, and the Canadian government took extraordinary steps to incarcerate them. The public was unsympathetic to the Chinese despite the migrants' hazardous journey. A 1999 public opinion poll found that 70 percent of Canadian respondents rejected the idea of automatically granting the Chinese boat people's claim to be political refugees.[66] A minister referred to the migrants as "law-breakers" who abused Canada's generosity, and as a result had stirred up anti-immigration feelings.[67] By 2000, of the 599 Chinese migrants who came by boat in 1999, only 16 were granted refugee status, but the government spent $36 million in processing and incarcerating them.[68] In their analysis of the media reporting of the Chinese arrival, Hier and Greenberg argued that a racialized moral panic was created in Canada, with a large part of the public and the news media viewing the refugee system and the "illegal Chinese" as a threat to national security. In particular, the news media highlighted the potential threat of Chinese migrants in bringing infectious diseases to Canada, increasing organized crime, and using Canada as a conduit for illegal immigration to the United States. The moral panic toward the undocumented migrants created in the print media was out of proportion, and Hier and Greenberg attributed it to a racial backlash against the Chinese middle-class immigrants whose financial success has attracted negative public reactions, including stereotyping, resentment, and marginalization.[69]

The moral panic over the Chinese migrants unleashed some of the historical sentiments against the Chinese. But the social construction of the Chinese in this discourse tends to dwell on the greed of smugglers, the bogus nature of Chinese migrants, and their unacceptable means of coming to Canada rather than directly on the racial aspects of the Chinese.

Another incident in 2003 in Toronto also triggered harsh public responses toward the Chinese community. The outbreak of Severe Acute Respiratory Syndrome (SARS) in 2003 generated a public health panic in Canada. It was estimated that between March and June, more than 1,000 articles were published on SARS in the national and Toronto editions of the *National Post*, 366 articles in the *Globe and Mail*, and 20 in *Maclean's*.[70] The news media traced the origin of SARS in Canada to a Chinese Canadian family who had visited Hong Kong and brought the disease back to Canada. Since SARS was first discovered in Asia and brought to Canada by a Chinese family, the public was swift in associating the Chinese community in Toronto with SARS, and at times blaming the Chinese for the epidemic. The media reported cases of Chinese families in Toronto being shunned at schools, restaurants, and public places, where they were seen as a public threat.[71]

A study on the impact of SARS on the Chinese community in Toronto, based on interviews and media materials, provided a gloomy picture of how the Chinese were treated publicly during the outbreak of SARS.[72] For example, one respondent said: "My family members were not welcomed to sit with public during the whole subway trip. Non Chinese all sat a certain distance from us."[73] A health care worker also recounted: "People blamed the Chinese. Even my patient asked me if I'm from Hong Kong."[74] The Chinese and Southeast Asian Legal Clinic mentioned incidents in which landlords wanted to get rid of Chinese tenants; some Chinese respondents reported having exceptional difficulty in finding jobs after the outbreak of SARS because of the public perception.[75] A caller to a radio station used the term "dirty Chinese" and blamed the Chinese for SARS.[76] The news media reported that the Chinese community in Toronto was being shunned by mainstream society, and the business of Chinese restaurants declined substantially for lacking patrons.[77]

Even before the outbreak of SARS, the Canadian public had occasionally associated certain nonwhite racial groups with potential health hazards. For example, in a 2002 article entitled "Immigration Fuels Soaring TB rate," the *Times Colonist* (Victoria) reported that "most of the immigrants who come to B.C. arrive from countries where TB is rampant—India, China, the Philippines and Vietnam."[78] The paper also printed the comments of Dr. Kevin Elwood, director of tuberculosis control for the B.C. Centre for Disease Control: "The Chinese immigrants are particularly not interested in preventable drugs."[79] But the incidence of SARS indicates the scope and intensity of the public reactions toward the Chinese in Toronto. As the fear of SARS deepened throughout 2003, the public also constructed a negative connotation of the Chinese as being responsible for the epidemic and for threatening the health and security of Canada.

Conclusion

Historically, Canada has socially constructed the racial category of Chinese in relation to its European cultural framework of nation building. By the end of the nineteenth century, the notion of Chinese in Canada carried a deep-seated meaning in law, social relations, and racial ideology. The racial category of Chinese represented an undesirable race that had brought immorality and filth to Canada even though Chinese workers were believed to be frugal and industrious. The Chinese were also depicted as fundamentally different, racially inferior, and culturally peculiar if not untrustworthy, thus making them impossible to be assimilated with European Canadians. In particular, the public perceived the small number of Chinese women as having a low social image since many were believed to be prostitutes, slaves, or concubines who were accused of bringing health hazards and immorality to Canada.

The place of the Chinese in Canada improved substantially after the Second World War, as Canada witnessed the entrenchment of civil rights and later the Charter, which offers equal legal protection to all. Despite these developments, the notion of Chinese remains a meaningful racial category in Canada, although the content of the concept of Chinese has changed over time. Canada's guarded immigration policy after the Second World War toward Chinese immigration reflects its historical racial bias and its suspicion toward the Chinese of being potential Communist agents. Such political thinking contributed to maintaining the historical stereotype of the Chinese as undesirable and untrustworthy. It was not until Canada adopted a universal point system of assessing prospective immigrants based on education and skills in 1967 that Chinese immigrants were given the same opportunity of immigrating to Canada as other people.

The arrival of new Chinese immigrants from Hong Kong in the 1980s and 1990s and from mainland China after the late 1990s helped to create the image of the new Chinese middle class in Canada. These new immigrants brought substantial financial and human capital to Canada. By the 1980s, it was evident that the Chinese in Canada were beginning to be seen as financially successful, occupational mobile, and culturally sophisticated. But the mobility of the Chinese to white middle-class suburbs and their becoming property owners in affluent white neighborhoods triggered racial responses from some segments of Canadian society. Throughout the debates over Asian malls in Toronto in the 1980s, and later the controversy of "monster houses" in Vancouver, the Chinese were depicted as foreign elements destroying the environment, architectural heritage, and cultural fabric of Canada. Even the wealth of some Chinese immigrants was seen as coming from suspicious offshore origins that would only contaminate the cultural tastes and social harmony of Canada.

It would be a mistake to assume that the notion of Chinese as a racial minority was systematically and persistently being constructed in a negative light. But whenever incidents trigger a moral or health panic, the public seems to be quick to racialize the Chinese as a problem. The arrival of four ships on the west coast of Canada carrying 599 Chinese migrants in 1999 created a public outcry against the Chinese migrants. Sensational news reporting over a sustained period of two months also contributed to a negative image of lawbreakers and bogus claimants who took advantage of Canada's generous refugee system.

The outbreak of SARS in Toronto in 2003 also created panic and the pretext for the public to blame the Chinese community for the epidemic. Many Chinese in Toronto were shunned in public places because of the health threat they were believed to carry, and as a result, Chinese businesses suffered.

These incidents suggest that there have been deep-seated racial feelings toward the Chinese in the cultural framework of Canada. The entrenchment of rights and the passage of legislation advancing racial equality have created serious legal constraints on the articulation of race in Canadian society. However, under the conditions of moral and health panic, the legal constraints are easily relaxed to enable the notion of Chinese to be socially constructed, taking on new symbols and meanings while retaining some of the historical racial images of the Chinese in Canada.

NOTES

1. See Robin Cohen, *Global Diasporas* (Seattle: University of Washington Press, 1997); Lynn Pan, ed., *The Encyclopedia of the Chinese Overseas* (Singapore: Archipelago Press and Landmark Books, 1998).
2. See Lawrence W. Crissman, "The Segmentary Structure of Urban Overseas Chinese Communities," *Man* 2 (1967): 185–204; Maurice Freedman, "Lineage Organization in South-Eastern China," *L.S.E. Monographs on Social Anthropology* 18 (London: Athlete Press, 1958); William G. Skinner, ed., *Chinese Society in Thailand* (Ithaca, N.Y.: Cornell University Press, 1957); William G. Skinner, *Leadership and Power in the Chinese Community in Thailand* (Ithaca, N.Y.: Cornell University Press, 1958); William G. Skinner, *The Study of Chinese Society: Essays by Maurice Freedman* (Stanford, Calif.: Stanford University Press, 1979).
3. See Nicholas Van Hear, *New Diasporas: The Mass Exodus, Dispersal and Regrouping of Migrant Communities* (Seattle: University of Washington Press, 1998).
4. See Aihwa Ong and Donald M. Nonini, eds., *Ungrounded Empires: The Cultural Politics of Modern Chinese Transnationalism* (New York: Routledge, 1997).
5. See Crissman, "Segmentary Structure," 185–204; Michael A. Goldberg, *The Chinese Connection: Getting Plugged In to Pacific Rim Real Estate, Trade, and Capital Markets* (Vancouver: University of British Columbia Press, 1985); Freedman, "Lineage Organization;" Skinner, *Leadership and Power*; Skinner, *Study of Chinese Society*.
6. For a discussion of the concepts "race" and "racialization," see Michael Banton, *The Idea of Race* (London: Tavistock, 1977); B. Singh Bolaria and Peter S. Li, *Racial Oppression in Canada*, 2nd ed. (Toronto: Garamond, 1988); Peter S. Li, "Race and Ethnicity," in *Race and Ethnic Relations in Canada*, ed. Peter S. Li, 3–20 (Toronto: Oxford University Press, 1999); Robert Miles, *Racism and Migrant Labour* (London: Routledge and Kegan Paul, 1982); John Rex, *Race Relations in Sociological Theory*, 2nd ed. (London: Routledge and

Kegan Paul, 1983); Vic Satzewich, *Racism and the Incorporation of Foreign Labour* (London: Routledge, 1991); Pierre L. van den Berghe, "Race: Perspective Two," in *Dictionary of Race and Ethnic Relations*, ed. E. E. Cashmore, 216–218 (London: Routledge and Kegan Paul, 1984).

7. This section is primarily based on Peter S. Li, *The Chinese in Canada*, 2nd ed. (Toronto: Oxford University Press, 1998).

8. About 2,000 Chinese arrived by ship in 1881, and another 8,000 in 1882. The numbers are based on arrivals of Chinese passengers on vessels entering the port of Victoria. See Royal Commission Canada, *Report of the Royal Commission on Chinese Immigration: Report and Evidence* (1885), 397–399.

9. See Statutes of Canada, *An Act to Restrict and Regulate Chinese Immigration into Canada* (1885, c. 71); Statutes of Canada, *An Act Respecting and Restricting Chinese Immigration* (1900, c. 32); Statutes of Canada, *An Act Respecting and Restricting Chinese Immigration* (1903, c. 8).

10. See Statutes of Canada, *An Act Respecting Chinese Immigration* (1923, c. 38).

11. As a result of the 1923 act, only four categories of Chinese were allowed to land in Canada: members of the diplomatic corps, and children born in Canada of Chinese parents, merchants, or students. See Statutes of Canada, *An Act Respecting Chinese Immigration* (1923, c. 38, s. 5).

12. See Li, *Chinese in Canada*, 67.

13. See Peter S. Li, *Destination Canada: Immigration Debates and Issues* (Toronto: Oxford University Press, 2003).

14. See Kay J. Anderson, *Vancouver's Chinatown* (Montreal: McGill-Queen's University Press, 1991); Patricia E. Roy, *A White Man's Province: British Columbia Politicians and Chinese and Japanese Immigrants, 1858–1914* (Vancouver: University of British Columbia Press, 1989); W. Peter Ward, *White Canada Forever: Popular Attitudes and Public Policy toward Orientals in British Columbia* (Montreal: McGill-Queen's University Press, 1978).

15. See Royal Commission Canada, *Report of the Royal Commission on Chinese Immigration: Report and Evidence* (1885).

16. See ibid.

17. See ibid., xxi.

18. See ibid., xxvi.

19. See ibid., xxii.

20. See ibid.

21. See ibid., xxxv.

22. See ibid., xliv.

23. See Li, *Chinese in Canada*.

24. See Dominion Bureau of Statistics, 1911, *Census of Canada* (1913), Vol. 2; Dominion Bureau of Statistics, 1921, *Census of Canada* (1923), Vol. 1.

25. See Royal Commission Canada (1885), lix.

26. See Chuen-Yan David Lai, *Chinatown: Towns within Cities in Canada* (Vancouver: University of British Columbia Press, 1988), 207.

27. See Constance Backhouse, "The White Women's Labour Laws: Anti-Chinese Racism in Early Twentieth-Century Canada," *Law and History Review* 14, no. 2 (1996): 342. See also Ward, *White Canada Forever*, 8–9.

28. See Ward, *White Canada Forever*, 8.

29. See Backhouse, "White Women's Labour Laws," 342; Tamara Adilman, "A Prelimnary Sketch of Chinese Women and Work in British Columbia 1858–1950," in *Not Just Pin Money*, ed. Barbara K. Latham and Roberta J. Pazdro, 65–67 (Victoria: Camosun College, 1984).

30. See Anderson, *Vancouver's Chinatown*, 73–104.

31. See Li, *Chinese in Canada*.

32. See Peter S. Li, "The Emergence of the New Middle Class among the Chinese in Canada," *Asian Culture* 14 (1990): 187–194.

33. See Statistics Canada, *2001 Census of Canada, Public Use Microdata File for Individuals* (2005), Ethnic Origin (232), Sex (3), and Single and Multiple Responses (3) for Population, for Canada, Provinces, Territories, Census Metropolitan Areas and Census Agglomerations.

34. The term "middle class" has been used to refer to a segment of the labor force whose market value is premised upon superior professional and technical skills that are translated into substantial market advantage over the working class. The expansion of the advanced capitalist economy and the emergence of the information age have created a rising demand for workers with professional and technical expertise. But unlike the grand bourgeoisie or the upper class, which has ownership of the means of production and control over the production process, the new middle class is made up of employees with professional expertise and educational credentials that give them some control over the conditions of work, such as a degree of work autonomy, and, depending on the nature work, they may also have some control over the labor of others. See Nicholas Abercrombie and John Urry, *Capital, Labour and the Middle Classes* (London: Allen and Unwin, 1983); Guglielmo Carchedi, *Class Analysis and Social Research* (Oxford: Basil Blackwell, 1987); Nicos Poulantzas, *Political Power and Social Classes* (London: Verso, 1978); Nicos Poulantzas, *Classes in Contemporary Capitalism* (London: Verso, 1978); Erik Olin Wright, "Marxist Class Categories and Income Inequality," *American Sociological Review* 42 (1977): 32–55; Erik Olin Wright, *Classes* (London: Verso, 1985); Erik Olin Wright, *The Debate on Classes* (London: Verso, 1989).

35. See Li, *Chinese in Canada*, 124.

36. Statistics on the Chinese middle class for 2001 were calculated from Statistics Canada, *2001 Census of Canada, Public Use Microdata File for Individuals* (2005).

37. See Peter S. Li, "The Rise and Fall of Chinese Immigration to Canada: Newcomers from Hong Kong Special Administrative Region of China and Mainland China, 1980–2000," *International Migration* 43, no. 3 (2005): 9–32.

38. See ibid.

39. See Canada, House of Commons, *Debates, 3rd Session, 24th Parliament*, June 9, 1960, 4715–4716.

40. See Li, *Chinese in Canada*, 93.

41. See Statutes of Canada, *Canada Act* (1982, c. 11); Statutes of Canada, *Multicultural Act* (1988, c. 31).

42. See "The Chinese Centre Parking 'Chaos' Draws Ire of 500," *Toronto Star*, May 29, 1984.

43. See "The New, Upscale Chinatown Prospering in Scarborough," *Toronto Star*, November 21, 1988.

44. Ibid.

45. See "Ethnic Concentrations Causing Conflict," *Liberal*, June 25, 1995.

46. See "Mayors Condemn Comments on Chinese," *Toronto Star*, September 16, 1995.

47. See ibid.; "Bell Stands Her Ground," *Toronto Star*, August 22, 1995.

48. See "Only Some People Live in 'Ghettos,'" *Toronto Star*, August 31, 1995.

49. See "Markham Declares Truce with Chinese," *Toronto Star*, September 27, 1995.

50. See Statistics Canada, *Profile of Census Tracts in Ontario*, Part B, Catalogue 95–338 (Ottawa: Minister of Industry, Science and Technology, 1994).

51. See Peter S. Li, "Unneighbourly Houses or Unwelcome Chinese: The Social Construction of Race in the Battle over 'Monster Homes' in Vancouver, Canada," *International Journal of Comparative Race and Ethnic Studies* 1 (1994): 14–33.

52. See W. T. Stanbury and John D. Todd, *The Housing Crisis: The Effects of Local Government Regulation* (Vancouver: Laurier Institute, 1990).

53. "Hong Kong Connection," *Vancouver Sun*, February 18, 1989.

54. See Angus Reid Group, *Immigration to Canada: Aspects of Public Opinion* (Winnipeg: Angus Reid, 1989).

55. See David Baxter, *Population and Housing in Metropolitan Vancouver: Changing Patterns of Demographics and Demand* (Vancouver: Laurier Institute, 1989).

56. See "Hong Kong Connection;" "Big Houses," *Western Living*, November 1988, 31–41.

57. See "Hong Kong Connection."

58. See Li, "Unneighbourly Houses" 27.

59. See ibid.

60. See "White Flight, Chinese Distress," *Globe and Mail*, September 30, 1995.

61. See Sean Hier and Joshua Greenberg, "News Discourse and the Problematization of Chinese Migration to Canada," in *Discourses of Domination: Racial Bias in the Canadian English-Language Press*, ed. Frances Henry and Carol Tator, 138–162 (Toronto: University of Toronto Press, 2002).

62. See "Third Ship Spotted Off B.C. Coast," *Globe and Mail*, August 31, 1999.

63. Ibid.

64. Ibid.

65. See "Minister Condemns Smuggling of Humans," *National Post*, September 3, 1999. The harsh response toward the Chinese migrants was in sharp contrast to the welcome given a dog found in one of the boats. A reporter from the *Globe and Mail* wrote: "Canadians are welcoming with open arms a dog found aboard a smugglers' ship while the human passengers face deportation to China amid a public backlash against illegal migrants, the second boatload to arrive in a month." See "Migrant Mutt from China Given a Warm Welcome," *Globe and Mail*, August 18, 1999.

66. See "Third Ship Spotted Off B.C. Coast."

67. See "Minister Condemns Smuggling of Humans."

68. See "The Boat People's Big Gamble," *Globe and Mail*, July 22, 2000.

69. See Hier and Greenberg, "News Discourse."

70. See Carrianne Leung and Jian Guan, *Yellow Peril Revisited: Impact of SARS on the Chinese and Southeast Asian Canadian Communities* (Toronto: Chinese Canadian National Council, 2004).

71. See "Illness Spawns Some Shunning of Asians," *Globe and Mail*, April 3, 2003.

72. See Leung and Guan, *Yellow Peril Revisited*.

73. Ibid., 17.

74. Ibid.

75. See ibid., 17–18.

76. See ibid., 19.

77. See "SARS Brings Worries of Discrimination in Toronto," *Mingpao*, April 4, 2003; "Illness Spawns Some Shunning of Asians."

78. See "Immigration Fuels Soaring TB Rate," *Times Colonist*, November 21, 2002.

79. See ibid.

11

Recent Mainland Chinese Immigrants in Canada

Trends and Obstacles

LI ZONG

The 1990s and early twenty-first century witnessed large volumes of immigration from mainland China to Canada. Currently, mainland China is the largest immigration source country for Canada. Between 2000 and 2007, between 30,000 and 40,000 immigrants from mainland China entered Canada each year.[1] Most recent mainland Chinese immigrants, especially those arriving after 1990, have been well-trained and experienced professionals seeking new opportunities. Canada welcomes these immigrants mainly because of their potential to contribute to the country's population and economic growth. However, many mainland Chinese immigrants are disappointed and frustrated because they have not been able to achieve a satisfactory social and economic status in Canadian society. This has also caused concerns for the federal government because it has serious implications for the goals of shared citizenship, social inclusion, and social integration that the Canadian government tries to achieve through its reformed immigration program and policies.

This chapter reviews the trends of recent mainland Chinese immigration to Canada and examines obstacles that mainland Chinese immigrants face in integrating into Canadian society. Theoretical debates on the issue of occupational attainment for professional immigrants and covert racism will be addressed.

Trends of Immigration from Mainland China

The number of immigrants from mainland China to Canada was small in the 1950s and early 1960s. Those who came were mainly family members joining close relatives in Canada, particularly wives and children coming as family members of Chinese men already in Canada.[2] For example, between 1956 and 1965 only 4,890 mainland Chinese immigrated to Canada (see Table 11.1). In 1967, Canada changed its immigration policy by adopting a "point" system

TABLE 11.1

Mainland Chinese Immigrants in Canada by Landing Year, 1956–2004

Year	N	Year	N	Year	N
1956	1,516	1972	25	1988	2,770
1957	856	1973	60	1989	4,415
1958	894	1974	379	1990	8,116
1959	519	1975	903	1991	14,203
1960	183	1976	833	1992	10,548
1961	118	1977	798	1993	9,485
1962	244	1978	644	1994	12,513
1963	179	1979	2,058	1995	13,308
1964	184	1980	4,947	1996	17,532
1965	197	1981	6,552	1997	18,524
1966	4,094	1982	3,571	1998	19,781
1967	6,409	1983	2,220	1999	29,113
1968	8,382	1984	2,220	2000	36,716
1969	8,272	1985	1,883	2001	40,315
1970	5,377	1986	1,905	2002	33,231
1971	47	1987	2,625	2003	36,236
				2004	36,411

Sources: Numbers for 1956–1976 can be found at Leacy, F. H. (Ed.), Historical Statistics of Canada (1999) [computer file], Statistics Canada, Cat. No. no. 11-516-XIE Series A385-416 Immigration to Canada by country of last permanent residence, 1956–1976 (http://www.statcan.ca:8096/bsolc/english/bsolc?catno= 11-516-X&CHROPG=1). Number for 1977 can be found at 1977 Immigration statistics (1978), Employment and Immigration Canada, Cat. No. MP22-1/1977, p. 6, Table 3, Country of Last Permanent Residence and Destination of Immigrants (http://www.cic.gc.ca/english/pdf/pub/1977stats.pdf). Number for 1978 can be found at 1978 Immigration statistics (1980), Employment and Immigration Canada, Cat. No. MP22-1/1978, p. 6, Table 3, Country of Last Permanent Residence and Destination of Immigrants (http://www.cic.gc.ca/english/pdf/pub/1978stats.pdf). Number for 1979 can be found at 1979 Immigration statistics (1981), Employment and Immigration Canada, Cat. No. MP22-1/1979, p. 6, Table 3, Country of Last Permanent Residence and Destination of Immigrants (http://www.cic.gc.ca/english/pdf/pub/1979stats.pdf). Numbers for 1980–2002 are compiled based on data from Landed Immigrant Data System, 1980–2002 [datafile], Citizenship and Immigration Canada (Provided on CD). Numbers for 2002–2004 can be found at Facts and figures 2004: Immigration Overview— Permanent and Temporary Residents (2005), Citizenship and Immigration Canada. Cat. No. Ci1-8/2004E-PDF, pp. 34, Table: Canada-permanent residents from Asia and Pacific by top source countries (http://www.cic.gc.ca/ english/pdf/pub/facts2004.pdf)

to screen independent immigrants. The point system provided an equal opportunity for immigration from Asian countries. At the same time, the Cultural
Revolution, particularly in its early years (1966–1970), brought social turbulence
to mainland China, and many mainland Chinese who had relatives in Canada
wanted to leave China to seek a more stable future in Canada. Both pull and
push factors motivated a relatively large number of mainland Chinese (32,534)
to immigrate to Canada between 1966 and 1970 (see Table 11.1). However,
between 1971 and 1978 the number of immigrants from mainland China
decreased because of political pressure and restricted migration control in
China. It was not until 1979, after China adopted an open-door policy and began
to relax its restrictions on the exit of Chinese citizens, that many mainland
Chinese were able to leave for Canada and the immigration flow to Canada
began to increase again. Between 1979 and 1989, 35,366 mainland Chinese
immigrated to Canada.

The 1989 student protest movement in China, which led to the tragic incident at Tiananmen Square, triggered a sudden increase in mainland Chinese
immigrants. The Canadian government enacted a special program (known as
OM-IS-339) to protect Chinese students and visiting scholars who were in
Canada at the time and who participated in demonstrations in Canada to support the student movement in China. The policy allowed thousands of Chinese
students, visiting scholars, and their family members to obtain landed immigrant status on compassionate grounds. Between 1990 and 1991, 22,319 mainland Chinese became landed immigrants in Canada (see Table 11.1). In the
following two years (1992 and 1993), another 21,998 mainland Chinese immigrated to Canada. Since 1994, annual immigration from mainland China has
continued to increase, reaching 40,315 in 2001. In total, between 1994 and 2004,
293,680 mainland Chinese immigrated to Canada.

There were different trends between immigrant arrivals from Hong Kong
and from mainland China between 1980 and 2000. According to Li, between
1980 and 1986 the immigrants from Hong Kong and mainland China never
exceeded 8,000 a year from either source, although Hong Kong tended to have
a much larger volume of immigration than mainland China for most years.[3]
Between 1986 and 1994, the volume of annual immigration from Hong Kong
continued to increase and in 1994 peaked at 44,000. However, after 1994 the
number of immigrants from Hong Kong declined every year, and by 2001 fewer
than 2,000 immigrants arrived from Hong Kong.[4] In contrast, the annual number of immigrants from mainland China has increased dramatically since 1989
(see Table 11.1). Between 1997 and 2000, the number of mainland Chinese immigrants nearly doubled—from 18,524 a year to 36,716—making mainland China
the largest single source of Chinese immigrants to Canada.

In terms of the composition of mainland Chinese immigrants, there are three
broad categories into which they can be classified: economic-class, family-class,

and humanitarian-class.[5] Between 1980 and 1989, the annual number of economic-class immigrants (principal applicants and their dependents) from mainland China was small. However, starting in 1990 it has been increasing dramatically (see Table 11.2). The economic-class of immigrants includes entrepreneurs, investors, self-employed people, and skilled workers and professionals. Although the annual number of immigrating entrepreneurs, investors, and self-employed people increased between 1980 and 2002, the total annual numbers of these categories were relatively very small compared to the numbers of skilled workers and professionals (see Table 11.2). For example, the numbers of principal applicants who were entrepreneurs, investors, and self-employed people immigrating into Canada peaked at 197, 67, and 1,038, respectively, in 2001 (see Table 11.2). However, the peak for principal applicants who were skilled workers and professionals in 2001 was a staggering 13,342. Thus, most economic-class immigrants from mainland China were skilled workers and professionals. Between 1980 and 1989, the total number of principal applicants who immigrated to Canada from mainland China as skilled workers/professionals was only 5,909 (about 96 percent of the 6,127 economic-class mainland Chinese immigrants). Between 1990 and 2002, this number increased to 77,185, which is about 94 percent of the total number (82,354) of economic-class mainland Chinese immigrants. The same trend also applied to the economic-class immigrants who were dependents (see Table 11.2). This is expected because, as the number of principal applicants for the economic-class immigration increases, the number of their dependents as immigrants also increases due largely to those principal applicants who are immigrating as a family unit.

Table 11.2 shows the trend of mainland Chinese family-class immigrants between 1980 and 2002. The annual number of family-class immigrants from mainland China was less than 2,000 between 1980 and 1988, and starting in 1989 the number increased dramatically. Between 1989 and 2000, the annual number of mainland Chinese family-class immigrants increased from 2,930 to 9,016. The majority of immigrants from the family-class were primarily parents/grandparents and spouses. Between 1980 and 2002, 29,415 immigrants in this category (about 31 percent of the total number during the same period) were parents or grandparents, while 43,507 people (about 46 percent) were spouses.

For the humanitarian-class, the numbers were relatively low compared to the other two classes between 1980 and 1989. In 1990, however, numbers began to increase, with the highest number of immigrants to Canada in this class occurring in 1996 and 1997 (see Table 11.2). This increase has to do with the regularization program implemented between 1994 and 1998 by the Canadian government. In 1994, the Deferred Removal Order Class (DROC) was announced, allowing applications from refused refugee claimants who had not been removed after three years, subject to certain conditions. The DROC was particularly aimed at resolving the situation of over 4,500 Chinese claimants waiting in

TABLE 11.2

Immigrant Categories from People's Republic of

Family Class[1]	1980	1981	1982	1983	1984	1985	1986	1987	1988	1989
Spouse	310	280	454	336	286	248	233	321	303	307
Fiance	48	144	297	411	390	290	316	421	487	460
Son or daughter	178	199	44	28	28	12	17	33	37	511
Parent or Grandparent	875	1109	827	936	1060	990	959	1184	950	1644
Other family member	43	78	38	23	33	20	12	6	10	8
Subtotal:	1454	1810	1660	1734	1797	1560	1537	1965	1787	2930

Economic Class[2] – Principal Applicant	1980	1981	1982	1983	1984	1985	1986	1987	1988	1989
Entrepreneur	4	1	8	19	59	0	4	5	15	14
Self-employed	0	5	14	14	21	5	3	4	4	15
Investor	0	0	0	0	0	0	0	1	0	3
Skilled Workers	1509	1798	676	127	80	161	212	353	418	575
Live-in caregivers	0	0	0	0	0	0	0	0	0	0
Provincial/Territorial Nominee	0	0	0	0	0	0	0	0	0	0
Subtotal:	1513	1804	698	160	160	166	219	363	437	607

Economic Class – Dependant	1980	1981	1982	1983	1984	1985	1986	1987	1988	1989
Entrepreneur	4	2	9	20	35	0	3	5	18	11
Self-employed	0	3	10	25	19	3	0	2	4	20
Investor	0	0	0	0	0	0	0	0	0	3
Skilled Workers	1961	2913	1135	174	65	84	132	269	505	792
Live-in caregivers	0	0	0	0	0	0	0	0	0	0
Subtotal:	1965	2918	1154	219	119	87	135	276	527	826

China by Year of Landing in Canada, 1980–2002

1990	1991	1992	1993	1994	1995	1996	1997	1998	1999	2000	2001	2002
338	731	2355	3143	1942	1144	953	1791	1895	2445	2480	3258	3862
531	673	1056	1069	972	729	306	310	299	293	84	54	100
454	378	642	523	365	147	116	151	173	243	261	314	472
2002	2495	2173	2186	4053	3723	2188	2154	1787	1884	2313	2244	3771
11	45	316	328	483	673	684	523	913	694	605	610	811
3336	4322	6542	7249	7815	6416	4247	4929	5067	5559	5743	6480	9016

1990	1991	1992	1993	1994	1995	1996	1997	1998	1999	2000	2001	2002
21	19	20	22	32	71	103	128	153	159	179	197	117
12	15	14	21	27	38	49	41	50	48	55	67	40
12	13	11	38	20	33	64	130	228	271	665	1038	681
2819	6234	1742	808	1904	2497	4582	5132	5945	10072	12759	13342	9349
0	0	0	1	7	26	24	7	11	3	2	3	1
0	0	0	0	0	0	5	0	0	12	27	70	68
2864	6281	1787	890	1990	2665	4827	5438	6387	10565	13687	14717	10256

1990	1991	1992	1993	1994	1995	1996	1997	1998	1999	2000	2001	2002
18	26	44	49	63	135	211	273	289	310	362	407	252
15	21	23	32	38	58	71	56	76	94	84	95	68
7	11	28	55	66	88	187	303	525	635	1500	2388	1646
1710	2636	961	776	2376	3075	4936	5777	6007	11190	14650	15484	10738
0	0	0	1	3	11	12	16	1	1	0	0	0
1750	2694	1056	913	2546	3367	5417	6425	6898	12230	16596	18374	12704

(Continued)

TABLE II.2

Immigrant Categories from People's Republic of China

Humanitarian Class[3]	1980	1981	1982	1983	1984	1985	1986	1987	1988	1989
Government Assisted Refugees	4	8	22	19	18	18	11	8	7	13
Privately Sponsored Refugees	11	4	8	10	4	1	0	4	4	13
Asylum Refugees	0	0	0	0	0	0	0	0	0	0
Dependent Abroad[4]	0	0	0	0	0	0	0	0	0	0
DROC & PDRCC[5] – Principal Applicant	0	0	0	0	0	0	0	0	0	0
DROC & PDRCC – Dependent	0	0	0	0	0	0	0	0	0	0
Subtotal:	15	12	30	29	22	19	11	12	11	26
Other Category	1980	1981	1982	1983	1984	1985	1986	1987	1988	1989
Retireds – Principal Applicant	0	7	16	44	64	25	1	5	6	14
Retireds – Dependent	0	1	13	34	58	26	2	4	2	12
Subtotal:	0	8	29	78	122	51	3	9	8	26

Source: Landed Immigrant Data System, 1980–2002 [datafile], Citizenship and Immigration Canada (Provided on CD). 2004 Annual Report to Parliament on Immigration (2004), Minister of Public Works and Government Services Canada, 2004, Cat. no. Ci1-2004 (http://www.cic.gc.ca/english/pub/immigration2004.html#500).

Notes:

1. The family class includes the following persons: spouses; common-law partners; conjugal partners; dependent children; the sponsor's parents and grandparents; children under 18 years of age whom the sponsor intends to adopt in Canada; orphaned brothers, sisters, nephews, nieces, and grandchildren under 18 years of age; and any other relative if the sponsor does not have any of the previously listed relatives abroad or in Canada.

by Year of Landing in Canada, 1980–2002 (*Continued*)

1990	1991	1992	1993	1994	1995	1996	1997	1998	1999	2000	2001	2002
32	39	10	13	3	1	0	4	0	2	4	6	3
121	433	536	169	14	7	5	0	2	0	0	3	32
0	399	584	218	118	305	261	152	237	269	426	392	643
0	0	0	2	17	175	237	143	210	205	206	328	571
0	0	0	0	0	324	1874	878	583	151	35	9	3
0	0	0	0	0	47	663	555	397	132	19	6	3
153	871	1130	402	152	859	3040	1732	1429	759	690	744	1255
1990	1991	1992	1993	1994	1995	1996	1997	1998	1999	2000	2001	2002
8	18	12	9	2	0	1	0	0	0	0	0	0
5	17	21	22	8	1	0	0	0	0	0	0	0
13	35	33	31	10	1	1	0	0	0	0	0	0

2. The economic class includes skilled workers, business immigrants, provincial nominees, live-in caregivers, and their immediate family. There are three types of business immigrants: investors, entrepreneurs, and self-employed workers.

3. The humanitarian category includes Convention refugees (those selected abroad to resettle in Canada) and persons who were granted permanent residence after claiming asylum once in Canada.

4. "Dependents Abroad" refers to "dependents abroad of protected persons landed in Canada" (2004 Report to Parliament on immigration, 2004).

5. "DROC & PDRCC" stands for "defferred removal order and post determination refugee." (1980–2002 Landed Immigrant Data System)

limbo, usually because they were from moratorium countries—the federal government considered it too dangerous to deport people to such countries. China
was one of these countries at this time, and Chinese community organizations
in Canada began to advocate for permanent residency for failed refugee
claimants. Groups from Toronto, Montreal, and Vancouver, including many
nonstatus immigrants, drew public attention to this issue. Approximately 3,000
applicants from China, Iran, and other countries were regularized through this
program, but many more were rejected because they did not meet residency
requirements, had criminal records, or had serious medical conditions. In July
1999, a boat with 123 Chinese passengers arrived off the West Coast—the first of
four such boats to arrive over the summer. The public response was virulently
hostile. Most of the Chinese were kept in long-term detention, and some were
irregularly prevented from making refugee claims.

Mainland Chinese immigrants to Canada tend to settle in large urban centers. Table 11.2 shows that 66.6 percent of mainland Chinese immigrants who
entered Canada between 1980 and 2000 chose Toronto (41.3 percent) and
Vancouver (25.3 percent) as their intended destinations. Other favored cities
were Montreal (7.3 percent), Ottawa (4.2 percent), Calgary (3.8 percent), and
Edmonton (3.2 percent). Only a small proportion of the mainland Chinese
immigrants chose small cities located in Atlantic Canada and the Prairie
provinces of Saskatchewan and Manitoba.

Obstacles for Occupational Attainment in Canada

Between 1990 and 2002, over 77,000 well-trained and experienced principal
applicants who were skilled workers or professionals immigrated to Canada
from mainland China to seek better opportunities in Canada (see Table 11.3).
However, after entering the country, many of them found difficulties in obtaining the professional jobs they expected, and consequently they experienced
downward occupational mobility. According to a survey of 1,180 recent mainland Chinese professional immigrants conducted in the cities of Vancouver,
Toronto, Ottawa, Calgary, Edmonton, and Saskatoon between 1997 and 1999 (the
1997–1999 Survey), 79 percent of the respondents reported having worked as
professionals in China before immigrating to Canada.[6] However, only 31 percent
reported that they worked or had worked as professionals in Canada. Although
about 6 percent of the respondents became proprietors, managers, supervisors,
or administrators, 41 percent of the respondents had lower social status in non-
professional jobs, and 22 percent had never worked in Canada. About 75 percent
of the respondents reported that their occupations in their home country
matched their professional qualifications well, while only 23 percent reported
that their current (or last) occupation in Canada matched their professional
qualifications. About 41 percent of the respondents reported that they were

TABLE 11.3

Mainland Chinese Immigrants in Canada by Intended Destination, 1980–2000

Intended Destination	N	%
Toronto	89,653	41.3
Vancouver	55,003	25.3
Montreal	15,806	7.3
Ottawa	9,184	4.2
Calgary	8,344	3.8
Edmonton	6,929	3.2
Winnipeg	3,658	1.7
Hamilton	2,710	1.2
Victoria	2,343	1.1
Saskatoon	1,783	0.8
London	1,669	0.8
Halifax	1,485	0.7
Regina	1,043	0.5
Quebec City	871	0.4
Other areas	16,549	7.7
Canada	217,030	100.0

Source: Citizenship and Immigration Canada, 2001. *Landed Immigrant Data System.*

overqualified for their current occupations in Canada, and 29 percent said they had not worked since their arrival in Canada.[7]

There are two approaches in the literature on occupational attainment of immigrants. The first focuses primarily on individual barriers experienced by immigrants, including the inability to meet occupational entry requirements, a lack of Canadian work experience, and an inadequate command of the English language.[8] In the 1997–1999 Survey, 49 percent of the respondents reported that they have experienced difficulties with their command of English, and 34 percent also experienced difficulties in adapting to Western culture. Among those who answered "difficult" or "very difficult" with regard to command of English, 70 percent have experienced downward occupational mobility. Among those who answered "difficult" or "very difficult" in adaptation to Western culture, 65 percent have experienced downward occupational mobility. The language barrier can be overcome in time through personal effort. The survey shows that as the length of time in Canada increases, the percentage of downward mobility rate decreases.[9] This suggests that the linguistic abilities and level of adaptation of new immigrants improve when they stay in Canada for a longer period of time.

Although the individual approach has elucidated some personal difficulties, it has not explained how the structural factors pertaining to policies, criteria, and procedures for evaluation also contribute to occupational disadvantages for foreign-trained professionals. Failure to locate institutionalized barriers in social conditions and structural arrangements tends to assign blame to immigrant professionals themselves for failing to acquire professional jobs in Canada. A fundamental debate is over whether individual attributes or institutionalized barriers are mainly responsible for immigrants' occupational disadvantages.

The second approach stresses structural barriers such as unequal opportunity, devaluation of foreign credentials, and racism. It suggests that control of entry to the professions has caused systematic exclusion and occupational disadvantages for professional immigrants.[10] For instance, Boyd analyzes the differences between Canadian-born and foreign-born workers in the acquisition of occupational status. She argues that the Canadian-born receive a greater return for their education compared to the foreign-born because of "difficulties of transferring educational skill across national boundaries."[11] In their research, Fernando and Prasad report that among professional immigrants interviewed, particularly doctors and engineers, 71 percent had perceived barriers to full recognition.[12]

Many mainland Chinese immigrants perceived some structural barriers that affect their occupational attainments in Canada. The survey shows that 73 percent of the respondents believed that they could not enter into professional occupations in which they were trained because there is unequal opportunity for visible minority immigrants. About 77 percent reported that it was difficult for them to find professional jobs because of a shortage of opening positions in the Canadian labor market. However, the major systemic barrier identified by respondents is that their foreign credentials and work experience were devalued by professional organizations, government evaluation agencies, and educational institutions.[13]

Many mainland Chinese immigrants believe that they could not enter professional occupations in which they were trained because their foreign credentials were devalued. In the 1997–1999 Survey, 69 percent of the respondents reported that they experienced difficulties in having their foreign credentials recognized in Canada. Based on their own experiences and observations, about 78 percent of the respondents reported that "the difficulty in having their foreign qualifications or credentials recognized" was a major factor that affected or might have affected their chances to practice in their chosen professions.[14]

These immigrants thought that the greater the number of years of professional experience, the better their chance to get a job in their field in Canada. This assumption, however, turned out to be an illusion. In the 1997–1999 Survey, 94 percent of Chinese professional immigrants reported that they had professional work experience in China before immigrating to Canada; 50 percent had five to ten years of professional work experience; and 21 percent had more than ten years of professional work experience. Interestingly, Chinese professionals with more professional experience are more likely to experience downward mobility. In the survey, about 47 percent of the respondents do not believe that "the foreign work experience is compared to Canadian standards fairly."[15] They encounter a difficult situation in the Canadian labor market. On the one hand, nonrecognition of their foreign professional work experience disqualifies their entry into professional jobs, leaving them no chance to get Canadian work experience; on the other hand, the emphasis on Canadian work experience as a requirement for professional employment makes it difficult for them to qualify for professional jobs.

Covert Racism in Multicultural Society

The racism experienced by mainland Chinese immigrants in their everyday life is often expressed in a hidden form, which can be called "covert racism."[16] Covert racism is a contemporary expression of hostility toward racial minorities that goes undetected by conventional measures.

Since the implementation of Canada's multiculturalism policy in 1971, there has been a debate about whether multiculturalism promotes national unity in Canada. While Canadians generally support the values of equality and democracy, many have exhibited a remarkable degree of intolerance toward the increased presence of visible minorities in Canadian society. In the past two decades, the dramatic influx of refugees and immigrants from the third world and a large number of business and professional immigrants from Asian countries have produced a resurgence of racism in Canada. According to the 2003 Ipsos-Reid survey conducted by the Centre for Research and Information on Canada and the *Globe and Mail*, 74 percent of the respondents expressed the view that there is still considerable racism in Canada. The Ethnic Diversity Survey, conducted in 2002, shows that one in five minorities reported discrimination or unfair treatment, and 18 percent of Chinese respondents reported discrimination or unfair treatment.[17]

Racism has been generated and reproduced within complex historical and social contexts. Before World War II, overt racism based on the belief in racial superiority was dominant in Europe and North America. It was widely accepted that the Caucasian "race" was physically and genetically superior to other races, and was characterized by an inherent capacity for freedom and for an ability to create democratic institutions, capacities that they could impose in many other parts of the world.[18] With the expansion of capitalism and colonialism, the "innate superiority" of whites and the "natural inferiority" of blacks and other nonwhite peoples have been used to legitimate and justify racial oppression. Racism arose from initial unequal relationships as a dominant group sought to subjugate a subordinate group for the purpose of acquiring land, resources, or cheap labor. In Canada, racism was maintained toward racialized minorities such as the aboriginal peoples and Asian immigrants, and discriminatory laws, programs, and policies were entrenched in a social order that made prejudicial views appear as though they were natural and justifiable.[19]

After World War II, many changes contributed to the weakening of notions of racial superiority or inferiority based on biological and genetic factors. These changes include the struggle against colonial rule, the rise of nationalism, the development of sciences, and the abrogation of discriminatory laws and policies in many advanced capitalist countries. Thus, overt racism has become less acceptable in Western societies. The traditional idea of genetic inferiority or superiority may still be important in the fabric of racism,[20] but the discourse of racial inferiority is increasingly reformulated as cultural deficiency, social inadequacy, and technological underdevelopment.[21] An example is cultural ethnocentrism, which is a tendency to evaluate minorities' cultures based on the dominant group's imposed standards.[22] According to a survey conducted by the Angus Reid Group, about 13 percent of Canadians can be considered as "ethnocentrists," based on their negative attitudes toward immigrants and refugees. The basis of negative attitudes appeared to be largely cultural, as those expressing them were concerned that Canadian culture was under threat from an emphasis on multiculturalism and from a rapidly changing population resulting from high immigration levels.[23] In recent years, many scholars in North America have drawn attention to the emergence of a form of racism in contemporary social settings that can be described as "new racism."[24]

According to Weigel and Howes, the new racism is a contemporary expression of hostility toward racial minorities that goes undetected by conventional measures.[25] The new racism often contains an oblique attack on visible minorities in a covert or disguised form. Different from the past, when blatant and stereotypical forms of prejudice and discrimination were routinely directed at racial minorities with explicit hatred, the new racism usually disguises racist attitudes through behaviors that appear nonprejudicial or nondiscriminatory on the surface. To avoid embarrassing situations or possible physical or legal retaliation, racism now is usually expressed in somewhat more muted or polite tones, which are less likely to provoke outrage or indignation. Some scholars suggest that this new racism reflects a conflict of interest between opposing values in Canadian society.[26] "On the one hand is a commitment to abstract equality and justice (egalitarianism); on the other, an equal but often conflicting endorsement of meritocracy and universalism (individualism)."[27]

Since World War II, Canada has witnessed the abolition of overt exclusionary policies and laws such as repeal of the Chinese Immigration Act in 1947, the adoption of a multiculturalism policy in 1971, and constitutional guarantees of individual rights and freedoms in 1982. These changes help to promote a democratic and tolerant society, and the value of equality in Canadian society is widely propagated. However, economic, political, and social inequalities along racial and ethnic lines still exist, and covert expressions of bigotry and stereotyping remain.[28] The contradiction between democratic principles and racial inequalities at the structural level is reflected in the conflict between the egalitarian values of justice and racist attitudes. This is the basis of what Henry et al. call "democratic racism." According to Henry et al., democratic racism is a new ideology held by the public in contemporary Canadian society "in which two conflicting sets of values are made congruent to each other. Commitments to democratic principles such as justice, equality, and fairness conflict but coexist with attitudes and behaviors that include negative feelings about minority groups and differential treatment of and discrimination against them."[29]

The 1995 Vancouver survey confirms the coexistence of these contradictory values in the public, and the findings demonstrate the basis of a new ideology shared by many respondents in their attitudes toward Chinese immigrants.[30] Although people generally accept the value of racial equality, many are not prepared to accept nonwhite immigrants, such as the Chinese. About 79 percent of the respondents agree that "immigrants should have exactly the same job opportunities as Canadians," and 82 percent of the respondents agree that "minority groups in Canada should have equal opportunity for occupation, education, and promotion in society." However, European immigrants and Chinese immigrants are not equally supported by the public. About 73 percent of the respondents support admitting more European immigrants, while only about 47 percent of the respondents support admitting more Chinese immigrants. The negative attitude toward Chinese immigrants is not so much based on color or biological differences, but on perceived cultural differences. It is widely held that the different cultures brought by immigrants undermine national unity. The Vancouver survey showed that about 50 percent of the respondents disagree with the statement that "the establishment of multiculturalism policy has promoted a democratic and tolerant society in Canada." Many people in the survey believe that multiculturalism encourages cultural diversity and denies the existence of Canadian culture, and therefore creates and reinforces separateness and racial conflict. This concern is reflected in public attitudes toward recent Chinese immigrants in Vancouver.[31] Their comments reflect the belief still held by many Canadians that Anglo-Saxon culture as Canadian culture is the basis of national unity, and that immigrants must make conscious efforts to become "Canadian" by accepting and adopting the behavior of the dominant group. Most people would deny that race is important and almost unanimously would condemn racism as being wrong. In the 1995 Vancouver survey, about 59 percent of the respondents thought that ethnic origin should not be used as a criterion in admitting immigrants to Canada, and more than 82 percent of the respondents agreed that minority groups in Canada should have equal opportunity for occupation, education, and promotion in society. Yet at the same time, many people accept visible minorities and immigrants only on the basis that they can adapt to Anglo-Canadian culture. The same survey shows that about 59 percent of the respondents agree that "Chinese immigrants should adapt themselves to Canadian culture in order to become a real Canadian." Cultural diversity has always been a part of Canadian society, and it is an existing fact of life, and not something that can be changed artificially. Despite cultural differences, different racial and ethnic groups in Canadian society share core values such as democracy and equality. Some scholars suggest that although there is no empirical evidence to indicate that immigrants and their cultural diversity are posing any real threat to the dominant culture of Canada,[32] visible minorities and "immigrants are often perceived as undermining a British-dominated traditional symbolic order, on the grounds that visible minorities are seen as carriers of foreign cultures and norms which are believed to be different, if not incompatible, with the Canadian heritage and core values."[33] As Li points out, "the apparent growth of opposition to increased immigration to Canada and the intensification of negative sentiments towards immigrants, especially those from non-European origins, stem from the perceived threat to an established symbolic order and status hierarchy that are distinctly British dominated, and not necessarily from real conflicts between core Canadian values and the normative and linguistic diversities that recent immigrants are supposedly to have imported with them."[34]

Culture is dynamic and complex. The notion of "Anglo-Saxon Canadian culture" is vague and ambiguous, and the concept of "acculturation" or "assimilation" stressed in national unity is misleading and ill defined. Assimilation implies that there are certain objectives and widely agreed upon standards of behavior that are indicative of social and structural integration. However, in practice, it is unclear what types of behaviors indicate a person is assimilated.

Cultural diversity does not in itself create racial tension and conflict. It is differential power and unequal treatment that produce racial tension or conflict. Members of the dominant group often use their "standards" as a frame of reference for interpreting and evaluating the behavior of other groups. As Elliott and Flera point out, "Not surprisingly, these groups are rated inferior, backward, or irrational. It can be seen that although favouritism towards one's own group can promote cohesion and moral, it can also contribute to intergroup tension and hostility, . . . [and] to a proliferation of stereotypes about outgroup members."[35]

Finally, as regard to the multiculturalism policy, the real issue is not whether it harms or enhances national unity, but how the policy promotes mutual understanding and respectful relationship among different racial groups, and how it achieves a national solidarity and harmony within a culturally diversified society.

Conclusion

In the past twenty-five years, the number of mainland Chinese immigrants to Canada has increased dramatically, and they have brought significant financial and human capital resources to Canada. However, new Chinese immigrants have experienced great difficulties in accessing education-related professions in Canada. The problem of transferring educational equivalences and work experience across international boundaries results in mainland Chinese professional immigrants taking jobs for which they are overtrained, resulting in downward occupational mobility relative to the occupations they held before immigrating to Canada. Recent mainland Chinese immigrants face both individual and institutional barriers to entry into their respective professions. Individual barriers such as linguistic ability and cultural adaptation can gradually improve over time through their personal efforts, community support, and programs and services provided by the Canadian government. However, immigrants themselves cannot resolve institutionalized obstacles, such as the devaluation of foreign credentials and work experience, unequal opportunity, and racism.

There are contradictory social values within a multicultural society that become an important ideological basis of new racism. On the one hand, Canadian people generally accept "racial equality" and "democracy" as central values in a social democratic society; on the other hand, cultural ethnocentrism prevails in society as reflected in negative attitudes toward Chinese immigrants. This essay criticized the discourse that cultural diversity threatens national unity and argued that national unity can be achieved in the context of cultural diversity. To make full use of the talents and skills of Chinese immigrants, Canadian governments at different levels should consider providing more assistance, including delivery of effective settlement services, to help Chinese immigrants adapt to the Canadian society.

NOTES

1. Citizenship and Immigration Canada, *Citizenship and Immigration Canada,* 2000–2004.
2. Peter Li, *Chinese in Canada* (Toronto: Oxford University Press, 1998), 96.
3. Peter Li, "The Rise and Fall of Chinese Immigration to Canada: Newcomers from Hong Kong Special Administrative Region of China and Mainland China, 1980–2000," *International Migration* 43, no. 3 (2005): 9–32.
4. Ibid., 14.
5. Immigrants to Canada are officially grouped into more than ten classes, but the various classes can be generalized into the three broad categories. The economic category includes skilled workers/professionals who are admitted on the basis of skills, education, language ability, and occupational background; business immigrants (investors, entrepreneurs, and self-employed) who must bring with them sufficient capital to start a business in Canada, and either provide jobs for themselves or employ other Canadians; and live-in caregivers. The family category refers to family members,

including spouses, fiancés/fiancées, dependent children, parents, grandparents, and assisted relatives of Canadian citizens or landed immigrants. The humanitarian category includes refugees, deferred order removal class (immigrants who at one time were ordered to leave Canada but subsequently had their deportation order canceled), and designated-class (immigrants admitted under special government programs, usually in response to political upheavals in the home countries). The retiree-class is not included in the three categories, and it is listed separately in the other category.

6. "Mainland Chinese professional immigrants" refers to those who received their professional training in China and worked as doctors, engineers, school/university teachers, and other professionals; who entered Canada as immigrants; and who were residents in Canada at the time of the survey. The data were obtained through self-administered questionnaires. The questionnaire included seventy-one questions on credentials, work experience before and after immigration, personal difficulties and perceived structural barriers in accessing professional jobs in the Canadian labor force, opinions on policy issues, and general respondent information. Findings of the survey were reported in Li Zong, "International Transference of Human Capital and Occupational Attainment of Recent Chinese Professional Immigrants in Canada," *American Journal of China Studies* 5, nos. 1–2 (2004): 81–89.

7. Ibid., 82–83.

8. Michael Ornstein and Raghubar D. Sharma, *Adjustment and Economic Experience of Immigrants in Canada: An Analysis of the 1976 Longitudinal Survey of Immigrants*, a report to Employment and Immigration Canada (Toronto: York University Institute for Behavioural Research, 1983).

9. Li, "International Transference of Human Capital," 83, 84.

10. See, for example, Monica Boyd, "Immigration and Occupation Attainment in Canada," in *Ascription and Achievement: Studies in Mobility and Status Attainment in Canada*, ed. Monica Boyd et al., 393–445 (Ottawa: Carleton University Press, 1985); Kathryn McDade, *Barriers to Recognition of the Credentials of Immigrants in Canada* (Ottawa: Institute for Research on Public Policy, 1988); Frank Trovato and Carl F. Grindstaff, "Economic Status: A Census Analysis of Immigrant Women at Age Thirty in Canada," *Review of Sociology and Anthropology* 23, no. 4 (1986): 569–687; Indhu Rajagopal, "The Glass Ceiling in the Vertical Mosaic: Indian Immigrants to Canada," *Canadian Ethnic Studies* 22, no. 1 (1990): 96–105; Helen Ralston, "Ethnicity, Class, and Gender among South Asian Women in Metro Halifax: An Exploratory Study," *Canadian Ethnic Studies* 20, no. 3 (1988): 63–83; Charles Beach and Christopher Worswick, "Is There a Double-Negative Effect on the Earnings of Immigrant Women?" *Canadian Public Policy* 16, no. 2 (1989): 36–54.

11. Boyd, "Immigration and Occupation Attainment in Canada," 405.

12. Tissa Fernando and Kamal K. Prasad, *Multiculturalism and Employment Equity: Problems Facing Foreign-Trained Professionals and Tradespeople in British Columbia* (Vancouver: Affiliation of Multicultural Societies and Service Agencies of B.C., 1986).

13. Li, "International Transference of Human Capital," 84.

14. Ibid., 83.

15. Ibid.

16. Li Zong, "New Racism, Cultural Diversity and the Search for a National Identity," in *The Battle over Multiculturalism: Does It Help or Hinder Canadian Unity?* ed. Andrew Cardoza and Louis Musto, 115–126 (Ottawa: Pearson-Shoyama Institute, 1997).

17. See Statistics Canada, *Ethnic Diversity Survey: Portrait of A Multicultural Society*, September 2003, Catalog No. 89–593-XIE, http://www.statcan.ca/cgi-bin/downpub/freepub.cgi, accessed July 24, 2008.

18. R. Horsman, "Origins of Racial Anglo-Saxonism in Great Britain before 1850," *Journal of the History of Ideas* 37, no. 3 (1976): 387–410; R. Horsman, *Race and Manifest Destiny* (Cambridge, Mass.: Harvard University Press, 1981), 9–77; H. A. MacDougall, *Racial Myth in English History: Trojabs, Teutons and Anglo-Saxons* (Montreal: Harvest House, 1982).

19. Li Zong, "Structural and Psychological Dimensions of Racism," *Canadian Ethnic Studies* 26, no. 3 (1994): 122–134.

20. T. Duster, *Backdoor to Eugenics* (New York: Routledge, 1990).

21. W. Rodney, *How Europe Underdeveloped Africa* (Washington, D.C.: Howard University Press, 1982).

22. Peter Li, "A World Apart: The Multicultural World of Visible Minorities and the Art World of Canada," *Canadian Review of Sociology and Anthropology* 31, no. 4 (1994): 356–391.

23. Angus Reid Group, *Immigration to Canada: Aspects of Public Opinion* (Winnipeg: Angus Reid, 1989), 7–8.

24. Jean Leonard Elliott and Augie Fleras, *Unequal Relations: An Introduction to Race and Ethnic Dynamics in Canada* (Scarborough, Ont.: Prentice-Hall Canada, 1992); Samuel L. Gaertner and John F. Dovidio, "The Aversive Form of Racism," in *Prejudice, Discrimination, and Racism*, ed. John Dovidio and Samuel L. Gaertner, 61–89 (New York: Academic Press, 1986); Frances Henry et al., *The Colour of Democracy: Racism in Canadian Society* (Toronto: Harcourt Brace, 1995); Irwin Katz, Joyce Wackenhut, and R. Glen Hass, "Racial Ambivalence, Value Duality, and Behaviour," in Dovidio and Gaertner, *Prejudice, Discrimination, and Racism*, 35–60; John B. McConohay, "Modern Racism, Ambivalence, and the Modern Racism Scale," in Dovidio and Gaertner, *Prejudice, Discrimination, and Racism*, 91–126; Russel H. Weigel and Paul W. Howes, "Conceptions of Racial Prejudice: Symbolic Racism Reconsidered," *Journal of Social Issues* 41, no. 3 (1985): 117–138.

25. Weigel and Howes, "Conceptions of Racial Prejudice."

26. Elliott and Fleras, *Unequal Relations*; Henry et al., *Colour of Democracy*.

27. Elliott and Fleras, *Unequal Relations*, 60.

28. B. S. Bolaria and P. S. Li, *Racial Oppression in Canada*, 2nd ed. (Toronto: Garamond Press, 1988); Vic Satzewich, ed., *Deconstructing a Nation: Immigration, Multiculturalism and Racism in '90s Canada* (Halifax, N.S.: Fernwood, 1992).

29. Henry et al., *Colour of Democracy*, 21.

30. The survey on public attitudes toward recent Chinese immigrants was conducted in Vancouver in 1995, and in total, 778 people were surveyed using a probability sampling method. Findings were published in Li Zong, "Chinese Immigration to Vancouver and New Racism in Multicultural Canada," in *Ethnic Chinese at the Turn of the Centuries*, ed. Guotu Zhuang, 443–463 (Fujian: Fujian People Press, 1998).

31. These are written comments made by respondents who completed survey questionnaire. See Zong, "New Racism."

32. Raymond Breton, "The Production and Allocation of Symbolic Resources: An Analysis of the Linguistic and Ethnocultural Fields in Canada," *Canadian Review of Sociology and Anthropology* 21, no. 2 (1984): 123–144; Peter Li, "Unneighbourly House or Unwelcome Chinese: The Social Construction of Race in the Battle over 'Monster Homes' in Vancouver, Canada," *International Journal of Comparative Race and Ethnic Studies* 1, no. 1 (1994): 14–33; John Mercer, "Canadian Cities and Their Immigrants: New Realities," *Annals of the American Academy of Political and Social Science* 538 (1995): 169–184.

33. Peter Li, *Literature Review on Immigration: Sociological Perspectives* (Ottawa: Citizenship and Immigration Canada, 1996), 24.

34. Ibid., 23.

35. Elliott and Fleras, *Unequal Relations*, 55.

SELECTED BIBLIOGRAPHY

Abelmann, Nancy, and John Lee. *Blue Dreams: Korean Americans and the Los Angeles Riots.* Cambridge, Mass.: Harvard University Press, 1995.

Abercrombie, Nicholas, and John Urry. *Capital, Labour and the Middle Classes.* London: Allen and Unwin, 1983.

Abrahamson, Mark. *Urban Enclaves: Identity and Place in America.* New York: St. Martin's Press, 1996.

Adilman, Tamara. "A Preliminary Sketch of Chinese Women and Work in British Columbia 1858–1950." In *Not Just Pin Money*, ed. Barbara K. Latham and Roberta J. Pazdro, 53–78. Victoria: Camosun College, 1984.

Aguilar-San Juan, Karin. "Gazing Colonial: Looking at the Vietnamese American Community in Boston and Orange County." *Hitting Critical Mass: A Journal of Asian American Cultural Criticism* 51 (Spring 1998): 89–106.

———. "Creating Ethnic Places: Vietnamese American Community-Building in Orange County and Boston." Ph.D. diss., Brown University, 2002.

Alba, R. D. *Ethnic Identity: The Transformation of White America.* New Haven, Conn.: Yale University Press, 1990.

Albarran, Alan, and David H. Goff. *Understanding the Web: Social, Political, and Economic Dimensions of the Internet.* Ames: Iowa State University Press, 2000.

Allison, M. T., and C. W. Geiger. "Nature of Leisure Activities among the Chinese-American Elderly." *Leisure Studies* 15 (1993): 309–319.

Anderson, Benedict. *Imagined Communities: Reflections on the Origin and Spread of Nationalism.* Rev. ed. New York: Verso, 1991.

Anderson, Kay J. *Vancouver's Chinatown: Racial Discourse in Canada, 1875–1980.* Montreal: McGill-Queen's University Press, 1991.

Anderson, Wanni W., and Robert Lee, eds. *Displacement and Diasporas: Asians in the Americas.* New Brunswick, N.J.: Rutgers University Press, 2005.

Angelo, Michael. "The Sikh Diaspora: Tradition and Change in an Immigrant Community." In *Asian Americans: Reconceptualizing Culture*, ed. Franklin Ng, 208–237. New York: Garland, 1997.

Angus Reid Group. *Immigration to Canada: Aspects of Public Opinion.* Winnipeg: Angus Reid, 1989.

Arenson, Ling Z. "Taiwan xinyimin zai meiguo de wenhua rentong" [Taiwanese Americans: The Construction of a New Group Identity in the U.S.]. In *Modernity and Culture Identity in Taiwan*, ed. Lu Hanchao, 208–237. River Edge, N.J.: Global, 2001.

Aronowitz, Stanley. "Postmodernism and Politics." In *Universal Abandon? The Politics of Postmodernism*, ed. Andrew Ross, 46–62. Minneapolis: University of Minnesota Press, 1988.

Ashkenazi, M. *Matsuri: Festivals of a Japanese Town*. Honolulu: University of Hawaii Press, 1993.

Backhouse, Constance. "The White Women's Labor Laws: Anti-Chinese Racism in Early Twentieth-Century Canada." *Law and History Review* 14, no. 2 (1996): 315–368.

Bacon, Jean. *Life Lines: Community, Family, and Assimilation among Asian Indian Immigrants*. New York: Oxford University Press, 1997.

Baldwin, C. Beth. *Capturing the Change: The Impact of Indochinese Refugees in Orange County; Challenges and Opportunities*. Santa Ana, Calif.: Immigrant and Refugee Planning Center, 1982.

Baluyut, Pearlie Rose S. "A Glorious History, a Golden Legacy: The Making of Filipino American Identity and Community." *Amerasia Journal* 42, no. 3 (Winter 1998): 192–216.

Bankston, Carl L., III. "Filipino Americans." In *Asian Americans: Contemporary Trends and Issues*, 2nd ed., ed. Pyong Gap Min, 80–203. Thousand Oaks, Calif.: Pine Forge Press, 2006.

Banton, Michael. *The Idea of Race*. London: Tavistock, 1977.

Bao, Xiaolan. *Holding Up More Than Half the Sky: Chinese Women Garment Workers in New York City, 1948–92*. Urbana: University of Illinois Press, 2001.

——. "Revisiting New York's Chinatown, 1900–1930." In *Remapping Asian American History*, ed. Sucheng Chan, 31–48. Walnut Creek, Calif.: AltaMira Press, 2003.

Barth, Gunther. *Bitter Strength: History of the Chinese in the United States 1850–1870*. Cambridge, Mass.: Harvard University Press, 1964.

Basran, Gurcharn S., and Li Zong. "Devaluation of Foreign Credentials as Perceived by Visible Minority Professional Immigrants." *Canadian Ethnic Studies* 30, no. 3 (1998): 6–23.

Baudrillard, Jean. *The Transparency of Evil*. Trans. James Benedict. London: Verso. 1993.

Baxter, David, *Population and Housing in Metropolitan Vancouver: Changing Patterns of Demographics and Demand*. Vancouver: Laurier Institute, 1989.

Baym, Nancy, K. "The Emergence of Community in Computer-Mediated Communication." In *CyberSociety: Computer-Mediated Communication and Community*, ed. Steven Jones, 138–163. Thousand Oaks, Calif.: Sage, 1995.

Beach, Charles, and Christopher Worswick. "Is There a Double-Negative Effect on the Earnings of Immigrant Women?" *Canadian Public Policy* 16, no. 2 (1989): 36–54.

Beck, Ulrich. *What Is Globalization?* Trans. Polity Press. Malden, Mass.: Blackwell, 2000.

Bennitt, Mark, ed. *History of the Louisiana Purchase Exposition*. New York: Arno Press, 1976.

"Big Houses." *Western Living*, November 1988, 31–41.

Blake, C. Fred. "The Chinese of Valhalla: Adaptation and Identity in a Midwestern American Cemetery." In *Markers X, Journal of the Association for Gravestone Studies*, ed. Richard E. Meyer, 53–89. Worcester, Mass.: Association for Gravestone Studies, 1993.

Bodnar, John. *The Transplanted: A History of Immigrants in Urban America*. Bloomington: Indiana University Press, 1985.

Bolaria, B. Singh, and Peter. S. Li, eds. *Racial Oppression in Canada*. 2nd ed. Toronto: Garamond Press, 1988.

Bonacich, Edna. *The Economic Basis of Ethnic Solidarity: Small Business in the Japanese American Community*. Berkeley: University of California Press, 1981.

Bonacich, Edna, Ivan Light, and Charles C. Wong. "Small Business among Koreans in Los Angeles." In *Counterpoint: Perspectives on Asian America*, ed. Emma Gee, 436–449. Los Angeles: Asian American Studies Center, University of California, 1976.

Bonus, Rick. *Locating Filipino America: Ethnicity and Cultural Politics of Space*. Philadelphia: Temple University Press, 2000.

Boyd, Monica. "Immigration and Occupation Attainment in Canada." In *Ascription and Achievement: Studies in Mobility and Status Attainment in Canada*, ed. Monica Boyd et al., 393–445. Ottawa: Carleton University Press, 1985.

Brechin, Gray. *Imperial San Francisco: Urban Power, Earthly Ruin.* Berkeley: University of California Press, 1999.

Breton, Raymond. "Institutional Completeness of Ethnic Communities and the Personal Relations of Immigrants." *American Journal of Sociology* 70, no. 2 (1964): 193–205.

———. "The Production and Allocation of Symbolic Resources: An Analysis of the Linguistic and Ethnocultural Fields in Canada." *Canadian Review of Sociology and Anthropology* 21, no. 2 (1984): 123–144.

Brooks, James, Chris Carlsson, and Nancy J. Peters. *Reclaiming San Francisco: History, Politics, Culture.* San Francisco: City Lights Books, 1998.

Burgess, Ernest W. "The Growth of the City: An Introduction to a Research Project." In *The City,* ed. Robert E. Park, Ernest W. Burgess, and Roderick D. McKenzie, 47–62. Chicago: University of Chicago Press, 1925.

Bush, S. *Arizona's Gold Mountain: Oral Histories of Chinese Americans in Phoenix.* Tempe: Arizona State University, 2000.

Cadaval, O. *Creating a Latino Identity in the Nation's Capital: The Latino Festival.* New York: Garland, 1998.

Caldwell, John Thornton, ed. *Electronic Media and Technoculture.* New Brunswick, N.J.: Rutgers University Press, 2000.

Canada, House of Commons. *Debates, 3rd Session, 24th Parliament.* June 9, 1960.

Canada, Royal Commission, *Report of the Royal Commission on Chinese Immigration: Report and Evidence.* 1885.

Canlas, M. C. *SoMa Pilipinas: Studies 2000 (In Two Languages).* San Francisco: Arkipelago Books, 2002.

Carchedi, Guglielmo. *Class Analysis and Social Research.* Oxford: Basil Blackwell, 1987.

Castells, Manuel. *The Rise of the Network Society.* Vol. 1 of *The Information Age: Economy, Society and Culture Series.* Cambridge, Mass.: Blackwell, 1996.

———. *The Power of Identity.* Vol. 2 of *The Information Age: Economy, Society and Culture Series.* Cambridge, Mass.: Blackwell, 1997.

Chan, Kenyon S. "Rethinking the Asian American Studies Project: Bridging the Divide between 'Campus' and 'Community.'" *Journal of Asian American Studies* 3, no. 1 (February 2000): 17–36.

Chan, Sucheng. *Asian Americans: An Interpretive History.* Boston: Twayne, 1991.

———. *Not Just Victims: Conversations with Cambodian Community Leaders in the United States.* Urbana: University of Illinois Press, 2003.

———, ed. *Entry Denied: Exclusion and the Chinese Community in America, 1882–1943.* Philadelphia: Temple University Press, 1994.

Chang, Edward Tea. "Korean Community Politics in Los Angeles: The Impact of the Kwangju Uprising." *Amerasia* 14, no. 1 (1988): 51–68.

———. "The Post–Los Angeles Riot Korean American Community: Challenges and Prospects." *Korean and Korean American Studies Bulletin* 10, nos. 1–2 (1999): 6–26.

Chang, Edward Tea, and Jeannette Diaz-Veizades. *Ethnic Peace in the American City: Building Community in Los Angeles and Beyond.* New York: New York University Press, 1999.

Chang, Gordon H. "Writing the History of Chinese Immigrants to America." *South Atlantic Quarterly* 98 (1999): 135–142.

———. "Asian Americans and Politics: Some Perspectives from History." In *Asian Americans and Politics: Perspectives, Experiences, Prospects,* ed. Gordon H. Chang, 13–38. Stanford, Calif.: Stanford University Press, 2001.

Chang, Iris. *The Chinese in America: A Narrative History.* New York: Viking Penguin, 2003.

Chatterjee, Partha. *The Nation and Its Fragments: Colonial and Postcolonial Histories.* Princeton, N.J.: Princeton University Press, 1993.

Chen, Carolyn E. "The Religious Varieties of Ethnic Presence: A Comparison between a Taiwanese Immigrant Buddhist Temple and an Evangelical Christian Church." *Sociology of Religion* 63, no. 2 (2002): 215–238.

Chen, Hsiang-shui. *Chinatown No More: Taiwanese Immigrants in Contemporary New York.* Ithaca, N.Y.: Cornell University Press, 1992.

Chen, Yong. *Chinese San Francisco, 1850–1943: A Trans-Pacific Community.* Stanford, Calif.: Stanford University Press, 2000.

Chepesiuk, Ron. "Exporting High Tech Talent: Sino-American Deal Brings Chinese IT Workers to U.S." *Asian Week,* http://www.asianweek.com/2001_06_08/biz1_sfsc_headway_deal_html, accessed May 13, 2002.

Cheung, Freda K., and Lonnie R. Snowden. "Community Mental Health and Ethnic Minority Populations." *Community Mental Health Journal* 26, no. 3 (June 1990): 277–291.

Chiang-Hom, Christy. "Transnational Cultural Practices of Chinese Immigrant Youth and Parachute Kids." In *Asian American Youth: Culture, Identity, and Ethnicity,* ed. Jennifer Lee and Min Zhou, 143–159. New York: Routledge 2004.

Chin, Charlie. "Myths and Legends of Chinatown." *Asian New Yorker* (December 1990), 6+.

Chin, Doug. *Seattle's International District: The Making of a Pan-Asian American Community.* Seattle: University of Washington Press, 2002.

Chin, Margaret M. *Sewing Women: Immigrants and the New York City Garment Industry.* New York: Columbia University Press, 2005.

Chin, Rocky. "New York Chinatown Today: Community in Crisis." *Amerasia* 1, no. 1 (1971): 1–24.

Chin, V. F. "Finding the Right Gesture: Becoming Chinese American in Fae Myenne Ng's *Bone.*" In *The Chinese in America: A History from Gold Mountain to the New Millennium,* ed. Susie Lan Cassel, 365–377. Walnut Creek, Calif.: AltaMira Press, 2001.

Chinese Consolidated Benevolent Association of Chicago (CCBAC), comp. *A Century of Chicago Chinatown.* Chicago: CCBAC, 2000.

"Chinese Language Internet Users." Global Reach, http://www.glreach.com/, accessed February 26, 2001.

"Chinese Media Net." http://www.chinesemedianet.com/AboutUs.html, accessed February 26, 2001.

"Chinese Student Protection Act." http://www.ins.usdoj.gov/graphics/aboutins/annual/fy95/125.htm, accessed May 28, 2002.

Chinn, Thomas W. *Bridging the Pacific: San Francisco's Chinatown and Its People.* San Francisco: Chinese Historical Society of America, 1989.

Chun, C. A., and S. Sue. "Mental Health Issues Concerning Asian Pacific American Children." In *Struggling to Be Heard: The Unmet Needs of Asian Pacific American Children,* ed. V. O. Pang and L. L. Cheng, 75–87. Albany: State University of New York Press, 1998.

Chung, Angie Y. *Legacies of Struggle: Conflict and Cooperation in Korean American Politics.* Stanford, Calif.: Stanford University Press, 2007.

Chung, Tom. "Asian Americans in Enclaves—They Are Not One Community: New Modes of Asian American Settlement." In *Asian Americans: Experiences and Perspectives,* ed. Timothy Fong and Larry H. Shinagawa, 99–109. Upper Saddle River, N.J.: Prentice Hall, 2000.

Chu Tam Anh. "The Role of the Youth in Building a Community Oversees." *Non Sông* (1990): 61–65.

Citizenship and Immigration Canada. *Citizenship and Immigration Canada, 2000–2004.*

"CND." http://www.cnd.org/, accessed March 13, 2001.

Cohen, A. P. *The Symbolic Construction of Community.* New York: Tavistock, 1985.

Cohen, Lucy M. *Chinese in the Post–Civil War South: A People without a History.* Baton Rouge: Louisiana State University Press, 1984.

Cohen, Robin. *Global Diasporas*. Seattle: University of Washington Press, 1997.

Collet, Christian, and Nadine Selden. "Separate Ways . . . Worlds Apart?: The 'Generation Gap' in Vietnamese America as Seen through the *San Jose Mercury News* Poll." *Amerasia Journal* 29, no. 1 (2003): 199–219.

Coolidge, Mary. *Chinese Immigration*. New York: Henry Holt, 1909. Reprint, New York: Arno Press, 1969.

Cordova, Fred. *Filipinos: Forgotten Asian Americans*. Dubuque, Iowa: Kendall, 1983.

Cortinovis, Irene E. "China at the St. Louis World's Fair." *Missouri Historical Review* 77 (1977–1978): 59–66.

Crissman, Lawrence W. "The Segmentary Structure of Urban Overseas Chinese Communities." *Man* 2 (1967): 185–204.

Cunha, M. W. "Festivals and the Social Rhythm Considered in the Light of Functionalist Theories." Master's thesis, University of Chicago, 1943.

"CyberAtlas: Chinese-American Lead the Way online." http://www.nua.ie/surveys/, accessed February 26, 2001.

Danico, Mary, and Linda Trinh Võ. " 'No Lattés Here': Asian American Youth and the Cyber Café Obsession." In *Asian American Youth: Culture, Identity, and Ethnicity*, ed. Jennifer Lee and Min Zhou, 177–190. New York: Routledge, 2004.

Daniels, Roger. *Asian America: Chinese and Japanese in the United States since 1850*. Seattle: University of Washington Press, 1988.

———. *Coming to America: A History of Immigration and Ethnicity in American Life*. New York: Harper Collins, 1990.

———. *Guarding the Gold Door: American Immigration Policy and Immigrants since 1882*. New York: Hill and Wang, 2004.

Dearing, Emily Gaborne. "The Family Tree: Discovering Oneself." In *Filipina/o Americans: Transformation and Identity*, ed. Maria P. P. Root, 287–298. Thousand Oaks, Calif.: Sage, 1997.

Desbarats, Jacqueline, and Linda Holland. "Indochinese Settlement Patterns in Orange County." *Amerasia Journal* 10, no. 1 (Spring/Summer 1983): 23–46.

DeWilde, Steven R. "Vietnamese Settlement Patterns in Orange County's Little Saigon." Master's thesis, California State University, Long Beach, 1996.

Dion, K. K., K. L. Dion, and A. W. P. Pak. "The Role of Self-Reported Language Proficiencies in the Cultural and Psychosocial Adaptation among Members of Toronto's Chinese Community." *Journal of Asian Pacific Communication* 1, no. 1 (1990): 173–189.

Do, Hien Duc. "The Formation of a New Refugee Community: The Vietnamese Community in Orange County, California." Master's thesis, University of California, Santa Barbara, 1988.

Dominion Bureau of Statistics. *Census of Canada* 2 (1913).

———. *Census of Canada* 1 (1923).

Dreer, Herman. "Negro Leadership in St. Louis: A Study in Race Relations." Ph. D. diss., University of Chicago, 1955.

Dreiser, Theodore. "The Chinese in St. Louis." In *Journalism*. Vol. 1 of *Newspaper Writings, 1892–1895*, ed. T. D. Nostwich, 239–249. Philadelphia: University of Pennsylvania Press, 1988.

Durkheim, Emile. *The Elementary Forms of the Religious Life*. New York: Free Press, 1995.

Duster, T. *Backdoor to Eugenics*. New York: Routledge, 1990.

Ecklund, Elaine Howard, and Jerry Z. Park. "Asian American Community Participation and Religion: Civil 'Model Minorities?' " *Journal of Asian American Studies* 8, no. 1 (February 2005): 1–21.

Ehrlich, Walter. *Zion in the Valley, the Jewish Community of St. Louis*. Vol. 1, *1807–1907*. Columbia: University of Missouri Press, 1997.

Eljera, Bert. "Big Plans for Little Saigon." *AsianWeek*, May 17, 1996.

———. "Filipinos Find Home in Daly City." In *Asian Americans: Experiences and Perspectives*, ed. Timothy Fong and Larry H. Shinagawa, 110–115. Upper Saddle River, N.J.: Prentice Hall, 2000.

Elliot, Jean Leonard, and Augie Fleras. *Unequal Relations: An Introduction to Race and Ethnic Dynamics in Canada*. Scarborough, Ont.: Prentice-Hall Canada, 1992.

Erdamans, Mary Patrice. *Opposite Poles: Immigrants and Ethnics in Polish Chicago, 1976–1990*. University Park: Pennsylvania State University Press, 1998.

Espana-Maram, Linda Nueva. "Negotiating Identity: Youth, Gender, and Popular Culture in Los Angeles's Little Manila, 1920s–1940s." Ph. D. diss., University of California, Los Angeles, 1996.

———. *Creating Masculinity in Los Angeles's Little Manila: Working-Class Filipinos and Popular Culture, 1920s–1950s*. New York: Columbia University Press, 2006.

Espinosa, Hennijay. "Filipina/o Community Center: Working for a United and Empowered People." *Manila Bulletin USA*, January 19–25, 2006.

Espiritu, Yen Le. *Filipino American Lives*. Philadelphia: Temple University Press, 1995.

———. *Home Bound: Filipino American Lives across Cultures, Communities, and Countries*. Berkeley: University of California Press, 2003.

Espiritu, Yen Le, and Thu-Huong Nguyen-Võ, guest eds. "30 Years Afterward: Vietnamese Americans and U.S. Empire." Special issue, *Amerasia Journal* 31, no. 2 (2005).

Everard, Jerry. *Virtual States: The Internet and the Boundaries of the Nation State*. New York: Routledge, 2000.

Fan, Tin-chiu. "Chinese Residents in Chicago." Ph.D. diss., University of Chicago, 1926.

Farber, C. "High, Healthy and Happy: Ontario Mythology on Parade." In *The Celebration of Society: Perspectives on Contemporary Cultural Performances*, ed. F. Manning, 33–50. Bowling Green, Ohio: Bowling Green University Popular Press, 1983.

Fernando, Tissa, and Kamal K. Prasad. *Multiculturalism and Employment Equity: Problems Facing Foreign-Trained Professionals and Tradespeople in British Columbia*. Vancouver: Affiliation of Multicultural Societies and Service Agencies of B.C., 1986.

Fitzgerald, Maureen H., and Alan Howard. "Aspects of Social Organization in Three Samoan Communities." *Pacific Studies* 14, no. 1 (1991): 31–54.

Flewelling, Stan. *Shirakawa: Stories from a Pacific Northwest Japanese American Community*. Seattle: University of Washington Press, 2002.

Floyd, M. F. "Race, Ethnicity and Use of the National Park System." *Social Science Research Review* 1 (1999): 1–24.

Fong, Joe Chung. "Transnational Newspapers: The Making of the Post-1965 Globalized/Localized San Gabriel Valley Chinese Community." *Amerasia* 22, no. 3 (1996): 65–77.

———. *Complementary Education and Culture in the Global/Local Chinese Community*. San Francisco: China Books and Periodicals, 2003.

Fong, Timothy P. *The First Suburban Chinatown: The Making of Monterey Park, California*. Philadelphia: Temple University Press, 1993.

———. *The Contemporary Asian American Experience: Beyond the Model Minority*. Upper Saddle River, N.J.: Prentice Hall, 1998.

Fong, Timothy, and Larry H. Shinagawa, eds. *Asian Americans: Experiences and Perspectives*. Upper Saddle River, N.J.: Prentice Hall, 2000.

Freedman, Maurice. "Lineage Organization in South-Eastern China." *L.S.E. Monographs on Social Anthropology* 18. London: Athlete Press, 1958.

Freeman, James A. *Hearts of Sorrow: Vietnamese-Americans Lives*. Stanford, Calif.: Stanford University Press, 1989.

Fugita, Stephen S., and David J. O'Brien. *Japanese American Ethnicity: The Persistence of Community.* Seattle: University of Washington Press, 1991.

Fukuyama, Francis. *The End of History and the Last Man.* New York: Penguin, 1992.

Gaertner, Samuel L., and John F. Dovidio. "The Aversive Form of Racism." In *Prejudice, Discrimination, and Racism,* ed. John Dovidio and Samuel L. Gaertner, 61–89. New York: Academic Press, 1986.

Gates, Barbara T. "A Root of Eçofeminism: Ecoféminisme." In *Ecofeminist Literary Criticism: Theory, Interpretation, Pedagogy,* ed. Greta Gaard and Patrick D. Murphy, 15–22. Urbana: University of Illinois Press, 1998.

Gjerde, Jon. *Major Problems in American Immigration and Ethnic History.* Boston: Houghton Mifflin, 1998.

Glen, Everlyn N., and Stacey G. H. Yap. "Chinese American Families." In *Minority Families in the United States: A Multicultural Perspective,* ed. Ronald L. Taylor, 115–145. Englewood Cliffs, N.J.: Prentice Hall, 1994.

Glenn, Evelyn Nakano. *Issei, Nisei, War Bride: Three Generations of Japanese American Women in Domestic Service.* Philadelphia: Temple University Press, 1986.

Gittell, Ross, and Avis Vidal. *Community Organizing: Building Social Capital as a Development Strategy.* Thousand Oaks, Calif.: Sage, 1998.

Glick, Clarence E. *Sojourners and Settlers: Chinese Migrants in Hawaii.* Honolulu: Hawaii Chinese History Center and the University Press of Hawaii, 1980.

Gold, Steven J. *Refugee Communities: A Comparative Field Study.* Newbury Park, Calif.: Sage, 1992.

Goldberg, Michael A. *The Chinese Connection: Getting Plugged In to Pacific Rim Real Estate, Trade, and Capital Markets.* Vancouver: University of British Columbia Press, 1985.

Gonzalez, Juan L. "Asian Indian Immigration Patterns: The Origins of the Sikh Community in California." *International Migration Review* 20, no. 1 (1986): 40–54.

Gordon, Milton. *Assimilation in American Life: The Role of Race, Religion, and National Origin.* New York: Oxford University Press, 1964.

Gramann, J. H., and M. T. Allison. "Ethnicity, Race, and Leisure." In *Leisure Studies: Prospects for the Twenty-first Century,* ed. E. Jackson and T. Burton, 283–297. State College, Pa.: Venture, 1999.

Grimes, R. *Symbol and Conquest: Public Ritual and Drama in Santa Fe, New Mexico.* Ithaca, N.Y.: Cornell University Press, 1976.

Guest, Kenneth J. *God in Chinatown: Religion and Survival in New York's Evolving Immigrant Community.* New York: New York University Press, 2003.

Gupta, Sangeeta R. *Emerging Voices: South Asian American Women Redefine Self, Family, and Community.* Thousand Oaks, Calif.: Sage, 1999.

Gyory, Andre. *Closing the Gate: Race, Politics, and the Chinese Exclusion Act.* Chapel Hill: University of North Carolina Press, 1998.

Hagihara, Ayako, and Grace Shimizu. "The Japanese Latin American Wartime and Redress Experience." *Amerasia Journal* 28, no. 2 (2002): 203–216.

Hall, Bruce Edward. *Tea That Burns: A Family Memoir of Chinatown.* New York: Free Press, 1998.

Handlin, Oscar. *Boston's Immigrants, 1790–1865.* Cambridge, Mass.: Harvard University Press, 1941.

———. *The Uprooted: The Epic Story of the Great Migrations That Made the American People.* Boston: Little, Brown, 1973.

Haraway, Donna J. *Simians, Cyborgs, and Women: The Reinvention of Nature.* New York: Routledge, 1991.

Harris-Hastick, Eda Fernella. "Korea and Its Voices in New York City: An Ethnographic Study of a Small Asian-American Community." Ed.D. diss., Columbia University Teacher's College, 1990.

Hartman, Chester. *City for Sale: The Transformation of San Francisco.* Berkeley: University of California Press, 2002.

Harvey, David. *The Condition of Postmodernity: An Enquiry into the Origins of Cultural Change.* Cambridge, Mass.: Blackwell, 1990.

Hayles, N. Katherine. *How We Became Posthuman: Virtual Bodies in Cybernetics, Literature, and Informatics.* Chicago: University of Chicago Press, 1999.

Henry, Frances, Carol Tator, Winston Mattis, and Tim Rees, eds. *The Colour of Democracy: Racism in Canadian Society.* Toronto: Harcourt Brace, 1995.

Hier, Sean, and Joshua Greenberg. "News Discourse and the Problematization of Chinese Migration to Canada." In *Discourses of Domination: Racial Bias in the Canadian English-Language Press,* ed. Frances Henry and Carol Tator, 138–162. Toronto: University of Toronto Press, 2002.

Hing, Bill Ong. *Making and Remaking Asian America through Immigration Policy, 1850–1990.* Stanford, Calif.: Stanford University Press, 1993.

Hirabayashi, Lane Ryo. "Reconsidering Transculturation and Power." *Amerasia Journal* 28, no. 2 (2002): ix–xxii.

Hobsbawm, E. "Introduction: Inventing Traditions." In *The Invention of Tradition,* ed. E. Hobsbawm and T. Ranger, 1–14. Cambridge: Cambridge University Press, 1983.

Hooks, Bell. *Where We Stand: Class Matters.* New York: Routledge, 2000.

Horsman, R. "Origins of Racial Anglo-Saxonism in Great Britain before 1850." *Journal of the History of Ideas* 37, no. 3 (1976): 387–410.

Horton, John. *The Politics of Diversity: Immigration, Resistance, and Change in Monterey Park, California.* Philadelphia: Temple University Press, 1995.

Huang, Jianji. *Chinese Students and Scholars in American Higher Education.* Westport, Conn.: Greenwood, 1997.

Hu-DeHart, Evelyn. "Latin America in Asia-Pacific Perspective." In *What Is in the Rim? Critical Perspectives on the Pacific Region Idea,* ed. Arif Dirlik, 251–282. Lanham, Md.: Rowman and Littlefield, 1998.

Hsu, Madeline Y. *Dreaming of Gold, Dreaming of Home: Transnationalism and Migration Between the United States and South China, 1882–1943.* Stanford, Calif.: Stanford University Press, 2000.

Huh, Kil, and Lisa Hasegawa. "An Agenda for AAPI Community Economic Development." *AAPI Nexus* 1, no. 1 (Summer/Fall 2003): 47–65.

Hune, Shirley, and Phil Tajitsu Nash. "Reconceptualizing Community, Pedagogy, and Paradigms." *Journal of Asian American Studies* 3, no. 1 (February 2000): 7–15.

Hurh, W. M., and K. C. Kim. "Religious Participation of Korean Immigrants in the United States." *Journal for the Scientific Study of Religion* 29, no. 1 (1990): 19–34.

Hurley, Andrew, ed. *Common Fields: An Environmental History of St. Louis.* St. Louis: Missouri Historical Society Press, 1997.

Iglauer, Henry S. "The Demolition of the Louisiana Purchase Exposition of 1904." *Missouri Historical Society Bulletin* 22, no. 4 (1965–1966): 457–467.

Ignacio, Emily Noelle. *Building Diaspora: Filipino Cultural Community Formation on the Internet.* Piscataway, N.J.: Rutgers University Press, 2005.

Inoue, Miyako. "Japanese-Americans in St. Louis: From Internees to Professionals." *City and Society* 3, no. 2 (December 1989): 142–152.

Iweig, David, and Changgui Chen. *China's Brain Drain to the United States: Views of Overseas Chinese Students and Scholars in the 1990s.* Berkeley: University of California, Institute of East Asia Studies, 1995.

Izumi, Masumi. "Reconsidering Ethnic Culture and Community: A Cast Study on Japanese Canadian Taiko Drumming." *Journal of Asian American Studies* 4, no. 1 (February 2001): 35–56.

Jacobson, Matthew Frye. *Whiteness of a Different Color: European Immigrants and the Alchemy of Race*. Cambridge, Mass.: Harvard University Press, 1998.

Jameson, Fredric. "Of Islands and Trenches: Neutralization and the Production of Utopian Discourse." In *The Ideologies of Theory: Essays 1971–1986*, 2:75–101. Minneapolis: University of Minnesota Press, 1988.

——. *A Singular Modernity: Essay on the Ontology of the Present*. London, Verso, 2002.

——. "The Politics of Utopia." *New Left Reviews* 25 (2004): 35–54.

Jebe, Walter G., Sr. *Images of America: San Francisco's Excelsior District*. Charleston, S.C.: Arcadia, 2004.

Jennings, James, ed. *Race, Politics, and Economic Development: Community Perspectives*. New York: Verso Books, 1993.

Johnson, Phyllis J. "The Impact of Ethnic Communities on the Employment of Southeast Asian Refugees." *Amerasia* 14, no. 1 (1988): 1–22.

Jones, Steven G. "Understanding Community in the Information Age." In *Cybersociety: Computer-Mediated Communication and Community*, ed. Steven Jones, 10–35. Thousand Oaks, Calif.: Sage, 1995.

——. "The Internet and Its Social Landscape." In *Virtual Culture: Identity and Communication in Cybersociety*, ed. Steven Jones, 7–35. Thousand Oaks, Calif.: Sage, 1997.

Kaeppler, A. "Pacific Festivals and Ethnic Identity." In *Time Out of Time: Essays on the Festival*, ed. A. Falassi, 162–170. Albuquerque: University of New Mexico Press, 1987.

Kaplan, Amy. "Where Is Guantánano?" *American Quarterly* 53 (2005): 831–858.

Katz, Irwin, Joyce Wackenhut, and R. Glen Hass. "Racial Ambivalence, Value Duality, and Behaviour." In *Prejudice, Discrimination, and Racism*, ed. John Dovidio and Samuel L. Gaertner, 35–60. New York: Academic Press, 1986.

Keane, M., A. E. Rogge, and B. Luckingham. *The Chinese in Arizona 1870–1950*. Phoenix: Arizona State Historic Preservation Office, 1992.

Keener, Minglan Cheung. "Chicago's Chinatown: A Case Study of an Ethnic Neighborhood." Master's thesis, University of Illinois at Urbana-Champaign, 1994.

Kelly, Gail. *From Vietnam to America: A Chronicle of the Vietnamese Immigration to the United States*. Boulder, Colo.: Westview Press, 1977.

Khandelwal, Madhulika. *Becoming American, Becoming Indian: An Immigrant Community in New York City*. Ithaca, N.Y.: Cornell University Press, 2002.

Khanh, Tran. "Ethnic Chinese in Vietnam and Their Identity." In *Ethnic Chinese as Southeast Asians*, ed. Leo Suryadinata, 267–295. Singapore: Institute of Southeast Asian Studies/New York: St. Martin's Press, 1997.

Kiang, Harry Ying Cheng. *Chicago's Chinatown*. Lincolnwood, Ill.: Institute of China Studies, 1992.

Kibria, Nazli. *Family Tightrope: The Changing Lives of Vietnamese Americans*. Princeton, N.J.: Princeton University Press, 1993.

——. "South Asian Americans." In *Asian Americans: Contemporary Trends and Issues*, 2nd ed., ed. Pyong Gap Min, 206–227. Thousand Oaks, Calif.: Pine Forge Press, 2006.

Kikumura-Yano, Akemi, ed. *Encyclopedia of Japanese Descendents in the Americas*. New York: AltaMira Press, 2002.

Kim, Illsoo. *New Urban Immigrants: The Korean Community in New York*. Princeton, N.J.: Princeton University Press, 1981.

——. "The Koreans: Small Business in an Urban Frontier." In *New Immigrants in New York*, ed. Nancy Foner, 219–242. New York: Columbia University Press, 1987.

Kinkead, Gwen. *Chinatown: A Portrait of a Closed Society.* Scranton, Pa.: HarperCollins, 1992.

Kitano, Harry, et al. "Asian-American Interracial Marriage." *Journal of Marriage and the Family* 46, no. 1 (February 1984): 179–190.

Kling, Rob, Spencer Olin, and Mark Poster, eds. *Postsuburban California: The Transformation of Orange County since World War II.* 1991. Reprint, Berkeley: University of California Press, 1995.

Krulfeld, Ruth M. "Cognitive Mapping and Ethnic Identity: The Changing Concepts of Community and Nationalism in the Laotian Diaspora." In *Selected Papers on Refugee Issues,* ed. Pamela A. De Voe. Washington, D.C.: American Anthropological Association, 1992.

Kurashige, L. "Made in Little Tokyo: Politics of Ethnic Identity and Festival in Southern California, 1934–1994." Ph.D. diss., University of Wisconsin–Madison, 1994.

———. *Japanese American Celebration and Conflict: A History of Ethnic Identity and Festival, 1934–1990.* Berkeley: University of California Press, 2002.

Kurashige, Scott. "Pan-Ethnicity and Community Organizing: Asian Americans United's Campaign against Anti-Asian Violence." *Journal of Asian American Studies* 3, no. 2 (June 2000): 163–190.

Kurien, Prema. "Becoming American by Becoming Hindu: Indian Americans Take Their Place at the Multicultural Table." In *Gatherings in Diaspora: Religious Communities and the New Immigration,* ed. Stephen Warner and Judith Wittner, 37–70. Philadelphia: Temple University Press, 1998.

———. "Religion, Ethnicity and Politics: Hindu and Muslim Indian Immigrants in the United States." *Racial and Ethnic Studies* 24, no. 2 (2001): 264–293.

Kwong, Peter. *Chinatown, New York: Labor and Politics, 1930–1950.* New York: Monthly Review Press, 1979.

———. *The New Chinatown.* New York: Hill and Wang, 1987.

Lai, Chuen-Yan David. "Socio-economic Structures and the Viability of Chinatown." In *Residential and Neighborhood Studies in Victoria,* ed. C. Forward, 101–129. Western Geographical Series No. 5. Victoria: University of Victoria, 1973.

———. *Chinatowns: Towns within Cities in Canada.* Vancouver: University of British Columbia Press, 1988.

Lai, Eric, and Dennis Arguelles. *The New Face of Asian Pacific America.* Los Angeles: UCLA Asian American Studies Center Press, 2003.

Lai, H. Mark. "Historical Development of the Chinese Consolidated Benevolent Association/Huiguan System." In *Chinese America: History and Perspectives, 1987,* 13–51. San Francisco: Chinese Historical Society of America, 1987.

Lavenda, R. H. "Family and Corporation: Two Styles of Celebration in Central Minnesota." In *The Celebration of Society: Perspectives on Contemporary Cultural Performances,* ed. F. Manning, 51–64. Bowling Green, Ohio: Bowling Green University Popular Press, 1983.

Lawrence, Susan. "Chinese Students Hit the Jackpot." *U.S. News and World Report* 115, no. 11 (1993), 38.

Le, C. N. "Asian Small Businesses." *Asian-Nation: The Landscape of Asian America,* http://www.asian-nation.org/small-business.shtml, accessed December 6, 2005.

Lee, Erika. *At America's Gates: Chinese Immigration during the Exclusion Era, 1882–1943.* Chapel Hill: North Carolina University Press, 2003.

Lee, Jae-Hyup. *Dynamics of Ethnic Identity: Three Asian American Communities in Philadelphia.* New York: Garland, 1998.

Lee, Jennifer Lee, and Frank Bean, "Beyond Black and White: Remaking Race in America." *Contexts* 2, no. 3 (2003): 26–33.

Lee, Rose Hum. *The Chinese in the United States of America*. Hong Kong: Hong Kong University, 1960.

——. *The Growth and Decline of Chinese Communities in the Rocky Mountain Region*. New York: Arno Press, 1978.

Lemay, Michael, and Elliot Robert Barkan, eds. *U.S. Immigration and Naturalization Laws and Issues: A Documentary History*. Westport, Conn.: Greenwood Press, 1999.

Lesser, Jeff. *Negotiating National Identity: Immigrants, Minorities, and the Struggle for Ethnicity in Brazil*. Durham, N.C.: Duke University Press, 1999.

Leung, Carrianne, and Jian Guan. *Yellow Peril Revisited: Impact of SARS on the Chinese and Southeast Asian Canadian Communities*. Toronto: Chinese Canadian National Council, 2004.

Li, Peter S. "Ethnic Enterprise in Transition: Chinese Business in Richmond, B.C., 1980–1990." *Canadian Ethnic Studies* 26, no. 1 (1992): 120–138.

——. "Unneighbourly Houses or Unwelcome Chinese: The Social Construction of Race in the Battle Over 'Monster Homes' in Vancouver, Canada." *International Journal of Comparative Race and Ethnic Studies* 1, no. 1 (1994): 14–33.

——. "A World Apart: The Multicultural World of Visible Minorities and the Art World of Canada." *Canadian Review of Sociology and Anthropology* 31, no. 4 (1994): 356–391.

——. *Literature Review on Immigration: Sociological Perspectives*. Ottawa: Citizenship and Immigration Canada, 1996.

——. *The Chinese in Canada*. 2nd ed. Toronto: Oxford University Press, 1998.

——. "Race and Ethinicity." In *Race and Ethnic Relations in Canada*, ed. Peter S. Li, 3–20. Toronto: Oxford University Press, 1999.

——. *Destination Canada: Immigration Debates and Issues*. Toronto: Oxford University Press, 2003.

——. "The Rise and Fall of Chinese Immigration to Canada: Newcomers from Hong Kong Special Administrative Region of China and Mainland China, 1980–2000." *International Migration* 43, no. 3 (2005): 9–32.

Li, Wei. "Spatial Transformation of an Urban Ethnic Community from Chinatown to Chinese Ethnoburb in Los Angeles." Ph.D. diss., University of Southern California, 1997.

——. "Anatomy of a New Ethnic Settlement: The Chinese *Ethnoburb* in Los Angeles." *Urban Studies* 35, no. 3 (1998): 479–501.

——. "The Emergence and Manifestation of the Chinese Ethnoburb in Los Angeles' San Gabriel Valley." *Journal of Asian American Studies* 2, no. 1 (February 1999): 1–28.

——, ed. *From Urban Enclave to Ethnic Suburb: New Asian Communities in Pacific Rim Countries*. Honolulu: University of Hawaii Press, 2006.

Li, Wei, Gary Dymski, Yu Zhou, Maria Chee, and Carolyn Aldana. "Chinese American Banking and Community Development in Los Angeles County." *Annals of the Association of American Geographers* 92, no. 4 (2002): 777–796.

Li, Wei, and Emily Skop. "The Changing Face of America's Suburbs." Mimeograph. Tempe: Arizona State University, 2005.

——. "Enclaves, Ethnoburbs, and New Patterns of Settlement among Asian Immigrants." In *Contemporary Asian America: A Multi-Disciplinary Reader*, 2nd ed., ed. Min Zhou and John Gatewood, 222–236. New York: New York University Press, 2007.

Lien, Pefte, M. Margaret Conway, and Janelle Wong. *The Politics of Asian Americans: Diversity and Community*. New York: Routledge, 2004.

Lien, Pei-te. *The Making of Asian America through Political Participation*. Philadelphia: Temple University Press, 2001.

Light, Ivan. *Ethnic Enterprise in America: Business and Welfare among Chinese, Japanese, and Blacks.* Berkeley: University of California Press, 1972.

Light, Ivan, and Edna Bonacich. *Immigrant Entrepreneurs: Koreans in Los Angeles, 1965–1982.* Berkeley: University of California Press, 1988.

Lin, Jan. *Reconstructing Chinatown: Ethnic Enclave, Global Change.* Minneapolis: University of Minnesota Press, 1998.

Lin, Sam Chu. "How America Sees Us." *Asian Week*, April 27, 2001, News 1, http://www. asian-week.com/2001_04_27/news1_committee100survey.html, accessed May 3, 2001.

Lindberg, Richard. *Passport's Guide to Ethnic Chicago: A Complete Guide to the Many Faces and Cultures of Chicago.* 2nd ed. Lincolnwood, Ill.: Passport Books, 1997.

Ling, Huping. "Chinese Merchant Wives in the United States, 1840–1945." In *Origins and Destinations: 41 Essays on Chinese America*, ed. Chinese Historical Society of Southern California, 79–92. Los Angeles: Chinese Historical Society of Southern California and UCLA Asian American Studies Center, 1994.

———. "A History of Chinese Female Students in the United States, 1880s–1990s." *Journal of American Ethnic History*, 16, no. 3 (Spring 1997): 81–109.

———. *Surviving on the Gold Mountain: A History of Chinese American Women and Their Lives.* Albany: State University of New York, 1998.

———. *Chinese St. Louisans.* A series of thirty thematic articles published in the *St. Louis Chinese American News*, December 21, 2000, to July 19, 2001. www.scanews.com/history.

———. "Family and Marriage of Late-Nineteenth and Early-Twentieth Century Chinese Immigrant Women." *Journal of American Ethnic History* 19, no. 2 (Winter 2000): 43–63.

———. "Historiography and Research Methodologies of Chinese American Women." *Research on Women in Modern Chinese History* 9 (August 2001): 235–253.

———. "Hop Alley: Myth and Reality of the St. Louis Chinatown, 1860s–1930s." *Journal of Urban History* 28, no. 2 (January 2002): 184–219.

———. "The Rise and Fall of the Study in America Movement in Taiwan." *Overseas Chinese History Studies* 4 (2003): 21–28.

———. "Governing 'Hop Alley': On Leong Chinese Merchants and Laborers Association, 1906–1966." *Journal of American Ethnic History* 23, no. 2 (Winter 2004): 50–84.

———. *Chinese St. Louis: From Enclave to Cultural Community.* Philadelphia: Temple University Press, 2004.

———. "Growing up in 'Hop Alley': The Chinese American Youth in St. Louis during the Early-Twentieth Century." In *Asian American Children*, ed. Benson Tong, 65–81. Westport, Conn.: Greenwood Press, 2004.

———. "Reconceptualizing Chinese American Community in St. Louis: From Chinatown to Cultural Community." *Journal of American Ethnic History* 24, no. 2 (Winter 2005): 65–101.

———. *Chinese in St. Louis: 1857–2007.* Charleston, S.C.: Arcadia, 2007.

———. *Voices of the Heart: Asian American Women on Immigration, Work, and Family.* Kirksville, Mo.: Truman State University Press, 2007.

———, ed. *Emerging Voices: Experiences of Underrepresented Asian Americans.* New Brunswick, N.J.: Rutgers University Press, 2008.

Ling, Huping, and Allan Austin W., eds. *Asian American History and Culture: An Encyclopedia.* New York: M. E. Sharpe, forthcoming.

Lipietz, Alaine. "From Althusserianism to 'Regulation Theory.'" In *The Althusserian Legacy*, ed. E. Ann Kaplan and Michael Sprinker, 99–128. London: Verso, 1993.

Lipsitz, George. *The Possessive Investment in Whiteness: How White People Profit from Identity Politics.* Philadelphia: Temple University Press, 1988.

————. *The Sidewalks of St. Louis: Places, People, and Politics in an American City.* Columbia: University of Missouri Press, 1991.

Liu, Haiming. *Transnational History of a Chinese Family: Immigrant Letters, Family Business, and Reverse Migration.* New Brunswick, N.J.: Rutgers University Press, 2005.

Loo, Chalsa M. *Chinatown: Most Time, Hard Time.* New York: Praeger, 1991.

Lopez, David E. "Language: Diversity and Assimilation." In *Ethnic Los Angeles,* ed. Roger Waldinger and Mehdi Bozorggmehr, 139–164. New York: Russell Sage Foundation Press, 1996.

Lopez, David, and Yen Espiritu. "Panethnicity in the United States: A Theoretical Framework." *Ethnic and Racial Studies* 13, no. 2 (1990): 198–224.

Lopez-Romano, Sylvia Silva. "Integration of Community and Learning among Southeast Asian Newcomer Hmong Parents and Children." Ed. diss., University of San Francisco, 1991.

Low, Lisa. *Immigrant Acts: On Asian American Cultural Politics.* Durham, N.C.: Duke University Press, 1996.

Luckingham, Bradford. *Minorities in Phoenix: A Profile of Mexican American, Chinese American, and African American Communities, 1860–1992.* Tucson: University of Arizona Press, 1994.

Lukács, Georg. *History and Class Consciousness.* Trans. Rodney Livingston. 1923. Reprint, London: Merlin Press, 1971.

Lydon, Sandy. *Chinese Gold: The Chinese in the Monterey Bay Region.* Capitola, Calif.: Capitola, 1985.

Lyman, Stanford M. *Chinese Americans.* New York: Random House, 1974.

————. *Chinatown and Little Tokyo: Power, Conflict, and Community among Chinese and Japanese Immigrants in America.* New York: Associated Faculty Press, 1986.

Ma, Eva. *Hometown Chinatown: A History of Oakland's Chinese Community, 1852–1995.* New York: Garland, 2000.

Ma, Grace Xueqin. *The Culture of Health: Asian Communities in the United States.* Westport, Conn.: Bergin and Garvey, 1999.

MacDougall, H. A. *Racial Myth in English History: Trojans, Teutons and Anglo-Saxons.* Montreal: Harvest House, 1982.

Manalansan, Martin F., IV. *Cultural Compass: Ethnographic Explorations of Asian America.* Philadelphia: Temple University Press, 2000.

Masson, Jack K. "Conflict and Tragedy: Canada's East Indian Community." *Amerasia* 15, no. 2 (1989): 27–48.

Matloff, Norman. "Political Networking." *National Review* 49 (July 28, 1997), 37–38.

Mazumdar, Sanjoy, Shampa Mazumdar, Faye Docuyanan, and Colette Marie McLaughlin, "Creating a Sense of Place: The Vietnamese-Americans and Little Saigon." *Journal of Environmental Psychology* 20 (2000): 319–333.

McClain, Charles. *Asian Indians, Filipinos, Other Asian Communities and the Law.* New York: Garland, 1994.

————. *In Search of Equality: The Chinese Struggle against Discrimination in the 19th Century.* Berkeley: University of California Press, 1996.

McClellan, Janet. *Many Petals of the Lotus: Five Asian Buddhist Communities in Toronto.* Toronto: University of Toronto Press, 1999.

McConohay, John B. "Modern Racism, Ambivalence, and the Modern Racism Scale." In *Prejudice, Discrimination, and Racism,* ed. John Dovidio and Samuel L. Gaertner, 91–126. New York: Academic Press, 1986.

McDade, Kathryn. *Barriers to Recognition of the Credentials of Immigrants in Canada.* Ottawa: Institute for Research on Public Policy, 1988.

McKeown, Adam. *Chinese Migrant Networks and Cultural Change: Peru, Chicago, Hawaii, 1900–1936.* Chicago: University of Chicago Press, 2001.

McLaughlin, Colette Marie, and Paul Jesilow. "Conveying a Sense of Community along Bolsa Avenue: Little Saigon as a Model of Ethnic Commercial Belts." *International Migration* 36, no. 1 (1998): 49–63.

Mercer, John. "Canadian Cities and Their Immigrants: New Realities." *Annals of the American Academy of Political and Social Science* 538 (1995): 169–184.

Michaels, Robert Daniel, "The Structure and Spatial Morphology of the Ethnic Commercial Enclaves of Little Saigon and Koreatown in Orange County, California: A Comparative Study." Master's thesis, California State University, Long Beach, 2000.

Miles, Robert. *Racism and Migrant Labour.* London: Routledge and Kegan Paul, 1982.

Miller, Douglas, and Douglas Houston. "Distressed Asian American Neighborhoods." *AAPI Nexus* 1, no. 1 (Summer/Fall 2003): 67–84.

Miller, Stuart Creighton. *The Unwelcome Immigrants: The American Image of the Chinese: 1875–1882.* Berkeley: University of California Press, 1979.

Min, Pyong Gap. "A Structural Analysis of Korean Business in the United States." *Ethnic Groups* 6 (1984): 1–25.

———. *Ethnic Business Enterprise: Korean Small Business in Atlanta.* New York: Center for Migration Studies, 1988.

———. "The Structure and Social Function of Korean Immigrant Churches in the United States." *International Migration Review* 26 (1992): 352–367.

———. *Caught in the Middle: Korean Communities in the New York and Los Angeles.* Berkeley: University of California Press, 1996.

Min, Pyong Gap, and Jung Ha Kim, eds. *Religions in Asian America: Building Faith Communities.* Walnut Creek, Calif.: AltaMira Press, 2002.

Miyoshi, Masao. "A Borderless World? From Colonialism to Transnationalism and the Decline of the Nation-State." *Critical Inquiry* 19 (Summer 1993): 726–751.

Monrayo-Raymundo, Angeles, and Rizalene Raymundo, eds. *Tomorrow's Memories: From the Diaries of Angeles Monrayo-Raymundo, January 10, 1924–November 17, 1928.* Honolulu: University of Hawaii Press, 1998.

Mormino, Gary Ross. *Immigrants on the Hill: Italian-Americans in St. Louis, 1882–1982.* Urbana: University of Illinois Press, 1986.

Moy, Susan Lee. "The Chinese in Chicago: The First One Hundred Years." In *Ethnic Chicago: A Multicultural Portrait,* 4th ed., ed. Melvin G. Holli and Peter d'A. Jones, 378–408. Grand Rapids, Mich.: William B. Eerdmans, 1995.

Nagasawa, R. *The Elderly Chinese: A Forgotten Minority.* Tempe: Arizona State University, 1980.

Nagel, J. *American Indian Ethnic Renewal: Red Power and the Resurgence of Identity and Culture.* New York: Oxford University Press, 1996.

Nakanishi, Don. "The Next Swing Vote? Asian Pacific Americans and California Politics." In *Racial and Ethnic Politics in California,* ed. Bryan O. Jackson and Michael B. Preston, 25–54. Berkeley, Calif.: Institute for Governmental Studies, 1990.

Nakano, M. T. *Japanese American Women: Three Generations 1890–1990.* Berkeley, Calif.: Mina Press, 1990.

Nee, Victor G., and Brett de Bary Nee. *Longtime Californ': A Documentary Study of an American Chinatown.* New York: Pantheon Books, 1972.

Ng, Franklin. *The Taiwanese Americans.* Westport, Conn.: Greenwood Press, 1992.

———, ed. *Asian American Family Life and Community.* New York: Garland, 1998.

Ngai, Mae M. *Impossible Subjects: Illegal Aliens and the Making of Modern America.* Princeton, N.J.: Princeton University Press, 2004.

Ngin, Chor-Swang. "The Acculturation Pattern of Orange County's Southeast Asian Refugees." *Journal of Orange County Studies* 3/4 (Fall 1989/Spring 1990): 46–53.

Nietzche, Friedrich. *The Will to Power*. Trans. Walter Kaufmann and R. J. Hollingdale. 1901. Reprint, New York: Vintage Books, 1968.

Noyes, D. "Group." *Journal of American Folklore* 108 (1995): 449–478.

Okamoto, Philip Motoo. "Evolution of a Japanese American Enclave: Gardena, California. A Case Study of Ethnic Community Change and Continuity." Master's thesis, University of California, Los Angeles, 1991.

Olney, Douglas P. "We Must Be Organized: Dual Organizations in an American Hmong Community." Ph.D. diss., University of Minnesota, 1993.

Olson, Audrey L. *St. Louis Germans, 1850–1920: The Nature of an Immigrant Community and Its Relation to the Assimilation Process*. New York: Arno Press, 1980.

Ong, Aihwa. *Flexible Citizenship: The Cultural Logics of Transnationality*. Durham, N.C.: Duke University Press, 1999.

Ong, Aihwa, and Donald M. Nonini, eds. *Ungrounded Empires: The Cultural Politics of Modern Chinese Transnationalism*. New York: Routledge, 1997.

Ong, Paul, ed. *Beyond Asian American Poverty: Community Economic Development Policies and Strategies*. Los Angeles: LEAP Asian Pacific American Public Policy Institute and UCLA Asian American Studies Center, 1993.

Ong, Paul, Edna Bonacich, and Lucie Cheng, eds. *The New Asian Immigration in Los Angeles and Global Restructuring*. Philadelphia: Temple University Press, 1994.

Ong, Paul, and Suzanne Hee. *Losses in the Los Angeles Civil Unrest*. Los Angeles: UCLA Center for Pacific Rim Studies, 1993.

Ong, Paul, and David Lee. "Changing of the Guard? The Emerging Immigrant Majority in Asian American Politics." In *Asian Americans and Politics: Perspectives, Experiences, Prospects*, ed. Gordon H. Chang, 153–172. Stanford, Calif.: Stanford University Press, 2001.

Ong, Paul, and Anastasia Loukaitou-Sideris, eds. *Jobs and Economic Development in Minority Communities*. Philadelphia: Temple University Press, 2006.

Orleans, Leo. *Chinese Students in America: Policies, Issues, and Numbers*. Washington, D.C.: National Academy Press, 1988.

Ornstein, Michael D., and Raghubar D. Sharma. "Adjustment and Economic Experience of Immigrants in Canada: An Analysis of the 1976 Longitudinal Survey of Immigrants." In *A Report to Employment and Immigration Canada*. Toronto: York University Institute for Behavioral Research, 1983.

Orr, Elisabeth. "Living Along the Fault Line: Community, Suburbia and Multi-Ethnicity in Garden Grove and Westminster, CA 1900–1995." Ph.D. diss., Indiana University, 1999.

Orsi, R. A. *The Madonna of 115th Street: Faith and Community in Italian Harlem, 1880–1950*. New Haven, Conn.: Yale University Press, 1985.

Padawangi, Rita. "Indonesian Catholics in Chicago: Making Community in the Quest for Identity." Master's thesis, Loyola University Chicago, 2005.

Pan, Lynn, ed. *The Encyclopedia of the Chinese Overseas*. Singapore: Archipelago Press and Landmark Books, 1998.

Park, Edward J. W. "Competing Visions: Political Formation of Korean Americans in Los Angeles, 1992–1997." *Amerasia Journal* 24, no. 1 (1998): 41–57.

Park, Edward J. W., and John S. W. Park. *Probationary Americans: Contemporary Immigration Policies and the Shaping of Asian American Communities*. New York: Routledge, 2005.

Park, Jung-Sun. *Chicago Korean-Americans: Identity and Politics in a Transnational Community*. New York: Routledge, 2004.

Park, Kyeyoung. *The Korean American Dream: Immigrants and Small Business in New York City.* Ithaca, N.Y.: Cornell University Press, 1997.

Park, Robert. "Human Migration and the Marginal Man." *American Journal of Sociology* 33, no. 6 (May 1928): 881–893.

Pfeifer, Mark E. " 'Community,' Adaptation and the Vietnamese in Toronto." Ph D. diss., University of Toronto, 1999.

Portes, Alejandro, and Alex Stepick. *City on the Edge: The Transformation of Miami.* Berkeley: University of California Press, 1993.

Posadas, Barbara M. "Cross Boundaries in Interracial Chicago: Pilipino American Families since 1925." *Amerasia* 8, no. 2 (1981): 31–52.

Poulantzas, Nicos. *Classes in Contemporary Capitalism.* London: Verso, 1978.

———. *Political Power and Social Classes.* London: Verso, 1978.

Primm, James Neal. *Lion of the Valley: St. Louis, Missouri.* Boulder, Colo.: Pruett, 1990.

Putnam, Robert D. *Bowling Alone.* New York: Simon and Schuster, 2000.

Rajagopal, Indhu. "The Glass Ceiling in the Vertical Mosaic: Indian Immigrants to Canada." *Canadian Ethnic Studies* 22, no. 1 (1990): 96–105.

Ralston, Helen. "Ethnicity, Class, and Gender among South Asian Women in Metro Halifax: An Exploratory Study." *Canadian Ethnic Studies* 20, no. 3 (1988): 63–83.

Reeves, Terrance J., and Claudette E. Bennett. *We the People: Asians in the United States.* 2000 Census Special Report, censr-17. Washington, D.C.: U.S. Census Bureau, 2004.

Reimers, David. *Still the Golden Door: The Third World Comes to America.* New York: Columbia University Press, 1985.

Rex, John. *Race Relations in Sociological Theory.* 2nd ed. London: Routledge and Kegan Paul, 1983.

Rex, Tom R., and Katrian S. Walls. *Employment in Metropolitan Phoenix.* Tempe, Az.: Morrison Institute of Public Policy, 2000.

Reyes, Adelaida. *Songs of the Caged, Songs of the Free: Music and the Vietnamese Refugee Experience.* Philadelphia: Temple University Press, 1999.

Reynolds, C. N. "The Chinese Tongs." *American Journal of Sociology* 40 (March 1935): 612–623.

Richards, Rand. *Historic San Francisco: A Concise History and Guide.* San Francisco: Heritage House, 2005.

Rodney, W. *How Europe Underdeveloped Africa.* Washington, D.C.: Howard University Press, 1982.

Roediger, David R. *The Wages of Whiteness: Race and the Making of the American Working Class.* New York: Verso, 1991; rev. ed., 1999.

Rohsenow, John. "Chinese Language Use in Chicagoland." In *Ethnolinguistic Chicago: Language and Literacy in the City's Neighborhoods,* ed. Marcia Farr, 321–355. Mahwah, N.J.: Lawrence Erlbaum Associates, 2004.

Root, Maria P. P. *Filipina/o Americans: Transformation and Identity.* Thousand Oaks, Calif.: Sage, 1997.

Roy, Patricia E. *A White Man's Province: British Columbia Politicians and Chinese and Japanese Immigrants, 1858–1914.* Vancouver: University of British Columbia Press, 1989.

Rudwick, Elliott M. *Race Riot at East St. Louis July 2, 1917.* Carbondale: Southern Illinois University Press, 1964.

Rumbaut, Rubén G. "The Structure of Refugee: Southeast Asian Refugees in the United States, 1975–1985." *International Review of Comparative Public Policy* 1 (1989): 97–129.

Rush, John A. "The Generation Gap, as Analyzed by Reference Group Behavior, and Its Effects on the Solidarity of the Chinese Community of Sacramento." Master's thesis, California State University, 1969.

Rynerson, Ann M., and Pamela A. DeVoe. "Refugee Women in a Vertical Village: Lowland Laotians in St. Louis." *Social Thought* 10, no. 3 (Summer 1984): 33–48.

Saito, Leland. *Race and Politics: Asian Americans, Latinos, and Whites in a Los Angeles Suburb.* Chicago: University of Illinois Press, 1998.

Salyer, Lucy E. *Laws Harsh as Tigers: Chinese Immigrants and the Shaping of Modern Immigration Law.* Chapel Hill: University of North Carolina Press, 1995.

San Juan, E., Jr. *From Exile to Diaspora: Versions of the Filipino Experience in the United States.* Boulder, Colo.: Westview Press, 1998.

"SARS Brings Worries of Discrimination in Toronto." *Mingpao,* April 4, 2003.

Satzewich, Vic. *Racism and the Incorporation of Foreign Labour.* London: Routledge, 1991.

———, ed. *Deconstructing a Nation: Immigration, Multiculturalism and Racism in '90s Canada.* Halifax, N.S.: Fernwood, 1992.

Scott, J. C. *Weapons of the Weak: Everyday Forms of Peasant Resistance.* New Haven, Conn.: Yale University Press, 1985.

Sen, Rinku. "A Primer on Community Organizing and South Asians." *Amerasia* 25, no. 3 (1999/2000): 163–168.

Shah, Nayan. *Contagious Divides: Epidemics and Race in San Francisco's Chinatown.* Berkeley: University of California Press, 2001.

Shaull, S. L., and J. H. Gramann. "The Effect of Cultural Assimilation on the Importance of Family-Related and Nature-Related Recreation among Hispanic Americans." *Journal of Leisure Research* 30 (1998): 47–63.

Sheikh, Carol Ann Kohn. "Community Formation among Asian Indians in Southeast Florida." Master's thesis, Florida International University, 1998.

Shu, Yuan. "Information Technologies, the U.S. Nation-state, and Asian American Subjectivities." *Cultural Critique* 40 (1998): 145–167.

Shukla, Sandhya. "New Immigrants, New Forms of Transnational Community: Post 1965 Indian Migrations." *Amerasia Journal* 25, no. 3 (1999/2000): 19–36.

Shultz, A. *Ethnicity on Parade: Inventing the Norwegian American through Celebration.* Amherst: University of Massachusetts Press, 1995.

Singer, M. "On the Symbolic and Historic Structure of an American Identity." *Ethos* 5 (1977): 431–454.

Singh, Rashmi Sharma. "South Asian Diaspora in the US: A Trend?" http://www.indolink.com/Living/America/a1.php, accessed December 8, 2005.

Siu, Paul C. P. "The Sojourner." *American Journal of Sociology* 50 (1952): 34–44.

———. *The Chinese Laundryman: A Study of Social Isolation.* New York: New York University Press, 1987.

Skidmore, Thomas E., and Peter H. Smith. *Modern Latin America.* New York: Oxford University Press, 2001.

Skinner, William G., ed. *Chinese Society in Thailand.* Ithaca, N.Y.: Cornell University Press, 1957.

———. *Leadership and Power in the Chinese Community in Thailand.* Ithaca, N.Y.: Cornell University Press, 1958.

———. *The Study of Chinese Society: Essays by Maurice Freedman.* Stanford, Calif.: Stanford University Press, 1979.

Skop, Emily, and Wei Li. "From the Ghetto to the Invisoburb: Shifting Patterns of Immigrant Settlement in Contemporary America." In *Multi-Cultural Geographies: Persistence and Change in U.S. Racial/Ethnic Geography,* ed. John W. Frazier and Florence L. Margai, 113–124. Binghamton, N.Y.: Global Academic, 2003.

Smith, Susan Lynn. *Japanese American Midwives: Culture, Community, and Health Politics, 1880–1950.* Champaign: University of Illinois Press, 2005.

Sobel, Irwin, Werner Z. Hirsch, and Harry C. Harris. *The Negro in the St. Louis Economy, 1954.* St. Louis: Urban League of St. Louis, 1954.

Sobredo, James. "From Manila Bay to Daly City: Filipinos in San Francisco." In *Reclaiming San Francisco: History, Politics, Culture,* ed. James Brooks, Chris Carlsson, and Nancy J. Peters. San Francisco: City Lights Books, 1998.

Spickard, Paul R. *Japanese Americans: The Formation and Transformations of an Ethnic Group.* Farming Hills, Mich.: Twayne, 1997.

Stanbury, W. T., and John D. Todd. *The Housing Crisis: The Effects of Local Government Regulation.* Vancouver: Laurier Institute, 1990.

Statistics Canada. *Profile of Census Tracts in Ontario,* Part B, Catalogue 95–338. Ottawa: Minister of Industry, Science and Technology, 1994.

———. *2001 Census of Canada, Public Use Microdata File for Individuals.* 2005.

Stephens, John, and Sung-Ae Lee, "Diasporan Subjectivity and Cultural Space in Korean American Picture Books." *Journal of Asian American Studies* 9, no. 1 (February 2006): 1–25.

Surratt, Carla. *Netlife: Internet Citizens and Their Communities.* New York: Nova Science, 1998.

Swiderski, R. *Voices: An Anthropologist's Dialogue with an Italian-American Festival.* Bowling Green, Ohio: Bowling Green State University Popular Press, 1987.

Takaki, Ronald. *Strangers from a Different Shore: A History of Asian Americans.* Boston: Little, Brown, 1989.

Tal, Kali. *Vietnam Generation: Southeast Asian-American Communities.* Woodbridge, Conn.: Vietnam Generation, 1990.

Tchen, John Kuo Wei. *New York before Chinatown: Orientalism and the Shaping of American Culture, 1776–1882.* Baltimore: Johns Hopkins University Press, 1999.

Terada, Kazushige. "Railways in Japan—Public and Private Sectors." *Japan Railway and Transport Review* 27 (2001): 48–56.

Tiongson, Antonio T. Jr., Edgardo V. Gutierrez, and Ricardo V. Gutierrez, eds. *Positively No Filipinos Allowed: Building Communities and Discourse.* Philadelphia: Temple University Press, 2005.

Torok, John Hayakawa. "'Interest Convergence' and the Liberalization of Discriminatory Immigration and Naturalization Laws Affecting Asians, 1943–1965." In *Chinese America: History and Perspectives, 1995,* ed. Marlon K. Hom et al., 1–28. San Francisco: Chinese Historical Society of America 1995.

Trovato, Frank, and Carl F. Grindstaff. "Economic Status: A Census Analysis of Immigrant Women at Age Thirty in Canada." *Review of Sociology and Anthropology* 23, no. 4 (1986): 569–687.

Tseng, Yen-Fen. "Chinese Ethnic Economy: San Gabriel Valley, Los Angeles County." *Journal of Urban Affairs* 16, no. 2 (1994): 169–189.

Tuan, Mia. *Forever Foreign or Honorary White? The Asian Ethnic Experience Today.* New Brunswick, N.J.: Rutgers University Press, 1999.

Turner, V. *Dramas, Fields, and Metaphors.* Ithaca, N.Y.: Cornell University Press, 1974.

"The UCLA Internet Report: Surveying the Digital Future." http://www.ccp.ucla.edu., accessed November 2000.

"The UCLA Internet Report 2001: Surveying the Digital Future Year Two." http://www.ccp.ucla.edu, accessed November 2001.

U.S. Census Bureau. *1992 Economic Census, Survey of Minority-Owned Business Enterprises: Asian and Pacific Islanders, American Indians and Alaska Natives.* Washington, D.C.: Government Printing Office, 1996.

——. *1997 Economic Census, Survey of Minority-Owned Business Enterprises: Asian and Pacific Islanders*. Washington, D.C.: Government Printing Office, 2001.

——. The Foreign-Born Population: 2000. *Census 2000 Brief*. Washington, D.C.: Government Printing Office, 2003.

U.S. Census Bureau and U.S. Department of Commerce. *We the Americans: Asians*. Washington, D.C.: Government Printing Office, 1993.

U.S. Commission on Civil Rights, Wisconsin Advisory Committee. *The Hmong in Green Bay: Refugees in a New Land*. Chicago: U.S. Commission on Civil Rights, Midwestern Regional Office, 1998.

Vallangca, Caridada Conception. *The Second Wave: Pinay and Pinoy (1945–1960)*. San Francisco: Strawberry Hill Press, 1987.

Vallangca, Roberto V. *Pinoy: The First Wave*. San Francisco: Strawberry Hill Press, 1977.

Valovic, Thomas S. *Digital Mythologies: The Hidden Complexities of the Internet*. New Brunswick, N.J.: Rutgers University Press, 2000.

van den Berghe, Pierre L. "Race: Perspective Two." In *Dictionary of Race and Ethnic Relations*, ed. E. E. Cashmore, 216–218. London: Routledge and Kegan Paul, 1984.

Van Hear, Nicholas. *New Diasporas: The Mass Exodus, Dispersal and Regrouping of Migrant Communities*. Seattle: University of Washington Press, 1998.

Vergara, Benito M., Jr. "Betrayal, Class Fantasies, and the Filipina/o Nation in Daly City." In *Cultural Compass: Ethnographic Explorations of Asian America*, ed. Martin F. Manalansan IV, 139–158. Philadelphia: Temple University Press, 2000.

Visweswaran, Kamala, and Ali Mir. "On the Politics of Community in South Asian-American Studies." *Amerasia* 25, no. 3 (1999/2000): 97–108.

Võ, Linda Trinh. "The Vietnamese American Experience: From Dispersion to the Development of Post-Refugee Communities." In *Asian American Studies: A Reader*, ed. Jean Yu-Wen Shen Wu and Min Song, 290–305. New Brunswick, N.J.: Rutgers University Press, 2000.

——. "Managing Survival: Economic Realities for Vietnamese American Women." In *Asian/Pacific Islander American Women: A Historical Anthology*, ed. Shirley Hune and Gail Nomura, 237–252. New York: New York University Press, 2003.

——. *Mobilizing an Asian American Community*. Philadelphia: Temple University Press, 2004.

——. "What a Difference a Generation Makes: Negotiating Vietnamese American Womanhood in the Diaspora." In *Le Vietnam au Feminine/Vietnam: Women's Realities*, ed. Gisèle Bousquet and Nora Taylor, 323–336. Paris: Les Indes Savantes, 2005.

Võ, Linda Trinh, and Rick Bonus, eds. *Contemporary Asian American Communities: Intersections and Divergences*. Philadelphia: Temple University Press, 2002.

Võ, Linda Trinh, and Mary Danico. "The Formation of Post-Suburban Communities: Little Saigon and Koreatown, Orange County." *International Journal of Sociology and Social Policy* 24, nos. 7–8 (2004): 15–45.

Wang, Gungwu. *China and the Chinese Overseas*. Singapore: Times, 1991.

Wang, L. L. "Exclusion and Fragmentation in Ethnic Politics: Chinese Americans in Urban Politics." In *The Politics of Minority Coalitions: Race, Ethnicity, and Shared Uncertainties*, ed. Wilbur C. Rich, 129–142. Westport, Conn.: Praeger, 1996.

Wang, Xinyang. *Surviving the City: The Chinese Immigrant Experience in New York City, 1890–1970*. Lanham, Md.: Rowman and Littlefield, 2001.

Ward, David. *Poverty, Ethnicity, and the American City, 1840–1925: Changing Conceptions of the Slum and Ghetto*. Cambridge: Cambridge University Press, 1989.

Ward, W. Peter. *White Canada Forever: Popular Attitudes and Public Policy toward Orientals in British Columbia*. Montreal: McGill-Queen's University Press, 1978.

Warner, W. L. *The Living and the Dead: A Study of the Symbolic Life of the Americans.* New Haven, Conn.: Yale University Press, 1959.

Warren, Elizabeth. *Chicago's Uptown: Public Policy, Neighborhood Decay, and Citizen Action in an Urban Community.* Urban Insight Series No. 3. Chicago: Loyola University, 1979.

Warren, William H. "Maps: A Spatial Approach to Japanese American Communities in Los Angeles." *Amerasia* 13, no. 2 (1986/1987): 137–151.

Waters, Tony. "Adaptation and Migration among the Mien People of Southeast Asia." *Ethnic Groups* 8 (1990): 127–141.

Weigel, Russel H., and Paul W. Howes. "Conceptions of Racial Prejudice: Symbolic Racism Reconsidered." *Journal of Social Issues* 41, no. 3 (1985): 117–138.

Weinreich, P., A. J. D. Kelly, and C. Maja. "Black Youth in South Africa: Situated Identities and Patterns of Ethnic Identification." In *Environmental Social Psychology,* ed. D. Canter, C. Jesuino, L. Soczka, and G. Stephenson, 231–245. Dordrecht: Kluwer Academic, 1988.

Wilhelm, Anthony G. *Democracy in the Digital Age: Challenges to Political Life in Cyberspace.* New York: Routledge, 2000.

Wilson, Rob. *Reimagining the American Pacific: From South Pacific to Bamboo Ridge and Beyond.* Durham, N.C.: Duke University Press, 2000.

Wong, Bernard P. *A Chinese American Community: Ethnicity and Survival Strategies.* Singapore: Chopmen, 1979.

———. *Chinatown: Economic Adaptation and Ethnic Identity of the Chinese.* New York: Holt, Rinehart and Winston, 1982.

———. *Patronage, Brokerage, Entrepreneurship and the Chinese Community of New York.* New York: AMS Press, 1988.

Wong (Lau), Kathleen. "The Asian American Community in the Southwest: Creating 'Place' in the Absence of Ethnic 'Space.'" In *Asian Pacific Americans and the U.S. Southwest,* ed. T. K. Nakayama and C. F. Yoshioka, 79–90. Tempe: Arizona State University, 1997.

Wong, P., et al. "From Despotism to Pluralism: The Evolution of Voluntary Organizations in Chinese American Communities." *Ethnic Groups* 8, no. 4 (1990): 215–233.

Wong, Sau-ling C. "Denationalization Reconsidered: Asian American Cultural Criticism at a Theoretical Crossroads." *Amerasia Journal* 21, nos. 1–2 (1995): 1–27.

Wright, Erik Olin. "Marxist Class Categories and Income Inequality." *American Sociological Review* 42 (1977): 32–55.

———. *Classes.* London: Verso, 1985.

———. *The Debate on Classes.* London: Verso, 1989.

Xie, Yu, and K. A. Goyette. *The American People, Census 2000: A Demographic Portrait of Asian Americans.* New York: Russell Sage Foundation Press/Washington, D.C.: Population Reference Bureau, 2004.

Yamashita, Karen Tei. *Through the Arc of the Rain Forest.* Minneapolis: Coffee House Press, 1990.

———. *Brazil-Maru.* Minneapolis: Coffee House Press, 1992.

———. "Interview" by Michael M. Murashige. *Amerasia Journal* 20, no. 3 (1994): 49–59.

———. "Interview" by Michael M. Murashige. In *Words Matter: Conversations with Asian American Writers,* ed. King-Kok Cheung, 320–342. Honolulu: University of Hawaii Press, 2000.

———. *Circle K Cycles.* Minneapolis: Coffee House Press, 2001.

Yang, Kou. "Hmong Americans: Felt Needs, Problems and Community Development." *Hmong Studies Journal* 4 (2003): 102–124.

Yang, Philip Q. *Ethnic Identity: Issues and Approaches.* Albany: State University of New York Press, 2000.

Yao, Nancy. "From Apathy to Inquiry and Activism: The Changing Role of American-Born Chinese in U.S.-China Relations." In *The Expanding Roles of Chinese Americans in U.S.-China Relations: Transnational Networks and Trans-Pacific Interactions*, ed. Peter H. Keohn and Xiao-huang Yin, 85–96. Armonk, N.Y.: M. E. Sharpe, 2002.

Yeh, C. L. "Contesting Identities: Youth Rebellion in San Francisco's Chinese New Year Festivals, 1953–1969." In *The Chinese in America: A History from Gold Mountain to the New Millennium*, ed. S. L. Cassel, 329–350. Walnut Creek, Calif.: AltaMira Press, 2001.

Yin, Xiao-huang. *Chinese American Literature since the 1850s.* Urbana: University of Illinois Press, 2000.

Yu, Eui-Young. "Korean Communities in America: Past, Present, and Future." *Amerasia* 10, no. 2 (1983): 23–51.

———. *Korean Community Profile: Life and Consumer Patterns.* Los Angeles: Korea Times, 1991.

Yu, Henry. *Thinking Orientals: Migration, Contact, and Exoticism in Modern America.* Oxford: Oxford University Press, 2001.

Yu, P., and Berryman, D. L. "The Relationship among Self-esteem, Acculturation, and Recreation Participation of Recently Arrived Chinese Immigrant Adolescents." *Journal of Leisure Research* 28 (1996): 251–273.

Yu, Renqiu. *To Save China, to Save Ourselves: The Chinese Hand Laundry Alliance of New York.* Philadelphia: Temple University Press, 1992.

Zelinsky, Wilbur. *The Enigma of Ethnicity: Another American Dilemma.* Iowa City: University of Iowa Press, 2001.

Zelinsky, Wilbur, and Barrett A. Lee. "Heterolocalism: An Alternative Model of the Sociospatial Behaviour of Immigrant Ethnic Communities." *International Journal of Population. Geography* 4 (1998): 1–18.

Zeng, Ying. "The Diverse Nature of San Diego's Chinese American Communities." In *The Chinese in America: A History from Gold Mountain to the New Millennium*, ed. Susie Lan Cassel, 434–448. Walnut Creek, Calif.: AltaMira Press, 2002.

Zhao, Jianli. *Strangers in the City: The Atlanta Chinese, Their Community and Stories of Their Lives.* New York: Garland, 2001.

Zhao, Xiaojian. *Remaking Chinese America: Immigration, Family, and Community, 1940–1965.* New Brunswick, N.J.: Rutgers University Press, 2001.

Zhou, Min. *Chinatown: The Socioeconomic Potential of an Urban Enclave.* Philadelphia: Temple University Press, 1992.

———. "Are Asian Americans Becoming White?" *Contexts* 3, no. 1 (2004): 29–37.

Zhou, Min, and Carl L. Bankston III. *Growing Up American: How Vietnamese Children Adapt to Life in the United States.* New York: Russell Sage Foundation Press, 1998.

Zhou, Min, and Susan S. Kim. "Community Forces, Social Capital, and Educational Achievement: The Case of Supplementary Education in the Chinese and Korean Immigrant Communities." *Harvard Educational Review* 76, no. 1 (2006): 1–29.

Zhou, Min, and Jennifer Lee. "The Making of Culture, Identity, and Ethnicity among Asian American Youth." In *Asian American Youth: Culture, Identity, and Ethnicity*, ed. Jennifer Lee and Min Zhou, 1–30. New York: Routledge, 2004.

Zhou, Min, and John R. Logan. "Increasing Diversity and Persistent Segregation: Challenges for Educating Minority and Immigrant Children in Urban America." In *The End of Desegregation*, ed. Stephen J. Caldas and Carl L. Bankston III, 177–194. Hauppauge, N.Y.: Nova Science, 2003.

Ziegert, Sylvia Van. *Global Spaces of Chinese Culture: Diasporic Chinese Communities in the United States and Germany.* New York: Routledge, 2006.

Zong, Li. "Structural and Psychological Dimensions of Racism." *Canadian Ethnic Studies* 26, no. 3 (1994): 122–134.

——. "New Racism, Cultural Diversity and the Search for a National Identity." In *The Battle over Multiculturalism: Does It Help or Hinder Canadian Unity?* ed. Andrew Cardoza and Louis Musto, 115–126. Ottawa: Pearson-Shoyama Institute, 1997.

——. "Chinese Immigration to Vancouver and New Racism in Multicultural Canada." In *Ethnic Chinese at the Turn of the Centuries*, ed. Guotu Zhuang, 443–463. Fujian: Fujian People Press, 1998.

——. International Transference of Human Capital and Occupational Attainment of Recent Chinese Professional Immigrants in Canada. *American Journal of China Studies* 5, nos. 1–2 (2004): 81–89.

NOTES ON CONTRIBUTORS

LING Z. ARENSON, Ph.D., teaches history at DePaul University, Chicago. She has written on Asian American history with a focus on the interrelations between the Asian American experience and the international relations of the United States. She is currently researching on the experience of Chinese immigrants in the Greater Chicago area since the 1880s.

ANGIE Y. CHUNG, Ph.D., is assistant professor of sociology at the University at Albany. She is author of *Legacies of Struggle: Conflict and Cooperation in Korean American Politics* (2007). She is currently working on a project on ethnic suburbs and also adult American-born children of Asian immigrant families.

PETER S. LI, Ph.D., is professor of sociology at the University of Saskatchewan, Canada. His research areas are race and ethnicity, Chinese Canadians, and immigration. He has published more than seventy academic papers and eleven books, including *The Chinese in Canada* (1988, 1998), *The Making of Post-War Canada* (1996), and *Destination Canada* (2003).

WEI LI, Ph.D., is associate professor of geography at Arizona State University. Her research foci are immigration, and financial sector and community development. She coined the term "ethnoburb," describing suburban immigrant settlements in the Pacific Rim. She serves as the vice chair of Asian Advisory Committee for the U.S. Census Bureau.

HUPING LING, Ph.D., is professor of history at Truman State University. Her research focuses on international migration, and Asian American women and communities. A Ford Prize–winning author, she has published more than a hundred articles and ten books, including *Surviving on the Gold Mountain* (1998), *Chinese St. Louis: From Enclave to Cultural Community* (2004), *Chinese in St. Louis, 1857–2007* (2007), *Voices of the Heart* (2007), and *Emerging Voices* (2008).

HAIMING LIU, Ph.D., is professor of Asian American studies at the ethnic and women's studies department, California Polytechnic State University, Pomona. He is author of *The Transnational History of a Chinese Family: Immigrant Letters, Family Business, and Reverse Migration* (2005) and many articles on Chinese

American immigration, herbal medicine, agriculture, family, and transnationalism.

YUAN SHU, Ph.D., is associate professor of English at Texas Tech University. He has published articles in *Cultural Critique*, *College Literature*, and *MELUS*, among others. He is finishing his book project on Chinese American literature and culture.

ALLYSON TINTIANGCO-CUBALES, Ph.D., is associate professor of Asian American studies at San Francisco State University (SFSU) and senior research associate with the Educational Equity Initiative at the Cesar E. Chavez Institute. She is affiliated faculty in the Ed.D. program for Educational Leadership in SFSU's School of Education, a faculty/urban fellow with the Institute of Civic and Community Engagement, and founder and director of Pin@y Educational Partnerships (PEP).

LINDA TRINH VÕ, Ph.D., is associate professor in the department of Asian American studies at the University of California, Irvine. Võ is the author of *Mobilizing an Asian American Community* and the co-editor *Contemporary Asian American Communities: Intersection and Divergences, Asian American Women: The "Frontiers" Reader,* and *Labor versus Empire: Race, Gender, and Migration.*

WEI ZENG works in health care industry in Seattle after receiving her master's degree from the department of sociology at Arizona State University. Her research interests were family demography and race/ethnicity. Her research included examining various dimensions of race/ethnicity such as racial/ethnic differences of child development in the context of family.

MIN ZHOU, Ph.D., is professor of sociology and Asian American studies at the University of California, Los Angeles. Her main research interests include international migration, immigrant adaptation, ethnic and racial relations, and urban sociology. She has published widely on Chinese immigration, Asian American communities, and the new second generation.

LI ZONG, Ph.D., is a tenured associate professor of sociology at the University of Saskatchewan and an affiliated researcher of the Prairie Metropolis Centre in Canada. He is also adjunct professor for Xi'an Jiaotong and Lanzhou universities in China. He coauthored a book and published articles in the areas of immigration, racism, and China studies.

INDEX

Printed in the United States
215234BV00002B/2/P